Flying Uncle's Junk

Hauling Drugs for Uncle Sam

Also by Don Bloch

A Shadow at the Gate

Flying Uncle's Junk

Hauling Drugs for Uncle Sam

Memoir of a DEA Agent

Don Bloch

North Star Press of St. Cloud, Inc.
St. Cloud, Minnesota

Cover design by Joan Buerman
Author photo © Michael's Photography

ISBN: 978-1-68201-029-7

First edition: March 2016

Printed in the United States of America.

Published by
North Star Press of St. Cloud, Inc.
P.O. Box 451
St. Cloud, MN 56302

www.northstarpress.com

Editor's note:

This is volume two of Don Bloch's memoir. Volume one, *A Shadow at the Gate,* tells of Bloch's life as a farm boy, a seminarian, a hobo, and an Air Force pilot. This volume tells about his twenty years as a special agent/pilot with the Drug Enforcement Administration. It's helpful to have read *A Shadow at the Gate.* Without that, the reader will miss some of the humor, some of the irony, and the significance of some of the government blunders. Also, Bloch's ready sympathy for poor rural people, the references to Stearns County, and the flying terminology will be easier to understand. However, that reading is not essential. This book can stand on its own.

The introduction to Bloch's memoir is repeated here for those who have not read *A Shadow at the Gate,* and as a reminder for those who have.

Introduction

It is a mistake to take this book seriously. It is written from memory, and my life has been a hurricane of confusion. I was always trying to figure out what was going on—and failing. It started with my parents. They taught me to judge people according to their actions and their professions. But as I grew up, I found that my parents had greatly overrated some professions and had greatly underrated others. I lost a good deal of respect for many of the professions my parents esteemed, and I gained a good deal for many they did not. Among the losers were politicians, professors, reporters, and priests. Among the gainers were bootleggers, hoboes, snitches, and whores. This book is about how these things came to be.

Young men hunger for adventure. Sometimes they volunteer; sometimes it is forced upon them. Thirst for adventure drives young men to ignore danger and go with happy, childlike bliss into the unknown hazards of travel, love, and war. They volunteer for foolishness just to see where it leads. For a while I studied to be a priest, for a while I was an Air Force pilot, and finally I made a career with the Drug Enforcement Administration. That was a fine career for me because I had a great lust for travel. With DEA credentials, my fellow agents and I traveled all over the United States and into many foreign countries. We carried guns and rounded up outlaws. We spent enormous amounts of federal tax money on "The Great War on Drugs." We got paid to eat the world's best food, drink the finest whiskey, and sleep in the best hotels in dozens of cities, islands, and countries, where tourists pay thousands to do the same. I wish to thank the taxpayers of the United States of America for their generosity. I'd love to tell you that the millions—no billions—I helped squander on the anti-drug campaigns during those years did at least some good. But that wouldn't be true. When I left, we were worse off then when I got there. I also feel obligated to thank the foreign countries where my cohorts and I worked. They didn't throw us out at gunpoint as they should have.

Some of the things done in airplanes in this book are illegal, some are dangerous, some are both. They're set down only as history, not as recommendations.

This story is *gans und gar die Varheit* (the honest to goodness truth), as I saw it. But I know, from doing criminal investigations, that eye witnesses are often the worst witnesses. And there is a saying: "who writes history, makes history." If you're in this book and don't like the way it's written down, don't complain to me—write your own book. Or take solace in the fact that memories are fallible, or in this from Mark Twain: "The very ink with which all history is written is merely fluid prejudice." One can't avoid recording from one's own point of view.

Some of the conversations I have here are from my logs, and those are accurate; others are made up from memory and, although they're accurate as to the meaning, they are not (unless some miracle has occurred) as to the words. It's likely some names are misspelled, and some may be wrong. This is not intentional.

This much I have learned, this much I know. Life is full of contradiction and is rife with irony. The greatest of these is this: what a man wants most, and what he looks for all his life he already has, but does not know it. The restlessness, longing, wanting, of my life came from man's normal need to be free and at peace. Everyone wants this—rich man and poor man. Monks seek it in their monasteries, drunks in their drink, movie stars in their fame. But no amount of devotion, or drink, or fame can bring this to you, until you realize that you already have it at the core of your being.

The woods are lovely, dark and deep,
But I have promises to keep
And miles to go before I sleep.
~Robert Frost

Chapter One

VIETNAM, VIETNAM, HOW YOU formed my life! But for that war, I would not have been an Air Force pilot. I would not have made a career with the Drug Enforcement Administration and would not have traveled in all those foreign countries. Though I was never over there, the smoke that rose from the battlefields of that remote little country on the other side of the world directed the path of my working life. I had to join the military because of the draft. Because I became an Air Force pilot, I had to stay in until the government finally allowed me to go. Then a Laredo Border Patrolman told me, "Now you have no choice. You have to get a job with the federal government or those seven years with the Air Force will be wasted. When you retire, they'll add your Air Force time to calculate your retirement pay."

I was still eager for travel and adventure. I found out our federal government's drug-fighting bureau had offices all over the world, in well-known places like Paris, Frankfort, and Madrid, but also in such exotic places as Kuala Lumpur, Istanbul, and Quito. I was hooked. I applied with BNDD (the Bureau of Narcotics and Dangerous Drugs). By the time they hired me it was called DEA (Drug Enforcement Administration).

A mysterious thing happened a little while after I applied. At the time I was working as a real estate agent for Pemtom of Minneapolis. I had an office out in the boondocks near Eagle Lake in the northwest suburbs. With little business out there in the woods, I had plenty of time to contemplate that I was likely the worst salesman who ever held a Minnesota realtors license. I spent most of my time throwing darts at a board on the wall. One day I got a call from a man who identified himself as an officer of a federal organization in Washington, D.C. He asked if he could meet with me with reference to my application with BNDD. He said it had to do with internal security but could not say more on the phone. I was not to tell anyone (not even my wife) about his call or his pending visit. He said he would explain in person.

Now here was intrigue! Here was excitement. I heartily invited him for a visit. A week later this man flew into Minneapolis, rented a car, and came to my office. He had very official-looking credentials showing himself to be with the CIA, but he said he was temporarily working for BNDD. He questioned me about details on my application. Then he said they had a special mission for me, but he could not divulge any details until I had come to Washington, D.C. for some interviews and had passed a lie-detector test. It was the spookiest thing. How could I resist? He gave me money for airfare, for cab fare, for a hotel room, for meals, even for drinks. He made me promise not to tell anyone, not the boss, not the wife, not the dog.

I told my wife, Bea, I was going to Washington for a job interview and she was satisfied with that. In Washington I met with some more spooky guys in a small hotel room. They gave me a lie-detector test, asking questions to verify that my application told the truth, that I had studied to be a priest, had been an Air Force pilot, was not and had never been a drug user, and lots of stuff concerning my loyalty to the United States of America. They asked me if I had told anyone about the visit to my real estate office, and they asked if I was lying, which I thought was a strange question to ask since the polygraph was supposed to tell them that. After they decided I was indeed what they were looking for, and having sworn me to secrecy on the hotel's Gideon Bible, they finally told me what it was all about.

John Ingersoll was the head of BNDD. Ingersoll was a zealot like J. Edgar Hoover. He was always suspecting his boys of graft and collusion and all manner of corruption, but was rarely able to find the evidence. In late 1970 he went to the CIA for help in rooting out crooked agents, and in early '71 Richard Helms, then CIA director, approved a program to covertly recruit drug agents to infiltrate crooked agents for the sake of the security of BNDD. I was one of their first recruits. They were trying to get to me before I was hired and had a chance to see all that money on the street and get corrupted. They seemed to value the fact that I had studied to be a priest and I had volunteered to serve in the Air Force. To them this meant I must be of high moral character and also immensely patriotic. (I did not tell them otherwise).

They told me to choose an undercover name I would use when I called in to their secret number in Washington. The name had to have the initials "C.H." because I was their man from the Chicago region. I chose Catfish Hunter (a major league baseball pitcher at that time), but they said that was too common. I changed the last name to "Hire," because I had a student in the Air Force named Charlie Hire, and that would be easy to remember. We settled on "Catfish Hire" as the undercover name. I took out my notebook to write it down, but they said no. I was not to write down anything. I had to memorize their telephone number and my contact's name and was never to write it down.

They said they did not wish to hear about me being found in an alley somewhere with a bullet in my head. I was in total harmony with that sentiment.

My job would be to snoop out corruption among my fellow agents, gather evidence, and report to them in Washington. They stressed this must be kept top secret or life could get very exciting for me. They were confident I would be hired soon, because DEA was looking for pilots and I had a lot of flying time for my age.

Months went by. I called the secret number once when the Social Security Administration offered me a job. I wanted to know if I should take it or wait for DEA. The man in Washington said, "Take it. You'll be easier to hire when you're already working for the federal government. Any time you spend with Social Security will count towards your retirement pay." He was still convinced the Drug Enforcement Administration would be hiring soon and I would be near the top of the list because I was a pilot. So I signed up with Social Security, and after attending their oppressively boring training school in Rockford, Illinois, they sent Bea and me to Kokomo, Indiana, for my first assignment.

Kokomo was the worst town Bea and I ever lived in. It was a smutty, smoggy city with stagnant, gray air that stung the eyes and insulted the lungs. Smoke from factories did not rise, but spread itself around and seeped into our abode through every little crack in a window or margin of a loose-hung door. One gas refinery had built an enormous smoke tower supposedly to keep the fumes above the city, but it did little more than assure that pollutants were evenly distributed into the suburbs. People burned piles of damp leaves and garbage in their back yards in those days and left them to smolder and smoke all through the night. We lived at 531 East Taylor, a dingy, gloomy basement apartment with high, tiny slits for windows. We had to have lights on in the middle of the day, or feel around in the dark. When it rained, the place flooded, and we had to put our things up on the rickety table or the moldy couch. We paid twenty-two dollars a week for the privilege of staying in this paradise. I hated every minute of it. We had no money and, since I was just beginning to work for Social Security, we had no prospect of getting any soon—unless Bea robbed a bank, which she refused to do.

We weren't there long though. A teletype message came from the Drug Enforcement Administration, 1405 I Street, N.W. Washington, D.C., offering me employment as a special agent at $9,520 per year. They sent me to DEA Basic Agent School in Washington, D.C. It was a dismal excuse for training.

When I had graduated from U.S. Air Force pilot training, I was the proudest man in the world. When I graduated from DEA agent school, I was the most befuddled. The Air Force gave me a set of wings, which I would not have traded for a diamond mine in Africa. DEA gave me a gun and a badge and special agent credentials, all of which I would have traded for a pack of gum. The school instilled no pride in their organization.

They said at the school we should strive to be the "Outstanding Student," because then we would get to pick our first assignment. I made no attempt at that target, because I was sure from the beginning my roommate, George Coleman, would get that honor. He had been a cop in Baltimore for a long time and knew more about law enforcement than most of the school faculty. He had made undercover buys, done moving surveillance, put together cases, made arrests, and testified in court. He never lost his cool, and I could not have imagined a better man to have with you in a fight. Coleman was a crack shot and in top physical condition. He could max all the requirements in the gym (chin ups, push ups, swimming, rope climbing). He scored high on the academic tests. George Coleman was black, and DEA was eager to show they were fair to minorities. I prophesied that my roommate, George Coleman, would be number one.

I was a fool. Welcome to Basic Bureaucracy 101. Two women were in our class—the first two ever hired by DEA. One of the class counselors told me before the school was half over it was already preordained one of the women would be made the outstanding student. The director of DEA was eager to show what a fair and unbiased organization DEA was going to be. I did not believe the counselor. Neither of the women were anywhere near the top in academics, both had trouble doing the "required" exercises in the gym like chinups, pushups, and climbing the rope. The young woman finally given the honor of "outstanding student" needed remedial help on the firing range to pass the final. It was my first lesson in bureaucratic shenanigans. I discovered that in a bureaucracy prophesying is a tricky undertaking. I was a failure in that field. I retired from the prophesy business for good (one of two reasons you won't find me in the Old Testament).

I had an easy time of it at the school. Early on I made friends with Sal Dijamco from San Francisco. He was my guiding light. He had a law enforcement background and was streetwise as a New York alley-rat. He had no aspirations of being the outstanding student or of being outstanding in anything. He told me over and over, "This job is easy if you just remember this: keep a low profile, and don't front the money."

Sal and I sat in the back row of the classroom and kept that low profile. We didn't ask questions, we didn't volunteer answers. Sal cruised happily though the school. He studied just enough to stay in the middle. "You don't want to call attention to yourself by being near the top, nor by being near the bottom." Sal was a wise man that way, but later, back in San Francisco he did not always keep that low profile. He was once awarded the Administrator's Award of Honor, but he could not help that. He was shot while working undercover—a thing which I was confident he would have arranged differently if it had been left up to him. And I knew Sal. I was sure when they gave him his Award-of-Honor plaque, he was saying to himself, "Keep your damn plaque, just give me the money."

Braud and Holmes were two black students in my class. One day the three of us were on our way to Oxon Hill, Maryland, on a surveillance assignment. Braud stopped the car along Fourteenth Street to shuck and jive with the hookers there. After they had wasted half an hour spreading themselves around, I said, "Hey, guys, let's go. We have to get to work."

This is the response that came from Braud: "We have to get to work? Who's we? You have to get to work, white boy. We don't have to work. We're the right color."

That night I told Coleman about this. He told me that sort of thing was easy to explain. He said the federal government, in it's desperation to become integrated, was giving jobs to some blacks based strictly on the color of their skin no matter their qualifications, and that some of those blacks understood perfectly their position and were happy to take advantage of it. George had nothing but contempt for the kind. He said, "That riffraff makes it harder for other black men."

George was incapable of that kind of behavior. He outclassed men like Braud and Holmes by a mile. He outclassed most of us at the school. I was grateful to have George in the class, but I was disappointed that DEA would hire people like Braud and Holmes. George also told me Holmes had washed out of a previous class. He was too lazy to study, and he could not shoot worth a damn. He was being given a second try—a favor not normally granted to students who flunked.

"George asked me, "Do you have a college degree?"

I said I did. He asked, "Did they tell you that was a requirement?"

I said, "That was the very first thing they asked me, and they said I need not bother to apply if I did not have one."

"Well," he said, "you'll find that half this class doesn't have a college degree, nor the police background needed to get a waiver."

Twice Holmes was in the shooting booth next to me on the firing range. The first time it happened I thought it was pretty funny. We were given the order to load and get ready. When the order to commence firing was given, a thunderstorm erupted in Holmes's booth. There was banging, smoking, swearing, grunting, clicking, and everything that could possibly be associated with the working of a pistol (and much that could not), and all that action had remarkably little effect on the target that hung in front of his booth. Once in a while a hole would appear, but that was nearly always at the margins. When the din ceased, and the smoke cleared, the holes in that fortunate target were surprisingly few (considering all the sound and fury), and the holes were scattered about in such a random manner that one could not possibly conclude they had appeared there from a process that resembled the sighting and firing of a gun—unless it was with the shooter's eyes squeezed tightly shut.

The second time Holmes was next to me was when we were taking our final firing range exam. He was in the booth to my right. During the speed-firing round, as I was loading my pistol for the final six shots, the range instructor came to my booth and yelled by my ear (I was wearing ear muffs), "When you look up at your target, you'll see three holes in the upper right hand corner. Do not let that throw you. Those are not your shots."

Holmes graduated just like the rest of us.

The dumbest thing at that school came from the head of DEA himself, John Bartels Jr. He looked like a total nerd, and would have qualified for that category had he not lacked an ingredient normally associated with that title: intelligence. He was a little guy with glasses and with an innocent bewildered look. John Bartels Jr. had some loose screws. He gave the graduation speech. He told about all the agents who had recently been killed on the job. I had just spent the last several months convincing Bea the job of a special agent with the DEA was not any more dangerous than flying for the Air Force or working farm machinery in Stearns County, and there were plenty of jobs: soldier, game warden, steeplejack, that were far more dangerous. Just as I had her convinced, here comes Bartels with his idiotic speech. He said that DEA agents were four times more likely to experience a violent episode of shooting and killing than other federal law enforcement agents, including FBI agents. Was he nuts? Here seated before him were wives, sweethearts, and mothers, who were already concerned about this new career their loved ones had chosen, and he piled on more worries! He caused Bea a lot of needless anxiety. (Here I am many years later with not one bullet hole in me.) I thought Bartels was a jackass that day, and he never gave me a reason to change my mind.

Bartels did me one favor though. He ended that secret, sneaky program under which I had been named "Catfish Hire." I never liked the idea of spying and tattling on other agents, so I was glad when, after I had a few months on the job, a memo appeared that said DEA had ended the program. The memo said it was a program under which certain agents, known only to two agency officials, worked as undercover agents inside DEA and their function was to call in incidents of possible corruption in the ranks. The program was not working. The snitch agents were calling in vague charges against anyone they didn't like. I had never phoned in anything so I knew they weren't talking about me. I called the secret number to resign. The number had been disconnected. I never told anyone I had been one of those double agents. I threw away Catfish Hire, and never heard of him again.

Chapter Two

In the land of the Dacotahs,
Where the Falls of Minnehaha
Flash and gleam among the oak-trees,
Laugh and leap into the valley.
~Longfellow

IT WAS BITTER COLD that winter in Minneapolis. The Falls of Minnehaha were not leaping into the valley. They were frozen solid—stupendous icicles clinging to the limestone ledges like ancient white stalactites in the caverns of Lebanon. It was nighttime of the second day after Christmas. Special Agent Mark Kryger was buying amphetamine in south Minneapolis. The dealer was a man named Chapman. Kryger picked up Chapman, and they went to an old abandoned house where they were to meet the amphetamine source. Kryger had $1,000 of buy money, which he would show to the source, who would then get the amphetamine (or the speed or the crank, as it was known on the street) and deliver to Kryger at the house. Those of us on surveillance were planning to follow the source to see where he went to pick up the dope. We were hoping to identify Chapman's source. We had plenty of surveillance units scattered around the quiet neighborhood: DEA, Minneapolis police, Bloomington police, and Hennepin County narcs.

I had an eye on the front of the house. They had put me there because I was a rookie. All the action was taking place in the back where Kryger parked the undercover car, and where the source crooks parked when they arrived. It was very dark in that part of town—only a few dim street lights. The air fairly crackled with cold. I snuggled down in the seat of the car and pulled my parka close. I had no heat, because I could not leave the engine running. The smoke from the exhaust would draw attention to the car. I expected I would be there a long while. When the surveillance moved, they would likely still expect me to keep an eye on the house.

Surveillance reported over the radio that Kryger and Chapman had arrived and had entered. They said another car was there, an older model two-door, which they guessed would be the source, but in the darkness no one was able to get a plate number. From the front I could see nothing inside the house but one dim light somewhere in an inner room. Occasionally a shadow moved through the light. That was all.

Somebody said on the radio, "Anybody got an eye on the UC?"

Nobody answered. (The UC was the undercover agent.) I could see shadows move inside but could not identify them.

Time passed.

Suddenly I snapped to attention. I grabbed the microphone and said, "Something's wrong. The UC's running out the front door." But my transmission was at least partially blocked. Radios were crackling, stepping on each other so that only bits could be heard.

"Two men running out the back."

"What's going on?"

"Where are they?"

"Which car?"

I started the engine while Kryger ran to my car. I opened the passenger window, but he tore open the door, snatched the microphone out my hand and yelled, "It's a rip! It's a rip! They got the money. Stop the car that's leaving right now." Then he said to me, "Go, go, go. They're back there, take a right," he said, pointing. "I'm going back for Chapman."

I stomped on it. As I turned the corner, I saw headlights moving in from all directions. Two cars had blocked the street, and the robbers were just coming to a stop. I turned in behind them and hit the brakes. I might have stopped too far back, giving them enough room to back out, but my car skidded on the icy pavement and came to a stop behind them touching their bumper with a solid thump. I grabbed my revolver and jumped out. The robber-passenger was out and running across the street. I could see in the headlights he had a pistol in one hand. The driver opened his door. I heard the *pop, pop* of gunfire and saw muzzle flashes from the far side of the street. I ducked as a bullet whined over my head. All was chaos. Men shouting "Freeze!" and "Drop it!" and "Hands up!" The driver made no attempt to get out and run. He held up his hands as soon as he saw my gun. He said, "Don't shoot." I said, "Don't move."

I hesitated. Gunfire in all directions. More bullets whining in the air. Muzzle flashes winking in the darkness. I aimed my pistol across the top of the robber car, but in the darkness I couldn't make out who was who. The muzzle flashes were moving farther away. Agent Fekete had stopped right behind me. He came to the driver of the suspect car and shoved me aside. He grabbed the driver by his collar and hauled him out of the car and had him cuffed in seconds. He said, "Watch him close," and ran back to his car, got out a shotgun, and jammed it into my hands. He took off running, shouting, "Shoot him if he tries to get away."

In seconds all the agents had vanished and the street was quiet, leaving just me, the driver, and a bunch of cars parked at odd angles around the crook's car, some with lights on, doors open, engines still running. I put the driver into the back seat of his car. I turned off the ignition and put the keys in my pocket. I heard more gunfire coming from the next street. It sounded like children's cap guns. I was surprised at how little noise the guns made in the cold air. I was used to hearing gunfire inside on the firing range where it boomed and echoed like canons. Everything got quiet again. I wondered what was going on. The crook complained the cuffs were too tight, but I was not about to loosen them. I felt a little sorry for him. He wasn't dressed for the cold, and he looked miserable slumped and shivering in the back seat. I told him I'd loosen the cuffs as soon as some of the other agents returned.

A couple of our agents appeared across the street. One of them was Bloomington Police Officer Stone "Hey, Bloch," he said, "ask your prisoner the name of his buddy."

I did as I was told.

The prisoner answered, "Hey, man, this is no shit. I just now picked that guy up at the Amoco gas station. He wanted a ride. I don't know his real name. He called himself Coco or something like that."

"He doesn't know the guy's name," I shouted back to Stone.

At those words Officer Stone walked quickly toward me. He strode with a purpose. When he got to where I was standing next to the open car door, he snatched the shotgun out of my hands, racked a round into the chamber, stuck the muzzle hard into the belly of the prisoner and shouted, "Who was with you in the car!"

"Henry Roundtree!" screamed the prisoner at the top of his lungs—without the slightest hesitation, as he doubled up and squirmed, trying to get away from the shotgun barrel.

I was astounded. Just a minute ago he didn't know the guy's name. Stone slipped the shotgun onto safety, and handed it back to me saying, "Careful, there's a live round in the chamber."

"We're looking for Henry Roundtree," he shouted as he walked back toward the others. They all took off in search of Roundtree.

Some Minneapolis police cruisers came along to see what was happening. They were only too happy to take over the care of the prisoner. They moved all the cars off the street and secured the keys. Some of them drove off to help search for Henry Roundtree.

After a long while the agents came back. They had not found Roundtree and had given up. When we got downtown to our office, it was my job (being the rookie) to process the prisoner. I fingerprinted and photographed him, and the cops and I took him to the Hennepin County Jail. His name was Ben Carter. His screaming out the name of Henry Roundtree did not help us much. Minneapolis patrolmen who covered that area knew immediately who it was when Kryger told them about Roundtree's jacket, his work jacket from his dad's Amoco station, embossed on the front with his well-known street name: Junebug. Roundtree was not too smart that night.

Henry "Junebug" Roundtree was now a hunted man. Agent Kryger was already at the office drawing up an arrest warrant. Carter had given us information about where Roundtree might be hiding, but none of it helped us that night. When I got back to the office from delivering Carter to jail, the other agents were discussing the gun battle. In a few minutes some FBI agents arrived. It was their job to investigate incidents that involved a shooting by federal agents. They weren't happy getting called out at that time of the night. The DEA agents thought nothing of it. We were always working at night.

The adrenalin was wearing off, and it left me feeling exhausted. I wanted to go home to bed. The other agents wanted to go drink. However, we had to get interviewed by FBI agents. They were cranky because they'd have to go to the battle scene next morning and interview people in the neighborhood, hunt for bullet holes and gather other evidence to back up our story of what happened. They considered this grunt work and thought we should have been doing it ourselves. At one point we almost had another shooting right there in the office. One of the FBI agents started reading Agent Fekete his Miranda rights and Fekete blew a fuse and came across the desk at the man with murder in his eye. The FBI supervisor quickly intervened and said, "Ah, that won't be necessary," although I could tell he felt uncomfortable not reading us the Miranda rights. The FBI always followed the letter of the law.

Agent Kryger told of what happened inside the house. When Kryger and Chapman went in, Carter and Roundtree were inside. It was dark in there with only one light in the kitchen. Chapman wanted to talk to Carter alone, so they went into the living room. Kryger stayed in the kitchen with Roundtree. It was a casual conversation, about the weather, about Christmas—not about the amphetamine deal. After a while, Kryger heard Chapman and Carter arguing about money in the living room. Kryger walked in there to find out what the problem was. Carter was demanding money from Chapman which he claimed was owed on a previous purchase. Kryger was trying to mediate the argument, when suddenly Roundtree came into the living room with a gun, a four-inch Colt Python .357, which he directed at Chapman and demanded the money. (Roundtree was evidently the enforcer/ bodyguard.) Kryger felt under his coat for his pistol. Chapman told Roundtree Kryger had the money. Roundtree quickly turned the gun on Agent Kryger, and Carter told Kryger he'd better give Roundtree the money if he valued living.

Kryger said that he was already tightening his finger on his S&W 9mm, when a voice inside his head brought to mind Psalm 27:1 and he relaxed. That might be, but I think the voice in the head may also have mentioned the mountain of paper work and the months of investigation that would have followed that trigger-pull. Kryger gave Roundtree the buy money and Roundtree, still covering him with his pistol, told Kryger to get out, which Kryger did, running out the front to get to a radio.

Mr. Junebug may have been protected that night by more than just Psalm 27:1. The next time Kryger pulled the trigger on his 9mm, he was at the firing range. When the hammer fell on that shell meant for Junebug, there was only a click. The gun had a broken mainspring.

Not long after the shooting, Kryger got results in his hunt for Henry "Junebug" Roundtree. Roundtree was arrested in Chicago and hauled back to Minneapolis for trial. He was brought to the U.S. District Court in Minneapolis and charged with robbery of federal funds and with two counts of assault on a federal agent: one on Agent Kryger and one on Agent Bloch. Prosecutor John Lee had to have a specific name to put on the indictment. He could not just charge the assault on "some federal agents." The FBI's investigation determined I was as much as anyone in Roundtree's line of fire.

At trial, the jury found Roundtree guilty of one count of assault and one count of robbery. When the verdict was announced, Prosecutor John Lee came down to our office to report. He said, "Well, the jury determined it's okay to assault Agent Bloch. They found Roundtree not guilty on that charge. But assaulting Agent Kryger now, that was stepping over the line. They found him guilty on that count and guilty of the robbery."

Roundtree's attorney told how Roundtree escaped that night. He was running from the agents, occasionally turning to fire his gun. He saw a house with no lights with a screened porch in front. Seeing no pursuers just then, he thought it might be a good place to hide. Roundtree tried the front door but it was locked. He saw his pursuers coming onto that street. They were checking houses. He noticed a big rug covering the porch floor. He lay down on one end and rolled himself into the rug to the other end of the porch. When the agents came onto the porch they saw only a dirty rolled up piece of carpet. They did not bother to look.

Whenever there is a conviction in federal court, you can be sure there will be an appeal. There is not much chance of winning the appeal, but it is extra money for the lawyer, and every once in a while, when the appeals court judges have gotten out of the wrong side of the bed, they reverse the conviction. Roundtree appealed his conviction to the Eight Circuit Court in St. Louis. Judges and lawyers can't talk without loading up every sentence with "heretofores" and "aforementioneds." They can't make any statement without appending a volley of citations like: 18 U.S.C. 841 A, 1 and *United States v. So-and-So*, 1973, section this and paragraph that. And then adding a few precedents so the judge knows they weren't making it up themselves. However, hidden in all that legalese babble is a beautiful logic (when they are ruling in your favor, that is).

The appeal went basically like this: Roundtree said this was not a robbery but just a settling of a debt between him and Chapman. The court said, yeah, but Kryger was not the one who owed you the money, so taking the cash from him was a robbery, regardless of what Chapman owed. Then Roundtree said, but I should not have been held for stealing money that belonged to the United States, since I had no way of knowing Kryger had government funds. Kryger was pretending to be a drug dealer. The court said, well, that's your hard luck. The law says you don't have to know that little detail. Next Roundtree called Agent Kryger's identification into question and said the judge didn't give the jury proper instructions about how eyewitnesses are often wrong. The court said, no, we read over the transcript, and the judge did just fine on that point. Finally Roundtree said the robbery and assault were really only one crime and the judge should not have given him a separate sentence for two crimes. The court said, "You're wrong: two separate laws were violated." The one law was designed to protect federal law enforcement officers while performing federal functions. Just the fact that Kryger was a DEA agent, and was on duty, was enough. The other law was designed to protect those who have government property in their possession and merely requires proof the property taken belonged to the United States. The government proved that at trial.

The appeals court denied the appeal and Roundtree went to jail. The judge gave Roundtree three years for the assault and another three for the robbery. I don't know how much time he actually served, but I know that, under the law, he could have gotten a sentence at least four times as long. I remember being surprised he could get that kind of a sentence for taking money he didn't know belonged to the government, and for assaulting a man he didn't know was a federal agent, especially when that agent was holding himself out as a crook wanting to score amphetamine.

Chapter Three

THE ROUNDTREE SHOOTING happened two days after Christmas. I had been on the job a little over a month. With this happening so soon after I got on the job, one might think this kind of thing happened all the time. And movies and TV programs about drug enforcement give the impression the working life of a drug agent is one of constant gunfights, car chases, and undercover intrigue. Books written by agents do not lessen that impression. It is however, false. DEA life is, rather, many hours of boredom punctuated by an occasional interesting event that may be exciting. Most often they are not. In the DEA office, the boredom comes from the government's insistence that an agent fill out hundreds of needless, fruitless, foolish forms only an imbecile could take seriously (but there were enough of those to keep the system going). On the street, the boredom comes from having to do surveillance on a house or stationary car. The surveillance I did on the house in which Agent Kryger was being robbed that night was a very rare exception.

Often watching a suspect's house is a drudgery that goes on for days on end—a house that's apparently empty and where no one ever comes to visit, and from which no one ever leaves. Agents are soon convinced no one lives there, nor ever will, apparently. Only Charles Dickens could write about those boring times and make it worth reading. I'm not Dickens. I'm forced, therefore, to record only what I found interesting. Don't sign up with DEA based on these incidents.

That Roundtree gun battle was a fitting way to close that year of turmoil for Bea and me. We kept moving from town to town as I hopped from job to job, until we finally settled down to DEA and Minneapolis not long before Thanksgiving. At that time, turmoil was also the rule in DEA offices around the world. The recent conversion from BNDD to DEA caused confusion among supervisors about structure and ranking and among street agents about the objectives of the organization. The Controlled Substances Act Congress had passed in 1970 was supposed to clarify this, but it only added to the splendid bewilderment. Heroin was the number one target, but the flow of that had just changed. The French Connection had just been broken. Almost all the heroin in the country had been coming from opium poppies raised in Turkey, funneled into the U.S. through laboratories in France. That flow was broken when the Turkish government banned opium farming, and when narcotics officers in both France and the U.S. made a series of big heroin seizures costing the traffickers millions. The traffickers established new methods and new routes, and it was taking DEA a while to figure what those were.

The Minneapolis DEA office was in a transition too. The former special agent in charge (the SAC) had just left and taken several of his favorite agents along with him to St. Louis. Jack Walsh, our group supervisor, was in charge of our office temporarily. He'd soon be moved out, because Jim Braseth was coming from Chicago to take over as SAC, and Jim was bringing along his buddy, Dave Haight, to be group supervisor. Agent Jack Walsh and I got along immediately. He had been in the Air Force too, though not as a pilot. Jack considered me a greenhorn, but not a stupid one like most of the other agents did. Jack was smart, laid back, and unconcerned about bureaucratic details: my kind of guy.

But he drank.

One night I was on surveillance outside a nightclub in south Minneapolis. Minneapolis Narcotics Officer Boulger was inside working undercover. Most of the surveillance agents were inside at the bar where it was nice and warm and where they could drink beer and play pool while watching Boulger and the crook as they negotiated a cocaine deal. We were all set to follow the crook in case he went to the source. They had a radio inside and every so often reported what was happening. Every ten minutes or so a mike button clicked and "no change" came over the air. Jack's car was parked right near the front door. One of the agents, thinking this spot was too conspicuous, went inside, borrowed the keys from Jack and moved the car to the side of the building. Jack was too busy drinking to do it himself. The agent gave the keys back to Jack and told him where the car was parked.

As the night wore on, Jack got drunk. After a while other agents, knowing Jack would no longer be any good on surveillance, convinced him to go home to his wife. I watched Jack through my field glasses as he came out. He walked to the exact spot his car had originally been parked. He stood there gently swaying back and forth, trying to reasons things out. He kept looking down at his shoes as though the car might be found between his feet. I told the guys inside Jack was having trouble finding his car. Jack went back inside. The agents explained to him where the car was and he came back out and weaved his way around to the side of the building where he found the car. As he got into it, I went over to help him. He was stabbing around with his right hand trying to insert the ignition key. His left was groping around in the air for the steering wheel. Only one problem: those items were not within reach. He'd opened the wrong door. Jack was in the back seat.

But no matter how drunk Jack got, I had to admire the way he always showed up next morning early, clear headed, ready to work. That was not true for others. Drinking was a common problem in DEA, something true in most professions that have dangerous moments. A man would get his adrenaline up, then have to have a drink or two to calm down. After kicking in a door on a search warrant or having a struggle during an arrest—to the bar they go. After a while the need for drink is permanent.

Agent Dick Fekete, my first partner when I came to Minneapolis, was a prime example of this. Well, he was a partner in name only. He had already been with DEA a long time and could have been an enormous help to me, but since I didn't drink (much), and since I didn't know anything, we had little in common. He was supposed to pick me up mornings in his OGV (Official Government Vehicle—usually called a "G-car"). The idea was, by riding with a senior agent, a new agent would gain experience before going it on his own. The only experience I gained from my senior partner was disliking him. He was supposed to show me around town, share his knowledge of drug dealers with me. He did nothing like that. He picked me up a few times, but was so unreliable I soon used my own car to go to work.

He loved his G-car. "You see that gold Electra over there?" he'd asked me. "That's my G-car. If you ever touch it, I'll strangle you."

I laughed. Fekete smiled—a sardonic smile with lots of teeth and no humor. He glared, his cigar clamped tight in his teeth. He dragged on it heavily and expelled a puff of smoke at me.

"Just remember what I told you," he said and walked off.

I told Agent Terry Anderson of this conversation. He gave a wry grin and said, "Naw, he's not going to strangle you, but he might bend the barrel of his pistol over your head."

I was grateful for that information. If there's anything I hate it's to ruin a good pistol. Fekete carried a beauty: a long barreled .44 magnum.

The car Fekete was talking about was a late model, all gold, Buick Electra 225 that had been seized from a drug dealer. It was an enormous car. Fekete called it his "deuce-and-a-quarter." It had a big V8 engine with a displacement of over 400 cubic inches. In spite of its weight of two and a quarter tons, he could make the tires smoke by tromping on the accelerator. It was over eighteen feet long. Sitting behind the wheel, a person always felt like the hood ornament was in the next county somewhere. It was big. It was flashy. It was fast. It fit Fekete perfectly. He was a wide-shouldered, beefy man who walked around like he owned the world. He was a big Italian, about six foot four, 250 pounds, with a thick shock of hair, and a mustache like the front bumper of a Mac truck. When he made a fist, it looked like the hoof of a Clydesdale.

Fekete's love of his Buick turned out for the best. I used my own car or hitched rides with other agents for a while. Then one day the boss saw me get out of my car and asked "Whose car is that?"

"Mine," I said.

He asked me why I was driving my personal car to work. I told him about Fekete without it looking like a tattletale. I thought he would say, "Oh, yeah. We'll see about that," or "I'll set him straight." But he didn't. Instead he took me up to his office and looked over a board with car keys on hooks.

"The only car I can give you is that old gray Dodge Dart," he said apologetically.

It was great. I had my own G-car, a gray, compact Dodge Dart with no radio in it. It was considered the worst car in the fleet—a great advantage because no one ever wanted to borrow it. What's more, that car was almost invisible on the street. Its dull gray made it unremarkable. It was the best surveillance car I ever drove in my entire career with DEA. A flashy car like the Buick Electra was easily spotted and readily remembered when seen in traffic. I don't think I ever burned surveillance while driving that little gray Dodge. And it was a great undercover car, too. It had no police radio in it and didn't look at all like something a cop might drive.

The one thing Fekete loved even more than his car was his gun. He carried his forty-four in a shoulder holster. The barrel was so long it looked more like a rifle, and he had to pull it up out of the holster like he was reaching for a hook shot to clear leather. "This is a gun," he said to me. "That's a toy," meaning my weapon. I carried a little Smith and Wesson, stainless steel, Model 60. I liked it for undercover. It was small, light, and easy to hide. Fekete scorned it. He said a shot from that gun wouldn't stop a schoolgirl, and the entire contents of the cylinder couldn't give a grown man a headache. Besides, he said, with that short barrel you can't hit anything beyond five yards. That was true. The barrel of the Model 60 was so short, and the space between the front and rear sights so small it was almost a waste of time to aim it.

My pistol had room for only five cartridges in the cylinder. But I had read a study that showed almost all DEA gunfights took place at close range (less than ten yards) and the exchange usually involved three or four shots. That's because those fights were usually inside a building. After a couple of shots, somebody was down, and it was over. So I considered the Model 60 the ideal undercover gun. I carried hollow-point bullets, which were designed to expand on impact and tear a vicious hole in flesh and bone. I kept it hooked inside my belt on the right side of my belly. A little overhang of my shirt covered the handle. The only time a crook ever noticed that gun was when I purposely exposed it. I could always feel it riding there. It gave me great comfort whenever I got into an argument undercover. Sure, in a gunfight outside on the street it would have been nice to have a cannon like Fekete's, but then an M-16 would have been even nicer.

Normally a big man didn't intimidate me, but with Agent Fekete it was different. He made me nervous. Whenever he was around, things seemed to go bad for me. He liked to walk up and stand chest to chest with me to tell me what he wanted or let me know where I had screwed up. I felt like I was facing a rampant grizzly bear. Even after work, when agents stopped by the watering hole to have a drink, Fekete's presence ruined the occasion for me. He could easily beat me at pool even though I was the better player. I had learned to play a decent game of pool in college, and I frequently beat guys who could beat Fekete. But when I played Fekete, he always won. He could intimidate me just by being there, and my shots went bumping aimlessly around the table. He knew it, too—knew he could beat me by making me nervous. He was a total bully when I played him. He stood in my way and made me walk around him to take my shot. He loudly predicted I couldn't make a shot. He exhaled clouds of cigar smoke as I was aiming. He called me a pussy for getting nervous. I was miserable around him. I tried to avoid him, but at times I had no choice. He was always with the boss.

Agent Fekete was a drinker of enormous capacity. He was a good friend of Jim Braseth, our SAC. Braseth too, was able to hold liquor in prodigious amounts. When I wanted to talk to Braseth after hours (and sometimes during), I searched for him in the drinking holes around the federal building. The bar was always foggy with smoke, and Fekete's stogie, big as a tree trunk, was not the least contributor. I would listen for Fekete's loud voice and, walking in that direction, I'd find my boss. Agent Fekete, and usually Agent Terry Anderson (also well-versed in the art of potation) were there too. Dave

Haight, the new group supervisor, was often part of the group. I was not of this crowd because I could not hold my liquor. They looked upon me as a total amateur not worthy to be in the same bar with them. They were right.

Even Fekete's wife had occasion to make me uncomfortable. I was doing paper work in the office one evening after hours. I had been in court all day and had some files to ready for another court session in the morning. I could hear voices on the radio—the guys were out on a moving surveillance. Fekete's voice was among them, a bit surprising since he was usually in the bar by then.

The phone rang. I answered "DEA, Agent Bloch." The lady on the line identified herself as Mrs. Fekete.

She said, "Oh, I know you. You're Dick's partner."

I acknowledged that indeed I was and tried to hide my lack of enthusiasm.

"Do you know where my husband is?"

I told her he was out on surveillance.

"Oh, no need to lie about it," she said kindly. "I mean which bar is he in?"

"He's on surveillance with some other guys, I just heard him on the radio a minute ago."

"Then shouldn't you be out there with him?" The voice had turned frosty. "I want to know where my husband is!"

"Really, Mrs. Fekete, he's on surveillance. I just heard him on the radio."

Now she came on screaming, "You're just like the rest of those son-of-a-bitches! Always covering for each other!" Crash, she hung up.

The first time I suspected there was something really wrong with Fekete was when he wrecked his gold Electra. My phone at home rang at three o'clock in the morning. "You got my car over there?" It was Fekete. I struggled out of the fog of sleep, trying to make sense of the question.

"What?" I asked. I knew what he had asked, but it didn't seem possible. He knew darn well I didn't have his car. He knew I wouldn't go near that car. What was the purpose of this call, especially at this time? "I don't have your car," I said, still puzzled.

"Oh, okay. I thought maybe you took it. It's missing from the parking ramp." He hung up. This was not like Fekete at all. Something was fishy here.

As I drove to work the next morning I was still pondering the strange phone call. I thought Fekete had probably gotten drunk and forgot where he parked his car. But then why call me? Maybe he was with the boss and blamed me and had to call to make it look good. I knew something wasn't right. When

I got to the office, Fekete was not in yet, but his story from the night before was already all over the office. He had parked the car in the parking ramp across the street as usual. That was sometime after noon. When he went there that night (around bar-closing time) the car was missing.

I was suspicious of this story for one main reason: that phone call. But another thing not normal was that when Fekete went bar hopping, he didn't go on foot. He didn't leave his car parked in the ramp. I went to the guard shack of the parking ramp and talked to the guard. He had a good memory. He knew me after just one meeting, and from then on waved me through with a smile.

"You know the gold Buick Electra that belongs to our office?"

He nodded. "Sure." He knew every regular car in the lot.

"Do you by any chance remember if it went out of here last night?"

The guard looked at the ceiling and pursed his lips, then down at the floor and shifted the pursed lips to one side. He nodded slowly. "Yup," he said. "I remember. Went out about five o'clock or so."

"You remember who was driving it."

"Well, sure. That big Italian guy who always drives it."

"Would you swear to that?"

"Bull shit! I don't swear to nothin'. If you DEA guys got trouble between you, I ain't getting in the middle."

I couldn't blame the guard. Fekete was a scary guy. But Fekete was lying. I knew what happened. Fekete hated paperwork. He'd gotten himself into an accident and didn't want to fill out the mountain of government paper involved. So he hid the car and said it was stolen. But there was no way I could prove it.

The Minneapolis Police found the car later that day near some big cement grain silos in east Minneapolis. It was all smashed up. Both the front end and the rear were badly mangled. It was theorized some crook who hated Fekete had stolen the car and had smashed it out of spite. Terry Anderson was out drinking with Fekete that night. He backed up Fekete's story about the car being gone when they went to the ramp. I didn't believe it for a minute. I told Terry what I thought happened. He said I was wrong and Fekete was telling the truth. But I could tell he wasn't comfortable with the story. I told him what made me suspicious was that early-morning phone call from Fekete. "Dick was a fool to make that call," I told him. I wanted Fekete to know I was not his stooge.

Later that day Braseth called me in and told me that, since I was not the investigating agent on Fekete's stolen G-car, it'd be best if I kept my imaginations to myself. Fekete, of course, had heard what I'd been saying, and it didn't improve relations between us. He took to making fun of me whenever he had a chance. One of his favorite antics was to make fun of my balding head. My hairline had begun receding back in college, and by then it was well advanced on either side. Fekete often came into the office in the morning and would stand by my desk with his comb out and pretend to comb his thick mane to match mine. The other agents got a big laugh out of this. But for this antic Fekete would be repaid. He would be repaid far beyond anything I could ever have devised myself—even at my worst. His day of reckoning came during the time I was gone to Mexico on Operation Trizo. This happened two years later, but I might as well finish the Fekete story here.

I was on temporary duty to Culiacan, Mexico, for three months. (I'll get to that.) I got back on a weekend and went to work early the following Monday morning. I was the first one in the office. I had a backlog of paperwork to wade through. I was already well into the paper as some of the agents filed in. When Helena, our office secretary, came in, she walked up behind me and bending over whispered in my ear.

"Now, you can take your revenge on Fekete."

I looked at her and frowned. She was smiling delightedly. She obviously had some priceless gossip and couldn't wait to unload.

"What are you talking about?" I asked.

"He's lost his hair! Remember how he used to make fun of your hair? Now you can make fun of his."

"You mean he shaved his head?" I said, not believing for a minute Fekete would mow his beautiful thick mane—for he was vain.

"No, no." she laughed delighted at my disbelief. "I mean he has really lost his hair! It all fell out."

"Oh, baloney," I said. I was getting irritated. She was enjoying this so much. I thought she was pulling my leg.

"You just wait. When he comes in you'll see for yourself. He's bald as a cue ball. Remember he used to call you cue ball? He has some kind of disease that makes his hair fall out. You'll see."

I did see. Fekete came in. It was the first time I saw him in a hat. A few strands of hair hung limply from under the brim. When he removed the hat, a few more were visible. It looked awful. He had two or three little patches that contained perhaps a half-dozen hairs, but mostly single strands were scattered about so his bare skull gleamed through like a beacon. He was worse then bald. He would have looked better bald. I felt sorry for him and could not think of revenge. In a few weeks all his hair was gone including his eyebrows and chest hair. He looked like the shining, bald Mister Clean in the Proctor and Gamble commercials. Fekete pretended his bald head didn't bother him, but the fact he took to wearing a hat, and sometimes wore the afro wig we had in the office for undercover told me different. I found I liked Fekete much better after that, which showed me that a lot of the problem between us came from my own thin skin.

But I must give Fekete his due. He was a valuable agent. He was raised in Philadelphia, and had already been with DEA for six or seven years though he was no older than I. He had big-city street wisdom far beyond anything I would ever develop. He was fearless on the job and, sober or drunk, there was not a better man to have with you when you were kicking in a door or making a difficult arrest. When Dick Fekete projected his bulk against a door, it flew open—usually off the hinges. If by chance it was of reinforced oak and withstood the first assault, when Fekete clamped down on his cigar, and stepped back for a second try, one had best get out of the way because now the entire house was in jeopardy. And if a belligerent prisoner was refusing the cuffs, one confrontation with the flaming cigar and the blazing eyes backed by that hulking Italian bulk reduced the prisoner to a placid lamb who went eagerly to jail, happy to have iron bars between himself and that mad man. During my twenty years with DEA, many a time I wished Dick Fekete was with me.

He was later transferred to Philadelphia, and I was sent to McAllen, Texas. It was, however, not the last I heard of Dick Fekete. We had barely parted ways, when I heard he and two DEA drinking buddies had been arrested in a go-go bar in Camden, Pennsylvania, for being drunk and disorderly. But they were not only acquitted (they said they were on an investigation into prostitution and drugs), the city paid them a hundred thousand dollars in a settlement. About five years later, I met a Philadelphia cop in court in Houston. He told me Fekete was highly thought of by the police, and he had just made a big cocaine case against a major trafficker from South America. Right after that, some agents from Detroit came down to McAllen to testify in court on a marijuana case. They told me still another Dick Fekete story:

One day Dick was drinking in a favorite watering hole called the Waterside Café. A fight broke out in the kitchen between the owner and an employee, a hot-headed twenty-one-year-old kid (coincidentally named Ferretti). Ferretti snatched up a butcher knife. The owner yelled for Dick to come help. Dick went back there. The man with the knife turned toward Dick, who pulled his canon and, when the kid refused to drop it, put three holes through him. Dick got acquitted—justifiable homicide.

Nothing more about Agent Fakete for a few years. I met him once when we were both working Operation Snow Cap down in Santa Cruz, Bolivia. He still looked like Mr. Clean, only now he seldom wore a hat. His shiny head had become his trademark. His home station was Panama then, a coveted assignment in DEA, one which top notch agents got as a reward for good work. Dick and I were on the best of terms down there in Santa Cruz, like old pals. I even helped him interview an informant one day. The man couldn't speak English and Dick's Spanish was limited to rudimentary bar talk: *una cerveza mas*. About a year later, I heard Dick had gotten himself assigned to the Miami DEA office. That made sense. That is where all the action was, and Dick loved action.

When I next heard of Dick Fekete, I was already retired for several years and had forgotten about him. Then one day I read a brief story, buried in the back pages of the *St. Cloud Times*. I called the Minneapolis DEA office about the story, and they sent me some paper clippings from the *Miami Herald*. This time Dick was in real trouble. He was in jail—for murder.

On the 12th of December 1997 Agent Fekete was at a Christmas party in Miami. He was celebrating in his usual manner. Some of his fellow agents and Dade county policemen convinced him he'd had enough to drink and should go home. They also convinced him he was too drunk to drive. DEA Agent Shaun Curl offered to drive him. Agents said Dick was singing as they helped him into Curl's car. The way home was about twenty miles. During the trip, Dick for some unknown reason (he says he was blacked out) shot and killed Agent Curl. Curl was thirty-nine years old, had a wife and two children. Fekete was sentenced to fifteen years in jail.

That's the end of that story except for one thing. After agents retire and no longer fear for their jobs, they leak out things covered up before. Here's what happened to Fekete's Buick Electra. Agents Anderson and Fekete had been out drinking that night. They were bar hopping in Fekete's Buick. He had parked it in front of a bar. About midnight they came out and found they were parked in solid. The cars in front and behind were bumper to bumper with the Buick. Agent Anderson was for going back in the bar and trying to find the drivers, but Fekete said, "Bullshit on that. Get in." He put the car in drive, revved up the engine, and jumped off the brake. The big Buick moved only a few inches, but its weight was enough to drive the front car forward a foot. He dropped it into reverse and did the same to the car behind. He kept doing this. Each time the Buick slammed into the other cars it jumped ahead (or back) a little more. Fekete enjoyed it so much he made himself more room than he needed. When they finally drove away and discovered the considerable damage to the Buick, they hatched the plot about the stolen car. Fekete drove the thing to the grain silos, thoroughly smashed the car, then they drove off in Anderson's car. I have to say this: I would never have had the guts—even drunk—to pull this off. Fekete did it without batting an eye.

The tragic story of Agent Curl's death brought a lot of speculation about how this could have been allowed in DEA. Many said supervisors turned their heads because Fekete was such a valuable agent, but I think this is closer to the truth: most supervisors didn't recognize the problem because they had similar problems themselves. Drinking buddies don't recognize each other as dangerous. I'm sure Dick Fekete had many more buddies in DEA than I did, and those men saw him, not only as a great agent, but as a fun guy to have around.

I'm not trying to condemn anyone here. Our culture was different back then. In those days public drunkenness was not condemned as it is today. It was smiled upon. Even women got drunk in the bars on Friday nights, and we all had a big laugh. There was no MADD organization—mothers were not mad yet. Innocent television shows like *The Andy Griffith Show*, showed how delightful it could be when Otis got drunk. The famous comedian Foster Brooks entertained by acting drunk. Dean Martin acted drunk half the time on his variety show. Cops would stop a weaving car and tell the driver he had too much to drink and should be careful on the way home.

In those days men went on two-day benders, and then told stories about their drunken adventures. A few of those stories actually were funny. Here's one—a little comic relief after the Fekete tragedy—told to me by a DEA Compliance Investigator (he normally did not drink):

> When I got off work, I remembered that my wife had the bridge club over that afternoon. I went across the street to Joe's Bar to have a beer. I was killing time. I didn't like those snooty bridge-club women and wanted to spend as little time with them as possible. I thought I'd have one beer and sip it slow, but the bartender set me up two. It was happy

hour: two-for-one special. By the time I was half way though the second beer, I realized this was one of those special nights when the beer goes down really easy. It tasted good, and I didn't feel bloated like I always do.

Right about then, in comes a buddy of mine, who works at the pharmacy. Before I know it, he orders me a beer. The bartender sets up two more. When I finished those two, I knew I was getting tipsy, but I felt so good and, since I owed my buddy a beer, I ordered another. The bartender sets up two more. I thought I better go to the bathroom before I drank those two—to make room, you know. The floor in the bar was covered with peanut shells and puddles of beer. As I got off the bar stool I slipped and fell flat on my belly. I had trouble getting up, because my hands kept slipping on the peanuts. My buddy helped me up, but the whole front of my shirt and part of my tie was covered with barroom slop, which did not blend well with the white of the shirt and the yellow of the tie. Luckily I had left my suit jacket on the barstool. It was still clean.

After I finished my beers, I said goodbye to my buddy and drove home. I drove very slowly because I didn't want to get there before the ladies of the bridge club were gone. The stuff on my shirt had mostly dried, and I found I could hide a good part of it with my suit jacket. As I drove along, I found I had to pee again, and after a little while I also had to take a shit. I saw a nice bunch of bushes near the street and pulled over to the curb. I stepped through the bushes and found a little clear spot. I squatted and let go. Suddenly I thought of it. I had no toilet paper! I patted my pockets for a handkerchief. Nothing. With my left hand I'd been holding onto a branch of a bush to steady myself as I squatted, but in my search, my left hand forgot what it was doing and let go. I tumbled backwards and sat in the pile I had just made. I tried wiping with my finger but that didn't help much. Then I thought, well, I have to get the tie cleaned anyhow, so I used the tie to wipe my ass. It was an expensive tie, too. I wiped the tie on the grass and hung it around my neck. I drove home. I got lost for a minute and drove past my home and had to backtrack. I saw only one car parked near my house, so I figured the ladies must be gone. Well, the witches had carpooled that day and were just leaving as I entered the front door. I had to squeeze by them in the hall, and I saw them wrinkling their noses and shrinking back from me like I was an ax murderer or something.

Well, I got no end of hell from the wife. I deserved it, so I said little in my defense. I had no defense. I got a bad night's sleep and woke up with a grinding hangover. But that wasn't the worst of it yet. When I backed out of my driveway and started down the street to the office, my neighbor flagged me over.

"What the hell were you up to last night?" he asked. I never heard him sound so unfriendly.

I said, "What are you talking about?"

He said, "What am I talking about? I was sitting in the back of the house having a beer. I heard a car pull over to the curb, and heard a door slam. I thought I heard something in the bushes at the far corner of my property. I looked around the corner of the house, and just then you stepped out of the bushes and took a shit on my lawn! It was getting dark, but god damn it, I know it was you."

Chapter Four

I WAS SITTING AT MY DESK in the DEA office on the fourth floor of the Federal Building in downtown Minneapolis. A few other agents were just coming in. Helena was already there. She usually showed up early so she could read the *National Inquirer* and drink coffee before getting her typewriter warmed up. She was a kind hearted, sentimental old dingbat, who laughed easily, cried easily, and loved to quote the great wisdom of the *National Inquirer.*

She said, "Oh, isn't this beautiful. Listen to this, boys. It's so true. It says here that life is like an onion. You peal off one layer at a time and sometimes you weep."

No one paid her any attention. She added as she turned a page, "Isn't that just the truth, though?" Then Fekete looked up from his desk and, taking his cigar from his mouth yelled in an irritated voice, "No! Life is like a banana. Sometimes you eat it and sometimes they shove it up your ass."

Dave Haight came in. He signaled to me, "I wanna see you in my office."

Haight was the group supervisor. I had no idea what he wanted. The only other time he'd called me in was to talk about a case, and I had nothing new going. He was hanging up his coat, without looking around he said, "I read one of your reports yesterday."

That surprised me. I was convinced supervisors signed off on reports without bothering to read them. I waited.

"It had to do with that Norsheim cocaine case."

I waited.

"I don't normally put my personal opinions into the physical description section."

I said, "Ah, well, I don't either."

"Oh, really?"

He had in his hand a DEA 6 (an investigative report), signed by me. He opened it to the last page where the physical descriptions were. In a DEA 6 there was a standard way to write the physical description. It was always in the same order: "white male, 5' 9", 175 lbs, black hair, blue eyes," then peculiarities like: "he is missing one ear," or "has a tattoo of a spider on his neck" or "he always wears a cowboy hat."

Haight read, "Black male, 5' 11," 170 lbs, black hair, brown eyes. He is a big asshole, and he always wears a large silver chain around his neck."

I was astounded. "I didn't write that," I said.

"You dictated it."

"I didn't dictate that."

"Helena says you did."

"She's wrong."

"Take it up with her." He tossed the report on my lap. I left his office.

Helena typed all our reports. She could go smoking along at 120 words per minute while holding the phone receiver on one shoulder and gossiping with her friends or arguing with her teen age son.

I asked Helena about my report. She said, "That's exactly what you dictated on the tape. I played it back several times."

"Now, Helena," I said, "You know I wouldn't put something like this in an official report."

"I simply typed what you dictated," she sniffed.

I went to my desk. I ran the tape. It did not say, "He is a big asshole." It said, "He has a big afro."

The afro was a popular hairstyle back then, as were several other fads that were strange to me after being in the Air Force. Some of the agents adopted these styles. They thought they were cool (though they said it was for working undercover). Another fad for men was wearing heavy jewelry. Agent Fekete had a necklace that looked like a shiny, gold logging chain. You had to have a Rolex watch to be "in" as a DEA agent. They bragged about how expensive their watches were. I didn't like the fancy jewelry. In Stearns County, a man would be ashamed to have paid that much for a stupid watch, and if he paid a lot of money for a necklace, he hung it on his lady, not on himself. Some local drug agents even adopted those ridiculous platform shoes that were in vogue. Those shoes had started as little two-inch heals but developed into minor stilts, until doctors were calling them "elevated orthopedic nightmares." Those shoes routinely brought people to emergency rooms with sprained and broken ankles. They were great though when a crook had them on during an arrest because he couldn't run. And the bell bottom trouser of that time also developed into the ridiculous: loose, floppy flags hanging around the bottom of the leg—also great at arrest time for they too impeded running. The only fad of the time I liked was the short mini skirt. But I did not adopt that either.

At the DEA School they told us we would be working only on big cases. Small cases were to be handed over to the local police. Yet when the boss first assigned me a case, it was the smallest and most insignificant possible. Our compliance investigator had been complaining a doctor in north Minneapolis was writing prescriptions at an extravagant rate. He wrote as many as the rest of the doctors in the city put together. Pharmacists were calling in every few days saying something was fishy. The boss decided to send an agent up there, and since the case didn't look like it could possibly develop into a gunfight or a car chase, nobody wanted it, so, of course, it was assigned to me. The boss said, "Go up there and snoop around. Put together a case on the guy. He's got to be crooked."

Great. I was supposed to be buying heroin and cocaine from drug lords, mafia types, and world-class drug dealers. Instead, here I was investigating an over-zealous little doctor. I checked out some buy-money and recorded the serial numbers. You had to record all the serial numbers on buy-money in case the money ever needed to be traced. Tracing buy-money was often a way of nailing the source of the drugs. I drove up to Plymouth Avenue North where Dr. Sam Leonard had his office.

His dingy little waiting room looked like Christmas in a crack house. Scattered about the room on the floor and the chairs were skinny young men with long greasy hair and unshaven sallow faces, some sniffing and some chronically coughing. I saw some young girls too, with stringy hair, no makeup, clutching worn denim shoulder bags and sitting close to or leaning against one of the males. There was standing room only. Some of those in the chairs were asleep and some, leaning against the wall, appeared to be. Some stood in the middle of the room and stared blankly and said, "Hey, man," without inflection as I walked by. I had let my hair and beard grow since DEA school, so by now I looked like I fit in—except my face wasn't the color of the wallpaper.

There was no receptionist. The patients kept track of who was next. When I walked in, a young man (or boy—he looked like he might still be in grade school) said, "You're after me." It looked like I'd be there all day. The room was way too hot. It was winter, but someone had turned the thermostat to about 100 degrees, and the doctor's heater was going full blast. The place smelled like a bathroom in a bar. All the ashtrays were loaded with cigarette butts and gum wrappers. The furniture had cigarette burns, and there was gum stuck to the walls. I was turning to leave, but the school boy told me it'd not take long—the good doctor was very fast. He was right. Patients were spending less than five minutes in the corner room that served as his consulting office. I stayed and took to reading the graffiti on the walls.

When I went into Dr. Leonard's office, I found it was very small. I think it had been a storage closet. There was a little table and chair for the doctor, a small stool for the patient, and a book case with a few books and some doctor paraphernalia like tongue depressors, a microscope, thermometers, a little flashlight, hoses, and picture cards of various diseases.

Dr. Leonard MD was an aging little man with a stubble beard. He was over seventy, and looked it. The skin of his face was an unhealthy gray, but he had vigorous, snapping eyes sparkling with intelligence and constantly darting about as if he was playing a fast game of pinball. His skinny body seemed packed with energy. He moved in nervous fits and starts like a chipmunk.

"Where's my ten spot?" he said, holding out his hand.

They had told me in the waiting room I must hand Dr. Leonard a ten dollar bill as soon as I walked into his office. I had purposely waited to see if he would ask. I pulled the required bill from my pocket and slapped it into his hand. He tucked it in his shirt pocket and said, "Okay, what do you want?"

On that first visit, I went through a long song and dance about why I needed amphetamines. I said I often drove truck at night and it made me sleepy. I didn't want to have an accident. My story was so compelling, I thought, he almost had to give me the drugs. But all that was unnecessary. He was already writing a prescription for Dexedrine before I finished.

Anslinger and the Bureau of Narcotics and Dangerous Drugs had only recently managed to get amphetamine listed as a Schedule II drug, which meant it ranked up there with cocaine. The good doctor was running amuck. He was dispensing prescriptions like Santa does candy. I learned one didn't need much of a story to get drugs.

"I want some amphetamines," I demanded on my next visit.

"Didn't I just give you some a few days ago? What happened to them?"

"My girlfriend had a party with her friends, and they used them all up." My excuses became more brazen with each visit. I wanted to make sure a jury would realize this man was a real pusher not just a misunderstood medicine man.

"Don't let that happen again," he said indifferently as he wrote out another prescription.

I ordered uppers one day, downers the next.

"I need some barbituates to help me sleep."

"Why do you have trouble sleeping?" he asked as he wrote.

"I think sometimes I take too many uppers."

"Try to cut back on the uppers," he said, as he handed me a prescription for downers.

When I asked for cough medicine with codeine, he looked at me over his glasses with his sharp brown eyes. "Okay, but don't come back for more tomorrow. You know the DEA is watching me."

I felt like saying they were doing a lousy job, but I took my prescription and left. I thought I was spending a lot of money on Dr. Leonard, but Braseth seemed to think it was nothing. He'd read my reports and shake his head. "Boy, this bastard is a real dope dealer, isn't he? Ask him for heroin and see what he does."

I asked. The good doctor simply said, "Nope, don't have it." He gave me another bottle of cough syrup instead.

It'd be nice to report that, eventually, we arrested Dr. Leonard, but that wasn't what developed. After a while Braseth told me to take my case to the U.S. Attorney for prosecution. Oh, that U. S. Attorney was vicious in his punishment. With unwavering dedication, the proud office of the U. S. Attorney in Minneapolis, Minnesota, insisted Dr. Leonard retire: they had his license revoked.

That was the big Dexedrine case that started my career as a special agent for the Drug Enforcement Administration of the United States of America. I can't think of a favor we could have done Doctor Sam Leonard that would have served him better. He should have retired long ago to his cabin in northern Minnesota. For years he could have been out fishing and puttering around a golf course. Instead he was spending his time in a small, stinky office serving patients who really only needed a shower.

Dr. Leonard, you have the United States taxpayer to thank for your timely retirement. You'd probably have died in your office. And you taxpayers can thank me for wasting that money buying gas, buying drugs, and giving Dr. Leonard his ten spots. But that was nothing. It was a minimum drop in a maximum bucket, as you'll see.

Chapter Five

THE EASIEST WAY TO MAKE A CASE was through an informant. But people did not readily volunteer for that line of work. You could end up dead. The drug trade was a violent business in those days, though not in the ostentatious way it became later. Hits were done for revenge then, not for sending a public message. Hits were done late in the night in back alleys with silencers, not in broad daylight on main street with the loud clatter of machine guns. Dead bodies just turned up quietly and mysteriously with no exhibitionism. Even the great drug trafficker, Plukey Duke, died quietly in the back seat of a car at the Minneapolis–Saint Paul International Airport. The body might not have been found for days had it not been winter and someone saw large, red icicles of blood hanging from under the car. Dead bodies made informants think twice before going to work for DEA.

A dead body turned up in the Pat Morris case. I think this was Task Force Agent Boulger's case. I remember it because the arrest got a bit exciting, and because a corpse was an addendum to that case. Patricia Caldwell was an attractive Minneapolis hooker—at least she was at one time before she became a hopeless heroin junkie and no longer cultivated her good looks. She lived from needle to needle, turning tricks only for money to buy the drug. One of her sources was Pat Morris, who sold probably the highest quality heroin in the Twin Cities. Morris sold to dealers who cut his stuff and sold it on the street at a good profit. He did not sell to small-timers—except for Pat Caldwell. Morris personally delivered to her apartment though she lived in public housing in a seedy part of town. The Minneapolis narcs somehow turned her into an informant.

On this particular day, Pat Morris was to deliver a pound of heroin to Pat Caldwell. When Morris left his place we were on his tail. To keep Caldwell cool, our agents moved in for the arrest long before Morris was anywhere near her apartment. They had blocked the street, but as Supervisor Dave Haight walked up to Morris sitting in his big pickup truck to inform him that he was under arrest, Morris stomped on the gas, jumped the curb, and cut over to the street across the corner of the parking lot. We were off to the races right in downtown Minneapolis. The race was short. Another unit came head-on to block Morris. He swerved to get around, but he was going too fast. His tires screeched, he skidded and crashed into the concrete base of a street lamp. We took away his pound of heroin, his pickup truck, and his freedom (at least for a while).

Bea and I had a next-door neighbor in St. Louis Park, a doctor of medicine: Doctor Cassius Ellis. He was a good neighbor, a good friend, and a good doctor. When we needed some doctoring done, we went to Cassius. He was a fat, jolly man—and he was black by the way, and so was his wife, and so were his children (I add this because a reporter once called me a racist when he noticed I had arrested several blacks without arresting several whites for balance). Cassius frequently asked me about my job. He was very interested in drug enforcement. He was worried his children might get into drugs when they got older. I trusted him completely and often told him in detail about arrests we had made. Cassius was also Pat Caldwell's doctor.

Not long after the Morris arrest, I was raking leaves in our back yard, when Cassius called me over. He told me Pat Caldwell had committed suicide. They had found her lying peacefully in her bed, everything normal (except for the fact she was missing a few vital signs like heart, lung, and brain function). They said she had taken an overdose of heroin.

Agent Boulger did not believe that. He believed Pat Morris had hired Michael Ayd to give Caldwell a hotshot (a dose of heroin strong enough to kill her). I thought that was a very good guess. Boulger played a tape for me which was a recording of Ayd talking to an informant. Ayd was describing how he had killed someone else with a hot shot, and the excitement and pleasure in his voice as he told it made my skin crawl. He was a stone cold murderer. Later when Michael Ayd was brought to trial on a drug case, Boulger wanted to play that tape to show what kind of a citizen Ayd was. The judge refused to allow it. He said the tape was so prejudicial any jury, even one made up of serial killers, would find Ayd guilty of anything after listening to that tape.

Most of the informants we had were drug dealers we had arrested. They preferred facing the danger rather than jail time. It was rare a good informant just waltzed in, but it did happen. I had one I named Lenny. He was a tall, flashy black man with a diamond set in gold in one front tooth. Lenny lived by his wits on the street. He sometimes cruised Hennepin, lining up hookers with customers and collecting commissions. He sold small amounts of marijuana and PCP (Phencyclidine). He kept several women in apartments around the city. The ladies collected welfare checks (often in both Minnesota and Wisconsin) and sometimes turned tricks when Lenny needed extra money. The welfare checks, which were supposed to support the women and their children, went to Lenny. He gave the women an allowance—whenever there was any left. Lenny used most of it to pay for the apartments, buy drugs, gamble, and spend on other women. Lenny knew all the secrets of getting checks from the government for housing, food, and fatherless children. The women named Lenny as the father and claimed he had run off. Lenny dressed in expensive clothes, and flashed money around to impress his street buddies. He also flashed (whenever he smiled), that gold tooth with a large diamond. Every street bum in south Minneapolis knew Lenny and looked up to him like a guru. They respected him for his ability to make a high living by defrauding the government and avoiding the police.

Lenny came to our office one day to snitch off some other black dude because the dude was cutting in on one of his women. The accusations Lenny was making against the dude were basically the same things Lenny was doing himself. The problem solved itself when the woman disappeared with the dude. They must have left town, because if they had stayed anywhere in the Twin Cities, Lenny would have found them. Lenny kept coming around as though he liked me, but Lenny didn't really "like" anyone. He used people like tools. He kept contact with me because he thought I might come in handy if he got into trouble, which was exactly what he did a year later when he sold a gram of heroin to Mike Campion and Jim Hessel, who happened to be undercover agents with the Minnesota Bureau of Narcotics.

I learned a lot from Lenny about life in south Minneapolis. We used to go to Rhines's Café, a dive on the corner of Thirty-fifth and Fourth Street, to eat platters of red beans and rice. Voodoo was the owner, cook, waiter, and chief gossip in the place. He always wore bib overalls and dirty white T-shirts. He cooked real street food, farmer food, using huge platters for plates and topping off his dishes with two greasy pork hocks that leaked streams of flavor into the rice and beans on which they rested. He had a grill going in the back from early morning to late night, and a big deep fryer in which he made chitlins that he dipped in hot sauce and sold for fifteen cents a bag. He needed no sign, because the aromas emanating from the place beckoned beyond what any sign could do. Downstairs in the cellar Voodoo had set up a piece of plywood on two wooden barrels. The customers played craps down there, and on rainy days they played acey-deucey on a backgammon board that had all the paint worn off. There was a fruit jar on the shelf by the plywood in which a dime had to be dropped for each round of betting. That was Voodoo's cut. If we were upstairs having a beer at Voodoo's bar, and someone downstairs rolled a one-two, we'd know, because there would erupt from below a shout of "acey-deucey!" and Voodoo would go to the stairway and yell down for them to shut up or he would close down the game. He didn't want cops storming the place.

Lenny introduced me to his friends at Rhine's Café, some of whom were small time drug dealers. Lenny never introduced me to any big, powerful crooks, but he had no qualms about getting me in with dealers who had no clout. I could easily have made a case on a black man named Hiawatha who hung around Rhine's and sold theatre tickets impregnated with four hits of LSD, but Hiawatha was basically harmless and sold only enough to make a very sparse living. Braseth refused to spend money on a dealer like him.

One day Lenny told me I could score heroin from a black man named Jerome Ellison. Jerome was a heroin junkie who lived in an old house on Columbus Avenue South. I proposed the buy to Jim Braseth, but he didn't want to waste money on a small-time junkie. A few days later, however, he changed his mind. He'd talked to George Bent, the head of Minneapolis Narcotics. Unfortunately for Jerome, Nicky Frol was his heroin source, and the Minneapolis Police and the Hennepin County narcs wanted Nicky in jail. Braseth was always eager to promote good relations with the locals.

Nicky, a Russian immigrant, came to this country and found he could make a nice living by dealing heroin. That became his sole means of support. The cops took this as a personal affront. He was breaking the laws of this country and was not even a citizen. They wanted to make a case against Nicky and—as George Bent put it—"send his Ruskie ass back to Siberia where it belongs." When they heard I could score heroin from Ellison, they convinced Braseth it was worth a try to nail Nicky Frol. The Nicky Frol case was my baptism into the confusing and frustrating world of criminal conspiracy law.

Nicky lived in an apartment up on Yates Avenue in Brooklyn Park. He was very careful. He had a rule: you buy from whites, you sell to blacks, preferably junkies. In those days the narcs did not sell drugs in sting operations, and there were few black narcs. It was Nicky's belief a junkie would never burn his source, for a junkie wanted heroin more than life.

Since our main effort with Ellison was to get Nicky Frol, Braseth wanted me to wear the KEL (a body-worn mike) and to get Jerome to talk about Nicky. When everything was working right, a surveillance agent could hear the conversation between the undercover and the crook through the KEL, and could make a recording of it for use in court. We didn't use the KEL much because we had to get permission from higher up in the bureaucracy (always a pain, and good luck getting it by next Christmas). I didn't like wearing the thing because it was unreliable and had to be taped to the body under clothes, and the battery pack often got so hot it burned my skin. Also it was so big that if the crook patted me down, as they sometimes did, he could easily find it. Agent Kryger was our tech guy. He put the KEL on me and taped it on my lower back so it was as well hidden as possible. He showed me how to turn it on and warned me it could get hot. If I couldn't stand it, I should turn it off. If all else failed I should go to the bathroom and tear it off. The ability of the KEL unit to transmit a clear signal to surveillance depended on the distance between transmitter and receiver, surrounding buildings, topography, and the strength of the batteries. There were always times when the transmission was inaudible. Often the transmission would fade out when a car passed. If the undercover man was in some kind of trouble, it'd be a mistake to assume surveillance heard about it over the KEL.

I wondered what I would run into at Ellison's that day. No informant went with me to his house. Lenny had simply introduced me on the phone. Lenny said the time was right, because Jerome needed a fix, and his girlfriend had no money. Jerome was a main-liner, that is, he injected his heroin. You could smoke or snort heroin, but the hard-core user injected the stuff. Intravenous injection of heroin provided the greatest intensity and the fastest onset of the rush (the intense high). Jerome was not careful when he needed a fix. In Jerome's universe, the planets did not revolve around the sun, they revolved around heroin. He thought about heroin day and night. When he had no heroin, he spent all his time finding some, and he was reckless in the pursuit.

Jerome was eager to deal that day. His lady would not get paid from her job until the weekend. Jerome wanted to turn a deal immediately so he could get a cut of the powder to put in his arm. First he said I had to front the money, but when I said I wouldn't do that, he said I should come to his house, and he would have the source deliver there.

I pressed the button by Jerome's front door, assuming it was a doorbell. Hearing nothing from inside, I knocked. I waited. Knocked again. Then I heard soft footsteps, and a tall, thin blonde opened the door and told me to come in. All the shades were pulled. The gloom inside contrasted with the radiance outside. It was a beautiful sunny day in the springtime with trees breaking out, birds returning, lawns a cheerful green. Inside it was desolately dark, I could barely see anything. I was sunblind. I made out a big oak table covered with junk: books, boxes, ash trays, clothing pieces. The room had a melancholy look, as did the girl.

"I'm Don," I told her.

"I'm Willow. Jerome's downstairs. He's waiting for you."

She took me to the head of a stairway, and I went down alone.

Jerome was sitting on a wooden chair at a low bar. He was really skinny, even skinnier than Willow. He was a starving, burnt-out junky—eyes set in deep darkness, cheeks hollow, everything about his face conveying an impression of passionate hunger. Right away he wanted to see the money.

"I have to make sure you have the money before I call Nicky. It's the first thing he'll ask me."

I rolled down my right sock and showed him where I had the money.

"I have to count it," he said.

I gave him the roll, he counted and handed it back. (It wasn't but a couple of hundred dollars—I was buying grams, not ounces).

"I can't ask Nicky to come out here unless the money's right," he said.

"Well, let's get him on the phone," I said. "I've got customers waiting."

"Oh, you can't talk to him," Jerome said quickly. "Nicky won't talk to anybody but me. No, he won't allow it."

I knew that was probably true, but it didn't hurt to try. If I could talk directly to Nicky it'd make a much better case for court. But I also knew Jerome was afraid he'd get cut out of the deal and would lose his cut of the heroin. It didn't matter all that much to me. I was confident the surveillance outside would see Nicky make the delivery.

Jerome called Nicky. Nicky said he'd be right over with the dope. I figured Nicky would likely be coming from his apartment in north Minneapolis so I expected it'd take about half an hour. Jerome and I sat and talked. It was uncomfortable talking to Jerome. He never looked at me—not when I was talking to him, not when he was talking to me. He would look at the floor, the ceiling, the lamp, whatever, but he absolutely would not look directly at me. He was friendly in every other way, but his determination to avoid eye contact was creepy. To add to my discomfort the damn KEL unit was overheating and burning my back. (Later I found out I had a large red patch back there, and Bea told me there were several small blisters).

Willow came down for a cigarette, and I noticed Nicky did not look at her either. He just didn't like eye contact with people. Willow was a thin, willowy girl like Olive Oyl (Popeye the Sailor Man's girl friend). Her face, with prominent cheek bones and her sad, sunken eyes had a haunted look that somehow made her appealing. She had a deep sadness about her that made me want to put my arm around her and tell her everything would be all right. She worked somewhere in Minneapolis as a secretary, but all her money went into Jerome's arm—and into her own, if there was any left. She stared at my forearm with fascination. I looked down to find what she was seeing there. I looked back up and our eyes met.

"Your veins," she said. "They're beautiful."

No one had ever admired my blood veins. I had never heard such a compliment. A junky likes prominent veins. Their veins retreat into the flesh from constantly getting stuck with needles. I got that compliment again several times in the next few years. I had big, farmer veins like my dad. You could not see any veins on Willow's arms, or Jerome's, only black specks of needle tracks running all over like a labyrinth puzzle.

Willow disappeared. Jerome was restless waiting for his fix to arrive. He was constantly fidgeting. He got out a pack of matches and a spoon to cook the heroin. He reached down and got a mirror and a razor blade and laid them on top of the counter. He took a rubber cord he used for a tourniquet and played with it—tying it around his arm and untying it. He drummed the table with his fingers. He was making me nervous. He looked out the window.

"What kind of car does Nicky drive?" I asked and moved a little closer to Jerome so the surveillance would hear his answer.

"White Bonneville," he said.

He laid a syringe on the table and drummed some more.

He asked me if I was going to shoot up, and I told him I wasn't a user, just a pusher. He frowned and stared at the floor in front of my shoes for a while, but then nodded like he was satisfied.

After a while, he tied off his arm with the rubber cord to try to make the veins in his arm stand out. I could see only the needle tracks. They were clean tracks though, not like some junkies. I had seen arms covered with ulcers from using dirty needles or injecting bad heroin. Jerome took the syringe and started sticking it in his arm in various places. He cursed because he was having trouble finding a vein. Finally he found one and dark blood flowed into the syringe. He pulled the plunger all the way back and left the needle hang in his arm. I thought he was trying to gross me out, so I just watched calmly. I even moved my chair closer to let him know I wasn't afraid of a little blood. He waited a few seconds, then he shot the blood back into his arm. Well, I thought, maybe he just has an ugly way of testing his syringe. But he still left the needle in his arm. It hung there grotesquely. In a little while he drew blood again. When he shot the blood back in his arm again I asked, "What the hell are you doing, Jerome?"

He laughed. "I'm jerking off. Haven't you ever seen a junky jerk off with the needle? It gives you a rush."

It's not easy holding a conversation with a man who won't look at you and who keeps drawing his blood into a syringe and shooting it back in his arm, but I did my best. I kept bringing Nicky into the conversation.

"I've heard Nicky has good stuff," I said. "I hope he brings me some of his best. I don't want to lose customers."

"Oh Nicky's stuff's good," Jerome assured me. "You can step on it a couple times and still get a good rush for some. Straight, it makes your dick itch."

"What good is that?" I asked. "I don't have a need for an itchy dick."

Jerome laughed. "That's how you know it's really good. Makes your dick itch."

He drew blood into the syringe again.

"Nicky'll be here soon with the smack," he said. "He knows I'm waiting."

He shot the blood into his arm. The damn KEL felt hot on my back. This was taking too long. The surveillance was probably getting restless. I heard a car on the street. Jerome got up quickly and stood on tiptoes to look out the window. He said, "There's Nicky! Stay here. He'll freak if he sees you. He doesn't want to meet anyone."

He laid his needle on the bar, "Gimme the money."

I took my time getting the money out of my sock. I wanted surveillance to have plenty of time to see the white Bonneville and identify Nicky. Jerome grabbed the money out of my hand. He flew up the stairs. He came back down in seconds. He had with him a folded white paper. We poured out the brown powder on the mirror. Jerome took a razor blade and reverently separated a small amount of the powder. I had agreed he could take two hits. It was like a religious ceremony. We were both bent over the mirror. The room was quiet while he scraped tiny amounts of brown powder back and forth on the mirror.

He said, "There, is that okay?"

"That looks about right," I said. He had taken a generous amount, but I knew that a hit for a junkie like Jerome was far more than for a novice user.

I carefully wrapped up my part of the powder trying to keep my fingerprints off the paper, though I figured Nicky was probably smart enough to use gloves when he wrapped it up. Jerome put some water on his spoon and added a little heroin. He struck a match and held it under the spoon. The bottom of the spoon turned black and the liquid boiled around the edges. He propped the spoon on a rag to let it cool while he snaked the rubber tourniquet around his arm. He drew the liquid from the spoon into his syringe. He stuck the needle in his arm, drew some blood to make sure he had hit a vein, and then pushed the mixture into his bloodstream. His entire body relaxed visibly. He left the needle in for a few seconds then drew some blood to rinse it, shot it home, and pulled the needle.

He grinned. "Good shit," he said.

"Makes your dick itch?" I laughed

"It does" he said, and scratched himself to prove it.

The heroin rush comes quickly. Only seconds after the injection Jerome was already gone to paradise. He sat there grinning and nodding. That first rush doesn't last long, but it's followed by a state of deeply liberating euphoria. Jerome sat back in his chair, now completely at peace. Now he could meet my eyes with no trouble, but his were not there. He was far away. I could feel the tension leave the room.

Then I noticed that Willow was there, quiet as a shadow. She was looking at the spoon.

"I have to go," I said. "If my people like this stuff, I'll be back."

Jerome nodded with a sleepy half-smile. Willow stepped aside and let me pass.

I left the house and met Agent Kryger a few blocks away. Kryger had a Marquis Reagent test with him. We used those to field test heroin. We put a few grains of the powder into the little vial. It turned the vial's chemical mixture to a dark purple like good heroin was supposed to. It was the job of the surveillance to stay with the money until we knew we had heroin, then they could drop the surveillance. If the buy was turkey (not dope) it was their job to stop the car and take our money back. This time though, surveillance stayed with it until the white Bonneville parked at Nicky's apartment on Yates Avenue.

The case of United States versus Nickolas Frol was begun (I apologize for the attorney talk, and actually his real name was Nickolai—the attorneys always spelled it wrong). It was begun, but so far none of the surveillance agents could swear Nicky was actually the driver of that white Bonneville.

Braseth said, "You keep on buying until we nail Nicky." So I did. I made four buys from Jerome; the last one was a surprise—though not a pleasant one.

It was easy to set up the buys. A junky like Jerome needed money all the time. He took Willow's money, but that didn't reach. When Jerome wasn't sitting, nodding, smiling, he was driven by an overbearing need for the drug, and though a normal user might be able to get by with one fix a day, Jerome was far past that point. After that first buy he trusted me and began to initiate the buys himself. Late one evening he called me on the undercover phone at the office wondering if I needed smack. He said Nicky could meet him for a deal at a bowling alley in north Minneapolis. He wanted to sell three grams of heroin for $275. Jerome would get his commission from Nicky. It was late, but Braseth wanted to do the deal. We set off well towards midnight. The surveillance went to Nicky's. One unit followed me as I went to pick up Jerome.

I drove down to Jerome's house on Columbus where he and Willow got into my G-car and we drove up to the bowling alley not far from Nicky's apartment. Nicky's car was in the parking lot. It was a warm night near the end of May with low clouds and no stars or moon, only street lamps for light. The driver's side window of Nicky's car was open, but it was too dark to see. I gave Jerome $275 of the government's money, and watched him go to the white Bonneville and lean in the window. I saw a hand inside, but I could not make out the face. Jerome came back and handed me a green balloon. After I dropped Jerome and Willow, we field tested it and announced we had heroin. It was 3.2 grams, so Nicky was not skimping. Surveillance had seen the white Bonneville leave Nicky's and come to the bowling alley. On Nicky's return home one of the county narcs saw the driver at a traffic light and made a positive identification. We finally had a real case against Nicky. Up till then it was possible (not probable) that someone else was driving the Bonneville. Braseth wanted one more buy to cinch the case.

A few days later, Jerome called me again. I could feel the desperation in his voice. He was out of money and dope again. This time he had a special deal for me, a different source with higher quality heroin. The man had just sold a quarter gram to Jerome, and Jerome said it was the best stuff in town. He said the man would sell me a quarter ounce for $550.

He said, "You can step on it twice and still get high. You'll make a lot of money with this stuff."

To step on it meant to mix it with an adulterant. A step meant you mixed it half and half, doubling your dope (but also cutting your quality). To "cut" the dope also meant mixing it, but a cut was not necessarily a full step. All the dope bought on the street had been stepped on or cut. A dealer would cut the dope as much as possible in order to make the most money. But if he cut it too much, a junkie would not get a buzz, and he lost a customer. The adulterant used in the stepping process was any powder at hand and often dirty stuff that made junkies sick and gave them awful leprous sores from the needle. If a dealer said he had pure heroin or pure cocaine or pure anything, he was a liar. First of all, the stuff did not come pure from the illicit laboratories; and, second, if it were pure he'd be stepping on it several times before he sold it; and, third, if a junkie shot up pure heroin, it'd kill him for sure.

Surveillance went down to Jerome's house and found Stevie Smith's Cadillac parked in the neighborhood, so we assumed Stevie would be the new source. Braseth told me to go ahead, and we'd bust Stevie when he delivered. This would burn the Nicky Frol case, but Braseth had run the case by the U.S. Attorney, and he said we already had enough to prosecute Nicky. Besides, Stevie Smith was another well-known dealer we were eager to bust. He was more notorious than Nicky.

This deal was to take place on a street corner near downtown. Jerome said his man would park nearby and give him the dope. Jerome would deliver to me in my car, and Jerome would take the money back to his man. So we set up surveillance around that street corner. When they were all ready, I went up there with the money. I had a radio, but it was turned off and stowed under my seat, so I could hear nothing surveillance was saying. Suddenly Jerome was at the passenger door. He got in and shoved a green balloon, exactly like the one at the bowling alley, into my hands and said, "Quick, we have to get out of here. Heat's all over the place. Give me the money." First I tried to untie the balloon, but it was triple knotted and required a knife to open. Meantime Jerome was in a sweat. "Gimme the money! My man's nervous. He wants to get going. That stuff's good shit, guaranteed. I just shot some this morning."

I gave him the money and left that area. A few blocks away I tested the dope. It didn't turn the Marquis. It was turkey! I know if you are Sal Dijamco reading this, you'd be saying, "Dumb shit, you should have smelled a rat," but I was a Stearns County bumpkin, and I never did get what I'd call really street smart. I didn't have that nose for detecting conniving and scheming, or for suspecting and distrusting. But I should have listened to Dijamco: don't front the money. To add to my misery, when I reported "turkey" to the surveillance, they reported back they'd already lost Jerome. He had disappeared—into some alley, some shop, some car. Zip, gone. And they had never seen Stevie Smith's Cadillac in the area either. My money was gone (actually taxpayers' money), Jerome was gone—and we had no case against Stevie. Not only that, I would have to burn the case by going to Jerome to get the money back.

Agent Kryger went with me that afternoon to the address on Columbus. Kryger was a big man, and we thought to scare the money out of Jerome, but he said he had already spent it—and that was likely—so we arrested him, and that was the end of the whole case. Jerome swore he didn't know the man who sold him the heroin. He swore he too had been fooled. That was unlikely. However, even more unlikely was the idea Jerome could have engineered this clever rip off by himself. The Minneapolis Police said it had all the markings of a rip-off artist named Nevil, who made a living stealing from and defrauding traffickers. No one knew where Nevil lived, and they said he usually drove cars stolen from drug dealers.

Surveillance failed that day, but at least they'd done their job of getting Nicky that night at the bowling alley. Or had they? Sometimes surveillance failed to get the source because the evidence gathered by surveillance wasn't fascinating enough to satisfy the judges of the Eighth Circuit Court of Appeals. We took Nicky to court. After we all testified, Nicky got up and told the jury he was never in that white Bonneville and he was in the habit of lending his car out to various friends most anytime and had no idea who might have been driving on the occasions in question. Furthermore he did not deal heroin and wouldn't even know what heroin was if he had some right there in his hand. But the jury said, "Baloney on that, you're guilty."

We were happy for a while, until the Eighth Circuit got a hold of the case. I'll summarize their opinion: The Eighth Circuit Court of Appeals felt it was the stuff that came out of Agent Bloch's mouth at the trial that was baloney (if we may use that word here to mean "inadmissible"). Whatever Jerome Ellison said to Agent Bloch about Nicky did not count, because it was hearsay, and that was allowed only in a conspiracy. For such statements to be admitted there must be substantial independent evidence a conspiracy existed (and evidently the observations of the surveillance in this case were not enough to do that). If this leaves you a bit confused, join the club. All of us agents thought we had a case. Obviously the prosecutor, Assistant U.S. Attorney Dan Scott, thought he had a case or he wouldn't have brought it to court. Certainly the judge thought the testimony of Agent Bloch was admissible or he would have instructed the jury to disregard it.

It took me a while to unravel the mysterious conspiracy law. The conspiracy law was still so new that DEA agents, drug attorneys, and judges did not yet fully understand it. A new law had to be run through the system several times before it became clear how it would be applied. The case in which the conspiracy law had been the most recently and most extensively applied was in *U. S. v Nixon* (President Nixon and Watergate), but that was not a drug case, and who the hell understood that case anyway. The words written by Congress in making a law weren't nearly as important as the words written by the appeals courts in regard to the application of it. Later our office had another conspiracy case like Nicky's, but this time Agent Bloch's hearsay was admitted as if it were gospel. It was the case that netted the Lawyer Stephen Scholle.

But wait. First I must finish the story of Jerome Ellison. We definitely had a case on Jerome, don't you think?—hand-to-hand buys, definitely declared heroin by the DEA Regional Lab in Chicago, the United States Attorney eager to prosecute? Ah, well, that prosecution never took place. Jerome's lawyer found a shrink who was able to convince the judge that poor Jerome suffered from a kind of schizophrenia, or dissociative identity disorder, or some such thing, and it wasn't Jerome who sold the drugs to Agent Bloch, but Jerome's alter ego. I'm not kidding. Naturally the judge couldn't send Jerome to jail for he had nothing to do with the crime. And since I was unable to find a federal provision for arresting an alter ego, Jim Braseth told me to leave it alone and move on to the next case. End of *United States v Nickolai Frol*—wasted was the money to buy the heroin, to buy the gas used for surveillance, and to pay Lenny for the introduction. Wasted also the many man-hours of DEA, Hennepin County Narcotics, Minneapolis Police Narcotics, Minnesota Bureau of Narcotics, and United States Marshals—all wasted. However, all of us agents (having nothing better to do) had great fun working the case, and I'm confident the reader must be pleased to think he helped to defray the expense for our entertainment with his tax money.

LENNY DID BRING US a case against one really big drug dealer. Lenny knew all the drug traffickers in Minneapolis and St. Paul, but would not introduce me to the big ones like Plukey Duke. He valued his life more than our money. Only once did he agree to line me up with a big heroin dealer. That dealer was not in the Twin Cities, so Lenny felt it was not so dangerous. Lenny needed money bad one day, and he proposed to introduce me to a dealer in Battle Creek, Michigan, a man named Robert Rudolph. This was during that first summer after I started with DEA. I was still eager to travel, and since our Detroit office said Rudolph was a worthy target, I fully expected to go. But Braseth said no. He thought I was too green. He said I should send the informant to Detroit and let an agent there handle it.

I called Agent Cliff Best in Detroit. I did not know him, he just happened to answer the phone. In minutes he called back with eager approval, and I sent Lenny to make the introductions. Lenny and a Detroit undercover Agent named Hyman met with Rudolph in Battle Creek. Rudolph had a heroin source in Detroit named "Harry the Dago." They went back to Detroit to buy from Harry the Dago. (His real name was Peter McManus, and how in the world they got "Harry the Dago" out of that is a mystery to me.) McManus had a nasty reputation on the street. People who crossed him were often found floating in Lake St. Claire or the Detroit River with toes pointing downward. The Detroit agents bought several ounces of heroin from McManus at a bargain price of $1,000 an ounce. (I remember because it bothered me I had to pay double that in Minneapolis.) They arrested McManus and Rudolph.

Ten days later Rudolph was found dead. McManus, after his later conviction, appealed to the Sixth Circuit Court. He complained the District Court had refused to make the government divulge the identity of the informant. A defendant or his attorney was usually allowed to meet with the informant to prepare his defense, but after finding Rudolph dead, the judge had decided (for the health of the informant) to deny the meeting. The McManus appeal was denied. It was ironic that McManus, who had likely ordered the death of Rudolph, had killed the only man on the street who could have identified the informant for him. Otherwise the diamond tooth might have gone missing too.

Chapter Six

FOR A WHILE I HAD JOHN O'CONNOR for a partner. That was lucky for me. O'Connor was the polar opposite of Fekete. He was soft-spoken, polite, mild mannered, and he was not a drinker. The agents in our office, including the boss, did not think much of O'Connor, though, for two reasons. One, he didn't like undercover work; two, he was extremely frugal and would rather give up a finger than buy a round at the bar. He had not been raised in Stearns County and didn't know the code. Whenever it was his turn to buy, he vanished into the can or was out the back door. These defects did not bother me at all. I liked Agent O'Connor because he loved paper work. He often stayed late at night finishing reports, and those reports were always clear and concise and not full of self-aggrandizing horseshit. And the fact that he did not like to do undercover work was to my advantage. When there was undercover work to be done, I did it. This system was totally satisfactory to me. The big drawback about working undercover was the paperwork that followed. You had to copy all the serial numbers on the buy-money; you had to write a report giving all the details of what happened undercover; you had to "process the evidence," which meant writing some more reports, and getting a witness to sign, and locking up the evidence and sending it to the lab in Chicago the next day via registered mail, return recept requested. If there was any little mistake in all of this, it would come up in court and could jeopardize your entire case, as well as make you look like a dunderhead.

In those days undercover work was the bread and butter of DEA. Almost all cases required it. Most cases went like this: the undercover agent made a small buy, called a "buy-walk" (because we let the money "walk"); then one more buy-walk, and then he ordered as much dope as the seller could handle. We'd make the arrest upon delivery (that was a "buy-bust"). The serial numbers on all the bills of the buy-walks were recorded so the money could be traced. The buy-walk money was called "the dirty money," and if we could find any dirty money on the source when he was arrested, it was clinching evidence for court.

When O'Connor and I worked together, I did the undercover work and wrote a DEA 6 about it. O'Connor did the surveillance DEA 6 and helped process the evidence and fill out the forms. Best of all, he helped with the tedious work of making up that money list. We were a good team. After I had been on the job a year, I talked to Agent Ralph Arroyo, who had been with me in Basic Agent School. He said he hadn't made any undercover buys yet; he had only done mail deliveries. I had already bought heroin, cocaine, and amphetamines and testified in court. And Ralph was working in Chicago!

Because of his smooth manner, O'Connor was good with informants, especially females. He always seemed to have at least one lady snitch giving him information. One of them helped make a case against Harold MacMillan, a big drug dealer in Minneapolis. Actually she made the case indirectly by helping us get a search warrant for Vickie Gottry's house.

"Vickie is Harold's whore," Sergeant Johnson told me. (Johnson worked for Minneapolis Narcotics and knew everything going on in town.) "He got her strung out on heroin, and now she needs him. He supplies her. In return she turns tricks for him and keeps his drugs. She'll take a fall for Harold. But if we can get inside that house, maybe we can tie the dope to Harold somehow. That's a great warrant."

It was already late in the day when we got together the information for the warrant. Then I had to wait a long time in the magistrate's office to get it signed. If O'Connor had brought it up there, the magistrate would likely have given it a quick glance and signed. But it was the first time the magistrate had seen me, and he studied every word of it as if it were the rough copy for the U.S Constitution.

It was a cold, clear winter evening. Some brighter stars were already coming out as I left the federal building with the warrant. Street lights were coming on. Surveillance was sitting on Vickie Gottry's house on West Twenty-ninth Street waiting for the warrant. I delivered it to the supervisor, but we did not go in immediately. The snitch had said Harold had posted two guards with loaded guns inside the house. The guards would shoot anyone who came through the door without Harold's permission. This last little detail was of some concern to me. There was a rule that the agent who got the warrant had to lead the way into the house. There was good reason for this rule. It caused agents to be very conscientious in getting information about danger at the target house, and also in getting the address right.

I told the supervisor about the guards inside, and he said we would hold up the warrant while I got some marked units from the Police Department to join us. With police cruisers along, there could be no doubt it was the cops coming to the house and not some crooks wanting to rip off Harold's dope. If the two guards shot someone, they'd not be able to claim in court they did not know it was the police.

I went to the local precinct. I didn't like this assignment. I hated to ask these cops to come along on a dangerous warrant with the possibility of getting shot. It wasn't their case. They'd relish this no more than I did. I told the officer at the front desk what I wanted, and he directed me to a back room where half a dozen uniformed cops sat drinking coffee. I told them the bad news right up front. We wanted to hit the house where a woman named Vickie Gottry lived, and she had two armed guards ready to shoot anyone who tried to get in. This had an effect opposite what I had anticipated.

Every officer jumped to his feet. "I get the front door!" one shouted.

"Bull shit. You had the front last time. Jake and I take the front. You guys cover the back. Let's go."

I was never so relieved in my life. These men were professionals. They were eager to hit that house, eager for the danger. They knew all about Vickie and Harold and didn't appreciate that activity in their district. In no time we were in our cars, and I led a parade of three squad cars toward Vickie's house. I cinched my flak jacket tighter as I drove. I radioed we were coming, and, as we pulled up, everyone moved in—the cruisers with their strobes blinking, one with siren blaring. The rotating police lights of the cruisers lit up the street. Vickie's narrow little two-story glowed alternately red and white. Car doors were slamming all around. In the crackling cold air, I could hear the metallic *clack-clack* of shotguns as live rounds were jacked into chambers—and a sweeter sound I never heard. The lights went out inside the house as we came up on the porch. I had three uniformed cops right with me and several agents.

Under DEA rules we were required to announce ourselves. It was customary to stand to one side of the door when knocking, in case someone inside fired through the door. I stood to one side of the door and pounded on it. "Police, open up!" I shouted, but no one inside heard me because the officer behind me had already launched his body at the door, and the crash of the door flying open covered my greeting completely. The other officers brushed me aside as they stampeded into the house, so I was about the fourth or fifth person in there and had to fight for that position.

Though the lights were out, the room was bright with the light from officers' flashlights and from the red-and-white rotating lights of the cruisers flashing through the windows. Only a few feet from the door two black men sat on a couch. They had their hands in the air and looked scared. I saw no weapons and thought the informant had been mistaken. But one of the officers knew better. He reached under the couch by the first guard and pulled out a shotgun. Under the couch by the second guard was a .22 rifle. Both were loaded. The informant was right about the guns, but not about the guts of the guards.

The informant had told us Harold kept his heroin in the dresser in Vickie's upstairs bedroom. In a short time, agents located both heroin and cocaine up there. There was plenty of evidence the bedroom was Vickie Gottry's, and we found evidence that connected Harold MacMillan to the house. Vickie was not there. The guards at first denied knowing anything about the dope, but when officers put them against the wall and had cuffs on them, they both said it belonged to Vickie. You could tell they were afraid of Harold MacMillan because they vehemently denied knowing anything about him.

"You want us to go pick up Vickie?" one of the officers asked me, as though he knew her habits and was sure where he could find her. I said that if they could find her, they should bring her to the Federal Building.

"Oh, we can find her. Don't worry about that. We'll be there before you."

And he was right. When I parked in the lot behind the Federal Building, their cruiser was already parked in front. They had already bought themselves some coffee and were sipping from paper cups. They had Vickie in the back seat.

Vickie Gottry was a petite little woman barely over five feet. She was dreadfully skinny, had large child-like eyes, and her skin was pale as moonlight. She looked so frail I felt sorry for her as I fingerprinted and processed her to take her to the Hennepin County jail. She didn't smile, but she was friendly. She said she didn't care about going to jail. She talked easily, but would in no way implicate Harold MacMillan that night. However, later, when she heard the two guards had turned and were testifying against Harold, and that evidence from the house was enough to put Harold in jail, she agreed to testify for the government. She turned out to be a valuable informant and helped put several other dealers in jail besides Harold.

I got to know Vickie pretty well because, for a while, we had to guard her day and night. The word on the street was they would kill her before she ever testified in court. When I asked her one night why she sold drugs, she told me selling dope was addictive, just like using. It was exciting trying to outwit the cops. I was glad she was cooperating. I hated to put young people in jail. The first time I put a young man in jail, he wept, and I wept with him.

I did not take a crook's drug-dealing personally like many agents did. "How dare he break the laws of my country!" was the attitude of the zealots. But my grandfather had been a moonshiner, and I knew dear old granddad could have gone to jail for that. I had hobo friends on the West Coast who had been in jail. However, I did not allow sympathy to interfere with the job. Jim Braseth esteemed undercover work as the most important part of the job, and so I did a lot of it. And although I thought the zealots were a little crazy, those were the guys you wanted out there backing you. If you got into any kind of trouble, you could count on the zealot, whereas the slacker was likely to be asleep in his car. And if he was awake, he'd likely avoid anything dangerous. Even more likely, he'd be sitting at home on his couch watching TV and wondering at times (during a commercial) how the boys were doing out there on surveillance that night.

Often it is only by surveillance that a case could be made against the drug source. When an agent worked undercover, it was easy to see himself as the most important figure in the case, but surveillance was often far more important. Often only by surveillance evidence were we able to arrest the source—as happened with Nicky Frol. The failure of that case came from the Eighth Circuit, not from surveillance. Surveillance training was one of several areas where basic agent school failed. They were supposed to teach us how to do moving surveillance, but the instructors didn't know how to do it themselves, or they were so busy telling us war stories they never got around to making a proper job of it. When I first got to Minneapolis, I was a lousy surveillance agent and did not learn how to do it until Agent Bauer came from Detroit and showed us how.

A good moving surveillance had at least three cars. Only one man, "the point" or "eye" (since he had eye contact), had a visual on the crook. The others hung back. The point man had to be intelligent enough to know his safe distance (dependent on the amount of traffic, the daylight, and especially on how circumspect the crook was). The point man must especially know when to drop the point. Some agents got so carried away with self-importance when they had the point, they'd rather burn the surveillance than give up the point.

The reason surveillance was often the only way to nail the source of supply was because the drug dealer didn't want to introduce the undercover agent to that source. He'd be cutting himself out of the deal, losing his commission. And a smart source didn't want to meet the undercover agent. He didn't trust strangers. The smart source surrounded himself with a few trusted dealers and he sold his drugs only through them. That left surveillance as the only hope of nailing the smart ones.

Doing good moving surveillance is an art, and when there are three or more units driven by intelligent, dedicated agents performing that work of art, it is a pleasure equal to flying formation in jet airplanes. It can get very exciting, especially when the undercover agent is in the car with the crook, because then you have a heavy obligation to stay with that car for the protection of the undercover agent, but you also have a more-than-usual reason for keeping the surveillance cool. If you burn it, you might put the life of the undercover man in danger, and if you drop it, you don't know what is happening to your man.

When we were following a fellow agent, there was always great tension in the air, and even greater when he was temporarily lost—and there was always great relief when he was found again. You might think this an over-dramatization, but think how you'd feel if the undercover was lost, and then found dead. And if you think *that's* being over-dramatic, let me point out this very thing happened a few years later in New York, when young Agent Hatcher was undercover. It was in the spring of 1989. Hatcher met with a crook named Farace, a member of the Bonanno crime family. They were on their way to a restaurant to talk business. Farace was leading in his van. and Agent Hatcher was in an undercover car. Five surveillance agents in separate cars lost him. They lost Farace's van and Hatcher's car at a red light. Later they found Hatcher in his car with two bullet holes in his head, the motor still running, his foot on the brake. He had a wife and two kids.

The surveillance agents had some grand times in the Bob Priebe case. Agent O'Connor had an informant who introduced me to Bob Priebe. The informant said Priebe's source was an attorney named Scholle, who lived in a cabin by Lake Minnetonka. Jim Braseth got his hackles up anytime he heard an attorney was dealing, so we went after Priebe to get Scholle. Priebe had a Datsun 240z, and a lead foot. He picked me up in downtown Minneapolis and headed out for Lake Minnetonka with tires screeching around every curve (there were lots of them on that road back then) and with the speedometer pegged on any straightaway. We reached speeds of over one-hundred miles an hour. Agent Boulger, on one surveillance, blew a tire trying to stay with us, and that day the surveillance lost us. Priebe told me he felt safe when he drove like that because no cop could keep up with him. He said he could shake a tail faster than the chief of police could say, "Al

Capone." The surveillance had the devil's own time trying to stay with the bastard, but they couldn't just drop it because we wanted a case on that lawyer. Besides, the undercover man was in the car. Priebe dropped me at a gas station and sped off. He came back with the dope.

Priebe had a test for me: "Are you a drug agent?" he asked me. When I answered in the negative he was satisfied. "You see," he said, "they aren't allowed to lie. If they lie, that's entrapment, and they'll lose the case in court. Always ask your buyer if he's a drug agent."

I thanked him for the advice and was surprised he was so ignorant of the law, since his source was an attorney. He said his organization was the safest to deal with because they had a lawyer who knew how to get around the law and also because he, Bob Priebe, had a "sixth sense" that told him when someone was an undercover cop. It never failed him. Maybe he had something there. For some reason, after a few buys, Priebe would no longer sell to me. He said he was no longer in the business. We arrested him and took his 240z, but we couldn't flip him, so we didn't get the lawyer—not that time.

The following spring an informant introduced me to Barrie Watson. (If you follow this story closely, you might be able to figure out why, in this case, the Appeals Court allowed my hearsay testimony to stand when we finally brought Attorney Scholle to court.)

I met undercover with Barrie Watson to negotiate cocaine buys. Barrie, too, was not a big dealer, and we would normally not have spent time or money on him, but shortly after we met, Barrie told me his source was a lawyer named Steve and Steve lived close by on Lake Minnetonka. We were drinking beer at the Keg and Cork in Maple Plain at the time. Braseth was ecstatic. This must be that same old friend, Stephen Scholle, Esquire. Braseth approved all the buys I could get set up—whatever the cost.

Barrie was a pothead. His car always smelled of marijuana smoke, and his ashtrays always had tiny bits of stained cigarette paper from roaches he'd burned down to nubs. When Barrie sucked on a short, soggy roach, he made it sizzle and he stored the smoke in his lungs with great reverence until he was ready to pass out, then he expelled it with a *whoosh*. He was always half stoned—or sleeping. When I went to his place, he was either in bed or sitting on the couch drinking coffee and smoking. One morning I went there when he and a buddy had been using LSD. He was sitting at his table contemplating his blackened and battered old coffee pot with the awe of an entomologist finding a new species of butterfly. I told him I'd come back another time, and he smiled upon me with such joy and goodwill it was freaky.

A few days later I met Barrie again at the Keg and Cork. I had buy money on me. Barrie told me the lawyer had high-quality coke (cocaine) directly from Colombia. Barrie said he'd have to take my money to a man named Mike who lived in Maple Plain. Mike would go buy from the lawyer, who was a good friend of Mike's. Barrie said no way would I get to deal directly with Mike, let alone the lawyer. I told Barrie I was just a flunky for the money-man in my organization (which was no lie), and I'd have to call my man for permission to front the money. Jim Braseth had already approved that, but this gave me a chance to relay to surveillance about Mike and the lawyer. I called the office. They relayed the information to surveillance. Then I gave Barrie the money.

I had told surveillance Barrie would be easy to follow because he was so laid back and mellow, and so half-stoned. That was a mistake. Surveillance soon found they had to be very careful. When Barrie Watson got down to business, he miraculously rose out of his fog. On our first deal, he burned surveillance in a few minutes. They picked him up again later in Maple Plain just by chance. And they found when Mike, Barrie's source, was on business, he watched his rear view mirror more than the road in front of him. It wasn't until the third buy that we identified "Mike" as Mike Needham.

To show how good Barrie was at watching his rear, one night I met him for a buy at the Keg and Cork. It was already dark. Barrie liked to do his deals at night when it was easier to shake a tail. I stalled him for a time over a beer to let surveillance get set up. I fronted him the money, and he left to get the coke. In a few minutes he was back and returned the money. He said no deal. The place was crawling with heat. When I expressed doubt and said he might be seeing things, he said, "Come, I'll show you."

We went out to Barrie's car. As he drove through the parking lot he pointed out two of our surveillance units as possible suspects. He said they had followed him a few minutes ago as he left the parking lot. We drove out into the country a little way. Barrie knew the area like the back of his hand. He pulled the neatest little surveillance-detecting maneuver. We were in a heavily wooded area and approaching a T intersection on a straight stretch of highway. Barrie slowed down until he saw headlights far behind. Then he made a left turn onto the T, drove about a block, doused his lights, drove in the dark for another block, turned into a farm, and parked by the side of a chicken coop facing the road. In a few seconds, here came one of our surveillance cars. It made the left turn onto the T and went accelerating by us in a big hurry.

"Right there!" said Barrie. "That car was in the parking lot at the bar. And here comes another."

Sure enough, another of our cars turned and went smoking by. One, two, three, four. I knew they were calling each other on the radios, saying, "Does anyone have him. Where did he go? Do you see any lights?"

Well, the whole thing was so obvious there was no denying we had heat on us. Barrie and I decided we better call off the deal and try to find out what was going on. For a while Barrie was so paranoid he refused to sell to me. But after some time he relaxed again. He agreed to another deal. We were a lot wiser now. Surveillance no longer tried to follow Barrie. We found out where Mike lived. From then on, when I was buying from Barrie, surveillance set up on Mike's house and didn't try to follow Barrie. They just recorded the clock time when Barrie left me and when he arrived at Mike's.

The closest I came to meeting Mike was one day when I parked right by Barrie's house. I refused to front the money. I pretended to have been scared by all the heat that night. By then Barrie trusted me enough to agree. I flashed him the money, and he went to get the coke. This gave surveillance two shots at Barrie coming to Mike's: one to get the dope and one to deliver the money.

The surveillance on me saw Barrie leave, and a few minutes later surveillance at Mike's house saw Barrie arrive there. The cars on Mike lost him in traffic, but in a couple of hours he was seen coming back to Barrie's where I plainly saw him get out of his car and go into the house. Barrie came out and told me Mike had just arrived and was inside the house with the coke. I gave Barrie the money, and he returned in a minute with the powder. That was pretty good evidence for court, but we knew from our experience with Nicky even this wasn't good enough for the Eighth Circuit Court.

Barrie had told me the organization had a smuggler who made trips to Bogotá, Colombia, to pick up the "pure" cocaine but that I'd have no chance of meeting him either. Barrie told me other things about the organization, and surveillance had seen plenty to show that he was telling me the truth. We knew we had a case that would convince a jury, but we had the Eighth Circuit Appeals Court to worry about. This was just like Nicky's case. The remarks of one conspirator against another conspirator were inadmissible unless the conspiracy could be proved independently. To me this sounded like they were saying: "If you can prove the conspiracy without your evidence, then we'll allow the evidence." Well, why do I need that evidence, if I've already proved the conspiracy? But I was not a learned judge.

This meant that Barrie's remarks to me wouldn't be allowed in court unless we could prove the conspiracy without those remarks. And since I couldn't move up the ladder to meet Scholle or the smuggler, we were stuck. We had a good case on Barrie, but he wasn't our target. We needed someone with direct evidence of the involvement of the various members of the conspiracy.

We caught a lucky break. A man named Ray Thuftedal was arrested for selling cocaine. Ray was that someone we needed to take this case to court and to satisfy the Eighth Circuit. When Ray saw he was surely looking at jail time, he rolled over (cooperated). And when Ray rolled over, Jeffrey Kaufman, who had been arrested with him, rolled over too. Kaufman could confirm much of Ray's testimony.

Ray happened to be that smuggler who made those trips to Bogotá to buy the cocaine. He smuggled the drugs through Mexico in hollowed-out, scuba-diving batteries. Ray had received money on one occasion directly from Scholle for cocaine. Scholle at his cabin had helped Ray open the batteries and cut, weigh, and package cocaine for sale. Ray had met Mike Needham. Scholle had told Ray that Mike was his outlet for the distribution of cocaine. Ray Thuftedal had direct evidence against everyone in the conspiracy except Barrie, and we needed no help there.

On top of that, we had a trump card to play at trial that tied the whole conspiracy together very nicely. DEA had a new program called STRIDE (System to Retrieve Information from Drug Evidence). STRIDE examined the drugs sent by agents across the country to DEA's regional laboratories. They compared the samples and fed their findings into computers, which cranked out sheets of data that showed common elements. For example, if an agent from Austin submitted green amphetamine tablets with a peculiar shape to his lab in Dallas, and an agent from Minneapolis submitted green amphetamine tablets with the same peculiar shape to his lab in Chicago, STRIDE would alert the two agents their tablets were likely coming from the same source, and this could help to build a conspiracy case. Agent O'Connor put all this STRIDE and Thuftedal stuff together and took the case to the U.S. Attorney. We went to court.

Our STRIDE man showed up for court with a stack of computer printouts showing that, across the country, cocaine was rarely mixed with benzocaine. Dealers used lactose, mannitol, quinine, or any junk like powdered sugar, but they did not use benzocaine. Only two instances demonstrated benzocaine being used and those were from long ago. In the last three years not one submission of cocaine had benzocaine except in two recent cases: one was the cocaine taken from Thuftedal at his arrest, and the other were those Agent Bloch had purchased from Barrie Watson. This made it easy for the jury to infer a connection through the whole chain of conspirators. This was the kind of thing that made the Eighth Circuit Court of Appeals happy.

We went to court against Stephen Scholle loaded for bear. Scholle was a lawyer. Looking at the case, he must have known he was in a weak position. But he was getting advice from Doug Thompson, his defense counsel in court, and from Jack Nordby, who later did his appeal to the Eighth Circuit. Jack Nordby happened to be the same attorney who had appealed for Nicky and won. I think Scholle went to trial thinking that, even if the jury found him guilty of this conspiracy, he'd get it reversed by appealing to the Eighth Circuit like Nicky did. I also think that, at the time of trial, neither Thompson nor Scholle understood the full significance of the STRIDE computer readouts. It was a new thing. They got sandbagged and weren't prepared to mount a credible challenge.

The jury said guilty. The judge gave Scholle only two years!—professional courtesy, I guess. Scholle appealed, of course. Before the Eighth Circuit, Nordby used much the same arguments he had in the Nicky Frol case, but this time the court did not throw out the testimony of Agent Bloch. Scholle went to jail. Needham got eighteen months (he also lost on appeal). Barrie served no time. He rolled over. We did several more cases together, Barrie and I, but none as interesting as Scholle.

As usual, I have an addition to my story. Months later when, one night after work, I was having a beer with John Boulger. I wondered out loud about how Scholle might be doing in jail. Boulger said, "Oh, he's not in jail anymore. He found Jesus in jail and had a miraculous conversion. He promised he'd be a good boy from now on, and the judge let him go."

Oh, and also an addition to the Nicky Frol case: I did not hear anything more about Jerome Ellison for about a year. Then I heard he had been arrested for selling heroin to a Minnesota narc. That darned alter ego was at it again.

Chapter Seven

LENNY SAID A FLASHY WHITE PIMP was cruising Hennepin in a "triple pink Corvette." This was unusual—the white pimp part I mean, not the pink car. All high-profile pimps in Minneapolis were black guys. I watched for that car along Nicollet and Hennepin. I thought I'd pull him over and see who he was. I never got the chance. One day he just strolled into our office. He wanted to talk to an agent about drug trafficking on Hennepin. This man was weird! That he was a white pimp was the least of his weirdness. He came from California, where he had been a "high priest" in a Satanist church. He dressed all in pink, including very tight bell-bottoms of various shades of pink. His shirt was shiny pink silk that reflected light like a mirror. He proudly pointed out his Corvette—custom painted in three shades of pink—and which he had illegally parked in front of the federal building. He carried a Colt 45 Commander in his belt and wasn't shy about letting the handle show.

We called him the Fox because he was sneaky. The name pleased him, and he began to call himself the Fox when he phoned the office. He was a minor snitch for a while, providing little bits of drug information from time to time but nothing to lead to a federal case. He took great pride in the fact he had a DEA agent for a "friend." He never made a case for me, and I was very uncomfortable with his high-profile attitude. I was trying to pass him off to another agency. That is, I was trying to get rid of him—when someone got rid of him for me—and I mean permanently.

I found this note on my desk from Agent Kramer: "Call from sheriff in Wisconsin. Anthony Steele (that was his real name) committed suicide last Friday night the 26th of April 1974." The note had the sheriff's number. I called and got details. They had found the triple-pink Corvette in a ditch by a back road near the Wisconsin Dells. The Fox was in the driver's seat, deader than a doornail. The sheriff said, "evidently" Steele had been driving along the isolated country road alone looking at the scenery and, on impulse, had pulled his forty-five and shot himself in the head. My name and number was found in Steele's wallet. The sheriff had already sent Steele's personal belongings to me, as if I were the next of kin, and closed the case and would hear of no other theory regarding the death of Anthony Steele.

I didn't buy it. The Fox was a narcissist. That kind didn't commit suicide. He was "cruising with windows open"—he never did that. It would mess up his perfect hairdo. And the Fox would not go out to the country to enjoy the scenery. For scenery he cruised downtown. He didn't like the open spaces of farms and fields. The Fox's Minneapolis friend, Walter Harris, called Steele's mother in California the morning after the accident. He told her word on the street was that Anthony had been murdered. He said that, when Anthony left Minneapolis that afternoon, a girl from Mound had been with him.

But sheriffs always have the next election to think about, and an open murder case was a sticky commodity to have hanging around your neck at such a time. A case stamped "suicide" was over; a "murder" opened up months of hard investigative work. I would have looked into the case myself, but Braseth said, "Leave it alone. Good riddance. You have better things to do."

I sent Anthony's personal belongings to his mother. She said she was having the body cremated and would strew the ashes on some mountain in Germany as Anthony had requested.

A GOOD DEA AGENT HAD to work with informants. Most of the time the informant made the case, and indeed, before the conspiracy laws came along, this was considered the only way to make a case. Many agents convinced themselves their superior acting skills and clever thinking made the case. Almost always, the informant working in the background assuring the crooks everything was cool, kept the case going. We needed snitches. But Lord, working with snitches was a big pain. A snitch couldn't be trusted. He was, after all, betraying his friends. A good snitch was a skillful liar. That's how he convinced his friends. We had to watch a snitch closely, had to keep him at arms length and yet court him and con him to get out of him what we wanted. We became very familiar with an informant but could not afford to become good friends. It was an uncomfortable relationship with very few exceptions. Agents stupid enough to get involved with their informants often got into trouble when the informant turned on them. They sometimes lost their reputations, some even their jobs. Informants were a pain. They were always in debt, always asking for money, and always complaining about the electricity or gas being cut off at the house.

The strangest ones were those who volunteered. Not all of them were as weird as the Fox, but many were close. Our office had a female informant older agents called "Sweet and Sour." One day Agent Anderson was talking to her in the interview room when I walked in.

Terry made the introductions, "Don, this is Sweet and Sour."

I asked her, "Where did you ever get that name?"

Terry said, "Show him your tits."

She smiled and without the slightest disinclination, pulled up her sweater. On the one breast she had a tattoo that said "Sweet," on the other "Sour."

We saw a lot of very private tattoos on people because we always had to strip-search a prisoner before handing him over to the U.S. marshals or the Hennepin County jailers. One of the worst crimes an agent could commit was to hand over a prisoner with a weapon concealed somewhere. So we strip-searched, and part of that search was "bend over and spread 'em" to make sure the prisoner did not have something stuck up his behind. The most memorable tattoo I ever heard of was on a prisoner's big butt. The tattoo covered his entire rear end: on each cheek was a bright red devil with a black coal shovel. The two devils were shoveling coal into the asshole between them, from which issued bright flames of red, orange, and yellow.

Agent Terry Anderson had a volunteer snitch, and he was weird. He was a good snitch in that he made cases and was eager to testify in court. In every other way he was bad. He was a total egomaniac, decorated in gaudy tattoos, hung with heavy jewelry, wrapped in loud leisure suits, and topped with thick hair sprayed to the solidity of a football helmet. He had an enormous tattoo of a green dragon on his body he loved to show off especially to young ladies. The tail of the dragon started low on one leg. The body was wrapped around him, across his back and over his chest, with the red, multi-forked tongue sticking out his shirt collar on one side of his neck. If a lady asked about the tattoo on his neck, he'd immediately begin to unbutton (often to her dismay) to proudly display the head of the dragon on his chest, and if the lady was of strong constitution he'd display even more. This guy was exactly the kind of man I'd never associate with in real life, no more than I'd bed down with a giant lizard—and I'd prefer the lizard if it was a pretty one.

We called this snitch "Junior G-man" (he thought he was Dick Tracy and J. Edgar Hoover combined) or, for short, "Junior." Agent Terry Anderson had been in Minneapolis a long time, making arrests and testifying in court, so he was often recognized on the street. Whenever Junior brought in a case, and Terry thought someone in the target organization might recognize him, he had me do the undercover. I was still new and hardly known in town. I got to know Junior only too well.

Junior had poor judgment. In fact, he almost got me killed once. Terry and Junior were doing a cocaine deal, taking delivery at a fast food joint up at Forty-second Avenue and Highway 100. It was a buy-bust, and to keep Junior cool, we were arresting him too. It was my job to make a show of arresting Junior so the crooks would think he was in just as much trouble as they were. We did the deal on the back side of the building where there were no windows, so the fast-food customers wouldn't see the arrest. But Junior went wandering around like he was thinking of escaping, and I had to hold my gun on him and shove him into my car to put an end to his histrionics.

I was driving south on Highway 100 taking it easy, Junior riding shotgun. We were listening to the other agents on the radio finishing up the arrest. A police cruiser passed us. I looked in the rear-view mirror and saw another cruiser gaining on us. I knew immediately what had happened. Some Good-Samaritan customer sitting by a side window of the fast food place saw part of our show and, assuming I'd kidnapped Junior at gunpoint, called the police. I knew that the police, knowing I had a gun, would be trigger happy. I told Junior to shut up and do exactly as they said when they pulled us over.

They did. The cruiser in front slowed, the one behind pulled up alongside revealing a third cruiser behind. All three threw on lights and sirens at the same time. It was a shock even though I knew it was coming. They would have scared Batman. In a few seconds we stopped, and then there were four shotguns pointed at me and a voice yelling on the bullhorn, "Get out of the vehicle and get face down on the pavement in front of your car." The voice added, "Both of you!" because Junior was looking around and stalling and wondering what was happening. I was already on my belly. I yelled at Junior to get his ass down on the pavement and right now. He got down next to me, but then as the cops came near, he rolled to one side and started to explain. I heard an immediate clacking of shotguns, and I cursed Junior and told him to shut the hell up and lie still. The cops were on edge. Everything got quiet. One officer came up next to me. I told him I was unarmed, my pistol was in the car, that I was a DEA agent, and if he reached into my left shirt pocket, he would find my credentials.

The whole thing was cleared up in a minute. The officers were as nice as they could be, but one of the younger ones was mad at Junior for causing him to tighten his finger on the trigger. He told Junior he might be on his way to the hospital right now. I said, "Or better yet, to the morgue." I told the officers if they wished to take Junior down town and hang him from a street light they were welcome. They said they'd wait until next time.

ONE DAY TERRY LINED UP a cocaine deal. We decided I should do the undercover part. Junior and I met with the crook in a restaurant in north

Minneapolis. The crook said he couldn't sell me anything until the next evening. He needed time, he said, to check on me. The next evening was Friday. I tried to avoid setting up a deal on Friday nights, because everybody wanted to go for drinks. However, when the crook called the next afternoon, the boss said to go ahead and make arrangements for a buy-walk. The crook said he'd have the coke at his apartment in north Minneapolis, and it'd take but a minute to do the deal. I don't think he liked Junior either because he told me I need not bring him along.

The deal took a little longer than planned because the crook thought he had spotted surveillance in the parking lot. Which he had. It was one of our agents; he described him perfectly. However, after we talked a while, he calmed down and sold me the dope. A few blocks away, I pulled into an alley to do a field test so surveillance could drop it. I was in a hurry. The boys would be Friday-night thirsty. I was confident I had cocaine because Junior had already "field tested" the crook's powder several times with his nose, and had declared it high quality coke.

But the federal government didn't recognize Junior's nose as a valid field test. Another was required. Here was some more bad luck for me: headquarters had just sent us a new field test kit for cocaine. The old test was a little see-through pouch with a small vial of cobalt thiocyanate inside. You dropped a bit of cocaine into the pouch and busted the vial. As you shook it, it'd turn blue—that was a successful field test. The problem with that old test was that other substances made cobalt thiocyanate turn blue. One day I took some of Bea's powdered laundry detergent and gave it the test. It turned a fine shade of blue (I was pretty sure there was no cocaine in that). Now headquarters had sent us a new test supposed to be fool proof. It was a pouch with three vials in it (this test became known as the Scott's Reagent test, or just the Scott's test). I busted one vial at a time, shook, and noted the results. Each vial called for a specific reaction: first vial, blue; second vial, pink; third, layered pink over blue. I'd never done this test before but had memorized the instructions that morning, knowing I might be testing cocaine that evening. I kept shaking the pouch hoping it would layer out.

Damn it—the test was negative! I had a nice blue on the first vial. And yes, I got a pretty pink on the second. But the third vial would not give me the pink over blue layering.

Radio chatter: "What's happening?" and "Have we got real stuff?" The natives were getting restless. I did another test. Same results—not cocaine.

Dave Haight, the group sup, was out with us. "Thirty-five, what's up?" he asked on the radio (Thirty-Five was my call sign). I told him to meet me and explained the situation. He was the supervisor—let him make the call. We did another test. Dave wanted to call the test good after the first vial turned the stuff blue, but I told him the instructions emphasized: any variation from these results are considered a negative test. He said, "This is bullshit. You got one of those old test kits?"

I said, "No, you told us to throw those things away."

He rummaged in his trunk. He got on the radio, "Anybody got an old cobalt test with him? Thirty Five's got a whole chemistry set here and isn't getting results." (I guess he forgot that, only yesterday, he had told me I would have to use that "chemistry set" from now on.)

Terry brought over an old test kit, and in a minute we did that old cobalt test, and had an old cobalt blue color, and an old cobalt positive result.

"Okay," said Haight on the radio, "We got good stuff. It's Miller time."

That was Friday. The following Monday I sent the stuff to the lab in Chicago. A few days later they called Haight and informed him we had submitted some high-quality lidocaine with not the least trace of cocaine in the sample. So Dave comes and tells me I have to get the money back from the crook.

I said, "Okay, give me the dope, and I'll go get the money."

He said, "No, the lab keeps the stuff, even if it's not cocaine."

I said, "How in God's name am I going to get the money back. Do I tell the crook his coke was no good but I used it all up anyway? If I want my money, I have to have the package he sold me with maybe a little powder missing."

Damn! Typical bureaucratic BS: the supervisor's fault, but the street agent's responsibility. Terry Anderson and I got some of the money back, and the crook gave us the name of his source. We went to that source and got the name of his source. We arrested all three on a very weak and very unsatisfying charge of distributing what they thought was cocaine. I doubt if anyone did any time over this fiasco. I felt my supervisor should have.

You haven't heard the last of the lidocaine. Junior came in to get paid for the deal. He was outraged to find he would get nothing. Lidocaine was not illegal under the Controlled Substances Act.

Junior was going crazy. "I snorted that shit myself. It's some of the best coke I've had."

"Well, it's not worth anything to us," Haight told him."

"How can that powder be legal?" Junior raged. "It's just like cocaine. It should pay the same."

"Sorry, we can't pay for legal drugs."

Junior left the office steaming—and, as you shall see—scheming.

Chapter Eight

DURING THE HOLIDAYS AT the end of that same year, Junior was sniffing around Hennepin Avenue for drugs, for girls, for excitement. One fine afternoon as Junior was trotting along, he abruptly stopped short at a street corner and stood still, staring straight ahead intensely—in a trance like a pointer dog. Junior had just alerted on Albert Leon Willis, who was cruising along the street in his flashy blue Caddy with three of his flashiest ladies. The big gold stallion mounted on the hood gleamed splendidly in the sunshine, and the ladies inside gleamed equally in their diamonds, feathers, and furs. Mr. Willis had his white hat cocked at a rakish angle. The red feather of his hat stirred gently, for the window was open to allow in the air, which was exceptionally mild for a winter afternoon in Minnesota. The sun was glaring bright on the snow and melting it into little puddles on the sidewalk.

Mr. Willis stopped for a light at that same corner where Junior was still pointing. Junior's sensitive nose picked up the scent of incense of cannabis wafting from the open window. This, along with Junior's view of Al's main lady in the passenger seat sucking on a stubby hash pipe, made Junior wag his tail with pleasure—at least he would have, if he had been furnished with that appendage. Junior immediately accosted Mr. Willis with questions about how he and his ladies were enjoying the very fine weather, about the prices of ladies along Hennepin, and especially about the possibility of obtaining some of the very aromatic merchandise he had just scented. Willis invited Junior to a short drive and to an occasional pull at the hash pipe.

Al Willis was a pimp and a dealer of heroin and cocaine in the southern suburbs. He came daily to cruise along Hennepin and Nicollet with his ladies. Lenny described Willis's means of support somewhat more crudely, but succinctly: "Al pushes smack and blow in the south and runs holes along Hennepin." Al Willis sometimes sold marijuana, when his ladies did not need it all, but on this particular day he was low on the smoke, so he asked Junior if he knew where he might buy some. Junior said he didn't have any of that commodity for sale, but that he belonged to an organization that sold large amounts of heroin and cocaine. He hinted that, if Al was good to him, he might feel inclined to introduce him into the organization. Willis said he was interested in buying heroin, and he thought he might fit in well as a distributor for the organization. He said he had good drug connections in the Twin Cities, and also in Des Moines and Omaha. He showed Junior a roll of several thousand dollars in one-hundred dollar bills which he said was profit from a recent drug sale.

When Al dropped Junior at the street corner, one of the ladies in the back seat confided she had fallen madly in love with Junior—and with his dragon, too. Al wondered if Junior might wish to avail himself of that lady's charms. Junior declined reluctantly. He had pressing business. Junior got Al's telephone number in case he should need his services in the future—the lady was, after all, quite lovely. As Al drove off, Junior noted the license number (he had been working with us for quite a while by then).

Junior's pressing business was at the DEA office. He brought us his information. After Braseth checked with the Burnsville Police, he told me to open a case on Albert Leon Willis immediately. The police were eager, very eager to do Willis because he had moved his hookers into a high-classed white neighborhood in Burnsville, and complaints were coming in daily about apparent immoral happenings scandalizing the local women and children. Ladies that looked very much like hookers were bringing home seedy characters that looked very much like drunks. Willis claimed the ladies were dancers from Chicago who stayed with him whenever they happened to be in town, and the ladies had boyfriends who dropped in to say, "Hi."

A few days later Junior and I met with Willis. Junior had already laid out a basic story, so I had to go with that. I told Willis we were looking for a distributor in the black community of Minneapolis and St. Paul, and we might also need a man in Chicago. Before Willis could ask to buy heroin from the organization, I headed him off by telling him he would have to show he was not working with the police. He'd do this by selling me some heroin. I told him that, after we were satisfied he was safe to work with, I'd front him several ounces of heroin and eventually kilo amounts as we built trust between us. I told him our drug was of such high quality he'd be able to step on it several times and still sell it on the street.

Willis was intrigued. He wasn't immediately ready to jump into this offer, but after several meetings, he invited me to his house. I tried to cut Junior out of the deal, but Junior, not wanting to miss the action (all those leggy hookers), convinced the boss he was a vital part of this deal and must go along or it'd never work. The boss was afraid Junior might burn the deal if we cut him out, so I had to take him along. I didn't like having Junior along at any meeting with a crook because he spread himself all over the place, constantly butting in on conversations, even when the crook was in the middle of making self-incriminating statements. He just couldn't keep his mouth shut. I don't think Al Willis liked Junior all that well either because right after we got to the house that day in January, Al asked me to come into the bedroom where we could talk in private. Four of his ladies were there that morning, and they all gathered around Junior in the living room, entirely taken in by his alluring personality and by his charming dragon.

In the bedroom I sat in Al's stuffed chair. Al sat on his bed. We talked amiably about the organization and about how Al would fit in since he was black and would be a great asset for distribution. I told him my boss was eager to have him on board because the boss figured Al would be able to move large amounts of heroin and cocaine through his ladies. Al opened a side dresser drawer and pulled out two small tinfoil packets. One had cocaine, the other heroin. He offered me a snort. I said I wasn't a user. He offered to sell me those to show the organization boss he could be trusted. I told Al those packages would make him look small-time, and he should sell me at least an ounce of really good heroin. He said he would call me.

When we walked out into the living room, two of Al's ladies were sitting on the couch, and two, along with Junior, were kneeling at the coffee table. One of the ladies was bending over a mirror holding one end of a short straw to her nose and the other end to the mirror. A thin line of white powder disappeared up her nose.

"Good stuff, right?" Junior was directing a snorting party! He took the straw and passed it to the next lady. He started to cut another line of powder from the generous pile in the middle of the mirror. What the hell?

"Where did that stuff come from?" I asked angrily.

The delighted ladies all pointed to Junior and chirped about what fine blow it was. Junior was grinning broadly. I was absolutely stunned. I had heard about informants running amok, but this was ridiculous.

"Let's go," I said, giving Junior a shove. "We're here for business, not for a snorting party."

Junior grabbed the rest of the powder, and I pushed him out the door. He knew I was mad. The ladies were smiling and blowing kisses at Junior as we walked out. As soon as the car doors were closed, Junior was shouting: "It's not what you think! It's not what you think!"

I said not a word. I backed the car out of the driveway and gunned it down the street. After we were a few blocks away, I pulled the radio from under the seat and called off surveillance. I drove onto a side street, stopped the car, and turned on Junior screaming. "What the hell do you think you're doing?"

He was holding up both hands defensively, shouting, "Whoa, whoa. Listen to me before you go off. I didn't break any law. That stuff wasn't cocaine. It was that lidocaine shit." Junior's eyes were shining. He was giggling like a school girl, delighted with his own cleverness.

"Where did you get it?"

"I got it the same place you got yours. It's only lidocaine."

"You've just blown this case," I yelled.

"Oh, no," he said, "they'll trust us now more than ever."

"Look, you idiot! Lidocaine's a prescription drug. Are you suddenly a doctor?"

"You guys said it was legal!" Junior said, now subdued. He wasn't giggling anymore. "I don't see the harm."

"Have you ever heard of entrapment? You've set Al Willis up for a beautiful entrapment defense. Are you working for Al's attorney?"

When I dropped Junior off, I chewed him out some more. He said with his same old swagger, "Hey, no problem! If it comes up in court, we'll just deny anything like that ever happened. They won't believe the whores."

I looked at him in amazement. "You're going to be under oath."

"Well, I know that."

"Do you know what that means?"

"Yeah," he gave his cocky laugh, "It means those bumpkins on the jury will have to believe me."

God, was I mad. I could have shot that megalomaniac. I could still shoot him right now just thinking about it. I told Terry Anderson about his informant's little trick.

"Well, let's not worry about it," he said. "If Al sells you the ounce, it won't be a problem. He'll have to plead guilty on a hand-to-hand buy. It'll never get to court."

That turned out to be completely wrong, but I felt better for the moment. Maybe this would work out. I decided to bury the incident. I wrote a short DEA 6 stating I had talked to Al at his house, and he had agreed to call when he had the ounce of heroin. I didn't mention the lidocaine snorting. I also didn't mention the drugs Al showed me in his bedroom. I figured that way, if I was asked on the witness stand why I had not mentioned the snorting, I could say I put in the report only what seemed important at the time, and then I'd point out I hadn't mentioned the heroin and cocaine in Al's bedroom either, which is something defense counsel would not want to hear in court. I was thinking, for that reason, the defense attorney would not bring up the snorting party.

Al called two days later on a cloudy Friday morning in early January with snow threatening. That snow became a factor. Al was ready to sell me an ounce of high-grade brown heroin from "a very reliable source." He said he had a small sample I could test. He was waiting for me downtown at the new IDS Tower on South Eight Street. Two surveillance units followed me there. I met Al in the main lobby. I took his sample into the bathroom and ran the marquis on it. Excellent! I told Al I was happy. We agreed on a price of $1,600 for the ounce. Al told me that, under the circumstances, he was not charging any commission. (That, we figured out later, was a big lie.) He said he'd deliver an ounce of the same stuff to the Mobile Service Station at Thirty-sixth and Nicollet at one o'clock that afternoon.

I had already told Al I wouldn't front the money. He said his source would meet him at the gas station with the ounce of heroin. Al would come to my car and look at the money. He'd then go back to the source to get the ounce and bring it to me in my car. Then he'd take the money back to pay the source. Good plan! I could not have asked for better. Surely surveillance could nail that source; they'd see at least two meetings between Al and him.

The two surveillance units with me watched Al Willis leave the IDS Center and get into the passenger side of a brand new, custom-made, Cadillac Eldorado convertible, with a tall black man at the wheel. That black man was none other than Stevie Smith. We should have had more than two surveillance units there that morning. They might have followed Stevie to his heroin source. It had begun to snow heavily, and visibility was poor. The surveillance lost Stevie in downtown traffic. By the time we got back to the office, the snow was falling so thick we could hardly see across the street. But we had no trouble rounding up surveillance units for a noon meeting at our office, and for the buy-bust at the gas station. With any luck we were going to get Al Willis and Stevie Smith at one fell swoop. There were eager volunteers from most every local police department. Burnsville Police officers were high-fiving it even before we hit the street. I was subdued. I still had this knot in my stomach thinking about Junior and the damned lidocaine trick.

Luckily it stopped snowing and the sun came out as we left for the Mobile station. I put the buy-money in my sock and stuck a walkie-talkie under my coat. I put my revolver under the car seat. Surveillance got set up and directed me where to park. It had snowed a lot in the last several days, and the plows had stacked huge piles of snow wherever there was room. It was hard for surveillance to get a good view between these snow banks. They told me to park across the street to the south of the station where they had the best view.

There had been so much fanfare and such a big build up about the case all morning I felt really nervous as I parked the car. When I reached to turn off the ignition, I noticed my fingers trembled. I had my radio volume turned down low, and I listened as surveillance got set up. The guys all found themselves a good spot and waited.

One o'clock, and the radios were silent. No Al, no Stevie. What if Al didn't show? Maybe he or Stevie had seen surveillance? Hell, I could see two surveillance units from where I sat, and occasionally I saw others cruising by. I was getting paranoid. The crooks might have people in the gas station watching us. I wondered if my radio was working. I turned up the volume. Somebody, say something! I wanted to do a radio check, but that would make me sound like a nervous Nellie. Nothing but silence. I tried to settle back, but I couldn't keep from constantly looking around.

Finally my radio crackled alive, and someone sang the words, "Oh happy day," followed by a report that Stevie Smith's Cadillac had just turned off Lyndale onto Thirty-sixth. He was driving very slowly. Now all radios came alive. Everyone wanted to know where Stevie was, what color his car was, what he was wearing. Then someone interrupted and said Al Willis's blue Fleetwood was two blocks north, heading south on Nicollet. I could feel the excitement building fast on the radios.

"Everybody keep cool," someone yelled. "Stevie's looking around a lot. He's running heat. He's watching his rear."

Suddenly, in front of me was Al turning the corner. He nodded as he went by but made no sign of stopping. I watched in my rear view mirror. He disappeared around the next corner out of my sight, but surveillance still had him.

"He's running heat. Don't follow him. You'll burn it! Leave him alone!"

"Stevie's parked. He's watching him go by."

"Where's Stevie parked?"

"West side of the station." Surveillance had this covered well.

"Okay, Thirty-Five, heads up. Al's coming back your way."

I turned off the radio and put it under the seat. I stuck the revolver between my legs. I patted my sock to make sure I had the money. Al pulled up behind me. I rolled down the window. When Al came up, I pulled out the money and flashed it to him. Al told me to stay there. He'd be back with the stuff in a minute.

Al walked away and disappeared around a snow bank. I wanted to turn on my radio to hear what was happening, but I didn't dare. No movement. Surveillance was sitting very still. I didn't see Al, or Stevie, or Stevie's car. I was glad Al had parked behind me so I could at least keep an eye on his Cadillac. After a while, he appeared around the snow bank walking to my car. He handed me the package. I opened it. The heroin looked the same as the sample. I paid him without question and drove out of the area. I parked near a school and turned on the radio to listen while I did the field test.

I heard: "Thirty-five isn't answering, but I saw Al hand him the package."

"Standby, standby! Don't bust them yet. Let's make sure he gets plenty of time to pass the dirty money."

"Where are they?"

"They're both inside the station."

"Isn't that Al walking toward the UC?"

"No, no that's someone else. And the UC's gone. Stand by! Thirty-five, you on?"

I said, "Yes, I have the stuff. It's good."

"Don't bust yet! Al's coming out now. Wait for Stevie."

"Al's going to his car. Let's block him right here before we get into a chase. I think they passed the money inside."

"Here comes Stevie!"

"Okay, bust, bust! Do it, do it!"

Then all was quiet.

I started up and headed back to the Mobile station. They had Al and Stevie wide-legged against Stevie's car, which was parked right by the station. They cuffed them both and put them in a Minneapolis police cruiser.

"Who's got the money list," came on the air.

"I've got the list with me," I answered.

"Bring it over. I think we got your money here."

We checked a wad of rumpled bills they had dug out of the snow where Stevie had been standing. It was eight one-hundred dollar bills of the buy money. Stevie was an old hand at this. He knew he could not be caught with the dirty money. When he saw the officers closing in, he bent over and stuck the money into the snow bank. But an officer saw him reach down and stick his hands into the snow. They searched that spot and found the dirty money. Al had the rest in his pocket. Al had lied big about not charging any commission. He was making fifty percent on this deal!

Here was another case where surveillance was more important than undercover. They saw everything. We wouldn't have had a thing on Stevie, if they hadn't seen him hide that dirty money. Stevie's clever move back-fired on him because it showed he knew it was dirty. We had a good case against two heroin dealers. We seized Stevie's Eldorado and Al's Fleetwood.

The trial was set for summertime. As spring warmed into summer and the nights grew shorter and shorter, I got less and less sleep. It had nothing to do with the shorter nights but everything to do with entrapment defenses. Entrapment haunted my nightmares along with long lines of lidocaine laid out on endless mirrors. The Willis case would have been a textbook example of good law enforcement were it not for that boneheaded, egomaniac informant. We had in our clutches two big heroin dealers in a case over which everyone was rejoicing, and over which I was getting ulcers. I worried, not only about losing the case, but about losing my reputation as a good, honest agent. It was no good declaring I had nothing to do with Junior's snorting party. It is assumed a drug agent has control of his informant in an undercover situation. My concern wasn't lessened when the U.S. Attorney's Office assigned Mel Dickstein as prosecutor. Mel was a greenhorn, fresh from law school.

I kept consoling myself we had the best judge possible in Earl Larson, and we had at least a solid case against Stevie Smith. I continued to hope the defendants would plead guilty. But as the trial loomed, that hope faded. Al hired a sneaky attorney named Ellis Olkon, and Stevie hired Ronnie Meshbescher, only about the best defense attorney in the state and maybe in the nation. Ronnie Meshbescher, always the gentleman, tall, thin, mustache and beard perfectly trimmed, impeccably dressed, serious and somber as an undertaker, let nothing slip by him. With him at the defense table, I would certainly be grilled about the whole lidocaine incident when they had me on the witness stand. I absolutely could not lie under oath. I just hoped Judge Larson wouldn't throw the case out of court and me along with it.

There were no motions for separate trials. Al's attorney was smart enough to know having Meshbescher at the defense table with him lent his case an air of respect and dignity, and Meshbescher was smart enough to know more defendants, more witnesses, more lawyers, meant more confusion—which could translate into reasonable doubt in the mind of a juror. So we all went to trial together. Sure enough, Al's attorney went for the entrapment defense.

Mel was not worried about Olkon. When I told Mel about the lidocaine, he got all upset for a few minutes, but on second thought, he said he did not think it'd be a problem. He said the entrapment defense was one of the hardest maneuvers for a defense attorney to pull off, and Ellis Olkon wasn't that smart. To claim entrapment one had to start by openly admitting to having done the crime as stated by the government. Then one had to show two things: that the government seduced you, enticed you, led you into doing the crime and that you were not the kind of guy who would normally do such a thing.

That first point was what worried me. Junior's little snorting party made that a good defense. The second point was much in our favor though. Al Willis had a criminal record. Under the law, Mel wasn't allowed to bring up that criminal record unless Olkon did, or unless Al took the stand. With the entrapment defense, Olkon would almost be forced to put Al on the stand. That would open the door wide for Mel to ask about his past. If Al lied about his criminal record, the record could be brought into court to impeach him.

But Mel was worried about Meshbescher. Mel was a brilliant young man, but he was fresh from school and was close to wetting his pants going up against the formidable Ronnie Meshbescher. So we went to trial with me worrying about Olkon and Mel worrying about Meshbescher.

The trial lasted several days—because of Junior. The defense kept him up in the witness chair as long as they possibly could. They wanted the jury to get a good look at the kind of informant the government employed in this case. I'd told Junior to wear his best suit for court. Idiot that I was, it didn't occur to me Junior's idea of a "best suit" was not like normal people's. I was not ready for what waltzed into the court room. Junior wore his loudest, shiniest leisure suit. He was a Christmas tree of jewelry. His fingers flashed every conceivable stone that sparkled or shone. His shirt was open almost to the navel to reveal part of his emblazoned dragon and a big gold medallion hung on a chain over the dragon. On one wrist a dazzling watch, on the other a snazzy gold chain with a diamond-studded name plate. He swaggered up to take the oath and looked around smiling as it was administered. He climbed to the witness chair like an ensign just promoted to admiral might climb to the bridge of his ship. He grinned as he plopped himself down, crossed his legs, and hooked one arm over the back of the chair. He was the picture of arrogance—a prosecutor's nightmare, a defense attorney's dream. I was pretty sure every juror in the room had the same reaction I did: a deep desire to kick Junior's ass.

The two defense lawyers rejoiced when they saw that picture in the witness chair. They were fairly salivating at the thought of cross examining this fool. Mel Dickstein and I wanted to crawl under the prosecution table. Mel hurried through direct to get him out of the courtroom as quickly as possible, but the cross-examination went on forever. I had told Junior he should keep his answers short and tell the truth no matter what. But Junior was his usual expansive self. He couldn't give a short answer. When he had the stage, he wanted to make the most of it. And Junior was not used to telling the truth. This was new ground for him. He kept backing himself into corners and trying to stutter his way out. As soon as a break came, I reminded him of how to testify and made him take off some of the jewelry and button his shirt. I told him not to act so arrogant, but that was like telling a snake not to slither.

Even Meshbescher asked Junior questions, though he had no real reason to, since Junior wasn't with us that day at the Mobile station and knew nothing about Stevie Smith and the delivery. To complicate matters, Mel Dickstein couldn't afford to engage in any redirect examination because that would keep Junior on the stand even longer and also give defense counsel another chance at him on recross.

Finally we got Junior out of the courtroom, and Mel wiped his forehead. Things went better as we got to the testimony of the agents and officers, and of the chemist from the Chicago lab. My time under oath on the witness stand was short. Since Olkon was claiming entrapment, he didn't challenge me about the buy of the heroin, and since I wasn't present at the arrest of Stevie, Meshbescher only asked if I'd met his client that day. But Meshbescher did carefully cross examine the surveillance agents and tried his best to find little inconsistencies among them.

Mel had instructed me to make a large map of the area around the Mobile station, which he used in court to make it easier for the jury to understand where the various agents were stationed and how they could see what was going on. I had made the map very pretty, using magic markers of different colors. The map showed the Mobile Station, the surrounding parking lot, and nearby streets. The streets were neatly labeled: Nicollet Avenue, Thirty-sixth Street, Lyndale Avenue. I had drawn a nice big sign "Mobile Service Station" and had even labeled some of the snow banks. When Meshbescher cross-examined, he had each surveillance agent put an X at his position on the map, "a large one so the jury can see," and had them draw a line from their position to where Agent Bloch was parked (and had them put an X there too, and another line to where Stevie was parked to show they had a clear view.

I didn't like all those markings on my pretty map. When the first X was made, I frowned at Dickstein and shook my head to say, "Don't let him do that," but Mel waved it aside. By the time testimony was done, my map was a hopeless confusion of X's and lines. Some lines had been X'ed out when there was a misunderstanding and the line had to be redrawn. Some of those "misunderstandings" were clearly Meshbescher tactics. The only one not asked to make markings on my map was the Chicago chemist. He testified that, yes, the ounce of brown powder sent in by Agent Bloch was indeed heroin—very good heroin—and he explained the difference between cocaine and lidocaine.

Dickstein rested. Olkon put on his case. He called Al Willis to the stand. Willis, dressed in a neat brown suit, was soft spoken and humble (nothing like Junior) as he told the jury how he had been entrapped, how he had never sold anyone any heroin before, and how he'd sold Agent Bloch the heroin because he liked him and because Junior was constantly threatening him if he didn't do the deal (that part wasn't beyond my belief). Next Olkon called one of Al's hookers to the stand. She did not look like a hooker that day, being neatly dressed in a little padded jacket and skirt that went well below the knee, no makeup except a little powder on the nose, and two impossibly rosy cheeks. She began to tell about the "cocaine" snorting party, but she made a little change. She said it was Agent Blocks (that's what she called me) who brought in the cocaine, Agent Blocks who laid out the lines on the mirror, Agent Blocks who encouraged the ladies to snort, and Agent Blocks who snorted a good deal himself. She started her testimony fast and nervously broken. She wasn't very believable. As she rolled along, she became more confident and relaxed. Soon she was doing a masterful job and was indeed quite believable.

I kept poking Dickstein that he should object to break her rhythm, but he shook his head and let her go to the end. Dickstein was smarter than I was. When Judge Larson asked "any cross," Dickstein got up and politely asked the hooker to "repeat your testimony starting at the point where Agent Bloch brings out the mirror." She did it—word for word without a hitch. It was so entirely obvious this was a memorized script, even that she had not been the author, that any credibility she had before was extinguished.

Stevie testified he had no idea what happened that day at the Mobile Station. He stopped in for gas, and all of a sudden these cops came and arrested him! He knew nothing of heroin or of hundred dollar bills hidden in the snow.

In closing, Olkon hammered home that poor, innocent Al was entrapped by the government. Meshbescher emphasized the "confusion that reigned there that day at the Mobile station" and kept pointing at my map for proof.

Judge Larson gave the jury the long instructions about entrapment. The trial was over on a Friday. The jury was still debating on Saturday morning. Dickstein and I sat around waiting. The jury sent a message to the court. They wanted to know if the informant could be considered an officer or agent of the government. Judge Larson said yes he could, if the evidence showed that. Then they sent another note and asked the judge if they could change their verdict once they had it written down. Judge Larson sent them new forms and told them indeed they could. More hours dragged by. Dickstein said this didn't bode well for our side. The longer a jury took, the better for the defense. Pretty soon, here they came with another question: they asked if lidocaine was a prohibited drug. Judge Larson told them they should decide that for themselves based on the evidence. I could tell this jury was agonizing over that snorting party, and I fervently wished, for the hundredth time, I might be allowed some day the privilege of throwing Junior from a top-floor window of the Federal Building with a large anvil tied to him to expedite the descent. As long as I was dreaming, I resolved I'd heave a grand piano after for insurance.

Judge Larson called us into the courtroom. The jury brought in their verdict. They found Al Willis guilty, but they were undecided on Stevie Smith—a hung jury! If they had brought in a hippopotamus, I would not have been more surprised. I had thought we might lose Al, but I was sure we had a tight case on Stevie.

We made two big mistakes in the prosecution of Stevie (in my opinion). We should have tried him separately, and we should not have allowed Meshbescher to make a mess of my map. I'm not saying this because I was emotionally attached to that map (although I was). I'm saying this because of what I learned from some jury members after the trial. When I came off the elevator into the lobby of the Federal Building, most of the jury members were standing in front of the elevator door. I had to pass right through the group.

I stopped and said to them with a severely injured air, "You guys cut Stevie Smith loose!"

I didn't mean to say it so loud, and I didn't mean for it to sound like a scolding; it just came out that way. All of them answered at once. "We *wanted* to convict him, but some held out!" The jurors who refused to convict said they based their decision on that messy map. They kept repeating there must have been so much confusion at the Mobile station that day no one could know beyond a reasonable doubt what really happened. One lady kept referring to the map as "Mr. Meshbescher's map" (that was fine by me, he could have it—I didn't care to ever see it again).

There was no reasonable doubt here. That part had been manufactured right there in the courtroom by Ronnie Meshbescher. Mel Dickstein didn't care to see the map again either. He'd had enough of Meshbescher, of Stevie, and of maps. He refused a retrial. He allowed Stevie to plead to a misdemeanor—a misdemeanor!

Chapter Nine

IT'S NOT ONLY AN INFORMANT who can screw up a case; a fellow agent can do it just as efficiently. I have to tell you about the Jackie Price case, a promising cocaine case that came out of Cleveland. First I have to set the stage. Within DEA was a little "good ol' boys" flying club made up of agent-pilots who used airplanes for surveillance and for undercover. It was a supremely cushy job. They got to fly airplanes and take credit for arrests and seizures without all the bother of doing DEA 6's and sending evidence to labs and dealing with crazy informants. They rarely initiated cases, rarely testified in court. I applied, but they said they weren't hiring. Getting into this little club didn't depend on how much flying time a person had, how much experience with different types of airplanes, or how skillful a person was, but rather on how many buddies you had in the club. (It was later called the "Air Wing," so I'll use that.)

On one case, I wanted to use an Air Wing airplane to fly to Duluth to meet a cocaine dealer looking for a pilot to fly loads for him. I called the Air Wing. They said they'd send up a plane, but that I couldn't fly it. Only Air Wing pilots flew Air Wing airplanes. I'd have to take their pilot along. They sent up Agent Jim Lunn from St. Louis in a T-41, just like the ones I used to fly in Laredo for the Air Force, except this one was loaded with electronic equipment.

We got airborne out of Minneapolis and I was surprised to find that Lunn was determined to fly VFR to Duluth, for the weather was closer to IFR. As soon as we got airborne, we were zig-zagging between clouds, straining to see in the mist. Jim was navigating by following the highway. There were patches of drizzle and constant wisps of fog. We should have been on instruments.

At one point Jim asked me, "Are there any large towers out this way."

"Why don't we just get an IFR clearance?" I asked.

"Oh, the weather's better farther north, he said. "Besides, this is more fun."

On the way back the weather was even worse. As we approached the Twin Cities it was definitely IFR. I called approach control and got us an IFR clearance for four thousand feet. After we leveled off, I could tell Jim was not comfortable flying instruments in the clouds. The plane had a steer-only autopilot, but Jim kept overshooting the course, and he wasn't good at maintaining an exact altitude. He impressed me as a good pilot while we were VFR, but now he appeared nervous and made jerky corrections. I fished out the approach plate and gave it to him, saying, "Let me fly for a minute so you have a chance to study the approach."

He agreed. I took the controls, trimmed up the airplane and slid my seat forward. I concentrated intensely, to show him I knew something of flying instruments. I kept the altimeter nailed in place. I watched the course like a hawk and made corrections slow and easy. Lunn didn't say a word about the flying, but in a little while he said, "I'll let you go ahead and fly it. I'll set in the courses for you and make the radio calls. That way all you have to do is fly."

Because of that Duluth trip, I checked into Jim Lunn's flying credentials. Not only did I have ten times more flying time than he did, I even had much more time in the T-41 than he had. This was confounding. Headquarters was constantly encouraging special agents with aviation skills to apply for Air Wing positions because they "wanted only the most aviation-qualified special agents in the Air Wing." And that mysterious CIA guy who interviewed me before I ever came on with DEA had said DEA was looking for pilots and I would surely be flying.

Shortly after that Duluth trip, an Air Wing supervisor name Justinic came up to Minneapolis one day for court. That night he and Terry Anderson went out for a drink.

Terry asked Justinic, "Hey, how come Don Bloch isn't an Air Wing pilot. He was in the Air Force, he's got thousands of hours, and he has every kind of endorsement on his pilot's license."

Justinic, far from taking any interest in what Anderson was telling him, responded by saying, "Oh, we don't like ex-military pilots. They're too one-dimensional."

I said to Terry, "Too one-dimensional? What the hell does that mean?"

"I don't know. I guess it means they're not going to make you a member of their little flying club."

The irony of this was that, years later when I *was* in the Air Wing and flew with their pilots, it was clear their best pilots by far were ex-military pilots.

It was obvious Justinic had never bothered to check my flying credentials. He told Terry, "Military pilots only know how to fly jets and many of them don't even have a propeller rating or a multi-engine rating." It was an odd statement to make in light of the fact that some Air Wing pilots didn't have a multi-engine rating. If Justinic had bothered to make even a rudimentary check, he would have found I had more ratings than anyone in the Air Wing, including himself. Pilot ratings were public information. Mine included the following: Airplane Single Engine, Airplane Multi-engine, Commercial Pilot, Airplane Transport Pilot, Instrument Pilot, Flight Instructor, Instrument Flight Instructor, Ground Instructor, Advanced Ground Instructor, Instrument Ground Instructor. I don't know if I had my seaplane rating then, but those will do. I was, however, missing one important rating: single or multi Air-Wing buddy.

There. I have set the table for the Cleveland case. Agents Charlie Carter and Chuck Banks of our Cleveland office had met with some Chicago Mafia members and laid the groundwork for penetrating a group importing large amounts of cocaine from Colombia. Banks and Carter flew into Minneapolis one day wanting to borrow an undercover car to drive to Rochester for a meeting with Jackie Price, who was part of that Chicago organization, and who had been chosen to handle the Cleveland deal. As far as the friends and family of the honorable Mr. Price knew, Jackie made his living as the proud owner of the Tire and Tube Supply Company located on Fifth Avenue in Minneapolis. As far as Cleveland knew, he hugely supplemented his income from the tire shop with money from drug deals.

The two agents discussed their deal with SAC Braseth. He suggested it would look better if I fly them down to Rochester and have Price meet them at the airport. The idea was to impress upon Price he was dealing with big money. That way it would cause no suspicion when they ordered a large amount of cocaine. We rented a V-Tailed Beechcraft Bonanza. The plane was in mint condition and loaded with electronics. I had used the plane before on an undercover deal with Agent Anderson. It was a great undercover airplane. Widely popular as a private airplane among lawyers and doctors, it was the rich man's airplane—perfect for this deal. Banks and Carter called Jackie Price and told him they would meet him at the Rochester airport. They'd be flying in with their own "private airplane" and their own "private pilot."

I considered it a great privilege to work with Carter and Banks. They were much older than I, and both had worked many an undercover deal. They had reputations as professional, honest, dedicated agents and were, furthermore, two of the nicest people one could meet. They looked like mafia types. It was winter and they wore expensive business suits and long wool coats, and had large diamond rings on their fingers.

Price was waiting for us at the airport as we taxied in. Wherever his money came from, Price liked to show it off. He drove a big Cadillac, wore a cashmere-wool coat that looked as expensive as his car and smoked a cigar as big as its tailpipe. He was an enormous man in both stature and girth, with a proportionately small head that almost disappeared behind his cigar.

We had our meeting in the airport restaurant. At first I sat at a separate table. The three of them talked awhile, and then waved me over. Price had told them he was interested in hiring a pilot to get loads of cocaine directly from Colombia's Guajira Peninsula. Though this was not part of our plan, Carter and Banks, seeing an opening here, had done a supremely skillful job of selling me. They had told Price I was the best pilot they'd ever hired. I had been with them for a long time, and they found me honest and dependable. I had flown several loads of marijuana out of Chihuahua, Mexico, for them. Best of all, they said, I could be depended on to keep my mouth shut. I had flown for the United States Air Force in Vietnam and had gotten into trouble with my commanding officer for selling drugs on base. They said I had been a user myself in those days, but now I wouldn't touch the stuff.

The two of them had laid down this whole story off-the-cuff, with no prior rehearsal. It was a great story, and I used it many times later when I was undercover as a pilot. Jackie Price took to it like a catfish to tallow-bait. He was ready to hire me as his pilot right then. The Cleveland agents and Price exchanged phone numbers, and the meeting broke up with both sides agreeing to stay in contact as they arranged the first trip to Colombia.

This was a great case for me. I had no informant to deal with, no arrangements to make with the crooks, and I got to fly airplanes. Carter and Banks did all the work. In a few weeks the whole thing was arranged. I was to fly into Cartegena, on the northern coast of Colombia and meet there with the Colombian cocaine source. The Colombians would show me the airstrip at which the cocaine was to be delivered. The airstrip was a jungle strip near the Guajira coast. I would go back to the states and get an airplane and fly down to pick up a load of fifty pounds of cocaine as a test run. If everything worked out on that run, I'd fly ton-loads in the future. Half of the fifty pounds was to go to Price and half to Carter in Cleveland.

Now this was real adventure! The northeastern part of Colombia is a peninsula that sticks out into the Caribbean Sea, with the Gulf of Venezuela to the south. It's the Colombian state of La Guajira, which we called the Guajira Peninsula. Its capital was Riohacha, which, like the entire peninsula, was as lawless as Tombstone, Arizona, in the early west. It was said even the National Police of Colombia were reluctant to go into that region because it was completely under the control of outlaws. The Guajira was sparsely populated in those days—all desert and jungle along the coast with the steep, craggy mountains of the Sierra Nevada in the western part. It had no industry except some antiquated salt mining and some antiquated coal mining, but it had a booming business in very modern drug smuggling. When the Colombian National Police did go in there, they went in heavily armed, did their business, and got the hell out. It was the favorite region for drug smugglers because there was little chance of getting caught.

I made arrangements to fly down to Cartagena to meet with the crooks. Cleveland got clearances from headquarters. They arranged with our office in Bogotá to send DEA Agent Tom Zepeda to Cartagena to act as a consultant and surveillance agent. Like Carter and Banks, Zepeda was an old timer in the drug business, and Zepeda had years of experience in South America. Everything was looking good.

But headquarters threw a monkey wrench into the works: I'd have to take along a DEA Air Wing pilot! I told Agent Carter I wouldn't do that. Jackie Price had told us no other people could be involved on this first run. The crooks in Colombia wanted to do this test run, and if everything went smoothly, we could get the larger loads—as much as we wanted. Bringing in another pilot at this point would not be making it go smoothly.

The Cleveland agents were completely on my side. They didn't want anyone new for this first trip. But headquarters told us flatly that, if we wanted our case to proceed, I'd have to take an Air Wing pilot along. Carter and Banks pleaded with them, but it was set in stone. Headquarters said I was a rookie agent with no experience in South America, and they wanted a pilot along who knew the ropes. I said, "Okay, fine, I'll take Chris Bradley." I knew Bradley. He was a good pilot, an experienced agent, and he looked the part. He had long hair, an unkempt beard, and an easy manner that would win over the crooks in no time. He wore his clothes loose and sloppy and gave the general appearance of having little regard for rules. But headquarters said, "You can't pick your man. We do that." They explained how complicated it was to go through Colombia's Customs and Immigration, and wanted a guide along who "spoke the language and knew his way around."

The next day I got a call from another section of headquarters (I think the man said he was the assistant chief to the deputy chief of the temporary head of the soon-to-be established South American Desk of DEA's Foreign Office section, blah, blah.) He gave me the name of an Air Wing pilot stationed in Miami who was to go with me. He made it clear the Miami pilot would be calling the shots. He said, "While you're in Colombia, he's in charge. He has the experience. He knows his way around."

I called Bradley to ask about that Miami pilot, but Bradley was on vacation. The only other Air Wing pilot I knew was Jim Lunn, so I called him. Jim said, "Oh, you mean Jimmy-jet. I don't know Jimmy-jet all that well. I guess he's a good enough pilot, but I don't know how he is undercover. I never worked with him."

I asked why he called him Jimmy-jet.

He laughed, "Oh, that's kind of to rub it in. He wasn't anything but an army helicopter pilot before, but he thinks he's such a hotshot pilot that we started to call him Jimmy-jet."

I said, "Oh, then he served in Vietnam."

Lunn said, "No, he got out of going to Vietnam. His daddy was a big cheese in the army."

That did not tell me much. Jimmy-jet sounded like a man impressed with his own skills, but that kind never bothered me—as long as he really had skills. I was still green enough to have a rosy picture of headquarters in spite of everything that had gone on before. I was a pitifully slow learner. I set off for Miami trusting, with the simplicity of a child, that all this was best for the case, best for my safety, and in general the best way these things are done when working in foreign countries. I had to admit having a Spanish speaker along would come in handy. My Spanish was poor.

Carter and Banks were disgusted. Not only did we now have to introduce a new man into the deal, but that man would be in charge at the most critical part of planning the first smuggling trip. Agent Carter thought this was all politics. The Air Wing just wanted one of their men along so they could claim credit for the fifty pounds of cocaine and any future success in the case.

I met Jimmy-jet at the Miami airport in the waiting room of Avianca Airlines, Colombia's long-established national carrier, which we were flying to Colombia. My first disappointment in Jimmy-jet came from his physical appearance. I don't mean he was ugly or dirty. No, in fact he was quite dapper, with stylish clothes and neatly trimmed hair and moustache. He reminded me of a neat version of Chief Inspector Jacques Clouseau of the *Pink Panther* movies, except he was so much smaller. I guess I was hoping for something like a sumo wrestler to intimidate crooks with, but Jimmy-jet looked as harmless as a kindergarten teacher.

Small as he was in physical appearance, Jimmy-jet was dreadfully large in self-esteem. At the beginning I didn't blame him for this. After all, he was the man headquarters had chosen from all those Air Wing pilots to go on this mission. Therefore, he must be an agent of great value. He immediately made it clear that a lousy fifty-pound cocaine case was far below his normal standards, that he was there only by orders. In Miami, he said, they usually turn "these smaller cases" over to the local police. He added that these cases were often "ginned-up" by agents up north when the weather got cold in the hopes they might get to spend time in Miami at government expense. (He hit home there. I was enjoying the weather immensely.)

Having delivered himself of that opening salvo—a thorough mugging of the Cleveland case—he mostly held silence while he contemplated a spot on the ceiling at the far end of the Avianca waiting room. He said very little. I didn't have the impression his reticence was shyness, but rather his habit of contemplating matters of such vast importance he didn't wish to waste time bestowing upon common mortals the honor of sharing his meditations. When he did turn his head to examine his surroundings, he did it with insufferable dignity, looking around as if inspecting to see if Avianca's functionaries were performing properly.

When Jimmy-jet broke his silence, it was always to complain about something—anything. He was deeply disturbed by the fact we didn't have undercover passports. He said he never used his real name when working in these undercover situations. Next he found it outrageous we didn't have diplomatic credentials. He considered those credentials absolutely essential for working undercover in a foreign country. I had no idea what he was talking about. As far as using my real name undercover, I did that all the time. I had a whole set of undercover identifications in the name of "Donald Hendry," but those stayed mostly in my desk. When one goes to court, the crooks find out who you are anyway. You don't swear on the Bible to tell the truth, and then begin your testimony by lying about your name. As far as having "diplomatic credentials"—I didn't know what those were until later. I had one impression about Jimmy-jet: he was convinced other people were always wasting his time.

On the flight down to Colombia, I began to suspect Jimmy-jet not only didn't understand Spanish, but had never before flown on Avianca. When the stewardess brought us our lunch trays, I asked her in Spanish about the little ceramic bowl of water on the tray. She answered in Spanish that the bowl was for washing our fingers before handling our food. As the meal progressed I noticed Jimmy-jet was drinking out of his fingerbowl, but I said nothing. He was the expert. After a while, when the stewardess was passing, Jimmy-jet held up his bowl and asked for more drinking water. The stewardess explained to him (now speaking perfect English) what the bowl was for and said she would bring him a glass of water.

We stayed at the Dorado Hotel in Boca Grande, a suburb of Cartagena. It was one of the best hotels in the city. The crooks had recommended it. Agent Tom Zepeda was already there when we arrived. He had flown in a few days earlier from Bogotá to enjoy the weather and snoop around the town. Zepeda's hotel room was at the end of a hall on the top floor from which he could see most of the hotel's parking lot and half the town. I visited him in his room as soon as we got there. I thanked him for coming and apologized for disturbing his routine.

He said, "Nice beach, pretty women, good beer—yeah, I'm really suffering here."

Zepeda was a tall, handsome man, who looked a lot like Anthony Quinn. He had the same husky voice and laugh, and I'm sure he was highly successful with the ladies. He spoke Spanish like a native. It was flawless and so was his whisky, which he bestowed liberally upon himself in the lazy afternoons, and upon me whenever I visited his room.

During the next two days, Jimmy-jet and I had several meetings with the Colombian cocaine dealers. Their leader told me that once this first fifty-pound deal was done and paid up without trouble, I'd be able to get planeloads of cocaine or marijuana any time I wanted. He said right now they had seven tons of marijuana sitting at a strip in the Guajira, and he could get any amount of cocaine he wanted from the labs in Medellin.

From his room, Agent Zepeda watched the parking lot with his binoculars and occasionally walked through the lobby to get a look at the crooks as they came and went. By the end of the first day, he had one of them identified. The man was a known trafficker, and the National Police would be happy to arrest him, if we could make our case.

If we could. You can guess what Jimmy-jet was doing all this time: complaining. We were in the pretty coastal town of Cartagena, Colombia, where American tourists went for winter vacations. The rich ones anchored their yachts in the sheltered harbor a few blocks from the main street. The sun was shining, sky and sea endless blue, dark-eyed señoritas in bikinis on beaches, the crooks buying the beer. All of it insulted the sophisticated tastes of Jimmy-jet. The beaches were dirty, the women ugly, the beer flat, the hotel room too small. Not one thing came up to his lofty standards.

He remained aloof at our meetings, mostly sitting apart on a couch and engaging in his favorite pastime of contemplating a spot on the ceiling at the far end of the room. The problem was not that he didn't understand Spanish; most of the conversation was in English (except when the crooks were commenting to each other about Jimmy-jet). The crooks were friendly and intelligent. In a short time, I liked them better than I liked my DEA Headquarters-appointed partner.

The Colombian crooks weren't impressed with Jimmy-jet either. "What's wrong with your friend?" they asked.

After the first meeting, one of them said to me very politely, "Tell your friend to take off his sunglasses during our meetings."

Jimmy-jet refused! They were evidently his favorite army-issue sunglasses from his helicopter flying days. The irony was that he had his name and rank stenciled boldly on the side of the glasses in letters large enough to be read from across the table. He objected to using his real name undercover, yet refused to quit advertising it.

At the next meeting one of the Colombians said to me, "I still don't know what your friend looks like under those sunglasses."

I said, "You're not missing much. He looks like a weasel."

He stared at me for a moment, then he began to smile, then to chuckle. "You know," he said, "if I looked like a weasel, I guess I'd wear sunglasses too." He seemed to relax, and I thought they had accepted Jimmy-jet. That did not last long.

When the Colombian crooks said they wanted to fly us out to the jungle strip where the pick-up was to be made, so we'd be sure we could find the right place, Jimmy-jet refused that too. The crooks told me to dump this guy, and I was put in the agonizing position of having to defend and praise a man I did in fact intensely dislike. I told them he was such an expert navigator and pilot I couldn't do without him. Oh, I had to bite my tongue!

I took Jimmy-jet aside and tried to reason with him. But he just would not go to look at that airstrip. This made no sense. What pilot would pass up a chance to look at an airstrip he was to use in the near future? And the crooks said there were eight different jungle strips in that same area, which could easily be confused. (Remember, there was no such thing as GPS in those days.) But Jimmy-jet said we could not be sure their airplane was safe, that they had done the last one-hundred-hour inspection, or the last annual. He reminded me he was in charge and was responsible for my safety. Then he added this disgraceful comment: "Don't worry about it. If this is a legitimate case they'll be calling and begging us to come. If they don't call, it's because they never had the dope in the first place." So there you are. He had his ass covered like a true bureaucrat. If the case went well, he could take credit. If it didn't, we had a lousy case to start with.

The crooks proposed driving out to the strip. That made no sense either. The strip was near Rioacha, more than a five-hour drive and some of that through the rugged Sierra Nevada Mountains. Besides, I wanted to see the strip from the air, not from the ground. (It's amazing how different a strip, even a familiar one, will look from above.) Anyway, it made no difference. Jimmy-jet refused to go either way. The crooks left the meeting disgusted. They said they'd be back the next day to see if anything had changed.

I asked Tom Zepeda to talk to Jimmy-jet, but he said, "I can't interfere in your case, unless you guys try to do something the State Department wouldn't like."

"Is there any diplomatic reason why we can't fly out there with the crooks?" I asked.

"No reason at all. It makes sense to have the crooks show you where to pick up the dope. Not only would it make sure you have the right field, but we could be checking out who owns the field, and the DAS agents could get geared up to move in for an arrest." DAS was their name for the Colombian National Police. It stood for Departamento Administrativo de Seguridad (Administrative Department of Security). DAS agents were like our FBI, but they also had some powers similar to our CIA and our Secret Service agents.

Zepeda asked me, "Do you think their airplane's safe?"

I said, "Hell yes. Don't you think Colombians love their asses as much as we love ours? They won't go up in an unsafe airplane anymore than we would. He won't go, no matter what. That's what headquarters gave me for a partner."

Zepeda put a confidential hand on my shoulder. Looking me in the eye, he said with a big beaming smile, "Welcome to DEA."

Nothing changed overnight. Jimmy-jet still refused to go see the strip. The crooks were still confused. They drew me a map of the area by Rioacha showing the airstrips and highlighting the one we were to use. They said they would call my bosses in Cleveland when they had the cocaine ready to go. We shook hands and parted with some tension still between us. I was not happy. I felt like a job-seeker who'd just been told, "We'll give you a call when there's an opening."

We never made that trip to the Guajira. The Colombians were suspicious. The DAS agents never arrested any of them. The Cleveland agents did arrest Jackie Price however, and got some of his money. Somehow Banks and Carter convinced Price everything was fine and the test-run was ready and I was set to fly in the load. They had Price front $50,000 as a down payment for his share. They arrested him when he delivered the money and charged him with conspiracy to smuggle cocaine.

I still trusted (for I'm a slow learner) that headquarters had not sent me down there with a complete dud. I still believed Jimmy-jet must have made a lot of big cases in his day since he looked down his nose at a mere fifty pounds. This was back in the mid-seventies when fifty pounds of cocaine was a big case anywhere, even in New York, especially when it was only for a test run with bigger loads to come. It's true that, a decade later, a ton of cocaine seized in Miami barely made the newspaper, but that was a long way off. My still-rosy picture of Jimmy-jet was later destroyed by Agent Jose Marin, who I met in Colombia on Operation Funnel. Agent Ken Curry, Jose, and I were talking over a beer in the bar of the Hotel Petecuy in Cali. Jose described Jimmy-jet as a "prima donna," and he added, "Most of those Air Wing pilots are." Curry seconded the opinion.

Jose said, "I don't think he's made a big case of his own."

I said, "Isn't he supposed to be an expert at undercover work in Colombia?"

Marin laughed at that. "He's expert at claiming credit for other people's seizures, like all those Air Wing pilots." Curry seconded the opinion.

I was an idiot. To think that at times when Jimmy-jet was complaining, I was blaming the Cleveland agents. Several times I had said, "Well, this isn't my case. It's those Cleveland guys who put this together." I was ashamed of myself. Jimmy-jet was not worthy of carrying the briefcase of either Agent Carter or Agent Banks.

Like I said, I'm a slow learner. I clung to the belief Jimmy-jet must be, at the very least, a brilliant, top-notch, meticulous pilot or the Air Wing would never have recommended him. That fond belief, that shiny illusion, was tarnished years later, when I actually flew with Jimmy-jet. I was ordered down to Miami to get checked out in their Piper Aztec. Jimmy-jet did the check out. He was very nice to me and did a professional job checking me out—except when it came to starting the engines. He told me this aircraft was tricky to start, and he showed me how it was to be done. As I sat there in the pilot's seat with my mouth hanging open, Jimmy-jet put the mixture on number one to full rich and cranked until the engine was flooded. Then he pulled the mixture back, opened the throttle full, and did a flooded-engine start. The engine coughed and sputtered and lit, and sent a big cloud of smoke drifting away from behind us. The smoke advanced across the ramp while the lineboy gazed in wonder. This process was repeated for number two, and we were off.

In a short time we were back at the office having made the required landings. Jimmy-jet signed me off. He handed me the keys and the log book. He asked if I had any questions. I said no, except I was wondering about that strange procedure for starting the engines. He went on aggressive defense immediately.

"I suppose you know better. We don't know what we're doing around here. Go ahead and try it your way. But don't come back here asking where you should go to get the battery charged, when you've run it down."

I went out to the airplane, thinking I would do it his way, but as I climbed in and went through the checklist in the flight manual, I rebelled. The Air Force had pounded into me: always go by the Flight Manual. I started up according to the checklist. It fired right off with no problem, no cloud of smoke, no gaping lineboy. Agent Hal Kent and I used that airplane for a month flying out of Belize, and never had trouble starting it. My last illusion about Jimmy-jet drifted away like that cloud of smoke on the airport ramp. It's an eternal mystery to me why headquarters picked this reluctant agent to go on the Cleveland case when there were dozens of competent Air Wing pilots who would have been most happy to have that job.

Chapter Ten

IT WAS LUCKY MY FIRST DEA POST was near Stearns County. I couldn't have handled the pressure otherwise. Whenever the job became too much for me, whenever my spirit became gloomy and grim in the belief all humans were scheming, cunning, conniving vultures, whenever I needed my batteries recharged, Bea and I would take a few days off and drive back home to visit the folks. We'd spend time at my parents' home in Albany, or I'd go fishing with her dad on the small, peaceful lakes in the center of the county, or I'd spend an afternoon just talking to the old man as he sat in his easy chair smoking his ancient pipe and filling the air with the fragrance of Prince Albert Tobacco smoke.

We spent evenings at the kitchen table playing cards with neighbors and talking about the simple concerns of farmers: the height of the corn, the market price of slaughter steers and heifers at St. Paul, the quality of the alfalfa crop at the last cutting. There was never a mention of drugs or prostitutes, of guns or murder, of traffic or pollution, or any of the concerns of the city. I always found great pleasure in conversing with them for I loved to hear again their old German expressions and their English heavy with Teutonic accent. Even today I think with great pleasure of those simple people—their deep faith in their farms and their God. There was in them a profound contentment in following the ways of their fathers and grandfathers. They held no malice for others and were entirely convinced that others held none for them.

I had been raised in this atmosphere of contentment where the changes of weather, of fortunes, and of seasons were accepted with a deep trust that God knows best. The bitterest winds of winter, the sunniest days of spring, the stormiest hours of summer were all viewed with that same quiet faith. They ate their suppers gratefully without wishing for more or for better—grateful as cows ruminating in the meadow, peaceful as deer feeding in the moonlight. It was tranquil tonic for me to spend time back home.

After a few days of breathing the drowsy air of Stearns County, I was ready to saddle up again and face the turmoil in the city. And with that, I have another screwed-up-case story to tell. This story is short (as was the case—thank God).

One of our agents had an informant who came in with this unusual drug deal: the crooks would trade us three ounces of pure cocaine for a dozen M-16s. The informant said the crooks were working for David Fong, who owned a bar and restaurant (it was a great restaurant) on Lyndale at Ninety-third. Today that story might sound ridiculous. What could an honest, upright citizen like David Fong have wanted with an arsenal of automatic weapons? But in those days the agents, especially the older ones, were convinced all "Chinamen" were linked to either the On Leon Tong or the Hip Sing Tong, Chinese versions of the Italian Mafia. The boss found the story plausible. We informed ATF (Alcohol Tobacco and Firearms), since it was a gun deal. ATF got us the weapons; we loaded them in the trunk of the undercover car and were ready to go. The exchange (really the arrest) was to be made on the second floor of a parking ramp in downtown Minneapolis. Those of us covering the deal took along extra ammunition, and most of us took shotguns. The feeling was that, if the crooks were dealing for M-16s, they might already have some real fire power. If it was a rip, a shootout might become fairly exciting.

I was already at that parking ramp, looking for a hiding place behind a stairwell or a pillar, when I got an urgent call to get back to the office, right now. The operation had just been called off. As our undercover agent was leaving the Federal Building along with his covering surveillance, all of whom wore flak jackets and carried their weapons, a whole posse of FBI agents, equally arrayed, was doing the same. One of our agents asked an FBI agent what they were up to that afternoon.

The FBI guy said, "We have three ounces of cocaine and are going to trade it for a dozen M-16s."

That put an end to the famous David Fong M-16 case. Our DEA undercover agent was on the way out the door to meet their FBI undercover agent in that parking ramp, and both sides were loaded for bear and ready to make an arrest. The FBI had neglected a couple of things when they set up their side of this operation. They should have notified ATF (since it was a gun deal), and they should have notified DEA (since it was a drug deal). However, in their usual zeal to protect their turf, they had ignored such details. All of us were wearing jackets with DEA or FBI printed on them in large letters, but that was no guarantee nothing bad could happen. One shot fired by a nervous agent could have set off an O.K. Corral shootout, and somebody was bound to get hurt. In those days our "bullet proof" vests were no more than "bullet resistant" vests.

If the reader would like to speculate on who would have won such a fight, I'll point out a few things in our favor. We had on our side several veteran Minneapolis Police officers (in those days policemen were not reluctant to pull a gun as they are now). We had two US marshals and one of them was Leon Cheney (known as Hair Trigger). We had Dick Fekete (the big canon), and we had the ATF guys. Couple all that with the fact that FBI agents were always reluctant to fire their weapons (it caused them a mountain of paperwork and no end of investigative troubles), then you can make an educated speculation.

To give you an idea of what kind of man Deputy Cheney was: Back when we had that shootout with Henry Roundtree, he came down to our office next morning to complain he had not been invited along the night before to participate in the fun. We could only appease him by swearing we had not anticipated a gunfight. A few months later we went out at night on a search warrant—this time with Cheney along. I was guarding the back of the target house, Cheney was guarding one side. There were no lights on except in a front room. Cheney, with a double-barreled shotgun, was standing by a window high enough so he had to stand on tiptoe to look inside. He saw nothing but darkness in there. When our agents pounded on the front door and announced it was the cops coming in to serve a warrant, someone from inside put a couple of bullets through the door, and some of our agents promptly responded by adding a few more bullet holes (going the other way)—at which point the man inside surrendered. When Cheney heard the gunfire up front, he crashed the muzzle of his shotgun through the window pane and thundered the contents of both barrels into the darkness of the room. He told me he did it "to let them know they were surrounded." The gunfire exchange hit no one, though the boss got a flying splinter of glass in his eye and had to go to emergency to get it removed.

IT WAS ALSO LUCKY FOR ME my first post was in Minneapolis because there was no finer police force in the country than the Minneapolis narcs. I got to serve with men like Narcotic Officers Hitchins and Brademan, and with Task Force Agent Boulger, three of the finest. I remember how honored I felt to be considered a "fellow officer" with men of their caliber. At the time I assumed the cooperation we had in Minneapolis between the locals and DEA was normal. It was in fact, an anomaly. I found that out as I worked in later years in other large cities across the country while flying for the Air Wing. In most large cities there was competition and antagonism between the enforcement units. The feds would hide information from the locals and vice versa. But in Minneapolis the locals regularly brought us their cases and were happy to have a crook up on federal charges. They got better prosecutions and longer sentences in federal court than in Hennepin County court. The Minneapolis narcs were not jealous and were glad to share credit.

I got most of the credit for putting heroin dealer, Alfonso Davis, in jail, but that would never have happened had it not been for Minneapolis Officers Hitchins and Brademan. In those days heroin was known as the most dangerous drug on earth. There were still great, scary myths (many of them promoted by the government) circulating about the dangers of other drugs: marijuana turns you into a rapist and murderer; LSD short-circuits the brain; cocaine turns you into a raging maniac; PCP makes people claw their own eyes out. But the mother of them all, the big kahuna: heroin.

Alfonso Davis was considered the biggest heroin dealer in Minneapolis. I said I would start up a case with Davis as the target. That caused great mirth among the older DEA agents. They said the only way to start a case was to start with an informant, and my target was whatever dealer the informant could introduce me to, not whoever I wished for. That would have discouraged me, had I not learned something about conspiracy from Nicky Frol and Stephen Scholle, and had I not gotten encouragement from Officers Hitchins and Brademan. They took me aside and said, "Look here, if you're willing to work on putting together a federal case against Davis, we'll help."

I knew I couldn't ask for better help in the world. I immediately opened a General File on Alfonso Davis and wrote a report with all the information I could find about him. I described his house, his car, his friends, and his lovely criminal record. He had not yet been caught selling heroin, but he had a highly complimentary rap sheet congratulating him on such undertakings as assault, robbery, forgery, assault with a deadly weapon, bank fraud, armed robbery, interstate transportation of forged securities, and so on for more than a dozen convictions. During one of his robberies, he had engaged in the fascinating diversion of beating his victim with a pistol. My boss, Jim Braseth, upon reading my report, said, "Wow, this guy is a real sweetheart, isn't he? Yeah, if you can, put the bastard in jail." He let me take out a case number.

Mister Davis lived in a big house, among rich neighbors, up on the hill of Mount Curve Avenue, overlooking downtown. The residents of that hill had a lovely view especially at night when the lights of the city were on and even more so in winter when holiday lights of the neighbors blended with background lights of the city. Alfonso Davis's house looked like a castle, a huge place of thirty rooms, made of gray stone, and with a tall rounded tower on one front corner. And it was by no means the most expensive one on that hill. Alfonso was making the same stupid mistake many dopers made: as soon as they had some money, they had to show it off. He had no visible means of support, yet he drove a fancy car and lived in an expensive house in an upscale part of town. This always looked like mockery to a policeman. It was a disrespect he found hard to swallow. A policeman found it painful to put up with a heroin dealer to start with, but this one was "rubbing his nose in it."

While I was constructing my Davis file, Hitchins and Brademen were interviewing prisoners at the Hennepin County jail. Whenever they found one who knew Al Davis, they called me and said, "Go talk to this guy."

One day Hitchins said, "We got Eyeball here in the slammer. He knows every crook in Minneapolis. Go talk to him. Ask for Isaac Russell."

I took a handful of Hershey bars and a pack of gum with me to the jail. The police thought Eyeball was a heroin user. (Heroin addicts, when deprived of their drug, get a fierce craving for sweets). Eyeball said he was not an addict, but he accepted the candy, and ate it all, and started on the gum too, in the ten minutes we talked. If you ever wondered why they called a jail "the slammer," you need only to go visit the Hennepin County Jail for a few minutes. I heard the repeated startling crash of iron on iron as muscular guards slammed the big doors, and as spring-loaded bolts clanged into place. Between that banging and clanking I heard the rattle of leg chains as prisoners were taken in and out of their cells along the great halls.

Up front was a tiny interview cell where they brought Eyeball. The cell was divided by a wall with a small barred window. They put Eyeball on one side of the wall and, after searching me (though I showed them my credentials), they put me on the other. I spent very little time on that interview, because anyone walking by could see us, and anyone with good ears could hear us between the banging of the iron.

I decided Eyeball could help me. With the help of Hitchins and Brademan, he was released. A few of the Minneapolis Police had personal grudges against Eyeball. He was always causing them trouble, and they didn't think we should be using him as an informant. He should be behind bars. He was a suspect in several murders. He had been charged several times with assault, including one on a police officer. He had broken into houses and had taken people's cars. I could understand the police resentment, and I felt guilty about it, but Hitchins and Brademan pointed out that using priests, nuns, or altar boys as informants was not usually productive.

For more than a year I had the torture of having Eyeball for an informant. He made cases, yes, but he was always getting into trouble with the police, and I was always calling Hitchins or Brademan to bail him out. Considering the size of his reputation, one would think he was some kind of a giant. He wasn't. He was a skinny little black man, no more than five feet six inches. His nickname came from the scar that ran from the top of his forehead over one eye and down below the cheekbone. That eye was a ghostly, milky white and gave him a ghastly look. The eye was of no use except to scare people. He was extremely athletic and would sometimes, while walking along, jump up, summersault, and land back on his feet, hardly breaking stride as though it was the most ordinary thing in the world to do. Once when he and I were walking down the hall of an apartment building, he jumped up, kicked out the light bulb overhead, landed on his feet and kept striding along like a leghorn rooster.

The good part about using Eyeball as an informant was he never called and whined, "They're going to kill me" (which happened routinely with other informants). Quite the opposite: the crooks were more likely to be afraid Eyeball might kill them. Eyeball hung around with a sleazy street rat named Donnie Battles, who was kind of a bodyguard. Battles in winter always wore a long fur coat made of rabbit skin, and a pointed rabbit-skin hat, which made him look like Robinson Crusoe. Under that coat, Battles was likely to have a gun, or knife, or brass knuckles, or any instrument made for use in the entertaining pastime of maiming. He always walked around with his hands in his coat pockets—I should say it looked like he had his hands in his coat pockets, but those pockets had been cut out so he could get at the arsenal in his belt without the inconvenience of having to pull his hands out of his coat and reaching under it. Other street rats said that, at night, Battles carried a double-barreled sawed-off shotgun under his coat. He had the shotgun tied to his wrist with a leather thong, and he would swing the gun up through the front slit of the coat and point it at anyone who bothered him or Eyeball.

These two crooks (or as Agent Lewis would say, "stone crooks"—meaning they were thoroughly, entirely, nothing but, through and through criminals) roamed the streets of Minneapolis and had their noses into everything. That was why they were such a valuable source of crime information. Eyeball was so unafraid of other criminals, he used to set up deals right at his own house. I bought heroin from Holly Tyner, a wise old dealer, who was not in the least suspicious of me because Eyeball had set up the deal in a most homey atmosphere. How could Tyner harbor any suspicion? We did the deal in Eyeball's house, at Eyeball's kitchen table, with Eyeball's wife sitting across from us suckling her baby, the little guy making slobbering noises as he enjoyed his meal while Tyner and I negotiated close by. Normally these drug deals were done in back rooms and alleys, or in the privacy of a car, and with constant glancing over the shoulder.

Mrs. Eyeball was a petite little white girl with a gorgeous figure and beautiful face. She was always dressed neatly and her house was spotless. She was completely in love with Eyeball. She was an artist. She showed me a picture she'd painted of Eyeball, which hung on the wall in the bedroom. This girl had real talent. That picture looked just like Eyeball—no doubt about it, but she had somehow painted in a beauty and innocence that just was not there in the real man. The scar was there, the ghostly eye was there, but she had somehow managed to make him look innocent as a little boy at the Communion rail. A Hennepin County deputy had told me that she married Eyeball while he was serving time at the State Prison at Stillwater.

He said, "Her father's a hard-working, conservative contractor from St. Cloud, if I remember right. Imagine what it was like for him when she made the announcement."

The deputy imagined her saying, "Guess what, daddy, I'm getting married!"

Dad says, "Really, to whom?"

She says, "Well, you don't know him yet."

"Why don't you bring him around?"

"Well, it's because he's in Stillwater State Prison, and that's why we're getting married there. It'll be next Saturday."

If daddy's heart survived that shock, he had another coming when he first saw Eyeball.

Alfonso Davis wasn't easily caught selling heroin. He sold only to junkies. The credentials required to buy from him were tracks on the arms and legs. If a stranger wanted to buy, he had to first mainline in Alfonso's presence. This pretty much eliminated undercover narcotic officers. Few of us would be willing to inject heroin and, besides, in court it would make us look like fanatic fools, and could also set up an entrapment defense. Eyeball was disappointed when I informed him there was no way I'd shoot up. That meant Alfonso wouldn't sell directly to me. He'd sell to Eyeball, but no prosecutor wanted Eyeball for a star witness in a case. So we began to scout around for junkies who bought their stuff from Davis. I could buy from them and let the surveillance make the case against Alfonzo.

In fall, after mucking about on this all summer, we made the first buy. Dennis McDonald was a heroin addict who bought regularly from Alfonso Davis and sold some of the drug to get money for more. Eyeball introduced me to McDonald. I ordered up an ounce of heroin. When McDonald called and said Alfonso had the stuff ready, I met with him and showed him the money. Surveillance followed him to Alfonso's house and watched him go in. They watched him come out and come back to me. I paid McDonald $2,200, and surveillance followed him back to Alfonso's to deliver the money. Alfonso gave McDonald a gram of heroin for commission.

A month later I made another buy through an addict named Mason. Mason drove me right to Alfonso's house, but I had to wait in the car. This time I had to pay $2,500 for the ounce, and we learned later the extra charge was because Eyeball had set it up so he got a $300 commission. Mason took some of the heroin for his commission.

Braseth and I talked the case over with Assistant U.S. Attorney John Lee. When I told them I didn't think I'd ever get to buy directly from Davis, they decided we should end the case by issuing a search warrant on the Davis house and hoping to find dope and maybe some of the dirty money. I drew up a long warrant, much of it based on information from Officer Hitchins, and I heaved in everything I could, including Davis's long criminal record. The magistrate would not sign. He lined out large sections. I had it retyped, and this time he signed it.

Again, even though it was late in the evening, I found plenty of volunteers to go on the search. Minneapolis Police officers and Hennepin County Narcotics officers and Minnesota Bureau of Criminal Apprehension narcs were happy to go along. Alfonso was lucky. Even with that swarm of bees going through the house, we found no heroin. The only drug we found was about three quarters of a pound of marijuana. We found lots of drug paraphernalia like syringes, roach clips, scales, hash pipes. All over the house the agents found receipts that showed Davis was spending mountains of money. We also found six guns. They were loaded guns, and they were all illegal, for Davis was a felon. We found mannitol (which was the adulterant Davis was using to cut his heroin), and we found one bill of the dirty money.

With that, we went to court in front of the Honorable Judge Earl Larson, and I do mean honorable—he proved that he well-deserved that title. Prosecutor John Lee charged Alfonso Davis with four counts of narcotic offenses and six counts of firearms offenses, but Judge Larson severed the guns. He said we had to try those separately. I made sure McDonald and Mason knew how to dress and how to testify. I'd learned my lesson from Junior. They were both very good witnesses. They were good looking young men in their early twenties. They showed up dressed in business suits and ties, hair trimmed, clean shaven. They were humble as they told the story of how they became addicted, and how they supported their habit with heroin from Al Davis. John Lee did a masterful job of drawing them out. He knew this had good jury appeal. The two testified about how they got the heroin from Alfonso the day Agent Bloch bought from them. Then surveillance and Agent Bloch backed up their testimony with dates and times. The jury had to listen to Agent Bloch go through the boring procedures used in processing evidence and sending it to the Chicago lab. The chemist from Chicago confirmed the powder he got from Agent Bloch was indeed heroin, and that it was mixed with mannitol like the stuff found at Davis's house.

Lee rested.

When his turn came, Defense Counsel Resnick rested too! We went directly to closing arguments. Instead of witnesses, Resnick preferred to entertain the court with a long, dreary closing argument about how his client was framed by Agent Bloch. He tried to make the jury believe Agent Bloch was jealous of Davis because of his fancy house and car. As for McDonald and Mason, those two had memorized scripts fed to them by Prosecutor Lee. The proof of this was that, on direct, those two had ready, precise answers and perfect memories, but when he, Resnick, had them under cross, their memories failed, and they were not sure of dates, and they stuttered and contradicted. Those two were willing to tell lies for Prosecutor Lee in order to get lenient treatment for selling heroin to Agent Bloch. The problem with the stuttering argument was that Resnick's questions were so long and so confusing anyone would have stuttered.

Resnick's brilliant arguments fell on deaf ears. The jury found Alfonso Davis guilty of two counts of dispensing and distributing a Schedule One controlled substance (heroin), and one count of conspiracy to do that (the conspiracy between Davis, McDonald, and Mason). They found him not guilty on the charge of possession with intent to distribute (the marijuana found at his house). John Lee didn't care; that was a throw-away charge anyhow.

Several things about the Davis trial were new to me. Resnick, although claiming in his closing argument that his client was framed, did not put his client on the stand to explain what happened when McDonald and Mason came to his house. And Resnick went so far as to suggest that McDonald and Mason were selling heroin to Davis. That didn't lend creditability to his closing argument. Another thing was that Judge Larson sentenced Davis immediately. Normally sentencing took several weeks of dilly-dallying, while federal probation officers prepared a report about the convicted prisoner the judge used in deciding the sentence.

Judge Larson thanked the jury, dismissed them, and proceeded forthwith to read Alfonso Davis the riot act. Never before or after did I see Judge Larson get emotional. He was angry. He held Davis accountable for the addictions of McDonald and Mason as well as other youths of the judge's great city. He asked Davis why he had all those loaded guns at his house. He asked him point blank if he had threatened any witnesses (McDonald and Mason had received threatening phone calls from someone). He cited Davis's long criminal record and said, "Mr. Davis, I really think you're beyond any chance at all of rehabilitation." Then he sentenced Alfonso Davis to a whopping thirty years (ten for each offense—and the sentences were to run consecutively, not concurrently). This was the longest sentence I had ever witnessed for a drug dealer. He piled on a fine of $35,000.

Davis appealed (of course), but the appeal wasn't any better than the defense at trial, and had some of the same inconsistencies and contradictions. Resnick told the Eighth Circuit judges the severe sentencing was because Judge Larson took into account matters that had nothing to do with the trial: like the loaded guns and the witness threats. But the Circuit Court pointed out that Larson had not pressed Davis on the guns when he refused to answer, and that he seemed to take Davis on his word when he said he didn't threaten anyone. Besides, they said, if Judge Larson really wanted to stick it to him, he could have given Davis forty-five years instead of thirty. Then Resnick complained John Lee had interrupted him with objections during closing (that was true, but also perfectly legal, when the closer makes false statements). Resnick complained at one point the judge interrupted him (that also was true, and it was when Resnick was talking about how the jealous Agent Bloch had framed his client). Judge Larson said enough of that. "Agent Bloch has appeared in my courtroom many times and has never shown himself to be anything but an honest and upright law enforcement officer." (I could have kissed his gavel.) Resnick complained that Lee had made false statements during the prosecution's closing, but the Circuit Court said those statements were not "plain error," and since Resnick had not objected to them at the time, he could not use them on appeal.

Next Resnick said Judge Larson should not have allowed us to introduce the evidence showing how much Davis had paid for his house, for his jewelry, and for his multi-thousand-dollar brass bed (that bed stood up in that tall castle tower, which was the master bedroom). He also complained we had not properly established it was in fact Davis's residence. There was much more. It was the longest appeal I had ever seen. It was denied.

One more new thing for me about the Davis case: When it was all over—the trial and the appeal—Davis got another lawyer, Thorwald Anderson, and they petitioned the District Court to have the conviction set aside, because Davis "was denied effective assistance of counsel," which is the same as saying, "Resnick was a horseshit attorney." I thought Alfonso might have a point there, but he was the one who hired Resnick, not the government. When the District Court in Minneapolis denied his petition, he appealed to the Eight Circuit. They denied him too. Alfonso finally settled down to serving his time.

There is some real irony here. If the Justice Department had been using the asset forfeiture laws the way they did only a few years later, I would have been able to seize Alfonso's house, his car, his jewelry, his fancy brass bed, even his clothes, and he would not have been able to afford attorneys like Resnick and Anderson. He would have relied on a public defender supplied by taxpayers, and those attorneys would very likely have mounted a better defense.

Chapter Eleven

My relationship with Eyeball was now on a downward slide. I did not like the fact that he took a $300 commission out of the Mason buy, or that he at first denied it. We did a couple of other cases together—clean cases: two buys, a bust, and a guilty plea—but I watched the pair (Eyeball and Battles) closely. They knew it too, from the questions I asked before each deal, and they played it straight for a while. But soon they got cocky again, and one day they went too far.

They came in with a proposal to buy a pound of hashish from a Minneapolis dealer for eight-hundred dollars. They said the dealer was known on the street as "Red," and they claimed not to know his real name. They said I would not be able to do the undercover work, because the crook said he knew a DEA agent, and he gave a description that fit me exactly, so Eyeball suggested Agent Ron Tomcik do the job.

That suggestion was not surprising. Ron Tomcik was great undercover. No crook ever suspected Ron of being a narc, though some suspected him of being a user. He was so full of nervous energy, so hyperactive one could easily think he was high on meth or coke. One time Ron and I were undercover on a cocaine case. The two of us were sitting with two crooks in the living room of an apartment relaxing and chatting and drinking beer while waiting for a delivery. That is, three of us were relaxing. Relaxing was something Ron never did. He jumped up every few seconds, dashed to the window to look outside. He sat down for a minute, grabbed a magazine, turned a page, put it down only to take it back up and do the same thing. When anyone asked him a question he'd jump up and get right in the guy's face talking rapidly, his hands moving like pistons, his head bobbing at every word, and shuffling his feet like he was doing a soft shoe to keep time with his choppy sentences. One might think, well, he was nervous about working undercover. No, not at all. He was very experienced in undercover work. He was the same way during the day in the office or at night in the bar.

When we left the apartment that day, Ron and one crook led the way into the hall, the other crook took me by the elbow and said in a low voice, "Hey, your buddy got his nose a little too deep into the speed bag."

I asked, "What do you mean?"

He gave me a patient look and said kindly, "Look, I know your buddy's all hopped up on crank. Tell him no speeding while we do business. We can't have that. Always be careful on a deal."

The guys in the office called Ron "the Rocket." It eventually got to be a term of affection, but it had not started that way. When Ron first came to Minneapolis, the police called him "the Squirrel," as they saw him constantly snapping his head around in fanatic watchfulness and sending his long hair flying in all directions. "The Squirrel" became "Rocky the Squirrel" (from *Rocky & Bullwinkle* on TV); which was shortened to Rocky, and then, as they got used to him, to "the Rocket" (because they thought he might go off any moment).

Hashish is made from the top part of mature, female marijuana plants just before they go to seed. That part has the most THC (the stuff that makes you high). The manufacturer sifts out the leaves and stems until he has only a fine resinous powder left, and that gets compressed into little dark brown cakes. Break off a piece of the cake, put it in your pipe, and light up.

We called the stuff "hash." On the street it was often called "camel shit" because of its resemblance to animal dung. One had to be careful when buying hash in Minneapolis. There was very little good hash around. Some of it was so bad a person could get a better high from smoking the genuine camel product. Often it smelled moldy, and we knew it wasn't real hash. Real hash did not get moldy. Some of the street hash was no more than hydraulically compressed marijuana. Some was ground up marijuana leaves mixed with cooking oil, and some was total humbug: made from any leafy material like alfalfa or slough hay.

The stuff Ron, the Rocket, was to buy that day from Red, the crook, was touted to be one pound of "top grade Moroccan hash." Surveillance followed the Rocket with the two informants in the undercover car to the crook's apartment. We still didn't have the crook's name—just "Red." We had a description of his car, and we found that right away in the parking lot at the apartment. The plate came back to a name we didn't know. The apartment was listed as empty, but the informants said Red told them he had just moved in. After more than an hour inside, the Rocket came out alone. He drove off, and met with Dave Haight to field test the stuff. In a few minutes the surveillance was called off.

When we got to the office we found that they were still field testing. As more officers who knew something about hash filed in, more questions about the stuff came up. With more careful field testing, it became obvious that we did not have hashish. The surveillance had been called off too early. Rocket said they had passed around a hash pipe at the apartment to sample the stuff. Eyeball and Battles had both smoked the stuff and pronounced it excellent. The crook had smoked some too and thought it was the best he'd had. Rocket confessed he had "tried some" himself, but knew little about the taste of hash. Since all the experienced smokers thought it was good, Supervisor Haight (again doubting the chemical test) thought it must be good too. While we were field testing at the office, Eyeball called and asked when he could get paid for the deal. I told him to come later. I also told him to go to Red's apartment right now and keep him there for a few minutes.

We went back to the apartment to get our money. Eyeball and Battles were there. They said the crook was not answering his door. We got the key. The supervisor said no one was living there and offered to rent it to us at a reduced rate. We entered and found the place empty. There was no sign of habitation—no clothes, no groceries. A window near the fire escape was open. We had been fooled. A beautiful rip off. Rocket and the two informants had not noticed anything unusual when they were at the apartment with the crook. The car, which was inoperative (and had been so for months), was registered to a man living in another apartment, and he was not "Red." All we had was Rocket's physical description. The two informants didn't know anything more.

But I knew better.

Rocket had not noticed anything wrong—that part I believed, but Eyeball and Battles not noticing?—that was a lie. They were far too smart to be ripped off by some dumb honky. And they knew damned well this stuff was not hash. It was lawn grass and oregano and other kitchen spices: "parsley, sage, rosemary, and thyme" as Simon and Garfunkle would say, and it was as fake as that "acre of land between the salt water and the sea strand." And here was what confirmed it for me: when I called Eyeball and Battles to come in to get paid (really, I wanted to grill them about the deal), they turned me down. They said they wanted to hit the streets to look for Red. They said they'd get our money back no matter what, and would come in for payment in the morning. I say this confirmed it for me, but it did the opposite for supervisor Haight who listened in on the call: it made him believe they were telling the truth.

I had worked with these two schemers for so long I knew when they were working a con. They had been working with the government for so long they knew how stupid we were, and how easy we were with money. They had probably divided the money with Red right there at the apartment when the Rocket left. They expected to get paid on both ends. The government was to pay them as informants, and the crook paid them for setting up a sucker to buy the phony hash. It was most likely their "Red" had no idea he was dealing with a DEA special agent or he would never have been in on the con.

When I went to work next morning, after a night of pondering this, I was positive I had it right. It was the only way it made sense. And I was confident by now Braseth and Haight, trained on the streets of Chicago, would have it figured out too. But that wasn't the case. They were still reserving judgment.

Eyeball and Donnie came in to get paid. I could see Donnie was a bit nervous, but Eyeball's face radiated confidence, and his voice resonated with honest sincerity as he related the story about how he and Donnie had spent the night scouring the town for Red, trying in vain to get back the government's money. They had been unable to find Red. Eyeball calculated Red had left town knowing the wrath of the infamous Eye would be upon him after pulling off this dastardly trick. I said not a word until he had exhausted his repertoire. Then I said simply, "Game's up, Eyeball."

Eyeball looked at me with complete lack of comprehension. "What? What ya talkin' 'bout, man?"

"I said the game is up. You forgot something very important," I told him. "You forgot I've been working with you guys a long time now, and I've learned how things are on sneaky street. I know there's no way a pair of street-wise rats like you two are going to get ripped off by some phony dope dealer." I added, "Not only are you not getting paid for this deal, but you two owe the government eight-hundred dollars."

Well, you should have seen them. Both Eyeball and Donnie swore on the graves of their mothers and their grandmothers and any other mother they could summon at the moment. They'd been conned like the rest of us. I said I wasn't buying at all. They requested a conference with the boss. I said fine.

I wanted to blackball the two. "Blackball" meant that no DEA agent across the country would be able to use them as informants. To blackball an informant, one wrote a report stating this man had proven himself to be unreliable, dishonest, unprincipled, and traitorous—a description that fit Eyeball to a T.

But Eyeball was such a supreme con man he (with Battles backing him up) conned my bosses! After Braseth and Haight had their talk with the two, they were convinced the two scammers were telling the truth. I was flabbergasted! (I will change that word if I can find something stronger.) I'm not casting blame here. A good con man can fool anyone, and had I not had several months of schooling from those two, I would have been the easiest one to con.

My bosses were so convinced that they paid them for the deal. Other agents in the office were on the fence, wavering between thinking I was right and the whole thing was too clever for that pair to set up. But good old Officer Hitchins backed me to the hilt. I remember how he smiled and shook his head. "No way, no way," he said. "I wouldn't believe those two if it was their dying word. If they didn't set this up, I'm a communist." Officer Brademan agreed.

From that day on I refused to work with Eyeball, and I told him so. I would have closed the file on him, but again Eyeball was smart. He figured out a way to keep his foot in the door. In order to work his way back in, he came up with the most important information an informant could possibly surface: a hit on an agent. It was only a few days after the hash fiasco that Eyeball called. He said he knew I didn't want to talk to him but to just hear him out one more time. He told me the night before he had been at a bar in St. Paul and had heard there was a man from Chicago in town who called himself "the Gray Ghost." The Gray Ghost had put out a contract on the life of Group Supervisor Dave Haight.

Now Eyeball knew I didn't believe him. But he also knew I couldn't ignore information of this kind and I would have to pass it on whether I believed it or not. He was also pretty sure that, because of the importance of the information, he would get to talk to the boss and would be able to convince him that he was truly on the up and up, and get paid some more. Eyeball was right. I relayed the information. I relayed my skepticism. But Eyeball was called in. The bosses bought the story, and our agents began to snoop around for the Gray Ghost. The bosses paid Eyeball some money. Hitchins, Brademan, and I had a good laugh about this many a time over a beer (the Gray Ghost! Good Lord. Could Eyeball not come up with a better name?). It was all bullshit, and shortly the bosses realized it too. That was the end of Eyeball as our informant. He was blackballed, and his file was closed. Whew!

Months later, I heard that Hennepin County had a warrant out for Eyeball on a gun charge, if I remember right. They talked to me, and I gave them all the information in our files. I told them about his wife and baby, and where they had been living when I bought heroin from Holly Tyner, but they had already talked to Eyeball's wife and she had refused to give any information. I told them to look for Donnie Battles.

"You think Donnie would turn on his friend?" they asked.

I said, "Donnie will do anything for money."

For a long time after that I heard nothing about Eyeball. Then one day while we were running surveillance down on East Lake Street, one of the agents called me on the radio. "Hey, Thirty-five, come down here south on Cedar. You'll wanna see this."

When I turned the corner onto Cedar, I stopped. Half a dozen Hennepin County units with blazing lights were lined up on both sides of the avenue. Several deputies were in the middle of the street with shotguns pointed at a figure lying on the tar with his hands behind his head. It was Eyeball. I asked one of the deputies how they had found him.

"We had a snitch," he said, but he wouldn't tell me who it was. I guessed it was probably Donnie Battles. That night at the Spaghetti Emporium, some of the county deputies were celebrating. After they had oiled their jaws with a few rounds of whiskey they began to talk. One of them told me: "It was a lady that called us. I think it was his wife."

I hoped he was right. I hoped she had finally seen through Eyeball. I hoped she was no longer in love. I hoped she took her baby back home to Stearns County, never to return to the big city.

Chapter Twelve

IF YOU HAVE SUFFERED in a courtroom as a witness, as a juror, or as a defendant, you may not wish to be reminded. You might want to skip this chapter. But I must say something about the exalted federal court, because court is by far the most important part of a DEA agent's job (though it is not always recognized as such). All the undercover, the surveillance, the report writing, and evidence processing has one aim: bring the crook to court. If you are smart in all the other things, but stupid in court, you can quickly erase all the work you did on the street. If you think that when the arrest is made, the case is made and the rest is up to the attorneys and the judge, you are mistaken.

The lawyers we had for prosecutors were almost never career men. They came fresh out of law school and were prosecutors for a few years with the aim of gaining trial experience for their resumes. Then they'd move on to join a large law firm and make some real money. The result was an experienced DEA agent sometimes knew more about the drug laws and how to prosecute a drug case than did the green prosecutor. DEA Basic Agent School failed to teach this, and if they say Agent Bloch must have slept through that class, I can only say, that was their fault too. They should have put us on a witness stand and had us grilled by good defense attorneys. They should have had us act as prosecutor on a case. Instead they had DEA agents come in, tell us war stories and brag about the wonderful cases they had made in their illustrious careers. They pretty much let you think the court appearance was a cake walk.

I had to learn the hard way. I learned to testify by being humiliated on the witness stand. I learned how to prepare informants by seeing Junior screw up. I learned about conspiracy from Nicky Frol and Stephen Scholle. I learned about the entrapment defense from Al Willis.

A trial begins with impaneling a jury. The older agents in our office did not bother going to jury selection. They had seen it all before and thought the jury-selection process was BS (but they thought that about anything lawyers did). I went to jury selection to learn, and also for the entertainment. It was interesting to see which jurors were struck off the list. The first strikes were made by the judge himself. That was called striking "for cause," which meant there was a reason, like a physical sickness or a mental impairment.

The judge started by swearing the jury panel collectively. Then he asked them if anyone was not a citizen, sick, deaf. And he always asked if anyone knew the defendant or had ever associated with his family or done business with him. And so on. Obviously a person could be struck if deaf or if shown to be in poor health. Knowing the defendant caused dismissal because the juror likely had formed an opinion about him, which could prejudice the decision. Once I saw Judge Renner dismiss a juror simply because he had bought tires at the defendant's gas station, even though he said he did not know the defendant.

One day I was sitting in on jury selection in the Minneapolis District Court, Judge Miles Lord the sitting potentate, Earl Gray the defense attorney, John Lee the prosecutor. When Lord asked that standard question, "Has anyone ever done business with the defendant?" A young man stood up and timidly stuttered, "Ah, y-yes, your honor, I have."

Lord asked, "What kind of business did you do?"

The young man looked down, hesitated, cleared his throat. "I, ah, well, ah, I used to buy my marijuana from him."

Gray was out of his chair shouting objections before the man finished his statement, Lord was yelling, "Hold it, hold it!" John Lee was sitting next to me quietly chuckling, and the jurors were all in wide-eyed wonder over the fuss. Judge Lord called a sidebar. The argument was heated. Gray was turning purple. Lee was smiling. When the huddle broke, Lord dismissed the entire jury panel (who were entirely surprised), and we started over.

After "striking for cause" is done, the prosecution and the defense each gets "peremptory challenges." That means they can boot anyone off the jury for no reason at all. Any old hunch would do. In the old days the number of peremptory challenges varied, but usually each side got at least three, and they could strike for reasons not allowed today.

Defense attorneys would strike men of science, especially a chemist, because a chemist would not be confused with all those laboratory tests done on drugs by the DEA chemists from Chicago. Defense attorneys did not want a philosopher, because he might attempt to apply reason and logic to defense arguments. They didn't want men of principle, because they might stick to those in judging their client. They mostly liked unemployed and unhappy people. They never struck an artist, and for some reason they rarely struck a teacher, especially a female (that I never understood, because if I had done something bad, I would definitely not want Mrs. Finken, my grade school teacher, sitting on my jury). Gullibility is hard to measure in a juror, but defense attorneys seemed to consider that a virtue.

The prosecutor generally wanted the opposite. He usually preferred engineers, doctors, soldiers, and businessmen. He would have liked to have law enforcement officers on his jury, but those were always struck by the defense. The prosecutor did not want priests, nuns, and social workers. They had a tendency to blame society for the crimes instead of the poor defendant.

Both sides had standard beliefs about how jurors judged a defendant: Women were likely to judge a lady defendant more harshly then men would (that was especially true if the defendant was good looking). Minorities would go easy on their own kind. Young people were broader minded and less likely to convict. However, many of the strikes were purely arbitrary. Striking based on race or gender was still common back then. Now it's illegal. I once heard Agent Fekete upbraiding Prosecutor Joe Walbran about a strike he made: "Why the hell did you strike that pretty little red-head with the big tits? At least I would have had something to look at while you and the judge are boring everybody with your god-awful bullshit."

Finally the jury is seated, the trial begins. The judge gives some preliminary instructions and introduces everyone to the jury. Then the prosecutor gets up and tells the jury he's going to present such a pile of evidence any fool will conclude the louse sitting over there with defense counsel is guilty as sin. Next defense counsel gets up and says it is all a mistake. An innocent man is being hung (defense counsel knows his client is guilty, but he has to make the client believe he is getting his money's worth). He spends a few minutes edifying the jury with court clichés about the government "overstepping its bounds," getting "carried away with its own importance," and "trampling on the rights of the little man," and "needing a conviction." Then he sits down, leaving the jury in blissful ignorance as to what his defense strategy is, but leaving the client thinking he's being well-defended because he has heard his name mentioned several times in conjunction with such flattering titles as innocent, honorable citizen, church-going, and family man.

My favorite opening statement by a defense attorney came from the movie *My Cousin Vinney*. It cannot ever be matched for straight-forward compactness. When the prosecutor was done with his windy opener, the defense attorney got up, stood in front of the jury and, pointing at the prosecutor, said, "Everything that guy just said is bullshit. Thank you." He sat down.

The courtroom is a place of drama. That is why you see so many court scenes in movies. Much of the drama is because defense attorneys like to think of themselves as saviors of mankind, keeping innocent men from going to prison, while prosecutors view themselves as great crusaders in pursuit of justice for fellow citizens, and judges, having gone through years of seeing defense and prosecuting attorneys bow and scrape before him, come to consider themselves superior to the rest of mankind.

Only the witnesses have to swear to tell the truth, the whole truth, and nothing but the truth. The judge, the prosecutor, and the defense attorney don't. Lucky for them, especially for defense attorneys, because they would constantly be jeopardizing their eternal souls with hints, implications, allusions, and outright illegal testimony. The defense attorney's job is to distort, bend, and obscure the truth so that the jury doesn't find out what truly happened. Defense attorneys will deny this, but that does not stop them from doing it. They'll say it's the prosecutor who does that.

After opening statements, comes testimony. Witnesses are paraded in and out of the courtroom, exhibits are piled on the table one by one with introductions, explanations, instructions, with the usual tiresome and meaningless objections. When a witness for the prosecution takes the stand, the procedure goes like this: first the prosecutor examines him (that's called "direct"), then the defense attorney does (that's called "cross"). The prosecutor gets another chance ("re-direct"), and the defense does (re-cross). This can go on all day. They can re-direct and re-cross until the cows come home.

Unless his client has no prior record, the toughest decision the defense has to make is whether or not to put his man on that witness stand. The judge will hardly ever allow a defendant's prior record to be introduced. It might make the jury think the defendant really is a criminal, and they might vote accordingly. But if the defense puts the defendant on the stand, the prosecutor can ask about his criminal record, and if he tries to hide something, the prosecutor will pull from his briefcase a long sheet of paper and bring it up to the witness stand, dragging the end of it on the floor to show the jury how long this man's record is, and then impeach the defendant with his own crimes. The jury is suspicious of any defendant with a criminal record. However, the jury is suspicious of any defendant that doesn't get up there and say, "I did not do this."

The examining of the witnesses is the most important skill of the attorneys. Testifying on the witness stand is the most import skill of the DEA agent. The first time I took the witness stand, I was full of self-assurance. I had always been good at public speaking in high school and college, and had memorized every detail in the reports of the current case. It was Fekete's case, and I was expected only to testify about the small part I had played the night of the search warrant.

I took the stand that morning wearing my best suit and tie. I had carefully combed my hair and trimmed my beard, and was carrying my confident nose somewhat elevated. I was brilliant, I thought, on direct. The prosecutor asked exactly what I expected. I leaned forward in the witness chair and answered precisely according to the report. The jury smiled, and the prosecutor nodded as he said, "no further questions." I was thinking what a pleasant experience testifying was. One is the center of attention of all these fine people. Even the honorable judge seemed to pay close attention to what I had to say, and I imagined he smiled too.

I had noticed that, when Agent Fekete was done with his direct, defense counsel had declined to ask him anything, and the judge dismissed him, so I was surprised when defense counsel got up and said, "Just a few questions, your honor."

"Agent Bloch, you are new to this job, is that right?"

"Yes, sir."

"How long have you been out of Basic Agent School?"

"Well, ah, just a few weeks, or so, ah, a month . . ."

"And how many search warrants have you been on?" he interrupted.

"Well, at the school, ah, we did some . . ."

"Let's forget about the school. Let's stay with real life. Was this your first search warrant?"

"No, it was . . . I've been on one before, but this, ah . . ." My voice was now sounding squeaky for some reason.

"Did you identify yourself as a DEA agent when you entered?"

"Well, no, I, you see, Agent Fekete . . ."

"We have already heard Agent Fekete's testimony. The question is did *you* identify yourself as a DEA agent when you came in the door." He made it sound like I had done something wrong. This was not as comfortable as the rehearsed questioning by the prosecutor. I felt myself shrinking back into my chair. I glanced at the prosecutor. He was writing on a yellow pad.

Counsel asked again, "Did you identify yourself or not?"

"No."

"Now, Agent Bloch, oh, excuse me, it's *Special* Agent Bloch, isn't it?"

I acknowledged that, yes, I thought it was, at that. I looked at the prosecutor. He was watching the jury. I could not figure out where this was going.

"Tell us, *Special* Agent Bloch (he spit out the special), why are you called special." (I was shrinking more. For the first time I felt embarrassed to be called special).

"Well, I, well, it's just a title . . ."

"Objection you honor! (Finally the prosecutor exploded to his feet). "Counsel knows very well that the special simply means that the agent is allowed to carry a gun."

"Sustained (the judge with great pain). Counsel, if you have nothing for Agent Bloch, I will dismiss him."

"Just a few questions, your honor (bowing to the judge). Agent Bloch, are you aware you are not allowed to discuss your testimony with other witnesses at this trial?"

(Oh, Lord. He must have seen me out in the hall talking with Fekete.)

"Agent Bloch, are you aware of that rule?"

"Yes, yes, I know."

"Were you present at the pretrial conference conducted by the prosecutor yesterday morning?"

(How does he know about the pretrial meeting? I know where this is going now, and I don't have an answer.)

"Were you present at that meeting, or not?"

"Yes, yes, I was."

"And isn't it true that, at that meeting, you did discuss your testimony with the other agents and with the prosecutor?"

"Objection, you honor! Counsel knows that pretrial is excluded, and besides . . ."

"Sustained. Counsel, either move on, or come up here and explain where you're going."

"Sorry, your honor. I'll move on. Agent Bloch did you have a copy of the search warrant with you when you entered the house?"

"Agent Fekete had the search warrant."

"But did you *have* a copy of it?"

"Objection! What is the point?"

"Sustained. Counsel, I have already warned you."

"I'm sorry, your honor, I was getting to my point in a round-about way."

"Get directly to it."

"Agent Bloch, did you give the defendant time to answer the door before you broke into the house."

I began to sweat. This line of questioning could lead to real trouble. Fekete had tapped lightly and kicked in the door as he yelled "Police, open up." We were supposed to give the crook a "reasonable amount of time" to open the door. But that reasonable amount of time also gave crooks time to flush the dope down the toilet and to load their guns. We didn't even give a crook time to say, "Just a minute." It was *bam, bam!* "Police, open up." *Crash!*—down came the door. Most of our search warrants were done with the front door lying on the floor or hanging on one hinge.

I said, "I was not on the entry team. I was looking at the side of the house." That was all I could think of, but it satisfied defense counsel and I was happy when he started on another theme—happy for a moment.

"Agent Bloch it says in the report you informed my client he was under arrest. Is that correct?"

"Yes, it is."

"Did you have an arrest warrant?"

"No, I did not, I thought . . . Agent Fekete, ah, had . . ."

"Objection, your honor. We're still going nowhere."

"Sustained! That's enough now, Counsel. Can you try to ask at least one relevant question of this witness?"

"Agent Bloch Did you inform my client of his Miranda rights?"

"Yes I did." (I had him there.)

"Would you please tell the jury now, what those rights are?"

"I, yes, well, it's, you have the right to remain silent, and, ah, if you say anything (why was it so hot in this courtroom?), and, ah, if you say anything, then that might later be held in court against . . ."

"Objection you honor! Counsel knows agents are not required to memorize those rights. They read them off a card agents carry with them."

"Sustained."

"Agent Bloch, do you have your Miranda-Rights card with you?"

I began to pat my pockets. "I don't think . . . I forgot to bring . . ."

Defense counsel interrupted me with stabbing contempt: "I have no further questions of this witness" (he said witness as if he meant moron).

I had entered that courtroom carrying my nose high like a conceited giraffe. I left with my nose low like a depressed warthog. When I said to

Fekete, "That attorney made a fool out of me." He said, "You'll learn. Just remember when you're up there, all defense attorneys are stupid, and they're all crooks. That's why we call them criminal lawyers."

Well, it didn't make me feel any better to think I was made the fool by a stupid lawyer. When I apologized to the prosecutor for stuttering around, he said, "You did just fine. The defense attorney was being an asshole."

But I knew I didn't do just fine. I should have been able to answer those questions without help and without a stutter. I had prepared for direct examination, but had not prepared for cross. In the following weeks I sat in the back of the courtroom every chance I got to watch the testimony and to give myself the lessons absent at Basic Agent School.

Later, when I knew how, testifying became fun. I soon had ready answers for all the standard questions the defense attorney threw out like a net to see what he can catch. I found that, if I stumbled and stuttered, he smelled blood in the water, and, like a shark, he'd circle and come back for another bite at the wound. But if my answers were quick and confident, he'd turn away like a one that senses a hook in the bait. I learned to anticipate the questions of the defense attorney. I'd watch him during direct examination, and when I saw him scribbling on his pad, I knew on cross I could expect a question regarding whatever I had just said on direct. On cross I'd try to block the way or lead him into a trap where he'd ask a question that gave me a chance to unload an answer I could not give on direct because of restrictions imposed by the law or by the judge.

It took me a while to trust the prosecutor to clear up any confusion that arose during cross. When I got a question that needed clarification beyond yes or no, I'd glance at the prosecutor. If he was paying attention, I gave a short answer. If he was napping, I'd give a long answer and sometimes purposely throw in something that would wake him up. After a while I realized how foolish I'd been to be afraid of defense attorneys. Most didn't prepare for court. They didn't study our reports. They skimmed over some of the summaries so they had a vague idea what the case was about, and then came to the courtroom to wing it.

One thing many police officers did in court—something that didn't help them communicate with a jury: they used cop-talk, a form of often clumsy and unattractive English. Cop-talk started long ago in an effort to be precise and clear, but it had grown all out of proportion so by now it was so loaded with esoteric vocabulary and uncommon expressions it did just the opposite.

It was routinely used by police officers on the witness stand or when they talked to news reporters. It was sad to see a man, who could sit on a barstool and speak eloquently (even after several drinks) using short words and wonderfully clear sentences, mount the witness chair and shift to this muddy talk.

On the barstool he would say: I saw he had a gun.

On the witness chair: From my vantage point I was able to ascertain that the subject had in his possession a pistol of unknown caliber.

On the barstool: I couldn't tell what happened.

On the witness chair: I was unable to determine what had transpired.

On the barstool: Then I got out of my car and went into the house.

On the witness chair: At this point in time I exited my official government vehicle, proceeded to the residence, and entered there via the front door.

On the barstool: I saw the same man go in the store and talk to a woman.

On the witness chair: I was able to observe the aforementioned perpetrator enter the establishment where he was seen to engage a female subject in conversation.

The trial is a sparring match between two attorneys with the judge sitting as referee. Either contestant can stop the proceeding with an objection, which the judge overrules or sustains according to what he had for breakfast. Judge Larson was much more ready to overrule the defense, Judge Lord to overrule the prosecutor. The judge is supposed to make sure the rules of law are followed but usually allows wide latitude if the opposing attorney doesn't object. Leading questions and those without foundation are routinely allowed. But if the two lawyers hate each other's guts, or are in a bad mood, those questions will raise objections, which can make the trial a real trial (tedious and long).

"Agent Bloch, did you see a red 1970 Ford in the alley that night?"

"Yes, I did."

That short exchange is perfectly fine on some days. But suppose the defense attorney is crabby that morning because they ran out of cocaine at the party last night, and suppose the judge is insecure because he just got reversed again by the Eighth Circuit Court. Now the short exchange goes like this:

"Agent Bloch, did you see a red 1970 Ford in the alley that night?"

"Objection, without foundation."

"Sustained."

"Agent Bloch, what were you doing on the night in question?"

"I was on surveillance at the defendant's house."

"Did you see a red 1970 Ford in the alley?"

"Objection, without foundation."

"Sustained."

"Agent Bloch, what part of the defendant's property were you watching."

"I had an eye on the alley."

"And did you see a red 1970 Ford in the alley?"

"Objection, leading the witness."

"Sustained."

"Agent Bloch, what did you see in that alley?"

"Objection, leading."

"Sustained."

"Agent Bloch, did you see anything in the alley?"

"Yes."

"What did you see?"

"A red 1970 Ford."

That last objection could have been avoided if the prosecutor had simply asked the question this way, "What, if anything, did you see in that alley." All this may seem quite laughable, but those exchanges are conducted daily in courtrooms across this country with all the pomp and solemnity of a bishop and two celebrants at a cathedral High Mass.

When the testimony is over, they have closing arguments. The prosecutor will usually throw in the old saw that "all it takes for evil to thrive (he means the defendant) is for good men and women (the jury) to do nothing." Then he will add with an index finger in the air, "Do something today! Do your duty!" And now, pointing that finger dramatically at the defendant, "Find that man guilty as charged."

Then defense counsel will get up and say the prosecutor during this whole trial was trying to hide something and did not respect the jury enough to present them with a complete picture of what actually happened. The implication is, if the jury knew the whole picture they'd find his client innocent (but he refrains from coming up with that whole picture). It is standard for the defense to try to make the jury believe it's their duty to acquit if they have any doubt about the defendant's guilt. That's a lie—one told over and over in courts across the United States of America. The defense knows that the measure is not *any* doubt, but *reasonable* doubt.

In his final instructions, the judge tries to explain reasonable doubt so the jury can understand it, but he rarely achieves that goal. The judge always cautions the jurors not to allow their personal attitudes to influence the verdict. He says they must only consider evidence heard in court. He tells them they must not be influenced by sympathy, prejudice, or passion toward any party, witness, or lawyer in the case (which is like telling them they must suspend membership in the human race). Also, the instructions are so long and boring most jurors have entered a coma by the time the judge gets through the first half. It's not an easy task for a judge to read instructions and make them sound interesting to a jury when he has read those instructions a thousand times before. I don't know why lawyers want to become judges. It's a boring job. You sit on your butt all day. True, there is a great variety in the different hearings: initial appearances, preliminaries, arraignments, discoveries, and trials, but they all become routine after a while. I have seen judges napping in the courtroom. Many read the morning paper while attorneys spar. When you think the judge is up there making careful notes, he's likely working on the day's cross-word puzzle.

This is not to say the job is always easy, routine, and without variety. I once witnessed an exchange in a courtroom that illustrates this. It happened in Houston in the United States District Court for the Southern District. A lady judge was sitting, and I could tell as soon as I walked in that she was greatly exasperated.

She sighed deeply and said, "For the tenth time, Mr. Mitchell, do you have a job, do you have an income, do you have any means of support?"

The defendant was a tall, skinny man with a rough face and beard. He looked like Abraham Lincoln.

"No, I don't have a job. They won't give me one. I asked the man who runs the church, and he said to go away. You can ask me anything and I'll tell the truth."

"Very well. The court has determined you are financially unable to retain counsel. The court will appoint a public defender to represent you. You have the right to remain silent about your case."

"All that happened was, I was going to get just one joint from—"

"Hold on, Mr. Mitchell. Save that for your lawyer."

"Save what? I can't pay the lawyer. I got no savings."

"He will represent you for free."

"Well the doctor said I was sick. But he refused to drop the charges."

"Mr. Mitchell, your doctor has nothing to do with this court."

"They gave me shock treatment, didn't they? What was that for?"

"Mr. Mitchell, where are you currently living?"

"I told you, on the street. The last time I had a place was in, in . . . I think it was Waco. Is Waco the place they take stupid people?"

(At this point a man in suit and tie comes in, greets the judge, and walks to the defense table.)

The judge says, "Mr. Mitchell this will be your lawyer."

"This one? (He pulls back and frowns at his lawyer.) What's your name? Is it Tom, again? Okay, I can't remember names. Ever since the doctor gave me those shock treatments, I can't remember a thing."

"Mr. Mitchell can you promise to be here tomorrow morning at ten?"

"Promise! Promise? I'm on the street. I'll get lost. I don't have a watch." He turns to his lawyer. "Say, can you lend me a dollar so I can go to the Star Hope Mission for supper. How do I get there from here? Oh, I'll go downtown."

"Mr. Mitchell, we are downtown."

"I got three wives, and I don't know where any of them are at. They got money. I'm not lying, judge. They could pay you. I wish I knew."

"Mr. Mitchell you're charged with kidnapping. Talk about that with your lawyer."

"I know, I know. I remember the charge."

"Will you be here in the morning?"

"I promise. I'll be back." He snaps to attention and salutes the judge. She hangs her head in despair. "Just so they don't send me to that wacko-Waco town."

"Mr. Mitchell, forget about Waco. Talk to your lawyer about your case, and be here tomorrow."

"I'm sorry, I'm sorry. I promise I'll make it. I didn't mean to do anything bad." Raises his right hand. "I promise to tell the whole truth and nothing but the truth."

The judge called the next case on the calendar.

Chapter Thirteen

Often an order came from Regional Headquarters in Kansas City for Braseth to assign a Minneapolis agent to go somewhere. If no one wanted the assignment, it rolled downhill to me. That's how I got to go on a wiretap to Indianapolis, to Spanish school at the State Department in Washington, D.C., to Operation Funnel in Colombia, and to tech school in Washington, D.C. It was funny. Braseth would apologize for sending me, not realizing I was always looking for adventure and was eager to go. And he'd come up with brilliant reasons why I was chosen, though we both knew it was because no one else wanted the job.

What a wonderful assignment that Spanish school was, though. It was the summer of 1976, the nation's 200th anniversary, when tourists from all over the country were traveling to D.C. for the privilege of seeing parades and fireworks and ceremonies and to view the splendor of their nation's capitol. I was there all summer. Bea came to join me part of that time, and we had a great vacation. Gerald Ford was president, and I was a good friend of his scheduling secretary. The secretary had been a student of mine when I was instructing at Laredo Air Force Base. I got a personal tour of the White House and got to meet the president.

While Bea was there, we went to the John F. Kennedy Center for the Performing Arts to watch plays, operas, and ballets. I could get tickets from the secretary almost any time. We had the best seats in the house, always in the president's box. We chatted with senators and congressmen during intermissions. We sat through performances by some of the best artists in the world. I learned one important lesson: that artsy stuff isn't for me. Since that summer I've never gone to another ballet or opera or stage show. I'd much rather sit on the back porch of some old farm house and watch cows graze in the pasture or listen to hogs squeal as they fight over acorns. I wouldn't go to an opera even if I could avoid all the hassle of finding a parking spot, standing in line for a ticket, elbowing through crowds, and finding a way out of a teeming parking lot afterwards. I'd rather take a walk in the woods any day. And anytime some snobby lady tells me the reason I don't like the opera is because I've never seen one performed by really good singers in a really good setting, I tell her about the summer of 1976. The lesson I learned in Washington has saved me time, money, and frustration.

I did actually learn a little Spanish at that school, and, because of that, I got sent on "Operation Funnel" to Colombia, South America, the fall of that same year. Jim Braseth called me in and told me they had "a big operation" going down in Colombia and needed help. Region had picked me, he said.

I said, "Why are they sending me?"

Braseth gave me a sardonic grin, "I guess because of your superior record working in Colombia." (A rather snide reference to the Cleveland case—and totally uncalled for.) He handed me a teletype of my orders and said, "Report to the DEA office in Bogotá, and they'll tell you where to go."

They did tell me where to go. Don't ask me what Operation Funnel was all about. I still don't know. My best guess is it was an operation to "funnel" taxpayer money into bureaucrats' pet projects, many of which had little to do with stopping the flow of cocaine or marijuana (that was always the professed aim of these foreign operations, you know). All DEA's operations in South America were supposed to "interdict" the flow of drugs. "Interdict" and "interdiction" were favorite words at DEA headquarters. If you don't know what they mean, don't bother looking them up. You already know as much about interdiction as they did. I can tell you this: during the time I was in Colombia on Operation Funnel, I did absolutely nothing to impede, stop, or slow-down the transportation of as much as one ounce of marijuana or one gram of cocaine. However, I had some interesting times spending taxpayer money. During the time I was there, they were constantly changing my assignment.

I flew into Bogotá and went to the embassy to meet Agent Octavio Gonzales the country attaché (the boss of DEA operations in Colombia). He seemed completely taken by surprise. I showed him my orders, but that didn't clear the air for him. He kept shuffling papers on his desk, looking uncomfortable. I had the feeling he viewed me as a hindrance rather than a help. He buzzed his secretary. She came in with a teletype. After reading that, he nodded several times but still looked undecided. I had the feeling he wished I'd just go away. And a minute later that's what he told me to do. He told me to get a room at the Tequendama Hotel and keep in touch with the secretary. She'd have instructions for me shortly. I checked in at the Tequendama, and for two days I performed the vital function of viewing the sights of the city.

Bogotá, planted up on a high plateau on the side of the Andes Mountains, is close to nine thousand feet above sea level, and there must have been over three million people in the city back then. In the daytime it was beautifully clear all around with bright sunshine showing off the snowy peaks of the mountains, but by night it was miserable, damp and cold with a thick fog so I could barely make out the lights across the street. I thought I must be in London groping like Ebenezer Scrooge on the way home from his counting house. I spent peaceful mornings at the Tequendama reading the *Miami Herald* between naps. Afternoons I went to the museum at the university, and at night I visited the clubs and bars.

The best thing I saw in Bogotá happened at Sunday morning Mass. I can't remember ever having a better time in church. I found a little chapel near the hotel where I sat in the back pew. Mass began routinely. All was quiet except for the soft droning of the priest and an occasional mumbled answer from the sleepy (and very sparse) congregation. Sometimes a lady frowned at her fidgeting urchin. Sometimes I heard a little snore from one of the few men in attendance. It was still cool in the stone church, but warm sun was pouring in through the large open doors in the back. At the beginning of the offertory, a yellow dog came padding in through those doors. The sunshine on the tiled floor made it feel warm under his paws, and he decided this would be a fine place for a nap. He curled up and closed his eyes. Just before the consecration a black dog came in too. The yellow dog must have taken his favorite spot, for he gave the sleeping dog an offended look and a low growl. The yellow dog raised his head and returned the greeting. The black dog didn't take kindly to the yellow dog's remark and registered his disapproval by setting his hair up on the back of his neck, showing some fang, and rumbling deep in his throat.

The priest raised the host. Ding went the bell. The yellow dog was on his feet now, neck-hair up too, soft rumble too. Few of the congregation took note. They must have heard it before. The priest mumbled over the chalice. The priest raised the chalice. Ding went the bell. But that ding was covered. With a powerful snarl the yellow dog leaped, and the fight was on—a rocking, rollicking brawl with snarling, growling, yelping—with flying fur and slashing fang, the echoes in the church magnifying every sound. For a few seconds the priest, the altar boy, the congregation, and all the angels and saints in heaven watched the dog-ruckus. It was suddenly over when the yellow dog decided he had enough of this type of entertainment. He tried for a quick exit, but could get no traction at first on the smooth tiles. There was a desperate scraping of claw on stone, and then out he went like a rocket with the black dog on his tail.

I could tell this had happened before because the congregation quietly turned back to the altar with an air of business-as-usual, the apathetic drone of the priest continued, and sleepy Sunday Mass dozed on.

Octavio's secretary finally called me. Octavio was sending me to Florencia, the capital of the territory of Caquetá, which lay in the southern part of Colombia on the Orteguaza River. I'd be working with Agent Fred Duncan and Colombian DAS Group Number Five to find and destroy cocaine laboratories. The secretary said, "You won't have any trouble finding Fred. He'll be staying at the best hotel in town."

That turned out to be true. Fred and I stayed at the best hotel in the capital of the state of Caquetá, which was the largest and most important city in the southern part of Colombia. We were living in total luxury—by local standards, that is (not by standards of the States). The bathrooms at the hotel were little concrete cubicles with a pipe sticking out of one wall and a six-inch hole in the floor. There was no hot water. They didn't even pretend there was hot water. They had just one faucet to that pipe—cold. At least they were honest about it. Many Colombian hotels had two faucets, but you could run the water all day from either faucet and get only cold water. If a hotel did have warm water, it would take me an hour to figure it out because I'd assume the faucet labeled "C" was the cold, but, no, that was the hot (C for *caliente*).

At our hotel in Florencia the cold water that dribbled from the pipe was for our sink, shower, and toilet. We went in that cubicle naked, and shaved with cold water. The six-inch hole in the floor was the drain for our shower. It was also our toilet. We squatted over the hole to do our business, and then took a shower to clean up. The hotel had no phones. If we wanted to make a call, we had to go to the Telcom Office, run by the government. There we stood in line. When our turn came, we made our call at a little desk where the people behind us could listen to us yelling into the phone (necessary because of the poor connections).

If someone from the States wanted to get in touch with us, they had to call the Telcom Office. An office worker there took a message and delivered it to our hotel, if she had the time (and the inclination).

The good news was this hotel had electric lights. The bad news was our part of town got electricity only every second night. The other half of Florencia had electricity on the other nights. When we didn't have electricity, we read by candlelight or walked to where the DAS agents were staying. They were in the part of the town that had electricity on the nights when we didn't. They were even worse off. They slept in hammocks or on beds made of ropes. They had no shower and no toilet except an outside latrine (a trench among the trees). They had only two dim bulbs to light up their old wooden army barracks, which was on the verge of collapse. They viewed our hotel as incomparable luxury, and if Fred had been smart he would have been staying with the DAS agents at their barracks. It would not have been that much worse than our hotel, and it would have made for a much better relation between DAS and DEA. I didn't suggest this, however. I had my fill of trying to sleep in rooms vibrating with the snores of human males.

It was unusual for anyone in that town or the surrounding countryside to own an automobile. Mostly people traveled with horses, mules, donkeys, or ox-drawn carts. The roads were so bad only a very rich man would waste money on such a luxury as a car. One day the girl at the front desk told me there would be a parade that afternoon. She said, "I'll call you when it begins and we can watch it from the balcony." She seemed to think it was well worth my time. We stood together on the little second-floor balcony and watched three old pickup trucks and two cars circle the plaza below with drivers tooting their horns and passengers hanging out the windows, waving and shouting to the people gathered to watch this wonderful sight. That was their parade.

For a few days we hung around that quaint little town doing nothing. Augosto Suarez was the DAS chief. He and Fred met every day to consult about our next move in the great war on cocaine traffickers. Fred was fluent in Spanish, but he spoke Tex-Mex, southern border Spanish (I think he said he was from Laredo), and that hurt the ears of the Colombians, who prided themselves on speaking the purest Spanish outside of Spain. My understanding of Spanish was horrible, but when I talked, I spoke more like they did, (without the cursing and the slang). And I always used the polite form, because that's all I knew.

The DAS agents had a high-frequency radio they cranked up every morning to communicate—to attempt to communicate—with other DAS groups. Jaime Vega was their radio man. That position gave him tremendous status. Jaime would set up his equipment with great fanfare and spend at least an hour shouting through his flopping mustache into the microphone to make contact. Jaime's call sign was Piraña (piranha—the fish). I still remember some of the other call signs because I heard them hundreds of times every morning. He would call for "Temblon," or "Picuda," or "Ballena," and get no answer except some crackling static. The one he called the most was "Iscale," and from that Iscale Group, he would occasionally get a word or two between the static—nothing intelligible. But he would keep at it: "Iscale, Iscale! Piraña, *cambio*" (*cambio* means "over"). After an hour of that, he'd declare the signal was bad that day and would retire from the scene.

I liked Jaime and went there every morning to listen. I admired his perseverance and curiosity. Between calls he'd ask me questions about the United States, and I'd ask questions about Colombia. I could read and write Spanish very well, but could not understand spoken Spanish, unless it was spoken slowly and distinctly with no contractions or accent or slang—that didn't happen in real life. My understanding of their spoken language was so poor Jaime often had to write down what he wanted to communicate. Jaime called the United States "Gringolandia" and was convinced we were all rich and worked only for our entertainment. Fred did little to subtract from that conviction. He wore jewelry and name-brand clothes and seemed on permanent vacation.

Almost every day some of the DAS agents went down to the Orteguaza River to take a bath. I went with them in their roofless, fenderless jeep, which had every suspension spring broken and every shock busted so we felt every rock on the road like the kick of a mule. To enhance this charming ride, they carried a bag of rotted meat for catfish bait, which was so foul and evil-smelling it made my eyes water when the wind blew the fragrance my way. A nice little public landing by the river surrounded by orange and lemon trees hummed all day with the sound of insects and birds and rang with the laughter of women who came down to do the family laundry. The women sat in wooden canoes tied along the shore, and used the sides of the canoes as scrub boards.

Shortly after I arrived in Florencia, Augosto and Fred decided we should make an excursion to Puerto Rico, a small village northeast of Florencia, to see if anyone up there was in the business of making cocaine. We crowded eight of us into that little jeep with the broken springs and jounced along poking each other in the ribs with elbows and gun barrels, for we were bristling with weapons. They said only a few months before a bunch of guerillas had taken over the little town and were still hiding in the surrounding hills. The driver and front passenger sat on seats that had once been padded. The rest of us sat on hard board benches in the back—no, we sat on our hands—we had to, in order to reduce the spine-snapping jars as we bounded over rocks and potholes and washout canyons.

The road was no wider than a cow path and the rocks we climbed over were bigger than watermelons (on second thought, I'll reduce the rocks to coconuts, and widen the trail to a wagon trail). It was too narrow a trail for cars to pass each other, but that was no problem since we were the only car on the road. We didn't meet anyone the whole way, except an occasional burro. Our driver believed the faster he drove, the fewer bumps he'd hit, which was probably true, since the jeep was airborne half the time, but at that speed, the ones we did hit were like blasts of dynamite. The whole ride was a blur. My eyeballs jiggled in their sockets, and my teeth chattered as if I were naked at the North Pole. And to add to our enjoyment, one of the DAS agents got sick and kept puking out of the back of the jeep like he was marking the trail.

This road had no bridges, nor ditches, shoulders, or pavement—why, they didn't even have a traffic light! The little jeep plowed its way through several little rivers and kept refreshing us with little showers that helped cake us with road dust so we looked like old-time grain millers. Whenever we stopped to take a leak or fill our canteens, we looked at each other and laughed. We looked like old men with the ashen road-dust in our hair, eyebrows, and mustaches. Fred said very little. I suspect he was cursing himself for approving this operation, or at least for going along.

We got to Puerto Rico at dusk. Fred and Augosto met with a half dozen dignitaries of the town (half the population), and the rest of us went to the river to clean up. They called the river the Caguán. We bathed in the moonlight. The sky was completely clear, only a slight mist along the shore, the moon almost full, and strange equatorial stars winking above. We washed our clothes and hung them on branches by the water. We had our guns on a wide, flat rock used by the townspeople as a diving board. The DAS agents stayed near the rock and wouldn't swim far from their machine pistols. Only then did I realized how serious they were about possible guerilla attacks. I swam downriver a ways, and they immediately called me back. I wasn't showing off. I was trying to retrieve my bar of Ivory Soap, which went floating away, never to be seen again. I had brought that bar with me from the States exactly because it did float and was handy when bathing in a lake.

Fred and Augosto joined us at the river, but Fred wouldn't dive in. He washed himself on shore with a washcloth and later told me I was foolish to swim in that water. He said I was a sitting duck for guerillas. Besides snakes and piranhas lived in the river. I figured, if the DAS guys weren't worried about piranhas, why should I? We stayed the night in an abandoned shack. Augusto and Fred each had a rope bed. The rest of us slept on the floor. On the way back to Florencia the next day, we had another man on board (an informant, they said), so now we were nine, hanging over the sides of the jeep riding on one buttock. It made the ride even more fun.

A few days later I had a real problem. It was the last day of October, and the DAS agents were having a celebration—not for Halloween. They didn't know what that was. They were celebrating the birthday of the DAS organization. Augosto told me they were having a cookout feast down by the river. I was invited. The problem was he told me flatly Fred was not invited, and I shouldn't tell Fred about it. He said I should tell Fred I was going fishing for catfish with some of the DAS agents. Fred didn't like fishing. I had a choice of either insulting the DAS agents by turning down their invitation, or insulting Fred, for he was likely to find out. I went with the DAS celebration (how could I turn that down) and hoped Fred wouldn't find out or would not care.

We didn't go down to the Orteguaza as I expected, but to a little *quebrada* (stream) west of Florencia they called the "Charco Azul." The water there came from a nearby spring. It was cold and clear and very drinkable, not like the brown water of the Orteguaza. All the Group Five DAS agents were there by the river except Julio Lizarroso, the second in command under Augosto, and Juan Villamizar. Julio came along later with a mule team and cartload of ladies from town, including several very pretty señoritas and several old señoras, who, although not so pretty, became more and more attractive as they unloaded boxes of food and beer and began setting up for cooking the meal.

The men gathered wood and built two fires on the bank of the Charco Azul. They laid bottles of beer in the cold water between the rocks along the shore. I kept looking around for Juan Villamizar. He was my favorite DAS agent. He always took great care to explain to me what was happening. He spoke a little English, I spoke a little Spanish, and we both knew how to communicate by drawing pictures in the sand or using hand signals. He was a master communicator in any language. I believe he could have run for office in China, Greece, or ancient India.

Juan carried a long knife and was skillfull at carving with it. He could throw the thing with remarkable accuracy. He loved nothing so much as games with knives. I had given up on Juan, when here he came riding through the bushes on a floppy-eared mule, carrying on the saddle two racks of freshly butchered pork ribs, the blood still dripping from the meat.

The ladies had brought along three big, beautiful roosters, as brilliant in color as any pheasant or wood duck. It seemed a shame to kill them, but Juan and Julio and I took them downstream a little way. Juan cut off their heads, and we bled them into the water. We brought them back and gave them to the chattering women, who plucked them, sliced them open, and spread the carcasses wide with sticks. Juan whittled poles of green wood and skewered each carcass on a pole. They pounded one end into the ground next to the fire so that we could rotate the chickens as they roasted. The ladies washed out the gullets and crops, and stuffed them with rooster combs and waddles, with giblets, and with parts of the guts (I recognized chopped-up trachea for sure). They tied the ends, and the men skewered these bags of delicacies the same way by the fire. They cut the pork ribs into pairs and skewered them with onions like shish kabob and stood them next to the second fire. In that fire the ladies placed three large stones, and they set a pot of water to boiling on the stones. During the morning they leisurely trimmed off parts of chicken and pork and dropped them into the pot. They threw in large chunks of onions and some strange vegetables like platano, yucca, and arracacha. The arracacha was some kind of root, yellow when the ladies dropped it into the pot, but it turned orange as it cooked. Throughout the morning, whenever someone added wood to a fire, or even walked by, he would turn the skewers, and stir the soup with a stick.

This method of cooking was slow, but that was part of the celebration. The aromas of forest and of food had to be enjoyed along with the drink. We drank Costeña Beer and water right from the stream (it was better than the beer). Every few minutes they passed around a bottle of Aguardiente, a rather sweet liquor fermented from the juice of sugar cane (*guarapo,* they call the juice), and they flavored it with something that made it taste like liquorice. It was a powerful drink. It made my stomach feel good, but not my head. The ladies did not drink the beer, but when the Aquardiente bottle came around, they applied themselves with professional skill—some immoderately. This already cheerful group became even more cheerful throughout the morning.

The sun climbed hot in the sky, but we felt none of it. We were in full shade and cooled by the flowing cold water. Juan carved little pointed sticks we used as forks to harpoon things from the soup pot. As the outside of the meat became done, we carved off pieces and ate. After a while, someone broke into song. From then on, one group or another was always singing, always in Spanish, always unintelligible to me. The ladies sang one song while smiling and looking askance at me, and it set all the men to laughing. Julio told me it was a song that said the men of Caquetá were fine lovers, but the ladies preferred *gringos,* because they were not as lazy.

It was well after the noon hour when they took the meat from the fire and cut it up on banana leaves. We used leaves for plates and the sticks for forks. They had a few cups for the soup, which they passed around. The ladies had also made a dish that was very much like Mexican guacamole, except that it was chunkier and had diced, hard-boiled eggs in it. Some garnished their meat with it, some put it in their soup, and some ate it for desert. They also had a basket of "*roscones*" like a cross between a bagel and a donut with frosting on top.

That night I gave Augosto some money to help pay for the party, but I could have given him a year's salary and not made him a fair trade for the pleasure of that afternoon. In spite of the strange people, strange food, and strange customs, I felt as comfortable as I would have among the farmers back home in Stearns County, Minnesota.

Chapter Fourteen

IN A SHORT TIME we went on another expedition. This one made the wild goose chase to Puerto Rico look like a grade-school picnic. We took a trip into the heart of the jungle at the direction of Octavio Gonzales and the chief of the DAS in Bogotá. They had information a cocaine laboratory had popped up in the jungle along the Caquetá River. Several times the DAS agents had gone to snoop around Puerto Leguízamo (southeast of Florencia on the Putumayo River). They heard rumors cocaine was moving through that town. A navy lieutenant at Leguízamo had a lot of clout with the brass in Bogotá. He had the reputation for "getting things done." This lieutenant talked about the cocaine lab in the jungle and said he had a guide that could take us there. He said we had to move fast because his guide would soon be going back to Brazil. Octavio wanted Fred and me to go with the DAS agents on this trip so that DEA could claim credit when the cocaine lab got busted.

We set about packing. Augosto was called back to Bogotá, and Julio had to stay in Florencia. They put a reluctant Juan Villamizar in charge of this adventure. Good. That was my buddy, the communicator. Juan didn't trust the lieutenant at Leguízamo, but he had his orders. He and Fred flew to Leguízamo to talk to the guide and make arrangements for a boat. The rest of us finished packing. The DAS agents had a big tarp we cut into five-by-seven-foot pieces. Each man had a tarp and a blanket in which to roll his personal belongings. The tarps were raincoat and bedding.

The trip would take us about a week. There'd be a half dozen agents and the guide. But I was amazed at the meager supplies they were taking along—a little bag of salt and some cinnamon, a bag of onions, a jug of cooking oil, corn meal, a handful of garlic cloves, and the rest was nothing but coffee and sugar. A Colombian can live for months on coffee and sugar—lots of sugar. A Colombian cup of coffee (they called it a "*tinto*") was black as tar from the coffee, and thick as syrup from the sugar. A *tinto* could make your hair stand up, and it was funny to see macho DAS agents sipping this transmission oil from tiny, delicate cups like rich ladies at a tea party. They took along enough coffee and sugar to satisfy a marine regiment for a month. The amount of corn meal they took I alone could have consumed in two days. When I asked about the abundance of sugar and coffee, they smiled and nodded proudly. They said we would catch fish and shoot our meat on the way.

We were all armed with pistols and knives. Manolo was the only one who took a machine pistol. The others didn't want to drag a heavy gun and all that ammunition into the jungle so they had only revolvers. Manolo carried an Israeli Uzi with a metal folding stock. Manolo had been a boxer. He had the build of a fire hydrant and was tough as a tractor tire. We all wore boots; Manolo wore sandals. No ordinary human could travel in that area without mosquito repellant. Even our Indian guide used it. Manolo refused with the delicate excuse that repellant made his skin look bad. I would gladly have refused it too, if I had brought some along from home. The Colombian repellant ate holes in the cover of my notebook.

The other agents took our packs to Leguízamo, Jaime and I followed the next day with the radio equipment. No commercial airliners flew into that part of the world, but the Colombian military operated a couple of old DC-3s on an irregular basis. If you wanted to catch a plane, you did not check a schedule. You went out to the airstrip (if you could find it), and camped by the runway hoping it would show up, and then hoping it would have room. There were no tickets. If the plane was empty, a person could fly for almost nothing and bring along a dog, a chicken, and a cow (a small one, I think). If it was crowded, still no ticket, but bribe money was needed. The pilot or co-pilot would stand in the doorway of the DC-3 and look over the crowd. The people yelled and waved handfuls of paper money. The pilot would point his finger and wave on board the man that looked the most promising. When the plane was filled to capacity (enough room for the pilot to elbow his way to the cockpit), they closed the door. The remaining crowd walked sadly home and waited for another day.

When Jaime and I wanted a ride to Leguízamo, there was no room. No! Absolutely none. Then Jaime showed his badge. Suddenly there was room for both of us and our equipment, and our friends if we had any. We took off out of Florencia and headed southeast over thick jungle. The plane was loaded with people, some silent and aloof, some ragged, unshaven, and chattering like magpies. Several had dogs with them. The seats were long wooden benches bolted to the walls. I gave my seat to an old man (at least he looked old), who had a gorgeous, iridescent jungle fowl rooster with him, which he controlled with a dirty piece of twine tied to the rooster's leg. I clung to a strap on the wall, holding on like grim death in the turbulent air. The pilot's flying techniques were anything but smooth. Captain Tiggeman would have flunked him on take off.

We flew to a "town" called "Tres Esquinas," which was nothing more than a dirt strip alongside a few huts in a clearing by the river. I thought the pilot must be insane. As we approached Tres Esquinas, he executed the longest dragged-in approach I'd ever witnessed. For the last three miles we skimmed the very tops of the trees, with the gear nearly touching the upper branches. We flew over some thatched-roof huts in a little clearing. Jaime said that was a guerilla camp. The plane bounced and swayed in the updrafts. Patches of morning mist flickered by the windows. Several times the pilot made sudden turns one way, then the other. I could hear from the sounds of the motors he was making drastic power changes. As we dragged in low over a dirt road, I could see people running out to meet the plane. Two horse-drawn buggies galloped down that road like they were racing. The pilot finally set his machine down with an enormous, aircraft-carrier thud, and we went rattling down the bumpy runway that looked too narrow for the wing-reach of a DC-3. Tall palm trees just barely cleared the wingtips on either side. The pilot came back to open the door, and I frowned at him to let him know I didn't approve of his landing techniques, but he was busy shouting in Spanish at the passengers. I don't think he would have cared about my opinion if he'd noticed.

Jaime explained they recently had taken ground fire from the jungle in that area and now flew that dragged-in approach to make it difficult for the guerillas to draw a bead on the airplane between the treetops as it zipped by. We got to stretch our legs there for a minute at Tres Esquinas. The "terminal" was a thatched roof on poles with a dirt floor. A trio of pigs wandered among the passengers. Next to the terminal some women had a fire going. They were grilling food. I bought a smoky brown *arepa* corn cake and leaned against a tree by Jaime to eat. The place was filled with the fragrance of the cooking, of tropical plants and wood smoke, all mixed in with the perfume of pig manure and piles of rotting vegetation.

In a short time we took off again, crossed the Caquetá, and continued over heavy jungle to Puerto Leguízamo on the Putumayo. We slept that night in barracks provided by the kindly navy lieutenant. That lieutenant was a shifty-eyed, clean-cut, well-pressed soldier. He gave us a vigorous handshake, but was cold. He gave us a toothy smile, but it faded the second we looked away. He seemed to me sneaky like a fox, slippery as an eel, with the unblinking eyes of a snake. Jaime shared that opinion. He told me so next day as we walked to La Tagua, where the others were camped on the bank of the Caquetá. All was ready to shove off the next morning. They had rented a canoe—a huge thing made out of the hollowed-out trunk of a gigantic tree. They had also rented a motor and a man to operate it.

La Tagua was just a little village, no more than two dozen houses, but some of those actually had red tile roofs instead of the usual thatch. We slept the night in hammocks strung between the support posts of a large roof made of palm leaves. That was La Tagua's town hall, where they had their public meetings. Next morning, bright and early, with the sun still below the horizon and fog still on the water, we set off downriver for a week of fun.

I have to limit the story here or I'll never finish. Everything was so new to me that in a few days I had already filled my little green government memoranda book with wonders. We spent several days going downriver, two days trekking in the jungle, and several more days coming back upriver to La Tagua. The vegetation along the shore was so thick in most places it was hard to believe man had ever set foot there. The motor chugged along covering the sounds of the jungle. We flushed toucans and macaws along the banks. Sometimes a buzzard circled over us. Mile after mile we went, with no sign of human life. The air was heavy with humidity and oppressive with heat. Ahead of the canoe the water swirled as large fish got out of the way.

We filled our canteens from the spring-fed creeks that trickled out of the jungle along the banks. Sometimes the water tasted like moss, but it was cool and clearer than city water in the States and safer than hotel water in Mexico. Manolo did not carry a canteen but flopped down and drank like a calf from any stream and sometimes out of the muddy Caquetá. He said the brown water was more *saboroso* (flavorful).

When we stopped anywhere, as soon as the echoes of the motor died away into the forest, the sounds of birds and insects began to swell into a loud symphony. There were always strange animal tracks along the shore. Most any time we stopped, we had to build a fire to make coffee; but the agents did not sip like normal, but gulped it down and passed the cup. Off we went.

Nothing but endless green jungle dangling its vines over the moving water. Finally in the afternoon of the first day, we came upon a little farm on the riverbank. In my notebook I scribbled "Beraldo Rojas," but I don't know if that was the name of the place or the people living there. Two little canoes were tied to the bushes on shore. A dog barked ferociously and danced back and forth on top of the bank as we landed. A few stone steps led up to the buildings.

They called this farm a *trapiche*, the meaning of which I never figured out. It had a *molino* (a mill) to squeeze juice out of sugar cane reeds. Two short logs were set upright next to one another. They were geared at the bottom so when one turned, the other one did too. A pole was attached to the top of one of the logs and the other end to a little donkey. The donkey walked around and around in a circle, turning the mill. They fed long sugar canes into the slit between the logs and it squeezed out the juice which ran from a spout at the bottom into a pan on the ground. That donkey had made many a trip around that circle. He had worn a trench in the ground up to his knees.

Two brothers lived at the mill with a dark-skinned woman. I'm pretty sure the woman was wife to both men, but I didn't ask. I didn't want the Colombians to think I was being critical of their customs. They had three children: a boy of eleven, a girl of five, and a girl of three. The boy proudly wore a dirty army cap some soldiers had given him the year before when they passed through the region. The house was made of poles sunk into the ground, and the walls and roof were made of palm leaves. It had only three walls. One side was open to the river. The family slept in hammocks they strung inside the hut on the posts. All the family's belongings hung from the posts or rafter beams—pitchers made of gourds, several glass bottles, baskets made of palm leaves, bunches of tobacco leaves, coils of frayed rope, a home-made long bow, a quiver of arrows, and a skin from a big monkey. I also saw a bunch of green bananas and a string of dried onions. All around the beams were fish hooks of different sizes, thick fishing line, and fishing nets. The dirt floor was uneven but swept clean. In one corner was a big reed broom, and in another a tall stack of dried, leathery slabs of fish.

The surrounding area was all small fields of sugar cane hacked out of the jungle. I think the brothers spent all their time fighting the jungle, chopping it, burning it, cursing it. I could see edges of some fields where the jungle was winning, and clearings of new fields where the brothers were winning. All the palm trees showed charred places of a great fire.

The DAS agents squatted on their hams by the two brothers and talked. The donkey walked slowly round and round though no one was feeding the mill. I watched the dark woman in the hut. She was making us something to eat. She built a fire in her small iron stove. There was no chimney, just a hole in the roof. She put some rancid grease into a pan, and when it was hot she dropped in some of the leathery fish. She took down a basket of very dry, very hard biscuits and set it on their little table which stood part inside, part outside the hut.

The smell of the frying fish was not a bit pleasing, but what pleased me even less: as the woman was preparing the meal, the dog came in. He sniffed around the hut. When he got to the broom he cocked a leg and wet on it. The woman took no notice. She was busy putting the hot pan of fish on the table. When the dog got to the stack of dried fish, he cocked a leg and gave the fish at the bottom of the stack the same baptism he'd given the broom. I looked around. No one saw this. Fred was talking to the boy; the DAS agents still squatted with the brothers. (Colombians could sit on their haunches for hours, then get up and dance a jig.) I would have told the woman, but the dog did it in such a routine fashion I was sure he had done it before, and often. I took solace in the fact the woman had taken our fish from the top of the stack.

The main meal was awful. Bad taste, bad smell, bad color, bad texture. The biscuits were baked when mastodons roamed the earth. They tasted like limestone, and were almost as tender. But the whole meal was redeemed when she brought out dessert. She had cakes of brown sugar that she broke in pieces and handed some to each of us. It was delicious: rich with flavor like a mixture of dark brown sugar and molasses, but better than the brown sugar or molasses in the stores at home. And if eaten with a banana, why, it was manna from heaven. She had a basketful of those little cakes, and I bought some from her and rolled them in my pack.

As we were going down to the shore to continue downriver, along came a canoe up river. It was the sheriff from La Tagua with two deputies. They said they had a German prisoner lying in the boat. He spoke only German and Portuguese. There'd been a firefight in which one deputy was slightly wounded, and the German was shot in the stomach with a blast from a shotgun. They didn't think he'd survive the trip to La Tagua, but they seemed in no hurry. I went down to the boat. The man lay in the bottom with his eyes closed, white as a corpse. His stomach was a mess of jellied blood. I said to him quietly in German, "How are you?"

His eyes flickered open. He said, "I'll tell you how I am. I'm dead."

He stopped every third or fourth word to take a breath, but he kept talking. He said he wasn't afraid of dying, but he'd always wanted to return to the Fatherland to die. I said I better go, that he should rest, but he said, "No, stay. It's good to speak German to someone again." He closed his eyes. The sheriff and his men came and launched their boat. I told the German man goodbye, but he didn't answer. In a short time they were gone up the river.

During our whole trip, we met with only three other boats on that river. Two were loaded with green bananas, and the other, a mysterious phantom that appeared for a moment out of the fog one morning, was a dugout like ours, driven by a smoky gas motor and containing five very dark, bearded men, dressed mostly in skins, like ancient cavemen. They didn't smile, didn't shout, didn't wave. They dissolved like ghosts into the mist. When I asked who they were, the DAS agents gave a disinterested shrug.

We slept anywhere at night; we found a shelter or slept under the palm trees. The jungle darkness weighs one down in the night like a wet horse blanket. The thick canopy and the fog from the river block out the heavens. No stars, no moon, no meteor streak. Only the oppressive, dense dampness of black that makes one feel alone. You can see nothing. You can wave your hand in front of your face, but it's not there. Yet, you're not alone, for you hear all around you strange sounds that defy interpretation. When morning comes, a fog lies over the river that, lit by the rising sun, is as impenetrable as the blackness of the night. Then we would sit on the shore and wait, and watch the water swirling and gurgling around rocks and logs—for the river was high.

One night we slept in a pig barn. Someone's home had been there some time ago, but it had burned down. Another house had been started, but was never finished. The posts were still standing. Vines had crawled up to the tops of them and dangled there, looking around for further support. Young palm trees were coming up all over the yard. The pig barn (you could smell it) had a grass roof held up by four posts and fenced in with rusty wire. Under that roof was an attic of rough boards where some of us spread our rolls to sleep. The rest strung their hammocks between the standing posts of the would-be house. The pigs were gone; the people were gone. The place was unconditional, sad surrender to the jungle.

Paco (Francisco Barrera) showed me how to eat palm hearts. We'd find a young palm tree and cut the tender inside out of it. It has an ivory-colored cylinder that tastes like water cress. We had to select very young trees or the heart was woody and tasteless. Juan said people along the rivers lived on these palm hearts along with yucca, bananas, and fish. Some of them kept tame parrots around to eat when the fish ran out. He said parrots didn't taste good (I thought they must be a treat after eating their dried fish). Eating monkeys was common, he said, and when they found a tapir (somewhat like a pig), they felt God had smiled on them, and they feasted for days.

Evenings, as soon as we landed the canoe, Paco and I baited our hooks and caught fish from the back of the canoe. The fish looked like big bullheads, but they had stripes like zebras and spots like leopards. They called them *pintados*. It was fun to fish with Paco. He was as delighted as a little boy whenever we caught a fish and never tired of it. Paco fried them in oil, and we ate them with fried corn cakes. One night Paco caught a huge catfish, a *bagre*. That one fish fed the entire company.

We passed the mouth of a big river that flowed into the Caquetá from the north. They said it was the Caguán, and I thought we must be near Puerto Rico, but they said, "Oh, no. Puerto Rico is far, far to the north of here." The guide said we were looking for the mouth of the Quebrada Omancia (at least I wrote down "Omancia," but I never found it on any map). The Omancia was a little creek that fed the Caquetá, but we saw lots of little streams coming in left and right. How they could tell one from the other in this forever-changing vegetation was beyond me. But after a while the guide declared, "There it is!" We steered into a stream and entered a cave of green jungle. The stream was all closed in on top. Almost immediately we were blocked by a fallen tree. We chopped our way through that impediment, but in a few minutes the stream narrowed and was too shallow to navigate. We set out on foot looking for a path. We left the motorman to guard our stuff. For a while we hacked our way with machetes. We found a sort of path, which the guide said was the correct one. It looked like an animal trail to me. Juan said so too. We followed that deeper and deeper into the tangled bush. This was tiresome going. We were constantly ducking under branches or climbing over fallen trees. Vines dangled in our faces and often roped off the path so we had to cut our way.

On that trek our guide showed his mettle. He was a shriveled old man with deep lines in his face and hair all ashen gray. He had a thin, wiry, sinewy look like a monkey. I judged him to weigh no more then 125 pounds. His dark eyes were sunk so deep in his head I had to look twice to make sure he had eyes there at all, not just empty sockets. He looked to be at least twice the age of any of us, yet he outworked us all. When the path was blocked, we'd sit exhausted on a mossy log while he hacked through with his machete. This man was an efficient machine: he ate half as much food and had twice the energy of any of us. Juan said it was because he constantly chewed coca. Around his neck was a leather thong on which was suspended a small pouch from which he would, from time to time, extract a pinch of powder he would put in his cheek. The powder was made of ground-up coca leaves. This they said was the source of his magical energy. He was a silent man saying little when he worked, less when he rested. I misunderstood his name. I thought they had told me that his name was "Yucuna," and that was what I called him the whole trip. He always responded. After a while I noticed the others called him by another name, but I thought it was his nickname and didn't presume to be that familiar. Later I learned Yucuna was not his name at all, but the name of the Indian tribe to which he belonged.

Many of the DAS agents had been raised in the jungle, and some were superstitious. They believed in certain myths and warned me constantly about the dangers. They had already warned me about the *raya*, which was like a stingray. Wherever the river bank was muddy, they told me not to step in, because a *raya* might be hiding there. The *raya* had a poisonous stinging tail that could make a person very sick or even die. The myth about this *raya* was this: if a robber stole from your house, you could get revenge if you find his track. You cut off the tail of a *raya* and pierce a frog with it. Then you stick the tail with the impaled frog into the heel of the track of the robber. The robber will develop an infected, running sore in his foot that will soon kill him.

Walking in the jungle, whenever I ducked under a low branch I put my hand on the branch to steady myself. Paco told me not to do that. He said a common snake called the *cascabel* could climb among the vines and branches. You might put your hand on one and get fanged. Similar to our rattlesnake, it had mortal poison. Paco's lecture to me set off a discussion of a cure for snake bite. The best way, they said, was to kill that snake and eat the bile of the liver. Manolo's cure was to cut a cross in the flesh over each fang-wound and put raw sugar cane on it, and then drink a cup of kerosene (I think he was serious). All agreed the surest protection against snake bite and a warning against any danger was this: catch a live *cascabel*. They explained this wasn't hard to do with two forked sticks—one to hold down the head, the other the tail. You cut off the rattles and let the snake go. It must be kept alive. You then have to cross seven rivers (or one river seven times, makes no difference) to keep the snake from following your trail. Further insurance is to drop your shirt or your hat on the trail, because the snake will stay there and wait for your return. Eventually it'll give up and go away. You keep the rattles in your pocket. As long as that snake lives, those rattles will sound whenever danger's near.

Next they told me not to whistle. I had the habit of answering bird calls with an imitative whistle. Paco said, "Don't do that! You'll get a visit from El Silbón." Juan told me this gruesome legend: Long ago a son killed his father, and then boiled and ate the father's *tripas* (the insides, the guts). The ghost of the son now haunts the plains and open spaces of the jungle. He whistles from rooftops and tall trees. If you answer his whistle, he suddenly appears before you and beats you about the head and shoulders until you are black and blue.

We sometimes heard howler monkeys screaming in the tree tops. The first day out of La Tagua, as it was getting dark, we headed for shore. The motor was cut, and we coasted quietly. Suddenly we heard an ungodly, howling shriek, so loud that it rang in my head like a fire alarm and echoed so insistently up and down the Caquetá that I couldn't tell where the devil it came from. It was answered immediately by another and another, and for a moment I thought the anguished yowling must come from the mouth of Dante's hell. I looked at Juan. He was grinning. I knew it couldn't be danger. When the noise died, he said, "*mono aullador*" (their name for the howler monkey).

Next day as we walked along under the trees, I heard another howl from far away. I figured it was another howler monkey, but Paco, listening intently, held up a finger, and declared "La Llorona." Then Juan had to tell me yet another legend. La Llorona and her husband were of Spanish blood. She fell in love with an Indian. She bore a dark-skinned son by that relationship and drowned the baby in the river to hide her affair. Her guilt drove her mad, and she soon died. Now she haunts the forests along the rivers and lakes looking for her baby and wailing, "Mi hiijooo! Mi hiijooo!" (My son, my son). Her hair's white as snow and she's all dressed in filmy white so she blends with the mists along the river. They said only old people about to die can see her. But Manolo said dogs can see her too and will bark and howl pitifully when she appears. That's why one often sees a dog barking into the fog and hear one howling in the day when the mists are on the river. And if a person takes the tears of a dog and puts them in his own eyes he can see her too. I resolved not to try this experiment. I was content to leave her invisible, although I thought I might prefer a visit from La Llorona to one from El Silbón.

That afternoon we came across a rickety low rain shelter made of sticks and palm leaves. The guide announced this proved we were indeed upon the right trail. For the first time I thought he might be right. We were certainly on a trail made by humans, but the DAS agents were more and more dissatisfied with this trip. If we were on our way to a lab in the jungle, the trail should have been well-worn by the boots of men carrying in the coca paste, the chemicals, and the utensils, and by the men carrying out the bags of cocaine. But we had to admire that guide. He kept loosing the trail, but always he would find it again. He slogged along with the zeal of Christopher Columbus and looked completely honest and sincere.

Up ahead of us there came from the thickness of the jungle a sound like the low grunting of a pig followed by a coughing sound, like a man trying to expel food from his throat. Those sounds had the immediate attention of the entire group. All stood like statues looking in the direction of the sound. The guide stood with his ear cocked. Manolo shifted his weapon. I looked at Juan, frowning a question.

"*El tigre,*" he said in a low voice.

I didn't believe it. There were no tigers in South America. It was another of their myths. If there was a cat around here it was probably something like an ocelot or a bobcat. I didn't worry about it. We heard it no more and went on.

And then it began to rain. This was unexpected for we were not in the rainy season. No wind, but a hard rain roared on the leaves and splattered on the vines and splashed in our faces. It didn't increase nor decrease, but kept going at such a steady pace we gave up hope of it ever stopping—a constant, dismal, depressing rain. All through the afternoon it rained. The trail was lost again. Since the rain showed no sign of stopping, they decided to go back to the rickety shelter. Our "rain coats" leaked water here and there. They were fine for those quick little showers that fell for five minutes every afternoon, but were no match for this kind of ceaseless down-pour.

The shelter leaked as well. We had just enough room under there for all of us to lie down side by side with arms and legs straight like soldiers at attention. The rain rattled on the dry palm leaves and dripped through in a dozen places. None of us got much sleep. Everyone was wet, and they were all worried about El Tigre, because we had no fire to scare off the "big cat." At least I did not have that part to worry about.

Toward morning the rain slowed. I dozed. When I woke, it was just light. The rain had stopped, but water still dripped from the leaves, and shrouds of mist drifted among the trunks and vines. It was a dank, cool beginning for a tropical day. Everything was soaked. Fred was crabby. He looked like he'd been sipping vinegar all night. The whole company was squatting in a circle trying to light a fire. They had some dry matches but nothing dry for tinder to start a fire. Fred tried with a fistful of damp Colombian pesos, but they would only smolder, and go out. Manolo ripped off a piece of his bandana. That too only smoked. But I had dry paper. I kept my little notebook wrapped in a plastic bag, because I had found that sweat made the ink run, and we were always sweating on that trip. I hated to do it, but we were all chilled that morning. I ripped out a page and flame jumped up immediately. "*Mas, mas,*" they kept saying, and so I ripped out page after page. There went the story of the deadly frogs, the legend of El Duende, and a list of jungle plants you could eat. A quarter of my notebook went into the fire. Juan had carved a pile of shavings from the frame of the shelter, and when those got going, we fed the fire with the entire frame and parts of the roof. One might not think we'd want a fire in the jungle, but we all huddled around it as if we were in the Arctic, and were grateful as cavemen at fire's first discovery.

We spent an hour pretending to look for a trail, but most of us only searched for a break in the canopy where the sun could reach us. Spirits were low, and the men snapped at each other. They decided there was no cocaine laboratory. Even the guide surrendered. We gave the whole thing up and turned back. The return trail was easy to find. Even I could see where we had hacked our way. During that rainy night, lying stiffly on the cold jungle floor, my right knee had developed a problem that caused pain with every step. I was limping, but I kept up with no problem. I was eager to get out of that tangled thicket, and into some sunshine. When we reached the boat, we set out immediately for the Caquetá. What a relief it was to burst out of that green sepulcher-cave and into the bright sunshine and the wide open blue sky! We headed straight back to La Tagua.

I must tell of one thing that happened on the way back to La Tagua. It was evening. The sun was setting in a haze, and already long shadows lay across the river. As we rounded a bend, Paco, who sat in the bow of the canoe, pointed and shouted, "*Tigre, tigre!*" On the far side of the river a big spotted cat bounded out of the water and up the bank. It turned for a second, water dripping from its coat, then whirled and disappeared into the foliage. The damn thing was bigger than I was!

Ignorance is bliss. I had been a merry fool, happily humming my way through the jungle and thinking the others were acting like chicken-hearted children when they worried about a tiger. But this was the animal that concerned them. When they said *tigre,* they did not mean tiger; they were talking about the jaguar! And the jaguar that ran up that bank was a powerful-looking beast that could have had me for breakfast with enough room left for Manolo. I had a few nightmares after that in which I was running like a house afire through the jungle with jaguars after me. But it was a good lesson. From then on, any time I got sent to a foreign country, I checked out books from the library and read up on the place so I would not get sandbagged.

When we got back to La Tagua we were hoping for a ride to Leguízamo, but the heavy rains had turned the road into a swamp. It would take a week of dry weather before a truck could make it through. We set out on foot. I was still limping a bit and was carrying my share of our equipment. Manolo volunteered to carry my load, but I refused. However, my knee bothered me and I was trailing the rest. A man on a mule came along behind me. I waited for him and asked how much to rent his mule to get to Leguízamo. He wanted two dollars, which I gladly gave him. We tied my stuff on the saddle, and I rode the rest of the way with the owner walking behind. We also loaded Jaime's radio and the ammunition onto the mule, so the going was easy for everyone.

Back in Florencia, Fred was acting sulky. He had been that way most of the jungle trip. I was in high spirits because the pain in my knee had disappeared, and I had orders to go to Pasto up in the Andes Mountains to work with my old partner, John O'Connor. I spent most of the rest of my time in Florencia with the DAS agents. Juan said he was convinced our trek into the jungle was a diversion set up by the Leguízamo lieutenant. They had information now that indicated the lieutenant was involved in transporting packages of coca leaves and coca paste up the Putumayo to Puerto Asis, from where the stuff was shipped to cocaine labs in Cali and Medellin. The coca came from Bolivia and was stored on the Brazilian side of the border down by Leticia and Tabatinga. It was brought by pack mule to the Putumayo and then upriver in navy gunboats. Juan figured the lieutenant was expecting a shipment and had sent us into the jungle with his trusted guide to get us out of the way.

Chapter Fifteen

If I had hired a professional travel guide to plan a trip to Colombia for me, I don't believe he would have done as good a job on purpose, as the stumbling, bumbling bureaucracy did by accident. First they sent me down south to sample the steaming Amazon jungle. Then they sent me up to Pasto for a taste of the cold, dry air and bright sunshine of the high mountains, and next to Medellin to see one of the beautiful valleys of those great mountains of the Andes. I had only a few days in Pasto, and then I was suddenly needed in Medellín (I never found out for what). I flew into the valley of Medellin (the Aburras) on a SAM airplane (Sociedad Aeronáutica de Medellín) where good old smiling Agent Tom Zepeda met me at the airport.

"Nice flight?" he asked.

"Yeah," I said, "and some of my fellow passengers even had two legs instead of the usual four."

Tom said, "Chickens or turkeys?" He too had ridden those military flights with dogs and goats on board.

We did little more in Medellín than visit police stations. Agent Charlie Cecil was also there helping Tom. They were made for each other. Charlie was the only man I ever knew to be able to match drinks with Zepeda, though Charlie's tongue and legs got funny late in the day. Zepeda was always the same. He drank whiskey like Brits drink tea.

Tom Zepeda had an impossible job in Medellín. By that time Pablo Escobar had already graduated from stealing chickens and cars and tombstones, and was deep into the cocaine business. Pablo was bringing loads of coca paste from the south into Medellín where it was refined into beautiful white powder and sent to Miami. The local police said they couldn't find any cocaine labs. They kept telling DEA the labs were in the jungle. It was not that the police didn't know about, or recognize a cocaine lab. Some of them were moonlighting in Pablo's labs. Pablo was already a multimillionaire and he paid off the police. Tom Zepeda had a dangerous assignment. I don't think a DEA agent should have been stationed in Medellín at that time. Pablo Escobar could have had him killed for five American dollars with no risk to himself. But anyway, I got to see the city, which later became world famous for being the home of the organization of Pablo Escobar and the Ochoa brothers: the notorious Medellín Cartel.

After a month of this creative exercise in law enforcement, Octavio said I could go home. It was customary to have the agent in charge give an evaluation any time someone spent a month or more under his supervision. When I passed through Bogotá, Octavio handed me an evaluation to take home. He gave me the lowest evaluation I had ever received (excepting those verbal ones from my father back on the farm). When I questioned some of the marks, he said, "Well, you're not cut out for this jungle duty. Your health isn't good enough." I asked him what his basis was, and he said, "Didn't you have diarrhea? And didn't you walk lame for a while?"

I came out of his office fuming. The secretary said, "Oh, these TDY evaluations don't mean anything. The eval from your boss at home is what counts."

I said, "My health is better than his. At least I'm not fat." I added, "And Fred's, too (this had to come from Fred). I'll outlive them both."

I left Colombia still fuming. Octavio had kept me there just long enough so I missed Thanksgiving at home, and then gave me his shitty evaluation as a going-away present. I got home in early December and received an additional present: a mile-high stack of paperwork on my desk at the office. And I had another nice little remembrance of Operation Funnel: I scratched insect bites for a month. Funnel had introduced me to the friendly *zancudo*, which looks like a regular mosquito, but that's a disguise. The *zancudo* is a stealth mosquito. It's had Special Forces training and can take blood without your knowledge. When a mosquito is sampling your blood you can usually catch her at it. But the *zancudo* is a sneak and will escape before you know it's had a meal on your tab, and for a gratuity it leaves a generous red welt that itches for weeks. And it carries chemical weapons. If it's feeling really nasty, it'll give you an injection of yellow fever or dengue fever as a bonus. That *zancudo* of Colombia doesn't take a break over high noon like Minnesota mosquitoes do. It works all day and all night. It's fussier too, much prefers human blood to all others and, I'm convinced, considers O-negative (my type) a special treat.

I was still mad when I filled out my voucher for the trip. I sarcastically added the mule: "Rental of one mule . . . $2.00." I figured Dave Haight would question that, as would Jim Braseth, as would Kansas City, as would headquarters in Washington. It sailed through with no problem. I don't think anyone read that voucher, which was surprising, because they had a secretary at headquarters who went over the vouchers. I once had a secretary call me from Washington to complain about one.

She said, "I see here that on Monday morning the 25th you have nothing down for breakfast.

I said, "I had a bad stomach that morning. I didn't eat breakfast."

She said, "Don't do that! It just causes trouble. Now I have to send this back to you. You either fill in a breakfast or write down why you didn't eat."

I said, "Well, put in two dollars."

She said, "Thank you. But don't do it again. I'm not supposed to do this."

Here is the ironic part about this Operation Funnel. DEA at that time was eager to send us down the Caquetá River on the skimpiest evidence to find a cocaine lab in the Amazon jungle. They sent us down the river on the word of a crooked Navy lieutenant. The lab wasn't there. They were really in Cali and Medellín. A few years later, when Pablo Escobar and the Ochoa boys actually did set up an enormous cocaine laboratory in the jungle near the Caquetá, DEA ignored the informants, the tips, and the evidence. Strange boats never seen before were going up and down the Caquetá and the Putumayo. Airplanes flying routes never used before were tripping into apparently nothing but jungle. Strange chemicals were being shipped to places never heard of before. They allowed the Medellín Cartel to build a factory of such proportions it defied description.

The cartel's laboratory in the jungle was called Tranquilandia. It was actually a complex of about twenty individual laboratories. Finally some genius DEA agent in the States put a tracking device in a barrel of ether and traced it to Tranquilandia. When the DAS agents raided the place, they found ten thousand barrels (fifty-five gallon drums) of ether, the main chemical used to refine the coca paste. They found ten tons of cocaine (some of that was coca paste, but little is lost in the conversion), huge generators, scores of drying lamps, and enormous drying tables. They found bulldozers, trucks, eight landing strips, airplanes, helicopters. Long dormitories for the chemists, carpenters, plumbers, electricians, cooks, and waiters had been built, and pens for chickens, pigs, and herds of cattle to feed the workers. A cocaine factory of that size will never be seen again. If Octavio Gonzales had still been in charge, he would have sent an army down there at the first hint of a lab. Octavio kept a close watch on that jungle.

It seems that every DEA story I tell has some strange twist at the end. I'm not making these up. The story of Funnel was no different. I had been back less than two weeks, and it was getting on toward Christmas. I went across the street from our office in the evening to have a beer at the favorite watering hole. Braseth was there with some of the boys sitting at a table. I joined them, and right away Braseth says, "Hey, Bloch, you met Octavio Gonzalez when you were in Colombia, didn't you?"

I said, "Yes I did, the son-of-a-bitch."

Braseth exclaimed, "Whoa! Whoa!—oh, still sore about that evaluation, are you?"

"Why shouldn't I be? He sits on his fat ass, nice and safe in his fancy office in Bogotá and sends me out into the jungle with the jaguars and rattlesnakes, and when I get back he gives me a poor rating and says I'm not cut out for that kind of work—like it was my idea."

Braseth said "Well, hold on. You shouldn't be talking bad about him."

"Why not."

"It's bad luck to abuse the dead."

"What! What?"

"No joke. Evidently you weren't the only one unhappy with him."

"You mean somebody killed him?"

"The teletype came in yesterday. An informant came into the embassy to see him. He pulled a gun and shot Octavio dead right there in his chair in his 'nice, safe office.'"

He added, "Merry Christmas to all."

Chapter Sixteen

In those days, the town of Cabo San Lucas, on the southern tip of the Baja California peninsula, was a village of few people. In fact, the entire Mexican State of Baja California Sur had only a few people back then. The Mexican territory of Baja California Sur had become a state less than two years before. However, already a ferry ran from Mazatlán on the mainland to Cabo San Lucas on the Baja. And the road from La Paz to Ensenada had recently been paved. Drug smugglers liked to use that ferry and that road on their return trips from Mexico to the States. They preferred to clear customs at San Diego. The officials at San Diego did not look out so much for drugs as did those at Nogales and El Paso. No place in the Baja was anyone growing marijuana, and the land wasn't good for growing the heroin poppy. As long as someone wasn't a wild-eyed, long-haired, scruffy-bearded freak with a roach hanging from one corner of his mouth and driving a hippie van, San Diego officials waved people through on the assumption they were just tourists coming back from a few days lying on the beaches of Ensenada.

After a while DEA and U.S. Customs began to suspect what was happening. In the spring of '76, DEA sent a San Diego agent down to Cabo San Lucas, and Customs sent an inspector with his drug-sniffing dog. They worked with the Mex Feds (Mexican Federal Judicial Police) checking people coming off the Mazatlán ferry. One day the dog alerted on two smuggling rigs from Minnesota. Each rig consisted of a big pickup truck pulling a fifth-wheel RV camper. Each rig had a nice, clean cut young Minnesota man and a matching young lady in the truck. Each rig had two secret compartments that had about a thousand five-hundred pounds of marijuana hidden inside. The Mex Feds seized the rigs and put the men and women in jail. The DEA agent wrote a report about this and sent a copy to our office in Minneapolis.

In Minneapolis the agent reviewing this report determined the smuggling rigs were registered under a false name (Larry Lipschultz) and address. He made a note to that effect, then buried the whole thing in the General File room. He must have considered that, if Larry Lipschultz took all the trouble to make up a phony name and address, he deserved some privacy. I made a copy of that file and carried it in my brief case. They were bringing in three to six tons at a time, which, in those days, was colossal for Minneapolis. Whenever I had time, I tried to find answers to the questions: Who is Larry Lipschultz? Who financed this organization? Who made the arrangements in Mexico? Who built the compartments in the rigs? Who in Minneapolis was the receiver?

Somebody had taken a lot of money to Mexico to make that buy. The Mexicans didn't front that kind of dope. I had visions of a nasty mafia figure living in palatial splendor in one of our suburbs—or maybe a doctor or a lawyer with a secret life. I imagined tons of money, beautiful women, dangerous outlaws. A ton of marijuana was worth more than a quarter of a million on the street. Sometimes I imagined it might be a rotten politician supplementing his income. If I had known the truth, I might have put the file back where it had been resting peacefully for more than a year. But then we would have missed this whole story.

I wasn't an avid anti-marijuana crusader. I found that file by accident while looking for a file about a big heroin dealer—one that dealt in kilos instead of ounces. (A kilo is a little more than two pounds.) I never believed in "reefer madness" like Agent Harry Anslinger of the old FBN (Federal Bureau of Narcotics), who thought smoking marijuana turned young men into murderers and rapists. I'd been around enough marijuana smokers to disregard the "killer weed" theory. I knew smoking grass didn't cause young men to carry butcher knives, bounce off walls, and go into antisocial frenzies. It was almost the opposite. It made them listless, lazy, and hazy.

Agents didn't get much credit for spending time on a General File, so I tried to open a criminal case on the Cabo San Lucas bust. I went to Supervisor Dave Haight to get a number, but Haight said the other agent had already checked into it.

"What case?" he said. "What's to investigate? The people are already in jail, the marijuana destroyed—case closed."

I read off some of my questions, but he insisted there was no case because there was no dope. "When you go to court you have to have evidence to show the jury, physical evidence you can lay on the prosecutor's table in front of jurors. If this were a murder case, the prosecutor would want to see a bloody knife or a smoking gun. This is a drug case. He wants to see drugs. It makes the case real. The U.S. Attorney won't take a case with no dope."

"What if I can get the people in jail in Mexico to testify against the big guy here in Minneapolis?"

"They can't testify from a Mexican jail. Besides one of them is probably mister big himself, so he's already in jail. If they get out and agree to testify, you still have no dope on the table. Try to get yourself a prosecutor, you'll see."

Assistant U.S. Attorney Joe Walbran had the same mantra: "No dope on the table, no case." Most of our cases went like this: two small buy-walks, order big, bust on delivery; usually the crook pled guilty. And if the crook went to court: there was the dope on the table. Those were the cases the bosses liked. Those were the cases the bosses understood. And when we brought a case like that to a U.S. attorney, he snapped it up like candy. They liked "dope on the table," and got real shy around a pure conspiracy case. But the Eighth Circuit Court had done me a favor when they reversed the conviction of Nicky Frol. It made me study conspiracy law, and I saw that I didn't need a pile of dope on the table to make a case.

If I went to an assistant U.S. attorney, and he refused to prosecute, I was supposed to accept that decision and not go to another attorney. That was "attorney shopping," and it was forbidden. But we did it anyway. If we got turned down by day in the U.S. Attorney's Office, we tried again by night in the bar after buying a few. I went attorney shopping, but no one would bite.

I have to admit I had some selfish motives in this. For one thing the Minnesota winter that year was dragging on forever, and I thought I might be able to finagle a trip to sunny Baja California. For another thing, this would be a Class I case from the start. DEA had a rating system for cases. A routine case was rated Class III. If we had a big dealer involved, we could get our case jacked up to Class II. If he was really big, the regional office would give it a Class I. We got the most credit for working Class I cases. To make a case Class I, we had to submit all kinds of proof. Agents regularly fooled the regional office by tweaking the numbers, or tweaking the informant's information. But all that required paperwork. No tweaking would have to be done in this case. Just that report of the Cabo San Lucas seizure was enough to make it a Class I.

I was driving to work with Arctic winds sweeping down the fields and blowing snow across the icy highway. I determined to try Supervisor Haight one more time for a trip to sunny Baja. This time I limited my request to just one little trip to photograph the smuggling rigs and interview the prisoners at La Paz.

Supervisor Haight addressed my request: "Under what case number do I allocate the travel money?"

"Well," I said, "I don't have a case number, yet."

"I can't give you travel money if you don't have a case to put it under."

"But you didn't give me a case number."

"That's because you don't have enough evidence to open a case."

"I'm trying to get the evidence in Mexico."

"To get to Mexico you need a case number."

I said, "You have me in a catch twenty-two. To get a case number, I need the evidence. To get the evidence I need a case number."

Mr. Haight gave a rather wide grin to indicate his approval of this compact philosophical analysis of my situation, and gave a rather narrow movement of his right index finger to indicate the door as a signal the interview was over. When I started to walk out that door he said, "There's no reason to believe these guys'll talk, and we're not spending money on a lark. You've got a dozen other cases open. Work on them."

What really fried me was that I bet Agent Fekete or Anderson could have gone to Mexico merely by asking. They would have opened a case for them, and if it didn't turn out, they would have closed it. Simple. But I was a rookie.

I became obsessed. Other cases seemed boring. I was convinced the people arrested at Cabo were just drivers for the main man. Somebody very rich had excellent drug connections in Mexico. That somebody was sitting on his fat ass every night at Duffy's Tavern with a fancy woman on each arm, smoking a long cigar, and drinking Cuba Libres while his minions rotted in jail in Mexico. I got myself all in a fever.

Tom Nelson was one of the men arrested at Cabo San Lucas. His Minnesota license said he was from Remer, a little town up near Leech Lake. I drove up there and talked to his ex-wife. She said she knew nothing except that Tom got involved in this business right after their divorce. I got two impressions from her: one, she wasn't much disturbed about her ex being in jail, and two, she didn't like cops.

The other man arrested at Cabo was Roger Stege. I talked to Stege's girlfriend Irene, who worked at the phone company. She told me Roger was a carpenter and had done some work for a man named Darrell. I made a careful note of that. I traced the trucks and fifth wheelers back to the dealerships that sold them. They'd all been bought with cash on the barrelhead. The salesmen had only the name Larry Lipschultz. They said Larry was a clean-cut college boy who looked like John Denver. I searched every directory I could find: there was no Larry Lipschultz, no Darrell Lipschultz. After months of snooping, I was getting nowhere.

Again my buddies, Officers Hitchins and Brademan, helped me out. They interviewed prisoners at the jail to see if anyone knew a Larry Lipschultz. They quizzed their informants. They had one big, fat informant named Bob, who lived in north Minneapolis and made a living defrauding insurance companies. He bought cheap, old houses, heavily insured them, set them on fire, and collected the insurance. He found smashed autos in junkyards, transferred the titles to his name, insured them, then he "had an accident," and collected the insurance. To keep from getting caught, he kept switching insurance companies. The companies didn't pool their information in those days, and they did little investigating. It was easier for them to raise their rates than do investigations. Big Bob had been able to claim insurance money for the two smuggling rigs seized in Mexico.

Big Bob said a man named Brian was a player in the organization. He thought the last name sounded like Tarbo. I ran that name through all the systems in every form I could think of: Tarbeau, Tarbeux, Tarbow, and so on. Nothing. I thought it must be a nickname or a made-up alias like Lipschultz. I was stuck again. Finally I went through the whole dreary alphabet adding each letter, one at a time to Tarbo, and running each name through the systems. Just when I was ready to give up, I got to x. That made Tarbox. Tarbox? Who ever heard of a name like Tarbox? I ran it anyway. And then—bingo! I found a Brian Tarbox living in an apartment in Edina. He had no record, but he was all I had.

I have to say—another of those ironies of human existence—the big break in the case came, not through my investigative skill, but though my incompetence as a surveillance agent. I began to spend my free time doing surveillance on Tarbox, hoping he'd meet with Larry Lipschultz or a lawyer or with a man named Darrell or some big drug trafficker. I followed him to work in the morning, then went to the DEA office. At noon I'd grab a bag of French fries and watch his car for an hour. At night I spent hours watching the apartment until the lights went out.

That didn't last long. To do a surveillance with one car takes a certain amount of skill and genius, both of which I evidently lacked. Only a few days after I got started on this investigative technique, a young man came into our office late in the afternoon and said he wanted to talk to a DEA agent. He said he had information about a big marijuana smuggling organization. He was scared. He'd been paid a lot of money by the organization, and now someone was following him around. He thought they were planning to rob him. He'd already been robbed once. He was quitting the organization and quitting drugs. He'd testify in court. He was just married and wanted to settle down. His new bride was with him.

His name was Brian Tarbox.

I sat at the table in the interview room with pencil and paper. Brian sat across from me holding hands with his pretty little wife. It was obvious she was the big reason he had come in. When he faltered in his presentation, his memory lapsed, or his courage seemed to fail, she'd squeeze his hand, and that cleared his mind and gave him spine. He told about his trips to Mexico for the organization, about loading marijuana into fifth-wheel trailers, and his reception of sixty thousand dollars from a man named Darrell for making the trips. Shortly after he got the money, he had a knock on his door. When he opened it, two men burst in, breaking the chain lock. They had pistols and were masked. They demanded the sixty thousand dollars. Brian said he'd put it in the bank. They said he was lying. Brian denied that. Without ceremony, they tied Brian's hands and taped him to a chair with duct tape. They taped his legs apart to the arms of the chair and his neck to the back. One of them went to the kitchen and got a butcher knife. The other unzipped Brian's fly and took out his private parts. He grabbed the testicles and pulled the scrotum taut. He put the sharp side of the knife against the scrotum and said, "Where's the money?" Brian told him it was in the duct of the air conditioner. They took the money and left.

That's what scared him. These men knew he'd been paid, knew how much he had, and they knew it was in his apartment. He said he was so paranoid he couldn't sleep. It was affecting his work. When he drove his car, he watched his rear-view mirror constantly. A week earlier he noticed someone following him. Since then, he'd noticed it almost every day.

I said, "This guy following you around, what does he look like?"

He said, "I really can't tell. I see him only from a distance through the glare of the windshield. He wears a funny denim hat and drives a dirty yellow van (that was my hat and our surveillance van)."

Brian had spotted me almost immediately—that's how good I was! I didn't tell him until the end I had been following him around. But I liked his wife so much I couldn't bear to send her home in fear. Brian was both greatly relieved and astonished. He was relieved it was the cops and not the crooks following him, astonished I knew he was part of the organization that smuggled marijuana in fifth-wheel trailers. I made it sound like I knew a lot more than I did. That loosened him up. He'd been telling me he didn't know Darrell's last name, but now he recalled that name and several other details he'd left out. The organization had another truck and trailer rig. There had been at least seven smuggling trips into Mexico. His memory was good, but he didn't know a Larry Lipschultz.

When Brian and his wife left the office, I did five minutes research and then took out a case number under Darrell's name. It was the beginning of the case of *United States v. Darrell Lee Schaapveld.*

Big Bob told Officers Hitchins and Brademan an attorney was also involved in the smuggling. The two officers spent time investigating. They told me the informant might be talking about Attorney Jim Wegner, who had an office on Central Avenue Northeast. I checked on him and found Attorney Wegner owned a fifth-wheel trailer. I went to talk to him. He said he had just sold the trailer to a man who paid him cash. He believed the trailer was down in Arizona somewhere. The man's name was Larry, but the last name escaped him at the moment. He said his secretary would be glad to give me Larry's number. His secretary made a big show of looking for Larry's number, but was unsuccessful. When I confronted Wegner with my suspicion he was involved in a marijuana smuggling ring, he told me to take a walk.

I told Hitchins about this. He said, "Stand by. We'll go build a fire under old Jim Wegner." Hitchins and Brademan went to Wegner's office and told him he'd better cooperate. They said I was a top federal investigator and I was like a bulldog. "Once he has his teeth in a case, he never lets go." I laughed about this. Hitchins did too, but he said Wegner hadn't laughed.

Hitchens said, "I think he believed us. When we left his office, he had large sweat-patches under his arms, and his hands were shaking."

All of a sudden, when the bosses read my report about Attorney Jim Wegner, they took a great interest in the Schaapveld case. Braseth, who had several times in the last months asked me, "What the hell are you working on anyway? You haven't made an arrest in a year," was now patting me on the back for doing good work.

The next break came from the Federal Bureau of Prisons. On the *ABC Evening News* I saw a story about a prisoner exchange agreement the Bureau of Prisons had made with Mexico. The next day I asked Mary Schwab, the boss's secretary, what she knew about this. She said no one in the office had used it before, but she'd check into it for me. In a few minutes she had all the information and the forms I needed to try to get Nelson and Stege out of Mexico. Mary Schwab was the boss's darling. She practically ran the office. She was smarter than most of the agents and far more efficient. I got along with her from the first, not only because she was fun to get along with, but also because Sal Dijamco had told me, "Be sure you make friends with the boss's secretary. She is the most powerful person in the office." If there ever was a secretary made for DEA agents it was Mary Schwab. She was sex on wheels. Though devoted to her husband, she was a merciless flirt. When she smiled at me in the morning, I was glad I came in, and doubly glad I was a man. She'd answer the office telephone in her husky, breathy voice, "Drug Enforcement Administration," and make it sound like Mae West saying, "Come up and see me sometime." Like Braseth said, "She has a voice like a vibrating bed."

The exchange program worked like this: U.S. law enforcement agents identified prisoners they wanted to get out of Mexican jails. Mexican law enforcement agents identified prisoners they wanted out of American jails. Headquarters matched up the requests, and, if Mexico agreed, the exchange was made.

The prisoner exchange program wasn't popular with DEA agents. They found if they left one of their Mexican prisoners go home to serve his time in Mexico, the prisoner simply bought his way out of jail and went back into the drug business. And Mexican authorities were getting rich both ways. They were using the program to squeeze money from American prisoners. A prisoner couldn't get on their exchange list without cash under the table.

I paid no attention to these drawbacks. I immediately submitted the paperwork. I justified the request by pointing out that neither Nelson nor Stege had prior criminal records and were just mules (drivers, carriers, or transporters) for this big organization. As with all things that go through headquarters, it took a long time to get a response.

I was still attorney-shopping when a fresh, young attorney named Doug Kelley came to Minneapolis. I didn't like fresh, young attorneys. I liked old ones with experience. But I still had no dope on the table. I hoped a new guy might overlook that little detail. Kelley was bright, ambitious, clever, good looking—perfect for a prosecutor except for that lack of experience. He sat back and listened, but I could tell he wasn't eager.

"What happened to the marijuana?"

"They burned it."

"Did they send a sample to the lab to be tested?"

"No. Our agent wasn't that smart."

Kelley said, "Well. So we might be prosecuting on a load of horseshit?"

I said, "Look Doug, the DEA agent will say it was marijuana, the customs agent will say it was marijuana, and if you want, we can have a half dozen Mex Feds testify it was marijuana."

"Are any of them chemists? Did they run tests on the grass other than smoking it? The defense would tear them to pieces. We'd look like fools. We need an expert to testify that it was indeed marijuana, and not alfalfa—an expert who is right one hundred percent of the time. You need proof. Opinions and feelings and hunches don't count in court."

"We have the dog," I said, kidding. "He's an expert."

Kelley snorted and started a sneer, but that faded. He leaned forward, interested. He said, "Maybe you got something there. Would the dog ever alert on something that isn't marijuana, say lawn clippings, or a farmer's hay?"

Seeing a light, I said, "No. The dog doesn't make mistakes like that."

Kelley looked doubtful, "You check this out. If the dog's infallible, I'll take the case." He was getting excited. "We can have the dog come into the courtroom and find marijuana hidden under the witness stand. And we can give the jurors bags of alfalfa and show he doesn't alert on that."

Kelley liked the drama. He was already seeing his name in the paper. He had a friend named Jim Klobuchar who worked for the *Minneapolis Star*. (In those days the *Star* was the evening paper and the *Minneapolis Tribune* was the morning paper. The two later merged.)

I called the dog handler, U.S. Customs Inspector Landis, whose dog, Scuddley, had alerted on the marijuana at Cabo San Lucas. Scuddley had been sniffing out drugs for a long time. Inspector Landis said there wasn't the slightest chance the dog would make a mistake in the courtroom, though he said Scuddley had never "testified" before. I relayed this to Kelley. He immediately agreed to take the case, but he wanted me to go to San Diego and run some tests on the dog to make sure.

Suddenly I had a prosecutor and one of the targets was a lawyer. Money was no object. I could get help on the case any time I wanted. Other agents were doing surveillance. Other agents were doing interviews. I could travel where I wanted. When I told the bosses Kelley wanted me to go to California and meet the dog handler, it was approved without an eye blink.

I flew to San Diego. Landis said I could run any test on the dog. Landis had in his desk a small packet of marijuana wrapped in cellophane. He used the packet to play games of hide and seek with Scuddley. He stuck it into the back of the secretary's sweater collar as she typed away at her desk. He brought Scuddley into the room. The dog sniffed around the office for about ten seconds and then put his front paws on the back of the secretary's chair and alerted on her collar. Then Landis took out a towel, and he and Scuddley played tug-of-war for a while with it. That was Scuddley's reward for finding the packet.

I took the packet and sealed it in a zip-lock bag. I told Agent Landis to stay in his office and I'd call for him when I'd hidden the packet. I went down into the parking lot and hid the packet on top of the gas tank of one of the government cars. The exhaust pipe was still warm. I thought the lingering motor fumes would cover the odor of cannabis. Landis came out and walked up and down the rows of cars with Scuddley. When they got near that car, Scuddley leaped forward and alerted on the gas tank. That was good enough for me. I went back to Minneapolis and told Doug Kelley Scuddley was the expert he'd been looking for.

Kelley was happy. Happy enough to tell his buddy Klobuchar about a possible upcoming trial where a dog would come to testify. He told Klobuchar to keep it quiet. But Kelley should have kept in mind that Klobuchar was a reporter.

Just when things were falling into place, the great wisdom of the DEA bureaucracy sent me to Mexico on Operation Trizo. (I cover that later.) I was gone for three months. During that time Agent Haight and Agent Anderson made that trip to La Paz to do the interview of the prisoners, the same trip I'd been begging for. But they weren't prepared. Nelson convinced them he knew nothing about the organization, but Mr. Stege fed the two agents a lot of baloney, and they ate it up. They hadn't studied the case and, knowing nothing, were unable to separate fact from fiction. He told them the head of the organization was a man named Thomas Harris from somewhere in Minnesota. That Harris story was faithfully written down in a DEA 6. That false report would later come to haunt us at trial. They had made a basic mistake: don't write a DEA 6 if you don't know the facts.

By the time I got back from Operation Trizo the prisoner exchange had taken place. Nelson had agreed to testify and Kelley had already left him out on bail. Stege refused to cooperate so they sent him to jail up at Stillwater. I soon found Nelson really didn't know anything—that part of their DEA 6 was correct. But the Thomas Harris story—that was trouble.

I went to see Stege. I thought he was crucial to the case. I suspected he had built some of the secret compartments in the fifth-wheelers trailers. He wouldn't talk. When I asked him if he actually was choosing a couple of years in jail over testifying, he said, "Jail? You call this jail? This is a resort. I can do a couple of years here standing on my head. After what I went through in Mexico, this is plush vacation."

I said, "You think you're protecting your friends, but they betrayed you. You don't need friends like that. And I'll get them anyway, with or without your help."

He smirked. "If you're trying to convince me the government is my friend, you're barking up the wrong tree. I'll do my time. That way I'll be done with this whole thing. I'll get married, get back to work, and won't have to look over my shoulder all the time."

I was glad he mentioned getting married. I remembered his girlfriend Irene, with her long lashes and throaty voice, rich dark hair, calm, classy demeanor. She had looked beautiful in a plain gray dress that time I saw her. I thought, *Stege, you can't be crazy enough to choose prison with something like that waiting in the wings.* I went to see her right away. I laid the whole story in front of her, stressing that I was instrumental in getting Roger out of Mexico. She listened with a half-smile.

When I was done, she said in a clipped little voice, "Oh, really? Is that what he said? Well, let me check into this to be sure."

She stood up. She gave me her hand and said, "Agent Bloch, we're done here. I'll be going up to see Roger this weekend. I'll ask him to call you on Monday."

Monday morning I got a call from Roger Stege. He had changed his mind.

The first thing I asked him was, "Who is Larry Lipschultz."

He said he never heard of a Larry Lipschultz, but after I explained why I was asking, he said, "Oh, I know. That has to be Darrell. Whenever anything went wrong, Darrell jokingly blamed it on "that darned Larry Lipshitz." Darrell must have used that name, with a slight change, to register the fifth-wheelers."

There never was a Larry Lipschultz. That hunt was over.

With all these people cooperating: Nelson, Stege, Tarbox, Olson, it didn't take long to piece together the whole conspiracy. Darrell, fresh out of college, was the brains, the boss, planner, designer, director, producer, whatever. Only a few knew his real name. He made calls to them only from pay phones and used codes. If he said he was going fishing, it meant he was on his way to Mexico to arrange a load. If he said the fishing was good, it meant he had been successful in setting up a deal, and to get ready to make a trip.

Tarbox was a trusty old buddy from his college fraternity days. He made most of the contacts, passed out the money, and recruited people for the trip. Attorney Jim Wegner recruited some too, and the disgraceful fact was he recruited them from clients of his who were down on their luck and needed cash to pay his attorney's fees.

A fifth-wheel RV has its front part over the bed of the pickup truck that tows it. The hitch is bolted into the bed of a truck over the rear axel. That front part is the bedroom, with steps going up to it. Schaapveld had raised the floor of the bedroom, adding one extra step. The marijuana was secreted under that floor. Then he had the rear wall moved forward, and that created the space to hide the rest of the load.

Schaapveld put a half dozen *Playboy* magazines in the fifth-wheelers. He told the drivers that, when going through customs, both Mexican and American, they should leave the magazines in plain sight on the couch and table. Stege said it worked like a charm. The officials would come inside, sit down on the couch, ask a few questions, open one of the magazines, and begin looking at pictures. Occasionally they'd ask a question as they looked but seemed not to hear the answer. After paging through a magazine or two, they'd pronounce, "Okay, everything seems to be in order here." Americans would throw down the magazines, the Mexicans would keep them. End of inspection.

The trips were designed so, if anyone got caught, they could claim they did not know they were on a smuggling trip. They'd say they'd rented the rig, cash down, from a mysterious man named Larry (or Tom or Dick or Harry). They'd say they had gone on a vacation to Mexico, stayed a few days, and come back home. They knew nothing of secret compartments and weren't aware their fifth-wheeler was any different from others. If there was any marijuana in there, it must have been loaded some night when their rig was parked in the parking lot of their hotel, while they were sleeping.

Trips were made to either Mazatlán or Oaxaca. The drivers rented a hotel room for proof they didn't sleep in the trailers. Oaxaca is south of Mexico City, and rigs had to be piloted up and down steep inclines and over rough winding roads of high volcanic mountains. The Mazatlán trip was easier, but Oaxacan marijuana brought higher prices in Minneapolis. In the Twin Cities we heard marijuana names like "Colombian Gold," "Jamaican Blue," "California Juicy Fruit," but best of all: "Oaxacan Gold."

Soon Doug Kelley was ready for the arrests. I had identified Jean Neva as one of the drivers for the organization. She had been on a trip with Attorney

Jim Wegner. She refused to talk. We considered her a minor player and were ready to give her immunity. Doug had subpoenaed her to appear in front of the grand jury in St. Paul, but Jean didn't show up. The marshals couldn't find her that day. As Kelley and I were drawing up a conspiracy indictment against the defendants in the case, her name came up again.

An indictment has near its top a list of the indicted conspirators. It looks like this:

UNITED STATES OF AMERICA
v.
DARRELL LEE SCHAAPVELD
JAMES LOUIS WEGNER
BARBARA ANN KLANDE

And so on.

We had a dozen names on the list. Below that were listed the counts against them. In that part it says these people, these conspirators, did willfully and knowingly conspire, combine, confederate and agree together with each other and with . . . and here are listed the names of the unindicted co-conspirators (the people cooperating and are not being charged).

When we got to Jean Neva's name, Kelley said, "I hate to charge this lady. She got involved in this through her attorney, and she has a bunch of kids. Go show her the indictment. She'll change her mind. Tell her I said she can be on either list, top or bottom, her choice." That meant she could be on the top list and be charged with all that smuggling of marijuana, or she could be on the bottom list and not be charged at all. But she would have to co-operate and possibly testify.

Officer Wayne Brademan went with me to see Jean in Cumberland, Wisconsin. He said, "This is going to be easy. It's either sing or go to jail. With all those kids, she has no choice. Put it to her this way: 'Jean, there's going to be a hanging, and you can choose which end of the rope you want to be on.'"

Jean Neva didn't hesitate. When she saw the indictment, she knew which end of the rope was best for her. We had some papers along for her to sign. She grabbed the pen, but as she hovered over the paper, she stopped. She said, "Let me just call my lawyer, and see what he says." Her lawyer was there in ten minutes—all in a sweat. He took her aside, and they had a long argument. The lawyer was absolutely against her cooperating. I wish I remembered that guy's name. I'd gladly print it here in capital letters. We were promising Jean no prison time, no felony record, and we weren't even sure she'd be needed to testify in court. Her lawyer was either a stark idiot, or a hungry shark.

She chose the wrong end of the rope. We added her name to the upper list, so that now the indictment also read, "UNITED STATES OF AMERICA v. JEAN A. NEVA." She was arrested along with the rest of the gang, put in cuffs and brought before the court like any other criminal. But Jean did later realize she'd gotten bad advice. She didn't go to trial like some of the others. Kelley called me one afternoon and said Jean had just come in and wanted to plead guilty. She was appearing in front of Judge Lord in a few minutes. I went up and sat in the back of the courtroom. Jean was sitting in the front row. Lord called her to the podium and asked her what her intentions were. She said she was pleading guilty.

Lord said, "Where's your attorney?"

She said, "I don't need an attorney. I know I'm guilty."

Lord squirmed in his seat. "Normally we have an attorney here to make sure you know the consequences of pleading guilty. We'll set this for another time, and you come with your lawyer."

Jean said, "Why would I want my lawyer. I have gotten nothing but bad advice from him, and he's taken all of my money. I can't pay a lawyer, and I don't want a lawyer." She turned around and, pointing her finger at me, she said, "That man came out and offered to put me on the list of those who don't get charged. My lawyer told me to choose the other list, and so I got arrested and have been driving back and forth from my home in Wisconsin for my court appearances. I came all the way over here to plead guilty. I don't want a lawyer here to advise me to go to trial."

Lord said, "Get yourself a new lawyer."

"I have no money."

"Didn't you get paid by the organization for making a trip to Mexico."

"They paid me $2,000, and the lawyer took it all. I think they're all a bunch of crooks. He even took my wedding ring."

"Say that again?"

"He took my wedding ring as payment for his stupid advice."

Lord colored visibly, and I could see his jaws tighten. He grabbed his gavel. "I'm setting your hearing for two o'clock this afternoon. Your lawyer will be here. The United States marshals will make sure of that. They'll bring him here in handcuffs if they have to. There'll be no problem with your plea. You'll have a lawyer by your side, but he'll keep his mouth shut. He won't charge you a cent. He won't ask you for anything. If he does, he'll go directly to jail for contempt of court. If he ever bothers you in the future, call Doug Kelley, the prosecutor, and we'll take care it."

I'm pretty sure he could have taken that plea without an attorney, but Judge Lord was probably worried about the appeals court. Jean Neva got probation, and we never called her to testify. Things developed in such a way—strange way—that we didn't need her.

The boss wanted to make all the arrests at one time. He said it was to cut down on the number of fugitives, but I think it was mostly to make better headlines. There were no lack of volunteers. The officers met at our office in late afternoon. It was the 8th of December 1978, the Feast of the Immaculate Conception, but the room was spilling over. An officer filled every chair, some sat on desks, some leaned against the wall, and some sat on the floor. Officers came from the Minneapolis Police Narcotics, from Hennepin County Narcotics, from the Minnesota State Bureau of Criminal Apprehension, and from the Bloomington Police Department. The next morning the *Minneapolis Star* front page headline: "12 CHARGED WITH SMUGGLING 20 TONS OF MARIJUANA TO STATE." The article told about the arrests and gave special mention to James Wegner of Cleveland Street in Minneapolis.

It took us weeks to find Darrell. We would never have found him without help from Tarbox. There were warrants for him all over the country. The marshals had posters everywhere. No friend or relative knew where he was. No one heard from him. But then one day Tarbox called me and said he thought he had just seen Darrell's car at a little shopping mall. A few of us went out to make the arrest. We found the car and set up on it. I watched through my binoculars. I was supposed to identify Darrell before we moved in. We didn't want to make a mistake and warn him off. After a while a man came out and got into the car. But that man did not look one bit like John Denver. He had long hair and a beautiful, thick red beard. He looked more like he should be standing in the prow of a medieval Viking ship holding a spear and looking for monasteries to sack.

On the radio they were asking, "Thirty-five is that him?"

I said, "Wait. It does not look like him."

We waited until he was well away from the shopping center and I had a chance to pass him and get a good look. I still was not sure, but we pulled him over anyway. Lucky guess. It was the very Mister Schaapveld we were looking for. He was living out of his car. It was full of clothes, camping equipment, and food.

Two of the drivers that had made smuggling trips for Darrell to Mexico were Barbara Klande and Emma Lou Klande of St. Paul. They were an interesting pair, mother and daughter. The St. Paul police told me they were prostitutes and sometimes worked as a team. Only rich men could afford them. The police said they were bedding judges, lawyers, and doctors. I was there when we did the search warrant and made the arrests at their apartment on Lexington Avenue. I couldn't believe they might be prostitutes. They struck me more as rich, sophisticated, upper-class ladies. They wore modest, conservative clothes and little makeup. Both were very attractive—Barb in a serenely self-possessed way, Emma Lou in a pixie high school-cheer-leader way. It was hard for me to believe that Barb was a "cold blooded, vindictive bitch" as she was described by the police. She was soft spoken and calm. Their apartment had the furniture and artwork one might see in homes of millionaires. The police said some rich guy was paying the rent.

Barb had a bad reputation among the cops. When I told the Minneapolis narcs about the robbery of Brian Tarbox, they said, "That smells like that murderer Michael Ayd. Barb Klande knows him. I bet she hired him to get that money. Brian's lucky to be alive and double lucky to have his family jewels. Ayd might have sliced them off after he got the money just for the fun of it."

The Speedy Trial Act had been passed a few years earlier, but it did little to speed up the court processes—the usual motions, delays, appearances, hearings. Even more so in the Schaapveld case because we had so many defendants. But these were slowly pared down as the weeks passed. One by one they pled guilty. On the first day of February James Wegner appeared in the Federal Court House in downtown Minneapolis before Judge Miles Lord to plead guilty of conspiracy to import marijuana. He admitted he was along on three of the seven smuggling trips of the Schaapveld organization and had hauled in tons of marijuana. He confessed he had been involved in buying some fifth-wheel trailers. Under his plea agreement Wegner faced only five years (maximum) and a possible $15,000 fine. Judge Lord knew Jim Wegner's daddy, who appeared with Jim in court that day and promised his son would be good and wouldn't run. Lord left the attorney off easy. He allowed him to go free on his own recognizance, which meant he did not have to post bond. Other defendants in the organization also pled guilty, some became fugitives, some reached an agreement to testify in return for no prosecution.

Finally there were only three. The three that went to trial were Darrell himself, and Barbara and Emma Lou Klande.

Chapter Seventeen

YOUR HONOR, I OBJECT TO THAT. We would not be able to cross examine the witness."

Earl Gray was objecting to bringing Scuddley into the courtroom. We were sitting in Judge Lord's chambers for pretrial. (The judge's "chambers" is his office, but they call it a "chambers" to make it sound more highfalutin'). Kelley had just declared his intentions to bring the dog into court to show there really was marijuana in the fifth-wheeler trailers when they were busted at Cabo San Lucas. Gray was representing Barb Klande. Doug Thompson was present for Schaapveld, and Mark Peterson for Emma Lou Klande.

Judge Lord looked at Kelley for an answer to Gray's objection.

Kelley said, "Your honor, Mr. Gray is completely misrepresenting our intentions here. We plan to use Scuddley as a witness, but then we intend to allow Mr. Gray all the time he wants for cross examination."

The defense attorneys didn't think that remark was funny. All three objected to bringing a dog into court. To me their objections seemed insincere, though. As I watched the sparring between the lawyers, it was obvious all four attorneys, and the judge, too, were eager to drag this peculiar drama into the courtroom. They knew bringing a dog into federal court would cause a media sensation. Lawyers and judges always liked to have their names in the paper. They could all see the reporters crowding in, cameras flashing, their faces on TV, names and pictures in the paper. I could see on Lord's face the same look I had seen on Kelley's when I first mentioned the dog. Normally Lord sat back and looked bored during pretrial. He leaned forward on his elbows and was very attentive to the details of how Kelley wanted to use the dog.

Really, Scuddley was taking the place of the DEA chemist. Kelley was trying to show the dog's nose was as reliable as the chemical tests. The plan was to hide packets of marijuana in the presence of the jury, bring in the dog, and have him find the packets. We'd also use packets of alfalfa to show that Scuddley wouldn't make a mistake and alert on anything but marijuana. The defense attorneys had nothing to lose. They all knew the stuff found in the fifth-wheelers at Cabo San Lucas was marijuana, anyway. And if, for some reason the dog made a mistake, the prosecutor's show would blow up in his face. They all decided it was okay to use the dog. They were, in fact, eager to use the dog.

That day, behind the doors of the august chambers of the Honorable Judge Miles Lord, the case of *U.S. v Schaapveld* turned into a dog and pony show. True, the pony was missing, but that shortfall was more than satisfied by the number of jackasses that filled in. And I'm not talking here of defense attorneys only. Included must be the judge, the prosecutor, and especially newspaper reporters. Sadly I must also include myself because I saw this show developing and made no more complaint than a donkey, until it was too late.

The trial of *U.S. v Schaapveld* finally began at the end of the following April. By that time DEA had already reassigned me to the Texas border, and Bea and I were living in McAllen. I had to fly up for the trial. It was wonderful Minnesota springtime, warm and sunny in Minneapolis and painful to sit inside a somber courtroom. Judge Lord sat at the front behind his enormous desk, which made him look like an elf, for he was not a large man. To his left was the witness chair, and to the left of that sat the jury. In front of Lord's desk was the court stenographer who wrote down everything said (which is why we did not swear in court—profanity, I mean). Beyond her were two large tables. The one to her left was for the prosecution, the one to her right for the defense. Doug Kelley and I were the only ones at the prosecutor's table. The defense table was crowded—Darrel Schaapveld (now looking like John Denver again—clean shaven, wire rim glasses, hair trimmed) with his attorney, Doug Thompson; the lovely Barbara Klande (looking prim and proper as a small-town librarian) with her flamboyant lawyer, Earl Gray, Esquire; and Emma Lou Klande (looking fresh and pretty, and innocent as a rosebud on a June morning) with her counsel, Mark W. Peterson.

Schaapveld hadn't pled guilty in spite of an enormous pile of evidence against him. Thompson wanted to hear at least part of the prosecution's case to see which way the wind blew. He knew Kelley was a new attorney and wanted to see what he was made of. And he knew the dog was coming to town.

At trial one can usually tell early on what the strategy of a defense attorney will be by listening to the questions he asks when he cross-exams a witness. Thompson was using the age-old tactic of deflecting guilt upon the prosecutor's own witness. He wanted to make the jury think the real leader of the organization wasn't Schaapveld, but Tarbox. He did this by stressing and repeatedly drawing out testimony showing Tarbox making phone calls and paying drivers, and giving directions. He tried to minimize testimony about

Schaapveld setting up buys in Mexico. Gray, I could tell from the start, was planning to put Barb Klande on the witness stand. Peterson seemed to be of the same mind. I thought maybe the Klandes were so used to lying to their men clients and so used to being believed, they had no doubt they could lie their way out of this silly little jam.

Since Tarbox was a key witness, all three defense attorneys sought to make him into a sneaky, lying villain. Gray had his usual scattergun approach. He fired around in all directions hoping to hit something somewhere, but I could tell his overall strategy was to make Barbara look like an innocent little lady who thought she was just invited along on a vacation to Mexico because of her pleasing personality, that she never for a moment suspected the nefarious goings-on of this gang of criminals. Peterson's strategy was the same for Emma Lou, though his job was a little easier, because Emma Lou really did look like an immature little girl not entirely aware of what was happening. Both Klande attorneys wanted the jury to think their clients knew nothing about illegal drugs and certainly nothing about how those things could be smuggled. Both attorneys attempted to skew the testimony to make the jury think it was impossible their delicate little ladies could drive a huge clumsy rig like those used on the smuggling runs. Both emphasized the marijuana bricks were wrapped in such a way they couldn't tell what was inside without opening them. They were so tightly wrapped no marijuana was visible and no marijuana smell. So, even if the Klandes had helped load the bricks (which they did), they could have thought they were laying in food supplies, clothes, and tourist trinkets.

The trial slogged along with the speed of a three-toed sloth. If one of the three attorneys made an objection, and the judge sustained it, the other two would pop up and say they objected too. Then there'd be a big debate because an objection could be valid for one defendant and invalid for another. Then someone would say, "May we approach the bench," and they'd all gather up in a huddle for ten minutes while the jurors picked their teeth and studied their fingernails. Or the judge would say, "Why don't you jurors leave?" Then they could go out and have coffee while the attorneys spewed volcanoes of citations, and moved for mistrials, and objected to their own objections.

I saw Kelley was nervous. When he was questioning a witness and got an answer to one of his questions, he would say, "Oka-ay" to give himself time to think. Then he would ask another question and again say "Oka-ay," when he got the answer. But he did well. He was burying Darrell. As he skillfully led his witnesses through their testimony, Barbara's pushy, aggressive personality began to emerge. One after another the witnesses testified how, on those trips, she was always bossing people around. The jury slowly got the impression she might not be the innocent little lamb Gray made her out to be. She might actually be one of the leaders in the organization. And since the Klandes were always together on the trips, any impression the jury got of Barb stuck to Emma Lou. So now Peterson had to attempt to clean up his client by separating her from mom.

Kelley was good, and so were many of our witnesses. I watched in delight as the three famous defense attorneys tried to back our witnesses into corners only to see them slip out by simply telling the unvarnished story as it happened. When wrangling with smart defense lawyers, truth was the best weapon. In the pretrial briefings, Kelley and I told witnesses over and over: "Just tell the truth. Don't try to bend any facts to make yourself look better or to make someone else look worse."

It's a mistake to think lawyers are smarter than other people. Like college professors, they're often smart only in their narrow field of study and can in some ways be considered dumber than normal people. Give one of them a pipe wrench, a crowbar, or a pickax and he's not so smart anymore. Lawyers know how to yell out a citation in a courtroom, but what do they know about fifth-wheel trailers? All of the attorneys, including Kelley, assumed driving a big fifth-wheeler with a ton of cargo in the back on winding roads in the mountains would be difficult. When Kelley had a mechanic on the stand who knew everything about fifth-wheel trailers, he avoided going into that, thinking it might in some way help exonerate the Klandes. But when Gray got up to cross-examine, he tried to score on that very point—and got his nose burned. He violated the rule: don't ask a witness a question unless you know what the answer will be. The questioning went something like this:

Q: These big rigs are hard to drive aren't they?

A: No, they're very easy to drive.

Q: Isn't it true they get to swaying a lot when it's windy.

A: No, they're quite stable. A fifth-wheeler is more stable than the hook-behind trailer. It's much less likely to start swaying or to jackknife.

Q: But isn't it true that when you put a heavy load in the back, it does become unstable.

A: No. Not really. That's the beauty of the fifth-wheel setup. You have much better balance. Most of the weight is centered over the truck's rear axel.

Q: Isn't it true you have to have some practice and have to be in good physical condition to handle one of these rigs properly?

A: No, it's not. I've seen skinny, little old ladies, who never drove one before, wheel the thing out of our parking lot with no trouble at all.

Gray pursued that path no farther. I could have hugged the mechanic. I think Kelley could have too.

When Roger Stege got on the stand, they dredged up the old Thomas Harris story and tried to confuse the jury with it. Stege had to admit over and over the Thomas Harris story was a lie, one he had simply made up to satisfy Agents Haight and Anderson when they came to the prison at La Paz. He said he never told anyone the truth about the case until he began to cooperate with Agent Bloch. That true story was in my report. But they continued to try to make hay with the Thomas Harris report.

Peterson read off a line from the Harris report that contradicted my report. Stege said, "That was a lie."

Peterson read another line and asked, "Is this a lie too?"

Stege: "Yes."

Peterson read off some more. "And I suppose this is a lie too."

Stege: "Yes, it is."

The defense attorneys were driving home to the jury that Stege told a lot of lies. In closing arguments they could say our main witnesses were liars. But I don't think a juror present didn't understand a criminal sometimes lies to the police. The defense attorneys kept hinting the Thomas Harris story was the true one, and I had coached Stege about what to say on the witness stand.

When Peterson was pressing him hard on that issue, finally Stege, exasperated, declared loudly, "Yes, I must admit, Agent Bloch did tell me what to say on the witness stand. He told me to get up here and tell the truth!"

Stege was so forthright and so unruffled in admitting his former lies, and so sincere in insisting on his present honesty the attorneys who were pressing him appeared more deceitful than he did.

So everything went fine until the damn dog came to town. What a circus! All along the news media had given the Schaapveld case some coverage, but nothing like this. When Scuddley flew into Minneapolis, it was the Second Coming. News reporters were waiting for him at the airport. Inspector Landis came along with the dog, but you'd never have guessed it. Scuddley got all the attention. The *Minneapolis Star* had a picture of Scuddley that took up half the front page!—the story headline: "WILL THE WITNESS RAISE HIS RIGHT PAW."

This circus was dragged into the courtroom the next day. Believe it or not, the judge dragged it in. Out of nowhere, Judge Lord sent out the jury and pulled out the *Minneapolis Star* and began asking the attorneys if they had seen the picture and knew about all the publicity. It was as though he was inviting someone to move for mistrial. Well, it was like throwing bloody bait into shark water. Both Klande attorneys immediately moved for mistrial based on the prejudice caused by the article. Thompson asked for a recess so he could talk to Darrell, and then he went for mistrial too. I thought nothing of it. Defense attorneys were always moving for mistrial in order to impress the client, and to give them basis for a later appeal to the circuit court. So I was half asleep, when, like a thunderclap out of the blue, the Honorable Judge Miles Lord banged his gavel and declared a mistrial!

I was speechless. There was no sense saying anything. My entire repertoire of profanity wasn't fit to describe my feelings for Judge Lord. I was glad I didn't have my pistol with me in the courtroom. There was no *reason* to grant a mistrial. Lord hadn't even asked the jury if they had seen the article! All the hard work of preparation was flushed down the toilet. Start all over. I'd again have to be flying back and forth between Texas and Minnesota for the hearings and briefings and conferences. And there'd be even more delays now. The defense attorneys would definitely move for dismissal of the case based on double jeopardy. Even if Judge Lord denied the motion for dismissal the defense attorneys would appeal to the Eighth Circuit and try to get a dismissal there. That'd take months!

I flew back to Texas disgusted, dreaming of exhilarating ways to murder Judge Lord. I wished I'd never pulled out that General File and started the Schaapveld case. I lost all interest and wanted only one thing: for the case to be over. My home was in McAllen, but I'd be spending half my time in hotels in Minneapolis. I was to the point where I actually hoped Judge Lord would dismiss the case and have it over with.

After spending the amount of time required for an eminently sagacious judge to ponder a wonderfully serious motion for dismissal, Judge Lord decided double jeopardy did not apply and denied the motion. Then it took the defense attorneys more than a month to find the double jeopardy clause somewhere under the Fifth Amendment of the U.S. Constitution and to copy it down and send it to the Eighth Circuit Court in Kansas City so those judges could ponder it for at least a month as behooves wise judges of such high courts. They thought about it for the standard amount of time, then affirmed Judge Lord's denial. The trial was back on. I thought the Eighth Circuit would assign a new judge to the case (Larson, I hoped), but no, they wanted Judge Lord to officiate so they could be entertained by another appeal.

Summer was waning into autumn and some of the trees by the Federal Building in Minneapolis were already showing fall color when we finally went back to court. But then things got easier. Darrell pled guilty and agreed to testify. We didn't need the dog any more. Darrell could testify about the marijuana. He was expert enough for us. He told how he had learned about marijuana by smoking it at the University of Minnesota, how he made connections in Mexico during spring break, learned to bribe the Mex Feds met the growers on moonlit mountains at midnight to examine the product and negotiate the price, and how he paid his money to men whose names he did not know and whose faces he saw only in the dark. Darrell was a better marijuana expert than Scuddley, and Darrell was not nearly as boring as a DEA chemist. The Klandes should have pled guilty too when they saw Darrell was testifying, but they insisted on taking the stand.

Gray put Barbara Klande on the stand first, and she was good. She looked beautiful that morning and not a bit nervous. She should have been in the movies. If I hadn't known better, I would have believed her myself. Gray put her through her paces, and Kelley did not shake her. She could lie better than anyone I ever saw in a courtroom. She did it so calmly, so easily—not a tremble in the voice, not a diversion of the eyes.

Then Peterson put Emma Lou on the stand, but she wasn't good. She was pale and tense. She sat stiff and glanced at the jury out of the corner of her eye. She overacted like a grade-schooler in a Christmas play. Peterson should have cross-examined Barbara and left it at that. When Peterson asked Emma Lou if she knew marijuana was hidden in compartments of the fifth-wheel trailer, she squeaked out, "My goodness! No!" with the kind of horror a little girl might show when asked if she had shoved the bloody knife into the dead man's back. Emma Lou overplayed her hand, but she was cute.

If those two Klandes were hookers, they were the best-looking hookers I ever saw anywhere in the world. Officer Brademan once offered the opinion Gray and Peterson were taking their fee in trade, and were getting a bargain.

I said, "Gray told me they were getting paid strictly in cash."

Hitchens said, "Well, makes no difference. Either way the Klandes are getting screwed."

The Klandes were found guilty. That was the end of the Schaapveld case for me. I went home. But the newspapers of the Twin Cities continued to print stories about the great smuggling organization. The Scuddley story was like priming-water for the pump. From then on all the papers ran articles regularly. They interviewed some of the members of the organization. The Minneapolis DEA agents sent articles to me down in McAllen. They were trying to do me a favor, but I felt sick every time another article showed up in the mail. The reporters of the *Pioneer Press*, of the *Star*, and of the *Tribune* thought they were ever so clever when they had come up with headlines like, "TRIAL GOES TO THE DOGS," and "TALE WAGS DOG."

Articles came out on the case in the *Pioneer Press*, the *Minneapolis Star*, the *St. Paul Dispatch*, the *Minneapolis Tribune*, and also in smaller local papers. The headlines indicated what they found most intriguing: "MINNESOTA 'TOURIST' GANG FERRIES MARIJUANA NORTH," and "MINNESOTA SMUGGLERS GO BUST," and "MINNESOTA GANG BRINGS DOPE NORTH." The stories generated interest because the gang members were from Minnesota and because there were lurid stories about the torture inflicted by Mexican jailers: "MEXICAN JAILERS STRIP, BEAT, AND SHOCK CAPTIVES." Nelson told reporters how the Mexicans raped the women who were with Nelson and Stege at the time of the Cabo San Lucas arrest, how they released the women, then tortured the two men, stripped them, hung them by the wrists, doused them with water, applied the Mexican cattle prod method, beat them with sticks and wires. They forced their heads under water until they were almost drowned, placed pistols to their heads and snapped off shots on empty cylinders, and made themselves merry, while the two men were shaking with cold and fright.

Nelson said only a few of them spoke a little English, so even when he confessed everything he knew, they didn't understand what he was saying. There was no satisfying them except with money—and the two prisoners had none. After eight days of torture at Cabo San Lucas, they were transferred to the prison at La Paz. There were constant fights in the prison. Every day the Mexicans threatened to kidnap their families and hold them for ransom or some guard would point a cocked pistol at their temples and rattle along in threatening Spanish, not a word of which they understood. After a while, Nelson said, he was ready to die. When threatened with a pistol he told them to shoot. Ironically that ruined the fun for them That all but stopped the threats.

Nelson and Stege were in Mexican jail for two years. Schaapveld said he spent $120,000 trying to bust them out, including $40,000 to bribe a guard and $40,000 in lawyer fees, but nothing happened in spite of promises by the Mexicans. They got out only because of the prisoner-exchange program.

I SPENT MORE TIME on that Schaapveld case than on any other case during my career with the DEA. Darrel was probably the smartest crook I ever pursued.

None of the people in his organization had a criminal record. No phone records could be used in court. Darrell made all his calls from phone booths, then talked only code. He was brilliant in his selection of drivers, making it look like they were families on vacation, or a pair of young, clean-cut college students on spring break. On one trip a white-haired old lady and her little granddaughter were along. The drivers went through customs at the busiest port of entry at the busiest time of day. The hidden compartments were well done and were never noticed by any law enforcement officials until Scuddley came along. The strategy of leaving *Playboy* magazines scattered around inside the trailers to distract the officers was genius. Darrell had people all figured out, but he failed on the dog. He underestimated Scuddley's nose.

I later used that *Playboy*-magazine trick to smuggle guns into Belize for the DEA agents down there. It worked exactly as it had with the Schaapveld gang. The Belize Customs inspector "searching" my airplane sat on the couch of DEA's Merlin IIIB. He slowly paged through a *Playboy* magazine, asking me absent-mindedly if I had any guns on board. I said no. He left. Under the cushion on which he'd been sitting was an M-16. More guns were hidden behind the rear panel.

I got two awards for the Schaapveld case—I got zero satisfaction. I don't think Darrell was trying to hurt people by smuggling marijuana anymore than my grandpa was trying to hurt people when he was cooking moonshine in the willow thicket on the back forty. Darrell went to the University of Minnesota at a time when marijuana smoking was a college pastime. Dinkytown, the student hangout by the university, was always fragrant with the odors of cannabis. The smoking students considered themselves brave rebels, on the cutting-edge of social change. The professors considered themselves exceptionally enlightened and exquisitely cool when they smoked grass. Bob Dylan, the most famous U of M student of those days, was a pot connoisseur. Grass was everywhere in the jazz clubs, folk music clubs, and coffee houses. At the U of M marijuana was as acceptable as moonshine was in Stearns County during prohibition.

Darrell's little gang of smugglers made more headlines around the Twin Cities than mob hit men or serial rapists. Toward the end of February 1980, the *St. Paul Pioneer Press* dedicated a large part of its Sunday addition to the story and added a still longer story the next day. In the Sunday paper, the Schaapveld story shared front page with our American hockey team defeating the Soviet Union team in the "Miracle on Ice" and winning the 1980 Gold in the winter Olympics. The Schaapveld story stressed the gang members were "ordinary people, like your next-door neighbor." It was basically true. None of Darrell's gang was dangerous, except maybe Barb Klande (if the police were right). The older people in the case were simply greedy or needed money. The younger ones were looking for adventure. How is that different from most people?

I have no strange twist to add to this story. Judge Lord did that for me when he gaveled the mistrial. If Judge Larson had been on this case instead of Lord, that blunder would never have happened. Lord later became nationally famous for his rulings and his sermons in the Dalkon Shield case. He was praised by the media as a brilliant judge for his decisions. Ironically most people probably never heard of Judge Earl Larson, who was a great judge, but probably have heard of Judge Miles Lord, who in my humble opinion was not.

Chapter Eighteen

In Flanders fields the poppies blow
Between the crosses, row on row,
That mark our place; and in the sky
The larks, still bravely singing, fly . . .
~John McCrae

TO MAKE HEROIN YOU NEED poppies: *Papaver somniferum*. There are other kinds of poppies, but the somniferum ones get people high. That poppy grows into a beautiful flower, then sets seed in a nice, fat pod. Shallow cuts in the skin of that pod make it bleed a milky sap like the milkweed on farms and roadsides in Minnesota. The milk (or latex) oozes out onto the side of the pod, coagulates and turns darker. Those "opium tears," are a brownish gummy substance known as "opium gum" or "crude opium." A person can stuff this in a pipe if it's dry enough, set it on fire and smoke the hell out of it (or the heaven—some might say). I learned this from flying in Mexico with "El Professor" on Operation Trizo. We didn't smoke opium, the professor and I, but we observed it in the making.

Opium stirred into alcohol makes "tincture of opium." That is what the British called "laudanum," in the days of Sherlock Holmes. The compounds of opium gum can be separated with chemicals to produce things like codeine, papaverine, narcotine, and the best one: morphine (as any Civil War soldier would tell you). Those different compounds are called opiates. Heroin comes from the morphine opiate. Heroin, much more powerful than morphine, can be mixed with cheap powders like milk sugar or lactose and still give a buzz. It's not bulky so one can smuggle a thousand dollars worth in a watch pocket.

After the Turks quit raising poppies, many traffickers turned to Mexico—especially to the mountains of Sinaloa. Poppies grow best at higher altitudes cultivated by farmers in remote areas where law enforcement officials are not likely to come snooping around. Mexico had many such remote areas. The narcotrafficker got his best reception in the Sinaloa Mountains. There the *campesino* had a long tradition of rebellion against the government, and the Sierra Madre Occidental was still almost inaccessible. It had always been a lawless region filled with rebels, smugglers, and outlaws on the run from other parts of Mexico.

Kalashnikov AK-47 rifles were the law. That law was enforced by the big land owners, the ones who controlled the best farmland along the east coast of the Sea of Cortez (the Gulf of California). The Mexican government had been promising land reform, but never delivered. All poor people in that area despised the government. To make a living, the little *campesinos* (and a good many of the big ones) had been raising marijuana to sell to drug lords. That's where Schaapveld's marijuana came from. But now the *campesinos* were also raising poppies, and in some old barns drug lords had managed to put together labs for processing the poppies into heroin.

Most of the heroin made in Mexico when they sent me down there on Operation Trizo was "black tar" heroin. That black tar (or Mexican brown or Mexican mud) was a crude and unrefined form of heroin, but it was faster to make, and did not require the fancy lab equipment or the expensive chemicals needed to produce the pure white stuff that came out of the Golden Triangle of Southeast Asia. Mexicans weren't as fussy as Asians.

The American government complained about the poppy farms. The *campesino* did not understand the complaint. There had been a time during World War II, when the governments of both countries encouraged the growing of poppies. American soldiers needed morphine in the battlefields. Japan had taken over the poppy fields in the Far East, and Japan wasn't sharing.

Now poppies had been made illegal, but this was viewed by the Sinaloans as just another opportunity to make money. Their best smugglers were their greatest heroes. Many families had a long history of making a high living by smuggling illegal stuff into the United States. Lucrative products have always been smuggled across the border: guns, mercury, cigarettes, whiskey, and humans—to name a few. The best time came when the stupid U.S. government passed the Eighteenth amendment, prohibiting the sale of liquor in the States. Mexican *tequileros* floated rafts of booze across the Rio Grande at night and made rafts of money.

A *gomero* is a man who raises poppies. The Mexican word *goma* means gum. A *campesino* in Sinaloa who tried to follow the law made a stark living. The crops he raised were barely enough to feed his family and animals. He drove a miserable old pickup truck, which he maintained himself and often had to resort to his donkey when the truck was on the fritz. He could not have an accident or get sick because he couldn't afford medical care. But if this *campesino* became a *gomero*, suddenly he could afford a brand new truck, a doctor, medicine, and a Cuerno de Chivo (their nickname for the AK-47). The nickname means "horn of the goat" which they got from the curved, horn-like shape of the ammunition clip. A young Sinaloan farm boy wanted to become a *gomero* or maybe even a drug lord. A young Sinaloan farm girl wanted to marry a *gomero* or maybe even a drug lord.

The law forbidding the production of opium in Mexico was thoroughly and blissfully ignored in Sinaloa. The Mexican government made a few sporadic attempts in the direction of controlling the opium trade, but it was mostly for show. The poppy fields multiplied. The Mexicans stepped up their poppy eradication efforts occasionally when the American government stepped up the pressure. In the early seventies, the Mexican government started (with our money) Operation Condor to destroy the opium trade. They sent some of their soldiers and a few Mex Feds into Sinaloa to destroy poppy fields, but they were so poorly supported and so loosely monitored that corruption took over completely. Any farmer could pay a few pesos to have his fields left alone.

Then they got serious: they sent General Jose Hernandez Toledo. That general had a bloody reputation among Mexicans—a reputation he got from his participation in the infamous October 1968 student massacre in Mexico City. From that massacre he had also earned a reputation for getting results when his government wanted something done. The general, when he got the assignment to Sinaloa, predicted that in a few months the problem there would be solved. But this time the general was not dealing with a bunch of unhappy, rich students who wanted to be part of the cutting-edge protest movements of the '60s. The men of Sinaloa were a different breed. Violence didn't scare them. Gunfire was music to their ears. One night they kicked in the door of the general's hotel room and raked his bed with AK-47s. The lucky general was out walking off overindulgence in Tres-Rios enchiladas. After General Jose Hernandez Toledo had spent a few months in Sinaloa, he was ready to go home. When he left, things were pretty much the same as when he came. The general is likely dead and buried by now, the drug culture in Sinaloa is alive and well.

The U.S. government continued to complain about the Mexican heroin. In 1976 Mexico agreed to a joint operation with the United States (their "Operation Condor," our "Operation Trizo"). They allowed DEA pilots and personnel to come down to help with the destruction of poppy fields. This was hailed in the American press and by American politicians as the unselfish act of a good neighbor, but that wasn't the case. What really happened was that the new president, Lopez Portillo, recognized the great flow of American heroin money into Sinaloa was making the drug lords so rich and powerful they would soon be able to mount a credible revolution against the central government. He invited us in, not because he was nice, but because he was scared. The United States supplied Mexico with airplanes, helicopters, chemicals, and tons of money to hire pilots and spotters. Mexico hired helicopter pilots from Evergreen Aviation International in Oregon to spray the fields with herbicide. DEA Air Wing pilots flew Mexican and American spotters around to find the fields.

The reason I got sent to Sinaloa on Operation Trizo was rather complicated. The Air Wing was jealous of any flying done for DEA unless they were doing it. I had found that out on the Cleveland case with Jimmy-jet. On another Minneapolis case, we were trying to follow the crook to his source of supply. After several attempts, we were ready to give up. We didn't want to bust the crook; we wanted his source. But we couldn't follow this guy! He made repeated maneuvers to detect anyone following him, like circling the block several times, turning down alleys and doubling back, and stopping at the side of a busy highway for five minutes, then suddenly accelerating into the traffic. Agent Anderson suggested to the boss that he send me up in an airplane to follow the crook from the sky.

Braseth looked at me, "Can you do that?"

I shrugged, "Sure, but I have to have someone with me to watch the car. I have to watch for other airplanes."

Agent Jerry Kramer immediately volunteered to be the observer. That man had guts. He couldn't know what kind of a pilot I was. We went up. Lucky for me, Kramer was an excellent observer. He never lost the car. We watched as the crook did his maneuvers, while our ground surveillance hung way back out of sight. We watched him circling and doubling and parking and accelerating. It was fun. We watched the crook meet with the source. Ground surveillance closed in to photograph the meeting. Air surveillance made that case.

SAC Braseth was quick to see the benefit. This became routine. Agent Lewis had an informant who owned a Citabria, perfect for doing aerial surveillance. He had it stationed at the Anoka airport and let us rent it for ten dollars an hour. It was a little tandem two-seater. Agent Kramer sat in the back and I flew from the front. The plane was so narrow it was easy to look down on either side. It chugged along at a mere one-hundred miles an hour (top speed), but we didn't need speed for surveillance. The slower, the better. I loved that little airplane. I used to rent it myself sometimes on Saturdays just for the fun of it. It was fully aerobatic and, though not like playing with a jet, I could do aileron rolls, clover leafs, and spins with it.

One day the Air Wing called Braseth and said, "Hey, you can't be doing those surveillances. You have to use our pilots and our airplanes to do surveillance for DEA." Braseth told them to go to hell. He'd tried using them, but every time he called, they were too busy or said they couldn't make it up to Minneapolis until next week. The Air Wing sent me a form and said I was supposed to fill it out whenever I "flew on official duties." I showed it to Braseth. He said, "Shit-can it." Then they called Braseth and said if I'd fill out those forms, they'd pay for the airplane and would make me a "back up pilot." That title meant nothing for me, but it meant the Air Wing would be able to claim the arrests and seizures we made as part of their statistics.

If this seems funny, more humor is coming. Now I was a back-up pilot. After a while they called and told me I shouldn't be using the Citabria. It was too "dangerous"—that's what they said! You see, the Citabria was a "tail-dragger," which is to say its third wheel was not up at the nose like most airplanes, but back at the tail. The Air Wing supervisors didn't know much about tail draggers, so they labeled them unsafe. I asked what I should be using. They said a Cessna 206 or a 210. When I pointed out that instead of ten dollars an hour they would be paying seventy dollars an hour, they said that was fine.

It wasn't my money. From then on I rented a Cessna 210 (I like retractable gear). Now we were not only paying more, but using an airplane not nearly as handy on surveillance as the Citabria. The 210 was a four-seater, and to look down out of the right side I had to lean over and stretch my neck like a giraffe, and Kramer had to slide back and forth in the back seat.

That was my experience with the Air Wing up until Operation Trizo.

At first the regular Air Wing pilots thought Operation Trizo was a wonderful adventure, but after a while they got tired of Mexican food and of staying in second-rate hotels. They began to whine about being away from home all the time. I don't think it helped any that one of them had recently been killed when he flew into a box canyon and wasn't able to turn short enough to get out. That Air Wing pilot was Agent Jim Lunn, who had earlier flown with me on that undercover mission to Duluth. He took Agent Ralph Shaw from Calexico with him to that great Flanders Field in the sky where heavenly poppies eternally grow. I don't know what kind of investigation the Air Wing did on that accident, or what conclusions were drawn. I know if the U.S. Air Force had done the investigation, they would have ended their report with that standard, obvious and cold-blooded line: "The pilot allowed the aircraft to enter an attitude from which he was unable to recover."

DEA Air Wing supervisors drafted backup pilots to fill Trizo slots. I wanted to go, but I was up to my neck in the Schaapveld case. Braseth told headquarters I was needed in Minneapolis. But the Air Wing had more clout than Braseth. They kept reporting thousands of acres of poppy fields destroyed, which headquarters converted into tons of heroin and presented it to Congress as a measure of the success of Operation Trizo. That information converted into money for DEA, and that converted into influence for the Air Wing. Headquarters ignored Braseth and sent me down to Culiacán.

Culiacán was the capital of Sinaloa and also the capital of the opium trade. The Trizo supervisors briefed me before I went down there, telling me I was to "keep a low profile." They said the Mexican government didn't want the local people to know there were large numbers of United States law enforcement officials in their country. "We are strictly undercover down there," they told me and said I should pretend to be a tourist and not let on I was a DEA pilot. For motivation, they added that they had reports the narcotraffickers of Sinaloa had placed a twenty-five-thousand-dollar bounty, dead or alive (preferably dead) on any DEA pilot found in Sinaloa. They also reminded me I was a mere back-up pilot and should defer to the experienced Air Wing pilots when there were questions. I assured them I'd conform to those requests, since I had not a clue what was going on down there. I thought the twenty-five-thousand bounty was likely pesos and not dollars (the Air Wing was always exaggerating danger), but even so, I resolved to be as invisible as possible.

I went to Denver for some training. That was a joke. It wasn't about how to fly safely, but how to crash-land your airplane in the river and the forest. On the second day, the instructor asked me what I thought about the training. I told him he might want to spend a few minutes talking about flying safely instead of crashing safely. He said, "Good idea," and then spent the rest of the day talking about biorhythms, a pseudoscience popular at that time. He spent hours showing us how to chart our emotional, intellectual, and physical cycles, and advised us not to fly on "critical days." This was his idea of flight safety.

They gave me a Cessna 210 to fly to Culiacán. Like an American tourist, I wore a stupid straw hat, large sunglasses, and an obnoxious flowered shirt when I landed at Culiacán International. I got into a cab at the airport, and before I could give the driver directions, he said, "You desire to go to the Tres Rios. It is but a short trip."

I said, "How do you know where I want to go?"

"They all stay at the Tres Rios. You are from La DEA." (The Mexicans pronounced it "la day ah.")

I swear that cab driver knew more about Operation Condor (or Trizo) than I did. He turned sideways in his seat and spent the entire trip facing back at me and rattling on about Operation Condor. He hardly looked at the road in front of him. When he looked forward, it was mostly to glance in the rear view mirror to see if someone was following us. He told me the names of some of the Mex Feds I would be working with.

When I got to my hotel room at the Tres Rios, I began to read the local papers to see what was going on. Agent Johnny Walker lent me some he had saved from the past several days. Local reporters knew we were in Culiacán on Operation Condor, knew where we were staying, the tail numbers of our planes, and our call signs, the number of planes and helicopters—everything.

We used Condor call signs. When locals heard someone speaking to Culiacán Tower in English using a Condor call sign, they knew it was a "piloto de La DEA." I knew enough Spanish to make my calls in their language and did so, unless I had some unusual request that forced me to resort to English.

I was uneasy at first about all the warnings I'd received and all the obvious leaks I observed at Culiacán, but God was the flying great! We flew into some of the prettiest land I've seen in my life, and the Mex Fed assigned to fly with me was the best. He had been a history teacher in Mexico City. The other Mex Feds called him "El Professor." He loved Mexico, the land, the people, the culture. I couldn't have asked for a better guide to fly with in a strange country. He knew the geography almost as well as the history. And when it came to spotting poppy fields, he had the eyes of an eagle. The Professor and I recorded more poppy fields than any other team, and often we found tiny fields up in the mountains others had missed.

I should mention that, while my Mexican spotter was probably the best, my American spotter (a DEA agent) was probably the worst. He had no interest in the mission or even in seeing the country. He slept in the right seat most of the time. I told the Professor he could sit up front, but the Professor said he preferred the back seat where he could look out of both sides. So the two of us, the Professor and I, looked for poppy fields, while a DEA agent snoozed in the right seat and collected hazardous pay for doing so.

My DEA spotter was often late coming to the airport. One morning the professor says to me, "Why do we wait for this man? All he does is sleep."

"Get in," I said. And in a few minutes we were airborne. The spotter could not complain to the boss because then it would come out he was late for work and mostly slept in the airplane. Why would he complain? He could only claim hazardous pay on days he flew.

The first time I flew with the Professor, as I added power to take the runway, I saw out of the corner of my eye that he crossed himself and kissed his thumb. He did this every day for the first week he flew with me. I smiled to myself. I couldn't blame him. If I were flying in this rugged country with a strange pilot, I'd cross myself too. We flew over terrain with no place we could possibly land if the engine quit. We flew among the steep ravines and rocky gorges of the great Barranca del Cobre (Copper Canyon). Copper Canyon is more beautiful and, if you count all the different canyons together, much larger than our Grand Canyon of Arizona. In some places it's deeper. I think the main river is the Batopilas, or maybe the Urique. Both start with the melting snows high up on the Sierra Madre. The cold waters tumble down from the cracks and the crevices into the jagged ravines and gorges in hundreds of places, making very tall waterfalls. The lofty falls spray down into the canyons, misting the walls and watering the plants as they go and trimming the place with dozens of rainbows when the sun is shinning. The waters flow together and make up two big rivers that flow to the west. The rivers all join up to make the Rio Fuerte, which takes all that water and empties it into the Sea of Cortez.

The professor loved this part of the Sierra Madre and it rubbed off on me. This was the rugged country where the U.S. Army had hunted Pancho Villa for years (and failed to find him—as the Professor gleefully pointed out to me several times). The Professor had a name for every peak and valley. In a short time, I knew most all the major landmarks. He constantly pointed them out as we went along. I made notes in my notebook, and at night I studied the names and marked them on my chart. I still don't know which were official names, and which he made up. None of them were listed on my aeronautical chart except the Sierra Madre.

Because of my poor Spanish, we didn't always communicate. He said, "*El Espinazo del Diablo*," pointing to three tall peaks to the southeast of Culiacan. I thought it meant "Devil's Fork," which was fitting. But next day he said, "Los Tres Friales," (the three Friars) and seemed to be pointing at the same three peaks. I said, "Let's use one name for a landmark, or I'll get confused."

The professor had to draw me a picture on a piece of paper. He got it through my head that El Espinazo meant "the Devil's Backbone," and it referred to the entire ridge of mountains. Los Tres Friales meant "the Three Friars," and meant the three high peaks on that ridge. The Espinazo, part of the Sierra Madre, was the line of mountains that separated Sinaloa from Durango. The mountains north of that ridge, he called Sierra Tarahumara. He had Spanish names for any unusual rock projection. Soon I could find most of the mountain towns like Santa Magdelena and Choix just by the shape of the nearby mountains. And I could recognize most of the lakes and the rivers by distinctive curves the Professor pointed out.

One day our old mechanic, Wayne York, asked me if he could take the number two VOR out of my airplane because Johnny Walker was complaining his didn't work. I said, "You can take them both, for all I care, I don't use them anyway. You can have the ADF too." My bravado came from knowing the Professor never got lost. York said he wouldn't leave me without something to find my way back to Culiacán, but a few days later both VORs were gone, and the following day the ADF was missing, too. He was evidently using my plane for spare parts until the next shipment of navigation equipment came from the States.

I never had a problem finding Culiacán from the air. Three big rivers joined there. (That is where the Tres Rios Hotel got its name.) The Tamazula River came in off the mountains from the east, the Humaya down from the north. The two ran together in the town to form the Culiacán River, which went almost straight west to Navolato. If I was flying to the west of Culiacán, I simply found Navolato and followed the river east to Culiacán. I couldn't miss Navolato because the river made a very sharp bend there. To the east of Culiacán, I could easily find a big lake where the Mexicans had damned the Tamazula. I just followed the Tamazula to the west for twenty miles and voila! there was Culiacán again.

The name of that lake, by the way, was "Lake Sanalona." Often at night in the bar at the Tres Rios I heard the bragging of hunters and fishermen who came from the States to hunt and fish Lake Sanalona and the swamps west of Navolato. Happy hunters they were, totally unaware of the battles going on in Culiacán. They went out with Mexican guides in the afternoons and got drunk in the bars at night. I heard one man say, "I shot ninety mallards today and would have shot more, but I was afraid of melting the barrel of my shotgun."

We always flew mornings to avoid the stifling heat of the afternoon. The Professor was such a good spotter we could finish our assigned area in a short time and then go up into the Copper Canyon to look for the most hidden fields and go sight-seeing. One of the sights to see was man made. I thought it should have been listed as one of the Seven Wonders of the World, the railroad track that laddered its way up the Sierra Madre. A train ran out of Los Mochis in the mornings, and headed east on the tracks to the mountains where it began a most laborious climb up the steep grades.

I have to give the Mexicans credit for building those tracks. That took some real courage. Even riding that train must take guts. The tracks run so close along the edges of cliffs a passenger sitting on the canyon side at times sees nothing but an airy drop-off down into the vastness of the canyon (we're talking thousands of feet) with the Urique River boiling and foaming between boulders far below. The train starts that climb around the town of El Fuerte, which is near sea level, and, slow as a line of pack mules, it twists and turns its way up to the town of Creel, at over seven thousand feet. That's only a hundred-mile stretch to climb seven thousand feet! In places the climb is so steep it's a wonder the train doesn't slide backwards. During that climb, a train will cross dozens of bridges and go through dozens of tunnels—surely more than any train in the world.

One day, when a fierce wind was blowing down the canyon, I moved the plane in close, and by lowering half-flaps and riding the stall horn, the headwind held us to almost the same ground speed as the train. I brought the airplane over next to a passenger car and the people waved at us and we waved back. People were pointing and waving and more faces were appearing at the windows. It suddenly worried me all the people coming to one side of a car might cause a derailment on that narrow-gauge track. I dived out of the way. The Professor marveled at that slow-flight and told his comrades in the bar that night I had stopped the airplane midair. He thought this was proof I was a good pilot. I did not tell him any student could do it.

If we wanted to cool off, and had the time, we'd climb to the top of the canyon, where it was often so cold I turned on the heat. We were up at eight thousand feet. Over flat places up there we liked to fly low. One minute we could be skimming the ground with the sharp rocks only a few feet below the belly of the plane, the next the terrain plunged away from us six thousand feet, and we seemed high in the sky, looking down at the green Batopilas far below with white water falls on either side. Then a second later, wham!—we were back at low altitude on the flatland just barely missing the rocks and bushes. You could go from those bleak highlands flying in a snowstorm among stunted firs and pines with the heater on full blast, and in only minutes descend into the canyon and be flying in the lush tropics among papayas and palm trees with the heater off and the vents open to get some cooling air. God was the flying great!

Nearly every day while I was stationed at Culiacán the weather was sunny. I was there during part of the rainy season, which meant we often had quick showers, sometimes with the sun still shining. That would throw a big rainbow across the top of the canyon like a crown. We would wash the airplane by flying through the showers. Some days a light haziness dimmed the sun and made the poppy fields hard to see. On those days we flew low. But normally the Professor preferred to fly at higher altitudes. He said he could spot the fields better. He was always looking, switching sides constantly, as intent as the great Harris hawk that forever circles over those canyons. He would point down to a spot and say, "*amapola*" (poppy). If there was any doubt, we'd drop down. He made very few mistakes, but sometimes the field was cabbage and not *amapola*. Cabbage has the same glaucous-green color as the poppy.

The town of Culiacán sat in the middle of the best farmland in Mexico. That part of Sinaloa, between the mountains and the Sea of Cortez, was Mexico's breadbasket. Truck farming was the main legal industry. Sometimes we'd find a poppy field hidden among the tomatoes and cabbages, or a marijuana field among the sugar cane and corn. A marijuana field in this rich land was a beautiful thing to behold. The plants were a luscious dark green, tall as a man on horseback, and heavy with seed heads that bowed and waved in the sea-breeze like luxuriant tassels of corn. I didn't mind marking those big fields on our maps. It was a shame to spray such beautiful plants, but I knew they belonged to rich farmers or narcotraffickers who could easily afford to lose them (or could afford to bribe the Mexicans into losing the information about them).

But down in the remote valleys we often saw a *campesino* struggling behind a wooden plow pulled by an ox, or plodding along behind a rickety old cart that rolled on wheels made of rough wood. I wasn't gratified when we found a little poppy field in those areas. The Professor marked them on his map for spraying. He said, "They should be raising corn and beans." But he knew as well as I did they could make ten times the money with poppies.

And I felt downright mean when we found one of the fields of the Tarahumara Indians. In the farthest reaches of the canyons and mountains some Indians lived at that time who were part of the tribe of the Tarahumara. The Professor had no hope for their future. "They can't be civilized," he said. "The missionaries have all tried—Jesuits, Dominicans, Franciscans. All failed." But the Professor liked the Tarahumara's independent spirit and he affectionately called them "Tarahumaritos." They were very shy and usually disappeared when they saw our airplane. The first time I saw one in the open, he was standing on the very edge of the projection of a cliff that hung two thousand feet above the Urique. The wind was blowing a gale up there! His hair was fluttering behind him, his trousers flattened against his legs. He wore sandals, a wide purple belt, a headband of the same color, and had yellow ribbons tied into his hair that streamed behind in the wind. Arms crossed loosely over his bare chest, he looked skyward and ignored the airplane going by. The Professor said he was praying to the sun god, and that he might later sacrifice one of his precious goats as part of the ritual. The Professor said these men were the fastest runners in the world. I have to say, that man on the cliff did look like he could run. He was all sinewy muscle and lean as a greyhound. However, I had never heard of an Olympic race won by a Tarahumara. Well, the fact is, I'd never heard that name at all before.

The Professor said a few of the Tarahumara had moved into little mountain towns like Carichi and Chinipas. But here in the canyon they lived in caves or lonely little huts that leaned against the walls of the cliffs. We saw one woman standing in the low doorway of a pitiful hovel made of crooked branches and sticks, chinked with mud. It looked more like a beaver lodge than a human habitation. Some of them lived in long-abandoned silver mines. For food they raised corn and beans on the flat places. The professor said they lived on corn cakes and boiled beans, and feasted when a goat died. Sometimes on the grasslands we would see a girl in a brightly colored dress tending her sheep or goats. She would crouch down among her animals and watch the airplane intently as a cat. Only occasionally we saw a burro or a cow up there in the remote places. Most amazing was that some of the Tarahumara grew poppies among the cliffs and crags where no normal human could climb. Often with sheer walls around the field, it did not seem possible for a man to work his way up there, especially while carrying a hoe. Any misstep could send a man down a thousand feet onto bare rock. We found a few fields wedged so tightly between cliffs the helicopters would not go in there to spray.

The Professor was a character of contrast. He liked the Tarahumara, but he was all lawman and hated law breakers, so he marked their poppy fields like any other. He was on the one hand a dignified gentleman, but he could also be crude. When we turned final for the main runway landing south on

Culiacán's runway two-zero, he'd point out several houses belonging to rich narcotraffickers. One day as we returned from our search mission, he asked me which way we were landing. I said, "South on runway two-zero." He knelt on the back seat and peed into a plastic bag and sealed it with a rubber band. He asked me to open the window and go slow. As we went over those houses he dropped out the bag, chuckling like a naughty schoolboy.

After I was in Sinaloa a month, I got lonesome for Bea. I invited her to come down to stay with me at the Tres Rios. Bea was happy to come for it was winter in Minneapolis. Here she could lie by the pool and watch the fronds of palm trees swaying in the warm sunshine. She became friends with the army general's wife. They spent their time playing ping pong and swimming and babysitting the general's son. The other agents said they didn't have their wives come down because it was too dangerous. But there may have been a strong secondary reason: more beautiful women in Culiacán than I have seen in any city in my life—and having a wife on your arm limits your chances to flirt.

The Tres Rios Hotel was in the more peaceful northern part of Culiacán a little east of where the three big rivers joined. But it was close enough to the active central part of the city so, at night, when the noise of the traffic died, we could sometimes hear the rattle of gunfire coming from over that way. The press called Culiacán "Little Chicago," recalling the days of Al Capone. But these gun battles were not about bootlegging whiskey; they were about smuggling drugs. Rival gangs fought over possession of the crops, the heroin labs, and over the privilege of hauling the drugs to the States. Culiacán was only a day's drive from the Arizona border on Mexico's Highway 15. That border was not closely guarded. Compared to Asian heroin, Mexican brown was not only cheaper to manufacture but it was also much cheaper to smuggle. Profits were huge, Sinaloa competition mortal.

Sometimes the gunfire came from across the river to the north, which was the rich part of the town, called Tierras Blancas. A lot of the top narcotraffickers lived there. One morning the paper had pictures of a bloody corpse lying on the bridge that crossed the river into Tierras Blancas. The executioners had caught the victim in the middle of the bridge and cut him to pieces in a Kalashnikov crossfire. Next morning citizens all over town stood around holding open newspapers and discussing the night's events. On Culiacán street corners, in early morning light, one could always see men reading "*la nota roja*" (the red news), the latest crime news, so named because of all the blood splattered over the front pages (the blood was black, though—not in color). The "red newspapers" were like our *National Police Gazette* only bloodier. They had a much livelier variety to choose from. The narcotraffickers read the morning paper to see if any of their competition had been eliminated. The rest of the town read to see if any of their relatives had survived the night.

All over town one could see the cowboy drug culture. The narcotraffickers wore cowboy hats and heeled boots. They wore tight blue jeans and decorated leather belts with big buckles stamped with pictures of marijuana leaves or poppy pods, and they had those same pictures hand-embroidered on their cowboy shirts. They drove big late-model pickup trucks, ate at the most expensive restaurants. At night they went to the best nightclubs where they drank Cerveza Pacífico from Mazatlán and danced polkas to music romanticizing drug smuggling and drug killings. Groups of these young studs hung around together, proud, loud and aggressive. Rafael Caro Quintero, who later gained notoriety in Guadalajara for his hand in killing DEA Agent Camarena was a leading man in one of those groups.

The traffickers were all Catholic. They wore golden crucifixes on neck chains hanging next to silver coke spoons. They donated heavily to the Church, and one could see the money in the huge stained glass windows and the statues of gold and silver, could hear it in the very sound of the church bells—not that rusty-iron clang of poverty heard in other towns, but the rich ring of bronze and silver. The men did not go to church except for baptism, matrimony, and requiem, but their women went every Sunday, and prayed for the success of their narco men. The padre ceremoniously blessed the narcotrafficker trucks and did not mention *la nota roja* in his sermon.

The traffickers had their own "patron saint," though his canonization in Rome or even his beatification was not imminent—and is likely to remain so. Images of him dangled from medals on the chests of young men in Culiacán. On the west side of town near the railroad tracks was a little shrine to this saint. Wilted flowers lay there, and faded pictures of the Virgin of Guadalupe, a very bloody and slashed image of the crucified Christ, and a little white plaster statue of the man. Someone had painted the man's little mustache black and put a black knit scarf around his neck. This was Jesus Malverde, patron saint of narcotraffickers and banditos of any kind, anywhere. The saint had ridden his horse through the hills near Culiacán in the late 1800s. As with all good outlaws since Robin Hood, he robbed the rich and bestowed the booty on the poor, and irritated the government. The government hung him near this shrine in 1909.

"An insignificant outlaw," the Professor said.

"Well, then why do these people admire him so?" I asked.

The Professor's quick return: "Why do your people admire Billy the Kid and Jesse James?"

It was said the police had, for many days, left the body of Jesus Malverde swinging on the tree where they hung him—a redolent reminder to men of similar ambition. People say for the next ten years beautiful flowers, never seen before, grew around that tree, and miraculous healings have taken place at the shrine. They have a big party there every year to celebrate this holy man. When the government wanted to build offices on the site of the shrine, opposition was so fierce the building was delayed a long time. A compromise was reached when the officials agreed to provide land nearby for the shrine. They say all of Culiacán turned out to see the demolition of the rock pile supposed to mark Malverde's grave. When the bulldozer drew near, the rocks moved around, shivered and shook and made echoing sounds like the gnashing of teeth from the depths of hell. The bulldozer driver lost his nerve and had to get very drunk before he had the courage to continue.

Many businesses in downtown Culiacán were decorated with spray paint, looking like the sides of 1960s hippie-converted school buses. They had pictures of marijuana plants, poppies, roaches, and pipes. Street venders filled the air with the aroma of tacos, chili *rellenos*, and quesadillas. They sold chorizo, hunks of goat cheese, and roasted corn on the cob. One could buy a taco for twenty cents or for twenty dollars (the latter included a little packet of cocaine). They sold candy and ice-cream—and information about where to go to make arrangements for drug deliveries north of the border.

Among all these signs of adoration of the drug culture, the government posted its own signs nailed to telephone posts, street lights, and bulletin boards, and pasted in store windows and on the sides of empty houses. The government sign was in Spanish. Near the top was a colored picture of a poppy plant and some marijuana plants framing the face of a skeleton. A large headline read: *CAMPESINO: NO SIEMBRES AMAPOLA Y MARIHUANA.* (Farmer: don't plant poppy and marijuana). It went on to say: "Besides being a crime punishable by jail and by the loss of your land, it destroys your home and your family. By planting narcotics you are planting the death of women, men, and children." The signs also told the *campesino* to see the authorities, who would help them in the planting of corn, beans, safflower, and other products that Mexico needed. A line in larger letters said, "The government wants to help you!" At the bottom was a picture of two hands joined in front of a cornfield, and an exhortation: "Together we will make a better fatherland." It was signed: Secretary of National Defense. A very nice sign indeed, but also very much ineffective in Sinaloa. No *campesino* in that area believed what it said. No *campesino* trusted the government.

The citizens of Culiacán were proud of their Mexican heritage and did not think much of Americans, but they had one concession to Americanization: *Pollo Frito de Kentucky*. Yes, they had a Kentucky Fried Chicken place in their town, and it was always busy. After we ate the food at the Tres Rios for a few weeks, though it was excellent Mexican fare, that good old American Kentucky chicken was a feast for an emperor. One evening Bea and I were driving to the Kentucky Fried Chicken place. We stopped behind a truck at a stop sign. The truck pulled out onto the highway, and this insulted the occupants of an oncoming car. The car was fresh out of the showroom, all shiny and new, with windows blacked out—the kind the traffickers liked to drive. The driver blasted an angry horn, and as the car came alongside the truck, the windows opened and shouts were exchanged. The cowboy riding shotgun stuck a Colt .45 automatic out the window and worked the slide to jack a shell into the chamber. The truck pulled onto the shoulder, and the car sped on its merry way with the .45 waving goodbye. I did not follow them. I wasn't curious to find out who was directing traffic in Culiacán.

Another day Bea and I went to the airport to make arrangements for her return to the States. An Evergreen man had his little yellow VW parked there. I noticed three large-caliber bullet holes in the back. Bea said, "There're more holes in the windshield." Six holes in all. I talked to the Evergreen man. He said he'd gone into town to get some Kentucky Fried Chicken the night before.On his return, as he was entering a traffic circle, he almost hit a little Mexican jay walker. The man pulled an automatic pistol and put three bullet holes into the back of the car, and then, as the car came around to make the turn off the circle, the little guy was waiting there and emptied his gun into the front. The man from Evergreen wasn't curious either. He didn't stop to get acquainted. He drove back to the Tres Rios and ate the chicken in his room.

There was one matter the Professor and I never resolved between us. It was about the *mordida* (the bite), which was the Mexican name for a bribe. Agent Tom Gomez had told me Mexican officials routinely took bribes, especially at border crossings. So I asked the Professor. I was surprised when he admitted he would take a bribe whenever he needed the money (if the bribe was presented in proper privacy). I told him I'd never taken a bribe, nor did I believe any of the agents I worked with in Minneapolis had. He smiled at this.

"We take bribes, you take bribes," he said. "We admit it, you don't. Which is the more honest?"

The *mordida* was a supplement to an official's regular income. It was a tradition. The Spanish started it hundreds of years ago. The Professor pointed out that the Spanish Officers running the Mexican silver mines long ago had stolen a fifth of the profits. They considered it part of their pay. Even those who became enormously rich doing it were not considered dishonest—just smart. Nothing had changed. Some of the top law enforcement officials sent from Mexico City to Sinaloa during Operation Condor became extravagantly rich. They had plenty of opportunities to collect the *mordida*. But in Sinaloa there were also plenty of opportunities for officials to die when they got too greedy. And many did.

AFTER THREE MONTHS the Air Wing told me to go home. They said the boss needed me in Minneapolis for the Schaapveld case. Only a few more months later Trizo was shut down. That operation was hailed as a great success and a stellar example of cooperation between the two countries. DEA's history still has it that way. For a moment it did look like a partial success. In Minneapolis I could see a little difference. The price of Mexican heroin went up even as the quality went down—a sure sign the source had been hurt. But, as is always the case, other sources were quickly available. The price of heroin went down again.

It's difficult to overstate the adverse effects of Operation Condor/Trizo, and you'll never see DEA officials attempting it. Mexican federales and Mexican army troops made thousands of arrests. But they didn't arrest the big drug lords who had the money to pay the *mordida*. They arrested *campesinos*, *gomeros*, manufacturers. Hatred for the Mexican government increased. Contempt for Americans increased. Operation Condor will always be remembered in Sinaloa as the time when the Mexican government cooperated with the United States government to drive thousands of small farmers out of business. Many of the drug lords, who had funded schools, clinics, and churches in the little Sierra Madre towns, left. They moved to Guadalajara. The government did not fill that void in helping the poor.

Law-abiding farmers didn't escape those times unscathed. In the days of Condor, we didn't have GPS to mark the fields for spraying. We put an X on a map and the chopper pilot sprayed. An X on a map could easily be misread. Fields were sprayed that were as innocent as a strawberry garden by a convent in Rome. On windy days spray-drift killed rows of potatoes and carrots that grew too close to poppy and marijuana.

The Sinaloan drug lords that fled Culiacán for Guadalajara became even more powerful in Mexico. Officials in Jalisco were no more honest then those sent to Sinaloa. And those drug lords connected with drug lords of Colombia. Mexico became a shipping lane for Colombian drugs. The Colombians raised enormous fields of marijuana to make up for the restrictions in Mexico. They also began to cultivate poppy fields in the Andes Mountains. As drug users in the United States used more cocaine, violence in both countries escalated. Innocent people often died in the crossfire. One of the Culiacán drug lords who moved to Guadalajara was Rafael Caro Quintero. He became powerful enough to order the killing of a DEA agent there.

Operation Condor/Trizo had an adverse effect in the United States too. President Jimmy Carter went into cardiac arrest when he learned that all the spraying in Mexico was contaminating the marijuana crop. The source of this information was Jimmy's White House drug advisor, a British con man and bureaucrat extraordinaire named Peter Bourne. Peter's information came from that always reliable and unbiased source: The National Organization for the Reform of Marijuana Laws (NORML). Peter had an attitude about drugs generally characterized in those days as "mature" and "realistic." He and several of Jimmy's White House staffers liked to smoke grass to relieve themselves of the stresses of their tremendous responsibilities, and at times the product they smoked came from Sinaloa. NORML said that some poor pothead might get sick from bad grass. This made Peter (and Jimmy) anxious.

In the spring of 1978 NORML filed suit against DEA and Evergreen and the State Department, and anybody else they could think of. The indictment said we were spraying Paraquat in Mexico and some of the sprayed marijuana was reaching the market in the United States. On that point, I'm sure they were right—and I can add: not just some, a lot. When a marijuana field was sprayed in Sinaloa, the farmers didn't roll over and play dead. When they saw their plants drooping from the spray they quickly harvested. They shipped it to the States via their normal channels. They weren't stupid. They did not stamp it: "Warning: sprayed with Paraquat" on the bales.

We were supposed to be using 2,4-D to spray. It was more specific and didn't lay waste to everything in sight like Paraquat did. I do think the choppers had 2,4-D on board most days when they were after poppy. The problem was that often when we checked the fields sprayed with 2,4-D, we had to mark them for re-spraying. If a plant did not get a good dose, it would droop for a few days and then recover. Our government shipped us 2,4-D, but the Mexicans had plenty of money (our money) with which to buy all the Paraquat they desired. They had long been using Paraquat, and they considered it more effective. Which it was. Paraquat kills green plant tissue on contact, kills faster than 2,4-D and it is more rain resistant. The Mexicans didn't worry about the fact it was non-selective (killed the tomatoes, too) and might be toxic to humans and animals. The Mexicans didn't understand how the American Government could be concerned about making a pothead sick when it was robbing him of his source of supply, and was also putting him in jail.

And don't try to tell a Mex Fed that, before spraying, one must do an environmental impact study.

Anyway, the word got around. American potheads read headlines about NORML's lawsuit, and sales of Mexican grass dropped like a stone. Even the golden stuff from Oaxaca was out of favor. But of course our potheads didn't quit smoking. They turned to Colombia and then the Colombian Gold pot was considered the best in the world.

All these were results of our wonderful Operation Trizo. Let us bury Operation Trizo at this point with this engraving on the stone: "Trizo is dead. The Drug Culture in Sinaloa is alive and well." During my career with the DEA, almost every Mexican drug lord, including those powerful kings who gained their fame in Jalisco and even a few in Colombia, came out of Sinaloa. A new one is born every day in those rugged mountains of the Sierra Occidental.

Chapter Nineteen

> "The government of my country snubs honest simplicity, but fondles artistic villainy, and I think I might have developed into a very capable pickpocket if I had remained in the public service a year or two."
>
> ~Mark Twain

SNIDE REMARKS ABOUT BUREAUCRATS and bureaucracies have crept into this narrative. You don't know what a bureaucracy is. You think you know, but you don't. And when I'm done telling you, you still won't know, because you won't believe me. You'll refuse to believe that your fellow man can be this insane. Certainly if you're a Stearns County farmer, you have no idea. But then, that's irrelevant, because if you were a Stearns County farmer, you wouldn't be wasting your time reading this. You would be out with your cows, and cows don't form bureaucracies.

Don't think I'm pretending to understand bureaucracy. I can only tell you how one works. Nor is it something one should strive to understand, for that striving gives one indigestion, diminishes one's sense of humor, destroys one's faith in humanity, and may cause one at times to contemplate suicide. Nor am I trying to give the impression DEA was worse than the other federal agencies. Not at all. DEA was still young and hadn't yet had the time to load headquarters with the required amount of stifling bureaucrats who would rank it up there with agencies like Customs, OSHA, the FBI, and the State Department. But we were well on our way.

I was lucky to learn early on about bureaucracy. One night I stopped at the Spaghetti Emporium where Jim Braseth, Dick Fekete, and George Bent sat drinking beer and playing liar's poker with ten dollar bills. Bent was the head of Minneapolis Narcotics and had much experience trying to work with government agencies. I drank a few rounds with them, while suffocating on the exhaust from Fekete's cigar. I didn't play liars poker with those sharks; they were too fast for me, and ten dollars was a lot of money back then. Braseth had seen my frustration with the Air Wing when they told me not to fly a Citabria on surveillance and when they said a V-tail Bonanza was too dangerous to fly. He saw how upset I got with the help headquarters gave me on the Cleveland case. So he took some time to instruct me, with the help of Fekete and Bent, on the workings of the DEA bureaucracy. I went home that night thinking those three jaded and cynical, but I was still an innocent farm boy from Stearns County. I soon found out what they had told me was the unvarnished truth. It was a profound insight and for me a great liberation from the frustrations of laboring under bureaucratic supervision.

Those who work in a bureaucracy must expect some astonishing abnormalities, otherwise they'll be confused and unhappy all the time. Over the years, I made a list of some of the peculiarities that occur in a bureaucracy. This list is important because it gives a hint of how it is our government can spend so much of our tax money with so little result, can make so many laws that do so little good, and can be constantly making "new" arrangements that keep everything the same.

Here is my bureaucracy list:

- People who can't make decisions are eventually put in charge.
- More power brings less responsibility.
- The effectiveness of an operation is not judged by its results.
- The fastest road to further funding is failure.
- Spending money is encouraged, saving is not.
- A petition to do anything new is regarded with distrust and the petitioner is seen as a rebel.
- Any petition moves up the chain of command with the speed of shifting continents.
- How much one works isn't as important as how much one brags about it.
- Appearing to be wise or honest is more important than *being* wise or honest.
- A busy person is viewed with suspicion; *appearing* to be busy is much preferred.
- Common sense, though lacking, is always invoked in explaining policies.
- Rules are so poorly written they often encourage the very activity they were meant to limit (this may be accidental or on purpose).
- Contrary to the aphorism that two heads are better than one, the combined stupidity of the group exceeds that of any individual in the group. Thus the quality of any work is inversely proportional to the number of heads working on it.

Those are the complications of a bureaucracy. The individual bureaucrat is much more simple. He has one overwhelming trait: selfishness—which we can easily see in the following unique "qualities" of a bureaucrat:

- Is remarkably skillful in his ability to take credit for the achievements of others.
- Claims talents he doesn't have, while failing to recognize talents subordinates do have.
- Always prefers a fawning slacker to a rebel worker.
- Has no opinion of his own but will fiercely defend the opinion of the majority, or of his supervisor (as soon as he is sure what that is).
- Is brilliant in maneuvering himself into a position of leadership, but has no talent in that area.
- Is a genius in painting failure as success.

Bureaucrats are often extremely clever. The news media usually mistakes this cleverness for intelligence (which is like mistaking Hitler for Einstein). By this cleverness many bureaucrats gain political office. When this type of individual becomes a majority, his organization—if you can call it that—has become a hopeless bureaucracy (that's redundant—sorry). The reason private companies can't survive when they're run by bureaucrats is because they don't have the power to tax the public. All bureaucracies eventually collapse unless the public keeps giving them money.

Bureaucracies have one main illness: the people who make the plans are isolated from the people who have to carry them out. Big decisions aren't made by the man out in the field, but by a man sitting on a soft cushion behind an expensive desk in a big office. And the cushion-man makes those decisions, not based on what's happening out in the field, but on his *guess* of what's happening, and that guess is based on faulty information. The information comes from the bootlicking slackers in the field who tell him what he wants to hear. The agent actually doing the work has neither the time nor the respect for the cushion-man to call him with information. And if he does call, it's to tell the cushion-man how screwed up his operation is. He's therefore labeled a "bitcher," and his reports are summarily dismissed, while those of the fawning lackey are received as gospel. And if the cushion-man should, by some accident, receive correct information, he'll still make decisions based, not on logic and reason, but on politics and convenience.

Any operation that appears to be failing is given more money. No bureaucrat will ever say, "Gentlemen, this plan of mine is a mistake." The plan is always fine. It just needs more money. A success, no matter how small, is an indication of the importance of the operation; a failure, no matter how large, is an indication more money is needed. The operation grows and grows. More agents are shifted into the operation. More supervisory positions are created to direct field agents. Each supervisor clamors constantly for more money and more people. The bureaucracy grows and grows.

Bureaucracies are not planned. They somehow grow of their own accord. Even if you assembled the best comedians in the world, they wouldn't come up with anything like this. And the bureaucracy always develops into a good-old-boy club that recruits buddies rather than qualified people. The purpose for which it was originally formed is hindered by the very members supposed to carry out that purpose. "Safe employees" are favored. A safe employee doesn't come up with new ideas, make decisions on his own, or try to head off a problem that might occur in the future. He likes things just as they are. He toes the party line. He knows the bureaucracy doesn't want good work. It wants conformists.

There. That's a short introduction to bureaucracies—"Bureaucracy 101," you might say. All this will appear a fantasy sketch to the average civilian, but those who have had the pleasure and honor of working for the federal government or one of the similar state governments will recognize the truth of it. I put it here to keep readers from being astonished by the things recorded in this book. If you find yourself at some point in your reading thinking, "Wait, this can't be," or "He must be mistaken," read this introduction again. It is only a few paragraphs.

NOW, AS A VERY PLEASANT DIVERSION and a most stimulating mental exercise, we'll consider how the DEA bureaucracy used its dazzling wisdom to guide the course of my career as a special agent. Back when I went to DEA Basic Agent School, they gave us a class in "Career Management." There we were instructed on how to get the assignments we wanted. They said whenever an opening occurred, it was advertised in every DEA office in the world for several weeks to give people time to apply. Anyone could apply, but when the time was up, the announcement was closed—no more could apply. Then the selection was made from those who applied. The best qualified was always chosen. Selections were made strictly upon merit. For foreign assignments, knowledge of the language of the country was given first priority. The whole system was based on "fairness." They sprinkled the words "equitable," "fair," "and unbiased" over the class like holy water from the aspergillum at Sunday High Mass.

I can't say how wonderful this all sounded to me at the time. I had always been a hard worker and was sure I could compete with anyone. I still wanted to travel, and it appeared I had several sure options open to me. I wanted an assignment to Germany. I could speak German and I knew in DEA there were very few who could speak that language. I wanted to get back into flying, and I knew I was better qualified than most of the pilots already in the Air Wing. My career was made. I could have wept for joy, thinking how I was working for an organization of this caliber.

The school had given us this party line: what counts was not who you know, but what you know. I heard that slogan repeated over and over by DEA supervisors across the country. However, the street agents had another slogan: "It's not what you know, but who you blow." When I first heard it, I thought it crude and cynical. It took me a while, but I found the school party line was a sly deception, and the street line a penetrating truth. I found this out by putting in for assignments.

At first I put in for assignments with the warm, fuzzy feeling I might actually be selected for any one of them. But the older street agents told me, "You have to have a rabbi to get what you want in DEA." A rabbi was a hook at headquarters. I thought that also rather cynical. I stubbornly held the belief the party line slogan must be correct.

An opening occurred in Mazatlán, Mexico. I put in for that immediately, thinking I'd be working with Mex Feds like the Professor, and that Bea could lie on the beach in winter instead of huddle by the fire. On the day the announcement was closed, I called the secretary in Washington. She said only three people had applied, and I was the only one who could speak Spanish. She thought I'd surely get the assignment.

A few weeks later, another announcement for a position in Mazatlán appeared on the bulletin board. I called the secretary to see if I should put in for that assignment too, or if they'd use my old application for both slots.

She said, "Oh, this isn't a new slot. They're advertising the same position again. Agent Jose Marin forgot to put in his application."

I said, "I thought the announcement was closed once the time ran out."

She said, "Yes, that's the way it is supposed to work."

I asked, "Well, do I put in another application?"

"If you want to be considered, yes, but I doubt it'll do any good. I think Agent Marin will get the assignment."

"How can that be?"

"I'm just the secretary."

I put in. Agent Marin was selected. Later when I was TDY to Mazatlán on the Schaapveld case, I asked for Agent Marin. They said he was no longer there. He'd changed his mind. He didn't like that assignment.

An opening occurred in Germany. I applied. At that time I actually did have a rabbi in Washington—President Ford's scheduling secretary. It was that summer when I was going to the State Department's Spanish school. President Ford's secretary told me, "If you want any of the announced positions, give me a call."

I said, "How can you help?"

He said, "All I have to do is mention to the DEA administrator that President Ford would like to see you get that position, and it'll be done. Guaranteed. No questions asked. Just give me the call."

"It's really that easy?"

"All you have to do is pull the string."

I never pulled that string. I thought it unethical. I was such a baby agent. I didn't know morality was weakness, that honesty was foolishness, that virtue was childish. I believed the selection process must be fair. I could only pull that string if everyone else had the same string to pull. Another agent got the Germany assignment. He spoke no German, but they sent him to the State Department's German School, a three month course. At the end of the three months he still couldn't speak German. They sent him for another three months. He was still weak, but DEA sent him anyway.

Next I put in for Curaçao (one of the Dutch Antilles islands in the southern Caribbean). Agent Anderson looked over my shoulder and said, "Don't put down that you can't speak Dutch. Agent Rieff put down on his application that he speaks Dutch, and he doesn't know Dutch from Greek. At least you speak German. That's close enough."

I said, "I'm not going to sign my name to a lie."

"You have to exaggerate your qualifications on those things. Everybody does."

"Won't they test me in Dutch? I'd be in real trouble."

"Naw, they won't test you, and if they do, you simply say you don't want the assignment anymore. And don't worry about the language. All these foreigners speak enough English so you can get by."

Curaçao was a plush assignment. I had no chance from the start.

But now came an opening for a pilot in Bogotá. This was perfect for me. The advertisement said the applicant had to be an experienced pilot and had to speak Spanish. I knew only a few Air Wing pilots who could speak Spanish, and they did not apply. The secretary in Washington said, "You're the only applicant who's both a pilot and can speak Spanish. I don't see how they can pass you by."

They did pass me by, and here's how: Agent Ashton, Air Wing pilot, applied. He couldn't speak a word of Spanish, but he was an Air Wing pet. They canceled the position, sent Ashton to Spanish school for several months, re-advertised the position and chose him.

Even my induction into the Air Wing did not come about because someone at headquarters had a sudden epiphany about my qualifications. The Air Wing didn't like the fact they had to go through headquarters to send me to Mexico for Trizo. Braseth was still my primary boss, while I was only a back-up pilot, and Braseth didn't let them use me as they liked. So they made me a full-time, official Air Wing pilot. To do that, they had to advertise a new position for a pilot in Minneapolis. The Air Wing said I should put in for the assignment, and I'd be chosen. I would have the same office, same desk, same home. I wouldn't have to move. The only difference would be that my boss would be the Air Wing instead of Braseth. Braseth didn't resist this because it would mean Minneapolis would have an airplane stationed there. This time the assignment was a sure thing for me.

But whoa! Not so fast! Agent Leonard wanted that Minneapolis assignment. Agent Leonard was another Air Wing good ol' boy. He said his father was sick and he needed to be in Minneapolis to nurse him. (By coincidence the father had become ill just when the Minneapolis position opened.) Agent Leonard, who had less flying time and fewer ratings than I did and who had to be moved along with his wife and family, got the Minneapolis assignment. I never blamed Agent Leonard for this. In fact I admired how he was able to manipulate the bureaucracy. Why should he not take advantage? Agent Leonard's favorite saying, "The squeaky wheel gets the grease," showed his understanding of bureaucrats. And why should the bureaucracy not approve Agent Leonard's request? To save tax money? Don't be silly.

But now the Air Wing had to give me a pilot position somewhere. I was a DEA pilot, with no slot. They couldn't justify two pilots at Minneapolis. An opening for a pilot occurred in McAllen, Texas. The Air Wing said that would be my assignment. Putting in was a mere formality. They said to get ready to move. Bea and I were delighted when we looked into this. The winters were not cold down there. No more snow. Palm trees instead of pine trees. Bea could go shopping across the border and enjoy the beaches of Padre Island. We began packing our stuff.

Wait a minute. Hold the phone! Air Wing pilot Agent Jarrell wanted that assignment. Agent Jarrell had been in the Air Wing since it started—the ultimate good ol' boy. The Air Wing said they'd send me to Calexico where Maxi was stationed, and move Maxi and family to McAllen. I was now on my way to Calexico. Bea and I switched gears. We were still delighted. Calexico was not as lush a place and not near the beach, but still it was warm, and it was someplace new. Bea drew up our route on a map. We'd travel down through Denver and Colorado Springs where I had Air Force friends, and we'd go through Las Vegas where Bea's sister lived.

Surprise! Never mind. Maxi changed his mind. He wanted to stay in Calexico. I put in for McAllen again. And that's how I got my assignment. That's how I got a great DEA post. Nothing to do with fairness, nothing to do with merit—just stumbling, bumbling bureaucracy at work.

My assignment was in Hidalgo County, which had a lot of drug action. And it was right next to Starr County where more drug deals occurred per capita than anywhere in the world. It was in south Texas where the flying weather was great and near the Rio Grande where the smuggling was constant.

And now you know how the selection process worked in DEA. I assure you, not a bit of this has been overdrawn. In fact, I can't think how I could amplify what really happened. You may find all this entertaining. It wasn't entertaining for me at the time. I suppose it can be viewed as entertainment, as having a tooth pulled could be entertainment when considered from the perspective of the dentist. I can laugh about it now. It wasn't funny then. If you find yourself not believing some of this, refer to the first paragraphs of this chapter: Bureaucracy 101.

Now let us consider another favorite school mantra: "work hard, make cases, and you get promoted." DEA supervisors echoed this with: "Work really hard, make big cases," and they added: "keep your nose clean." Keeping your nose clean meant not getting into fights in bars at night, not losing your gun or badge, and (this one they didn't mention) sucking up to the supervisor. Again the street agents had a counter-slogan: "Big cases—big problems; little cases—little problems; no cases—no problems." The fact was if you didn't work hard, made a little case once in a while, and didn't bother to keep your nose clean, you did just as well. The DEA system promoted mediocrity and coddled the slacker. The three main ways it did this were these: the difficulty of firing someone, the performance grading system, and the overtime pay system.

The first way the system promoted mediocrity was the difficulty of firing someone. This was the trump card for the slacker. A supervisor had to spend hours and hours writing reports over long periods of time to get an agent fired. He had to have meetings with the boss, and the boss had to write more reports. And if they finally were successful in firing someone, they opened themselves up to the wrath of the United States Equal Employment Opportunity Commission (the EEO). Let me quote from the EEO manual: *If you are a federal employee or job applicant, the law protects you from discrimination because of your race, color, religion, sex (including pregnancy), national origin, age (40 or older), disability or genetic information. The law also protects you from retaliation if you oppose employment discrimination, file a complaint of discrimination, or participate in the EEO complaint process (even if the complaint is not yours).*

Now, even the dullest attorney will find in that quote a reason why even the most egregious slacker should not be fired. When a conscientious boss did manage to fire a slacker, the poor victim was always re-instated after a few months—with back pay (and chuckling about his nice vacation).

The second way DEA promoted mediocrity was by the performance grading system. This worked in the slacker's favor because of the laziness of supervisors. Performance reports had to be filled out by a supervisor for each agent in his group. To give a high grade, the supervisor had to write an essay justifying the grade. To give a low grade, same thing. But to give an average grade, he merely checked off a few squares and signed his name. So what do you think happened? Everyone was average! The shame of it was that in each group usually two or three agents were hard workers and made the cases. They should consistently have been graded high. Then two or three were always ready to help with surveillance and with writing the reports. They should have been graded average. Another two or three helped only when you kicked their ass. Those should have been graded below average. And finally, each group had two or three who did no work whatever. They should have been fired.

Ironically if one of those slackers put in for a position in another office, the boss would enthusiastically support him and would brag to the receiving office about what a great agent they'd be getting. If the agent got the position, his former boss had just "kicked him upstairs" and was proud of it. The real agents described this process as "fuck up, cover up, move up." The sad thing is the slacker frequently got kicked up all the way to headquarters, where his laziness made trouble for the worker agents in the field.

The third way the system promoted mediocrity was the overtime-pay system. This was frosting on the slacker's cake. DEA agents worked nights and weekends a lot. We sometimes did surveillance all through the night, all next day and the next night, catching a few minutes of sleep here and there while one man kept watch. For this overtime we got paid an extra twenty-five percent of our base pay. The system had at one time been set up so each agent had to keep track of his time, and the government paid him for overtime hours. But agents worked overtime so consistently, and often claimed more overtime than regular hours, that the government made a deal: we'd get paid an automatic twenty-five percent extra, if we would forego compensation for any overtime above that. So now an agent got the same pay if he worked fifty hours overtime or one hundred.

Every DEA agent was happy with this. The real workers agreed to it, because they hated filling out all that paperwork. They were too busy with their cases. The supervisors were delighted because they didn't have to check the paperwork. And the slackers! Oh, my, what a blessing! They could now sit at home and watch *Hee Haw* on TV, knowing they were getting paid the same as those simpleton fellow agents who were out working a case.

DEA agents could also receive another kind of pay. We called it "Haz Pay." The bureaucrats called it "Hazardous Duty Pay Differential." I received tens of thousands of dollars of tax money in the form of Haz Pay during my career as an Air Wing pilot. And I feel guilty about that (not enough to return the money, but I apologize). The rules for receiving this Haz Pay were defined under *Hazardous Duty Pay Entitlement of the DEA Personnel Manual, chapter 2550.61.A.-J., 255.63.D., and appendix 255.B.* I'm not trying to be funny. That is an exact quote from our manual, and you can smell the awful bureaucrat in it. The rules were written by two types of bureaucrats: those who had a vested interest (they could receive Haz Pay), and those who knew nothing about flying an airplane (they could be led into believing anything about flying was hazardous). As a result I got hazardous pay for things not at all hazardous.

You might say, "Well, then why did you claim it?"

Good question. If I didn't claim it, I was depriving anyone flying with me of Haz Pay—they got the same pay. And here was the real beauty of the way it was written: if we did something considered hazardous for as little as ten minutes, we got Haz Pay for our entire day! So if we worked ten hours that day, the manual said we were entitled to ten hours of hazardous pay even if only ten minutes of our work qualified. Furthermore, the manual was so poorly written it could be (and most certainly was) interpreted so that non-hazardous things still qualified. I quote from the manual, chapter 2550.6 section D: *Hazardous duty is work performed under circumstances in which an accident could result in serious injury or death.* Well, almost all the work we performed could result in an accident: cleaning your gun, driving a car, flying an airplane, or walking down the street. And most any accident could result in serious injury, could it not?

But no one ever claimed Haz Pay for cleaning his gun. No supervisor would approve it. Ironically several agents did get seriously injured doing just that (they neglected to take out the bullets). On the other hand, we all claimed Haz Pay for work that never injured anyone, but which the manual said was dangerous. In a later section of the same manual it gave specific examples "to clarify the conditions under which a pilot could claim hazardous duty pay." It said we could claim it if we flew less than 500 feet above the ground "where no suitable landing site exists." But a suitable landing site for one pilot might be fifty feet of plowed field, whereas another pilot might need several thousand feet of smooth concrete to make a safe landing. Under that rule a bungling, incompetent pilot qualified in situations where a skilled pilot did not. Again the slacker was favored.

DEA had a similar situation about working undercover. They never gave me Haz Pay for negotiating a gun deal in Minneapolis with Bill Cooper, who was once on the FBI's most-wanted list and was considered "armed and dangerous." But they did give me Haz Pay for flying undercover with a two-bit crook on board the aircraft. Was that more dangerous? Is the crook going to shoot me and then try to land the airplane by himself? Making an undercover buy in the airplane was much safer than making it in a car. DEA history proved that. But again I took the money—your money.

There are more examples, but enough. You get the idea. Oh, wait, one more. We could also claim Haz Pay if we flew slow (some Air Wing pilots called Haz Pay "low-and-slow" pay). The manual defined "slow" like this: "a velocity of less than 1.2 Vso (stalling speed in landing configuration)." It did not specify the loading of the airplane, so we all claimed Haz Pay when we flew those slow circles on surveillance with one spotter in the airplane no matter how skinny or fat he was. That was not dangerous! Ask any pilot (not a DEA pilot). I would have felt less guilty to get Haz Pay for flying with some of the incompetent pilots the Air Wing forced me to fly with, and some of them should have been getting Haz Pay anytime they flew an airplane alone.

DEA also passed out awards. They gave me some from time to time—large posters or wooden plaques with grand titles in colorful letters: Sustained Superior Performance, and Excellence of Performance, and Exceptional Performance. The only ones I treasured were the ones with money attached. The awards program, although it didn't necessarily favor the slacker, certainly did not cut him out. The supervisor put you in for the award. A supervisor's pet was just as likely to receive an award as the agent who did the work. The people who made the final decisions were desk jockeys who knew little about what was happening in the field and had no idea of who deserved an award or who deserved a kick in the pants. One year they gave Agent McCullough and me the Administrator's Award for flying a Merlin III B out of a jungle strip in eastern Bolivia. It was supposed that we had done something heroic, because the plane had been damaged (and fixed) and the strip wasn't like the main runway at La Guardia. It was embarrassing for me to get that award because I knew of two other agents who actually had done heroic things in the line of duty that year but were passed over because the number of awards was limited. They gave me $2,000 for being a "hero." The ironic part was I had just spent a month flying out of a much more dangerous jungle strip in central Bolivia. I would have been less embarrassed to receive the Administrator's Award for any one of the takeoffs and landings I made at that strip. We probably wouldn't have received the award had not Agent McCullough been a good friend of the supervisor who put us in for it. I should have split my part of the money with Agent McCullough.

Now, in this last case I do feel guilty enough to actually return the money to the government. I require only that the Attorney General send me a letter requesting the $2,000.00 back (along with the requisite Internal Revenue Service forms—already filled out), and a notarized letter from the IRS promising not to waste the money on frivolous projects like repairing roads and bridges, and building schools and hospitals. (They should have no problem making that promise.) I'm even willing to pay interest provided the IRS calculates that interests at the same rate they pay me when they withhold more of my wages then they were entitled to.

Every DEA agent can tell stories about delightful bureaucratic SNAFUs that occurred during his career. I have one here to underline the ridiculous results that accrue when brilliant bureaucrats, unaware of what's happening in the field, make their erudite decisions: It happened that Spanish-speaking agents of the FBI in El Paso sued their bureau for extra pay. They said they deserved to be paid more because they had a skill that made them more valuable to the Bureau. This, of course, ignored all the skills brought to the bureau by other agents: chemist, truck driver, pilot, lawyer, firearms expert, and on. The FBI went to court. The FBI lost. DEA Spanish speakers immediately formed up to sue DEA. DEA folded without placing a bet. The only question was: how do we determine who speaks Spanish. Should the local supervisor make the call or should Spanish tests be given?

My opinion was that the local supervisor should decide, since he'd be in the best position to decide who was using Spanish-speaking skills to further the DEA mission. I based this opinion on my own case. I could speak Spanish, but not the Tex-Mex Spanish of the border. That was a mixture of Mexican slang, Texas slang, and partially anglicized Spanish. My Spanish-speaking skill didn't help the McAllen office in the least. Agent Mario Alvarez on the other hand, was an absolute expert in Tex-Mex. There were several times when I had to call on Mario to interpret for me.

Most Spanish speakers wanted an "objective evaluation" to avoid supervisors giving the extra money to their pets. (They had very good reasons to be cynical.) So headquarters decided to give tests, but they did not use Tex Mex speakers to give the evaluations along the border. They used teachers from the State Department's Spanish school. The examinations were done by telephone. The teachers graded you on a scale from one to five, and headquarters paid you according to your grade: a Grade 1 got the least, Grade 5 the most. Guess what happened. I'd gone to the State Department School. I spoke the kind of Spanish the teachers liked—though I didn't speak it well. Mario could communicate like an expert on the border, but the teachers couldn't forgive him all that slang. The result was this: I got a higher grade, and though Mario's Spanish was worth far more in McAllen, he got paid less. Ah, the wonderful bureaucracy!

Before I leave this bureaucracy subject, I must pay tribute to those agents who thrived in the bureaucracy. I'm not talking about the dull bureaucrat. He doesn't actually thrive in the system, he hibernates there. I'm talking about the man who's able to manipulate the system in such a way as to get anything he wants. These are men of exceptional intelligence, men with keen insight into the workings of the bureaucracy. They actually understand it! They see its contradictions and hypocrisies as weaknesses to be exploited. Their thinking isn't complicated by moral considerations or bothered by pangs of conscience. They don't care about the bureau's "mission," they care about their own. This type of individual is usually a good con-man and a brilliant politician. When this man has a bureaucrat for a supervisor, he plays him like a puppet. This man is usually highly valued by his supervisor (although that supervisor can't give an example of where he's been of value to the agency). This man is comfortable and content in the system. He's happy with the way it works. His one great skill is milking the most out of it. He loves the bureaucracy like a farmer loves his Jersey cow.

I must also, before I leave, sympathize with the zealot. He was bitterly unhappy in this system. He hated drug traffickers with all his heart. He was totally dedicated to the mission, saw himself as a knight in shining armor on a crusade to stop the world from using drugs. The "thinking" of a bureaucrat was totally foreign to him. He was a man to be admired—and to be pitied in this system. When headquarters was slow to respond to a request of his, he became angry. When headquarters refused to fund one of his cases, or sent him help that stymied rather than helped, he was outraged. He thought there was a conspiracy against him. At times he was sure the DEA, the CIA, and the State Department were all conspiring to obstruct his cases. He believed any problem he had with headquarters was due to scheming, plotting, and conspiring.

He was wrong. Bureaucratic blundering is due to incompetence, stupidity, and laziness. A bureaucrat is no good at scheming and plotting except in his own interest. A conspiracy of bureaucrats doesn't work because the minute a bureaucrat sees a slight advantage to himself in leaking instead of covering, he leaks. The hell with the other conspirators.

A dedicated DEA agent was often not a happy one.

Chapter Twenty

McAllen, Texas. Every morning a breeze blows east off the Gulf of Mexico. It blows across Padre Island, around the lighthouse at Port Isabel, and travels northwest along the Rio Grande. It rustles the leaves in the palm trees along the river and in the towns where there is irrigation. Between the towns is desert sand and cactus. This area of south Texas, up to the Nueces River, was long ago known as the "Wild Horse Desert," but now irrigation has erased most of the desert look. The Golden Valley of the Rio Grande is a wonder of contrasts. You see areas with the lush green of bananas, palm trees, flowers, and vines, and only a mile away is stark burning desert where the vegetation is dry, prickly, and sharp: Spanish dagger, cactus, and greasewood. Here the roadrunner rules with the rattlesnake, the horned lizard, and the scorpion.

McAllen was a wonderful place in those days. The traffic along Highway 83 was still light, and the spaghetti interchange with Highway 281 had not yet been raised high enough to allow the thunder of the Mexican truck-traffic to boom across the town. I was lucky. McAllen was a better post than any I had requested before—and for which I'd been passed over. It was spring when we got there, and the air was full of the fragrance of citrus blossoms from the vast orchards of orange and grapefruit cultivated all over the town.

Bea went to look for a house. I was busy settling in at work and flying back and forth to Minneapolis on the Schaapveld case. Bea went with a realtor, mostly looking at houses in north McAllen where the other DEA agents lived. One Saturday morning she saw an ad in the *Valley Morning Star* for a house in south McAllen. We went to look. No one was home. It looked lonesome: the swimming pool empty, the lawn uncut, the doors all locked. Bea pressed her nose against a big sliding glass door, shading the sides of her head with her hands.

"I want this house," she said.

I said, "Shouldn't we look inside first?"

"That won't be necessary. I want this house."

I said, "Okay, go get it."

It was fine by me. I was too busy with other things to care where I lived. I didn't realize what a great buy Bea had made until we lived there a while. The pool was much bigger and deeper than most swimming pools in McAllen. It had a high privacy fence around it. Behind the fence to the east was a big empty lot. It had a large well-attended garden. I assumed it belonged to the neighbor, but the day after we moved in, old Mr. Baker, who lived two houses to the west, stopped in. He asked if he could continue to garden on my land. This confused me until he explained we owned all the land to the east up to the neighbor's fence, more than double the land I thought we'd purchased.

In our yard we grew orange, grapefruit, lemon, lime, peach, and tangerine. In the alley we had figs and blackberries. Behind the pool we had papaya and mango. All winter long from October to April the weather was like heaven. But don't move there yet. In summer, by noon every day, that morning breeze that blows across the desert becomes a hot gale that rattles the fan palms and hisses viciously in the feathery fronds of the cocos plumosa. It's a blowtorch of a wind that turns grasses brown and kills the plants not of the desert—unless they have irrigation. You can't step outside without breaking into a sweat. You have to mow the lawn and hoe the garden in the early morning or late evening. When the sun's high, the heat index every day is more than 100 degrees. You long for a cooling rain. You long for the sound of thunder. You pray for a hurricane!—anything to break the monotony of that desert climate.

A big water valve was built into our lawn. If we needed water, we called the Hidalgo County canal rider, and he opened valves to route water from the Rio Grande to our section of town. It cost two dollars. We opened our lawn-valve, and the water came bubbling up and flooded our property. All the properties were bordered with little six-inch ridges, like miniature dikes that held the water. The land was flat as a table. In a few hours the water covered most of our yard. The flooded areas grew like jungle. The higher areas remained desert. On the high ridges we had the Spanish dagger (which served as a nesting site for the mockingbird), prickly pear cactus (good with scrambled eggs), and the great agave (usually called "century plant" by the gringos and "*maguey*" by the Mexicans). It's from the agave they make pulque and tequila.

We had ornamental trees like Chinaberry, Norfolk Island pine, and Brazilian Pepper. We had a great, flaming bougainvillea vine that draped over our wall on the west side and an enormous trumpet vine that climbed the fence on the south side and kept making its way up the highline poles in the alley. Every few weeks I had to cut it back. Ornamental plants that Minnesota housewives mist and water and fertilize grew in the shade of our house without tending: pyracanthus, schefflera, pothos ivy, mother-in-law's tongue. The place was a riot of luxurious vegetation.

We had so much papaya Bea had a hard time giving it all away. She made papaya pies. Several times she brought a wheelbarrow full of papayas to Lalo Ramirez, our neighbor to the south. He had a large family, and they loved papaya. He grilled in his back yard every day and sometimes brought us roasted goat and turkey in return. At Christmas and Easter he brought us home-made tamales. Those were the best tamales I ever had. We were friends forever after that. Bea had bought us a wonderful home, and we had wonderful neighbors there in McAllen, Texas.

The Air Wing described McAllen as a "border town," so I expected it to be right on the river like Laredo, but it was about five miles to the north. The little hamlet called Hidalgo was tight on the river. That town had the port of entry. Across the river was the Mexican town of Reynosa. During the first ten years we were in McAllen, we crossed the river to eat and shop. Bea and her girlfriends routinely wandered around the Mexican border towns across from Progresso and Brownsville. But as the years went by so many kidnappings and killings and disappearances occurred in Mexico they no longer went across.

The first Christmas we were down there, the temperature climbed into the upper eighties. I thought that was great then, but years later I began to miss the changes of seasons. It snowed just once during the fifteen years we were there. The McAllen children were ecstatic that day. They frolicked and danced in the snow like young colts and were sad when it was gone next morning. They'd never seen snow before. Lalo told me the last time he saw snow in the valley was when he was a teenager, and Lalo was an old man.

The DEA office was only four minutes from our house. The first time I walked into that office and stopped at the door of Group One, I thought I must be at a rodeo. The agents were sitting at their desks pretending to be cowboys. They all wore big cowboy hats, cowboy shirts, blue jeans, leather belts with big buckles, and tall boots with high heels. Most of them were college educated but they purposely talked with a disregard for English grammar. They wanted to sound like cowboys. They drawled sentences like, "That cain't be right. It don't make no sense." Even the ones not originally from Texas had adopted the dress and the language. They made fun of new agents until they conformed. But when they made fun of my comfortable hush puppies (they called them "orthopedic shoes"), I got stubborn. I had a nice pair of custom-made steer hide boots, but never wore them except to court. When I found my sandals drove them into a mocking frenzy, I wore those on purpose. I had a black beaver cowboy hat I bought at Laredo when I was in the Air Force, but I never wore it in McAllen. I wore my old, washed out denim hat for spite.

My job now was to fly surveillance and undercover missions for the McAllen Office, and also for Brownsville, Laredo, and Corpus Christi. The Air Wing gave me a new Cessna 206 to fly, and I could at any time get from the Air Wing an Aerostar, King Aire, Navajo, Aero Commander—almost anything—to fly undercover or haul cargo. Here was another irony of the bureaucracy: When I first came to work for DEA, they had refused to recognize my flying abilities. I wasn't allowed to fly any of their junk, even their stupid little T-41 in which I had more time than anyone. Then after years of very little flying, when I'd nearly forgotten how, suddenly I could fly anything they had. At the beginning DEA had put me on the street until I had learned to do vehicle surveillance, make undercover buys, write investigative reports, prepare cases for court and testify on the witness stand. When I was thoroughly trained in those areas, they changed me to a job where I hardly needed those skills. Once I had become a good street agent, they took me off the street. Once I had forgotten most of what I knew about flying, they made me a pilot.

But it was great. I never did a surveillance report anymore because the agents on the ground, or the spotter in my airplane did them. I didn't have to prepare for court and I seldom testified. I didn't have to make cases anymore! Really, I was no longer a DEA agent, just a pilot. They could have found hundreds of retired Air Force pilots, Airline pilots, and ex-Evergreen pilots, who'd gladly have done my job for less money. I didn't tell the bureaucracy that.

Many DEA agents resented Air Wing pilots. We weren't real agents, they said. I didn't blame them. It was obvious I no longer had many of the responsibilities of a DEA agent. I no longer faced many of the dangers. When ground surveillance got into a high speed chase, I calmly watched from above in the sky. I no longer felt the fear of crashing into another car at the next corner, or missing the next curve. I made lazy circles in the sky while my spotter told the agents on the ground which way the target was fleeing.

And gunplay? I had no worry there either (unless someone fired warning shots in the air). One day there was a shooting as we circled on surveillance over Mission, Texas. I could see the crook lying on the ground with a puddle of blood widening by his head. My only job was to call an ambulance.

Because I was not a "real agent" and a Yankee to boot, I wasn't well accepted at first. The last pilot they had at McAllen had been a good-old-boy Texan. The fact he didn't like to work bothered them less than my not conforming to the dress code. Texans are rabidly loyal to their state. They get angry at the very thought there might be a place somewhere in the world as good as or better than Texas. Tanya Tucker sang, "When I die I may not go to heaven," and hinted she'd prefer Texas. This song was played on every jukebox from Houston to El Paso. It expressed what they all felt, whether they were from a fancy Dallas suburb or from some dusty, dirty little town like Muleshoe or Prairieville. They were always waving their Texas flags and seceding from the Union when displeased with Washington. Which was every day. And I couldn't blame them.

They were equally fanatical about the Dallas Cowboys. Football is a religion in Texas. Texans are more loyal to their football team than their country or their church. A high school football game on a Friday night shut down the town. Everyone was at the game. Little mom-and-pop businesses closed; big department stores were empty except for the clerks, who wished they were at the game. A college football game was as important as a war between the states, and a pro football game was a war between galaxies. I made bets with the agents against the Dallas Cowboys only for the fun of it. I wasn't a football fan. I wasn't loyal even to the Minnesota Vikings.

But I was soon friends at least with the worker agents among them. They quickly saw I was willing to fly on a case any time—nights, weekends, holidays. I was used to long hours from working the street in Minneapolis. I was always ready to do aerial surveillance or undercover work. We had several cases in a row that showed what a great asset the airplane could be. The worker agents were soon my buddies. The rest didn't matter.

The Valley weather was perfect for flying. We seldom had foggy days where I couldn't do aerial surveillance. But the great weather brought tourists from Minnesota. They came in droves. Called "snowbirds," they were roundly despised by the DEA agents. They drove along the streets at a snail's pace looking around as though lost and pointing at things as though seeing wonders and were always blocking the traffic, making it hard for surveillance agents to follow a target through downtown McAllen. That's when aerial surveillance was the most valuable.

One day we were watching a pickup truck parked in front of a house on the west side of McAllen. The informant said two men were to come out of the house and get into the truck. They'd have a half pound of cocaine with them. The plan was to follow the truck and arrest the two when they stopped somewhere and met with someone—a customer, we hoped. But the ground surveillance was too eager that day. They got tight on the truck. They didn't want to lose it in snowbird traffic. They didn't want to lose that cocaine. The spotter with me (Agent Watkins) kept telling them he had the pickup in sight and to back off. But they pressed it, and soon burned it. The pickup began to flee at high speeds, turning corners sharply and doing other tail-shaking maneuvers. As the truck came around one corner, the passenger flung a package out the window. The package hit the pavement and rolled under a white sedan parked by the curb. I climbed higher so I could keep an eye on the sedan while the spotter stayed on the pickup. Finally they got a unit in front of the truck and were able to put an end to the chase. The agents searched the pickup. No dope. There was all kinds of chatter on the radio: "Get the informant out here," and "We have to cut them loose," and "No put them in jail." Watkins asked me if I still had the white sedan. I said I did and that no one had been anywhere near it. Our package was still there. Watkins informed the ground units he knew where the cocaine was.

This was somewhat bold on his part. We knew where a package was that had been flung out the window, but there was always the possibility it was a gun, or marijuana, or a box of candy. Watkins said, "The cocaine's under a white sedan about a quarter mile to your north." The ground units did not believe him. He kept telling them to look under that car. Agent Beaupre went to look, but he did not have his heart in it. Watkins directed him to the car. Beaupre glanced under it and reported, "Nothing there." Watkins asked me if I had the right car. I said, "It's there. He didn't look."

Watkins got on the air and said, "Will somebody with some brains, look under that car. The cocaine's under there, in case you're interested."

Agent Tittle stopped by the car. He got down on his hands and knees and reached under the sedan by the front tire and pulled out a package. The field test showed positive for cocaine.

One morning Agent George Spaulding and I were working undercover up by Kerrville, a town in the Texas hill country. Spaulding had arranged for the crooks to deliver a large load of drugs to us at an airstrip by Fredericksburg. We had flown up there the day before in a Queen Air, and were waiting for a call from the crooks to say the load was ready. When I had shut down the day before, I hadn't found a Pitot tube cover in the airplane. (The Pitot tube is a little pipe that sticks out into the airstream and measures the air pressure which is read on a cockpit gauge as airspeed.) The pilot after every flight covers the Pitot tube so dust and dirt doesn't get in. I took off one of my socks and slipped it over the tube, but during the night a passing windstorm blew the sock away.

Toward noon George got the word the crooks were ready and waiting with the load at Kerrville. They were nervous and wanted us to get there right away. We jumped in the airplane and took off (no preflight). As I rolled down the runway, I checked the airspeed indicator. Something was wrong. We were not accelerating at a normal rate. However, looking outside and watching the runway slip by and listening to the sound of the engines, all seemed okay. I glanced at the airspeed. It had dropped to near zero! I grabbed for the throttles to abort, but then the airspeed jumped to sixty. I was eating up runway fast, and it was getting kind of late to abort. I decided to go for it. I kept the airplane on the ground and lifted off at the last second in case I wasn't getting normal thrust out of the engines. I could feel immediately that everything was normal. It was just that the airspeed indicator wasn't working. We had barely missed the trees at the end of the runway, and Spaulding looked at me in shock. I said, "Something's wrong with the airspeed indicator. I have to fix it."

I pulled up into a tight closed pattern, landed, shut down one engine, and set the brakes. I told George to keep his feet on the brakes. I got out and looked at the pitot tube. Some mud dauber wasps had packed mud in there and almost closed the hole in the pipe. I tried picking it out with my pocket knife but that was no good. I went back in the airplane and asked George if he had a paper clip. He dug one out of his brief case, and in a minute I had all the mud out of the tube. We took off. Everything worked fine. The deal went down as planned. Agent Spaulding was happy. When we got back to McAllen he told the guys, "Well, the airplane was broke, but he fixed it with a paperclip."

I don't remember whose case this was, but the crooks had used a Navajo to haul cocaine from Panama to Texas. If you used your airplane to haul dope, DEA could take it away from you. The McAllen agents were looking for the Navajo to put a lock on it in order to be able to seize it if the crooks were found guilty. Weeks went by. The judge kept putting off the trial at the request of the lawyers. One day I was doing surveillance for the Laredo office and I happened to look into one of their storage hangars. Way in the back I found that Navajo. I had maintenance pull it out. I jimmied the door lock, cranked it up and flew it to McAllen. We locked it up in a hangar and chained it. The lawyers for the crooks complained to the judge I had stolen their airplane. I had to go to court. I told the judge that DEA was planning to use the plane until the trial was over. I told him if an airplane stood unused in a hangar it would deteriorate. Soon the oil and hydraulic seals started to leak and when the airplane was put back into service it required a tremendous amount of expensive maintenance. I said we proposed to use the airplane and that, if the crooks were acquitted, we'd pay them for the flying time. It would be advantageous for both sides. The judge bought it. We got to use the airplane, and eventually seized it when the crooks were found guilty. I think that may have been the first time the court sanctioned such an agreement over an airplane.

One day I got a call from the Brownsville office. An Aero Commander, loaded with marijuana, had crashed in a field the night before. They had unloaded the plane but wanted to seize it. They were afraid the crooks might come in the night and haul it off. They had a guard out there watching. They wanted me to look at the plane and see if it was flyable. I told them to get a truck and haul it out. They said they'd already checked into that. They needed a truck and a crane to load it. The only road out there was too narrow for that.

The case agent and a mechanic took me out to the airplane. We wound our way on dusty farm roads past grapefruit and orange groves until we got to an irrigation canal. The crooks had tried to land on the narrow access road on one side of the canal. It was a rough, one-car trail just wide enough to allow the canal rider to pass in his pickup. The right main landing gear had collapsed, and the end of the right wing was crumpled like an accordion. But there was no damage to the propellers. The mechanic jacked up the right side and I ran the engines. They were fine. I checked the controls and everything worked. Six inches of the right aileron was crumpled but it moved up and down freely. I knew enough about aerodynamics that I wasn't worried about the crumpling of the wing. It might make the stall speed a little higher, but I wasn't planning to use normal speeds for take off and landing anyway. The canal road was straight for almost a mile. I could get a good feel for the airplane before lift off. And the runway at Brownsville was long enough so I could come in there at max gear speed. My only concern was that there might be structural damage to the main wing spar and the broken right gear could not be made safe for a landing. The mechanic removed access panels and inspected the wing spar. He said that showed no damage. He said he could bolt down the gear with iron bracings, but I'd have to fly to Brownsville gear down.

When everything was ready, I climbed in. I wanted the mechanic to fly with me, but he refused.

I said, "You said the plane was safe to fly."

He said, "I meant safe for a pilot, not for a mechanic."

I took off, accelerated to well above liftoff speed, listening and feeling for any trouble. There was enough canal road I could still abort, but everything felt good so I pulled up, and she flew without a problem. I climbed to five thousand feet and did a test flight like I used to in the Air Force. (I omitted the upside down part). I saw little problem with that airplane. The stall speed was only a bit higher, and she rolled sharply right in a stall. Everything else normal. I took her into Brownsville.

We had a storm that night. Next morning I got a call from the case agent. He said during the storm the right main gear had collapsed again.

I said, "Let me talk to that mechanic. I have a complaint."

The mechanic said, "What's your complaint? I told you that gear was certified for one landing, and you got that."

I HAVE WANDERED AFIELD HERE. My point was that the Valley working agents soon saw I could be an asset to them, so we got along well. I did sometimes screw up, but that only gave them something to laugh about. One day we had one of those deals where we had to "get up in the air right now, hurry, hurry, the crook is on his way to pick up the dope!" Watkins was the spotter. He and I scrambled like fighter pilots in wartime. I skipped the preflight and launched without the normal checks. As we were taxiing out at high speed, I suddenly noticed the line boy was running alongside the airplane yelling and making hand signals at me. I stopped and opened the window. He yelled above the sound of the engine: "You still have your towbar on the nosewheel!"

Watkins retold that story dozens of times.

The non-working agents of the McAllen office could never get past the fact that I was always going somewhere TDY. They said I spent most of my time on vacations. I could hardly blame them. The Air Wing kept sending me to beautiful Caribbean islands like Aruba, Grand Cayman, and St. Croix. The agents knew those places to be tourist havens for rich folk. And when I got sent to Bolivia, Colombia, or Peru, they thought I spent the time lying around fancy hotels and sunning by the pool. The working agents assumed I was working, the non-working agents assumed I was on "paid vacations," and they were jealous. They were on paid vacations themselves, but they at least had to pretend to work whenever the boss came around, and they didn't get sent to the Bahamas to do their gold-bricking on a beach in the sun.

I considered McAllen the best place for an Air Wing pilot to be stationed. I was lucky to be able to spend the rest of my DEA career there. After a long TDY it was wonderful to come home to the house and the pool and the plants. Bea took care of the yard while I was gone, and it was astonishing how quickly everything grew. Whenever I came home around the holidays, she had the house all decked out with Christmas lights and holiday trimmings, and if it was a cold, damp day, she had a crackling fire going in the fireplace. I loved the Mexican culture down there on the border, and I enjoyed the unique characters that lived there. That's the next chapter.

Chapter Twenty-One

WE WERE OUT ON A NIGHT-SURVEILLANCE circling south of McAllen. It was cloudy—not a star, not a sliver of moon. Near midnight we were watching a truck supposed to leave to pick up a load of cocaine from the source. I was flying with no running lights or strobes because we were out in the country and the crooks could easily notice a plane circling overhead if it was all lit up. I was in a gentle right turn, when I saw something moving against the lights of Reynosa. I was squinting at it to see what it might be, when I suddenly pulled up sharply and rolled into steep bank to watch a DC-3 pass not ten yards below us. We were so close I could see the green lights glowing in his cockpit.

The spotter said, "What the hell was that?"

I said, "It was one of those blankety, blank smuggling airplanes running in the dark without lights."

"Isn't that illegal?"

"Well, yeeah! He's supposed to have all his navigation lights on—running lights, beacon, and strobes, damnit—but he turned them off in Mexico and forgot to turn them back on when he crossed the border coming into McAllen."

"Shit! You should turn him in to the FAA."

I said, "Yeah, and he should turn me in for doing the same thing."

I did not turn anyone in, but I went to see Hal Atkins the next day and told him to spread the word that DEA sometimes flies out there completely dark.

Reader's Digest magazine used to have a section called, "My Most Unforgettable Character." When people want to describe a person unique in his habits, thinking, and actions, they'd say, "He's a real character." The Golden valley of the Rio Grande had plenty of that kind. Those electronic smugglers were among the most interesting.

Electronics smuggling into Mexico went on for years at McAllen. At the height of its activity the Atkins brothers, Hal and Earl, owned a whole fleet of cargo planes. The north ramp at McAllen-Miller was a museum of World War II airplanes. They had vintage World War II cargo planes and converted bombers as old as their crusty pilots, and several DC-3s were always being loaded in the late afternoons. Every night right after dark, someone parked on South Tenth Street near the departure end of the runway might think he was at an airport on the coast of England watching the pre-dawn launch on D-Day. One World War II plane after another roared over. They turned south, crossed the river, and disappeared into blackness as they doused their lights.

The Mexican government had placed an inordinate import tariff on TVs, radios, tape recorders—any kind of electronic equipment. If you took those items across the border legally, you had to pay more in tariffs and bribes than the things were worth. The Mexican government had originally established those tariffs to protect the Mexican electronics industry. But the Mexican electronics industry was crap. They turned out junk, and Mexicans refused to buy it. They wanted American electronics. The *contrabandista* (smuggler) pilots flew tons of it into Mexico every night. They broke no law on this side of the border. They cleared U.S. Customs just like any other flight. But as soon as they crossed into Mexico they were as illegal as robbers and kidnappers. It was legal in Mexico for anyone to shoot them down. They went at night, lights out, to remote strips where they met with receivers who paid cash. They landed on mountain strips lit only by torches carried in the nervous hands of peons, or by the lights of the receiver's truck parked at the threshold. When they were caught in Mexico they were put in jail—Mexican jail. Then they had to get together the money to pay off the authorities or rot.

However, some of these *contrabandistas* were also drug smugglers. Every night they honed the very skills needed in the drug smuggling business, so it was easy to make the switch. I had several informants among them. Their bravery and knowledge of smuggling routes was a great help to me.

These men were the ultimate adventurers—real historic characters. Why more hasn't been written about them, I don't know. Many had flown for the CIA in Southeast Asia during the Vietnam War under the banner of Air America. Some had flown for the Shah of Iran, and for the dictator Somoza in Nicaragua. They led exciting lives, equal and often beyond that of bush pilots and combat pilots. They attracted beautiful women with their money and devil-may-care attitudes. I'd often see them sitting in the bar at the Airport Sheraton with clusters of gorgeous ladies half their age.

The highest compliment ever paid me came from those smuggler pilots. Their chief mechanic, Chuck Purpera, called me to ask a favor. The smugglers had bought that damaged Aero Commander I had flown into Brownsville. Chuck wanted me to fly it to McAllen so he could work on it in his hangar. None of his pilots wanted the job. Chuck offered me two hundred dollars.

I said, "No way." Chuck wondered why, since I had already flown it to Brownsville. I said, "That flight was part of my job. If I get killed in the line of duty, my wife gets taken care of, but if it happens when I'm flying for you guys, she's out of luck."

The smugglers thought me courageous for flying that crippled Commander, but they didn't know I had once been a test pilot, and I had taught aerodynamics in the Air Force. They took the wings off their plane and had it trucked to McAllen.

ONE CHARACTER I HEARD ABOUT as soon as I came to McAllen was Doc Beckett. I never met him. He left the border shortly after I got there. I don't remember his real name. Everyone just called him Doc. His father owned a construction company in Donna, but Doc hung around Rio Grande City up in Starr County where he had been raised. Starr County was the most lawless county in the United States; still is, for all I know. The people were all of Mexican extraction. They worshipped men like Juan Cortina (the Red Robber of the Rio Grande), who rustled cattle, and fought the Texas Rangers and the U.S. Army long ago. Every family up there had at least one member in the drug business. They had that same cowboy culture I'd seen in Culiacan. They all hated the Border Patrol, Customs, and DEA. Every trafficker drove a pickup truck, late model, luxury conversion, tinted windows, custom painted tailgate, and lots of chrome. Their houses usually had high fences all around with trained attack dogs inside. The windows on the newer houses had one way glass (we called it doper glass). In the back yard they kept fighting cocks, and every second yard had a cock-fighting arena. Hanging in the foyer or living room of the house was at least one gaudy painting of a fighting rooster and one of a race horse. Many of them owned race horses and all were members of the American Quarter Horse Association.

Rio Grande City was the capitol of Starr County. Gringos were not welcome there. Normally when McAllen DEA agents finished a drug raid, they went to the nearest bar and had a drink. Not so in Rio. We left town as soon as the deal was over and went back to the relative safety of the lower valley. A couple of gringo agents hanging around a bar in Starr County could start up a lynch mob in a few hours. But Doc Beckett, who was as gringo as they come, had not only lived there awhile, but thrived. The Beckett family had come from the coal mining area of Kentucky when Doc was just starting school. He wasn't only a gringo kid, but one with a funny look because he was blind in one eye. So he had to fist-fight his way through school.

In Starr County, Doc was feared like Billy the Kid. He had a habit of shooting or stabbing people he didn't like. But he was loved like Robin Hood because he was generous with the money he made smuggling marijuana across the Rio Grande. The Border Patrol and Customs said Doc was the meanest and the toughest son-of-a-bitch on the border (which meant in the world). They said he'd killed several people, and had himself been stabbed and shot several times. One border patrolman told me, "He carries a greater percentage of lead in his body than a pencil." All the law enforcement officers knew him. They'd had several high-speed chases with him, and had several times made bullet holes in the lid of his trunk. They said he always carried a sawed-off shotgun and had two pistols stuck in his belt.

One night when I was looking at some pictures of Doc Becket on the wall of the Customs Office in Rio Grande City, a Customs Patrol Officer looked over my shoulder and said, "If you ever meet that guy, and if you have at least three men with you, go ahead and arrest him. You can be sure somewhere, in some jurisdiction, he's wanted for assault, rape, murder, a knifing, a shooting, a bombing, or for drug sales. And he sometimes misses Mass on Sunday, too."

They were finally able to arrest Doc when a "friend" of his turned snitch after being busted at the Falfurrias check-point. When they took Doc to court he swore he'd kill the judge and also the Starr County Sheriff. They couldn't seat a jury. Everyone claimed they were afraid they'd be killed. Doc had a feisty little Mexican buddy named Magdeleno, who had already killed four people. Even Doc's little brother was afraid of being killed because he had once stolen some money from Doc.

When he got out of jail, Doc moved to Guadalajara and ran his drug business from there. He once shot it out with the Mexican army, and when they threw him in La Loma prison up at Nuevo Laredo he terrorized everyone there—and that's saying something. When I was in the Air Force at Laredo, the Mexicans said La Loma prison housed the worst collection of murderers, cut-throats, and assassins ever assembled in one place, and they included in that collection the warden and the guards who tortured prisoners just for the fun of it.

I wished Doc had stayed in Starr County because he inspired lawmen to tell colorful Wild West tales, and some of them were true. The last I heard of Doc, he was back in the States safely in jail up at George West. I went through George West every time I drove up to San Antonio. I should have stopped at the jail so I could say I had once met the notorious Doc Becket.

THE VALLEY ALSO HAD INTERESTING CHARACTERS who weren't outlaws—well, a few. The DEA Office back then was on the east side of the airport. Every day I drove to work by way of South Second Street. On the west side of that street near Lindberg Avenue was a curious old house sitting on a large lot among tall palm trees and ancient live oaks. This place belonged to old Joe Beard. He was already eighty when I first met him. I called him "Weird Joe Beard," and the justification for that will become plain. Joe lived with his wife in a weather-beaten, old house by a horseshoe driveway. The roof leaked, the inside smelled of mold, patches of plaster fell from the ceiling. His children were constantly urging him to move to a fancier place. Joe was rich. He had millions. He'd sold large pieces of land in south McAllen at great profit. That land was now the site of big hotels and businesses, and also of the main McAllen hospital and the McAllen Medical Center.

When Joe was young, he started making money almost by accident. He came with his wife from Oklahoma to find work in south Texas. Joe was an avid fisherman, and he had a natural skill as a draftsman. He had made himself a map of the valley with all the country roads and with every little pond and oxbow and arroyo that might have a fish in it. There were no decent maps of the lower valley in those days. When oil was discovered, the oilmen came stampeding into the valley. They needed maps to find their way around. Joe made copies of his map and entered the map business. He soon had an office and was making money. He bought the cheap valley land as investment, for he didn't trust banks.

I passed by his place twice a day. One day I stopped. A sign on the street (a piece of torn cardboard) said, "PAPAYAS FOR SALE, 25, 10, AND 5 CENTS." Joe sat in his yard under a live-oak tree in dirty, patched trousers and a frazzled straw hat selling papayas and putting the coins into a dented tin cup like a beggar might. I sat with him, and we talked papayas, oranges, and grapefruit like old friends. We remained friends the whole time I was in Texas. Like me, he loved plants, and he especially loved papaya. I stopped at his home whenever I wasn't in a hurry. If it was a hot afternoon, his wife would invite us in and serve us lemonade and frozen bananas. The bananas we raised down in the valley were very small, but very sweet. The Beards froze their bananas and ate them like ice cream.

Joe kept a big garden. Mrs. Beard was always offering to sell me produce. One day she said in her screechy voice, "We have maters and okree." She meant tomatoes and okra. She had never lost that Oklahoma-hillbilly accent. She trapped rats inside her house and sometimes outside when she thought they were getting too thick. I once saw a rat up on the roof as I drove in, and I often saw them scurry away when we walked into the back yard. The Beards used canned meat, cat food, and pork and beans, and threw the cans into the back yard with some of the contents still inside. The rats cleaned the cans for them. Joe would use them (the cans, not the rats) for potting his garden plants.

The first time I saw Joe sitting under that live oak, he had a string around his neck from which was suspended a small piece of leather about two inches long and an inch wide. I assumed it was some kind of amulet—you know, a good luck charm. Mexicans often wore them down there. But a few days later I stopped in when he had a customer. They were haggling over a box of papayas. Joe had that leather piece under his nose hanging over his mouth, and as he talked the gusts from his words kept flapping the thing in and out like the exhaust cover on a John Deere tractor.

When the customer left, I said to Joe, pointing, "What the hell's that thing?"

He sheepishly pulled the thing down so it again hung around his neck like an amulet. He said, "Don, you see, I have the habit of standing with my mouth open and my lower lip hanging, when I'm thinking." (That was true. I often saw him staring stupidly with open mouth and hanging lip as he leaned on his hoe in the garden.) He said, "So I use this piece of leather to keep the inside of the lower lip from getting sunburned."

Joe and I both hated possums, because they loved papaya as much as we did. You could not let a papaya get fully ripe on the tree or a possum would get it every time. I had a live trap in my papaya orchard. When I got a possum I took it to the humane society in Edinburg. Joe had several live traps. When Joe got one in the trap he threw the trap into his pond "until the bubbles stop rising." He had a pond constantly fed by a valve connected to the canal across the street from his house. He never had to call the canal rider. He got all his water for free. It was an agreement he'd made when he sold the city his land.

Joe also got his gas for free. One day in fall, I stopped by. Joe was holding on to a long air hose and blasting the leaves off the driveway. When I got out of my car I could smell a foul odor like something dead. He was blowing the leaves with city gas! He said, "Why shouldn't I. It's free." When I told him that might be dangerous, he said, "I've been doing it for years."

That was my old buddy, Weird Joe Beard.

HENRY WAS ANOTHER VALLEY CHARACTER. He was a good friend of several agents in our office. That's because Henry ran Sophie's Bar on South Tenth

Street. When I say "ran," I use the term loosely, because Henry was not a business man. Why Sophie fell in love with him no one knows. She was a big, wide, bold blonde with a voice like whisky and smoke. Henry was a skinny, shy, elf. She had money. Henry had nothing. Moreover Henry was shiftless, ambitionless, and careless. When Sophie asked him if he wasn't finally going to do something with his life, he told her he had once considered that he might, under some circumstance, like to be a bartender.

She bought him the bar on South Tenth Street.

If one didn't know the location of Sophie's Bar, it was easy to miss on Tenth. It was out in the country hidden in a little glen on the east side of the road among palm, oak, and sagebrush. Inside was a long bar along one wall and a full-sized shuffle board table along the opposite wall. As with all good Texas taverns, stuffed animals were mounted on the walls among the flashing beer signs, including the usual "jackalope" (a jackrabbit with antelope horns) and the mandatory south end of a north bound deer.

Sophie's was to the McAllen Office what the Spaghetti Emporium was to the Minneapolis Office, the favorite watering hole of DEA agents, and was regularly attended after hours by local law enforcement. Some agents went there almost every night, and everyone went there to celebrate a big arrest or seizure. It was a relaxed place. Customers left their wallets and rolls of money lying on the tables, and Henry left the cash register open and unattended. In the back, among the oaks and palms were barbeque pits and tables and benches. Some group was always holding a *pachanga* back there—a south Texas outdoor party where people drank gallons of beer and ate enormous platters of barbequed beef. If someone was grilling, we could eat free if we bought a round of beer for the group. Usually a dart board hung on a tree, and officers were throwing darts for money.

Henry liked it best when only a few customers were in his bar. He liked to spend his days playing dominos and his nights sampling the merchandise. Large crowds set him on edge, and he drank more to steady his nerves. Then he'd pass out at the domino table, and some of the DEA agents would take him to Sophie's house (right next to the bar). If Sophie was still up, they'd toss him in his bed. If she was asleep, they put Henry on the couch and threw a rug over him. The agents tended bar for him until closing and locked up the money from the cash register in the evidence safe at the DEA office. The next morning they'd take it back down to Sophie's. Henry was grateful. Every once in a while he'd make a big pot of chili and invite the agents down for lunch.

I FIRST MET THE CROP DUSTER character in the Rio Grande Valley. The farmers of the lower Rio Grande Valley raised produce for northern markets. They had to spray those crops with pesticides because it never got Minnesota-cold enough down there to kill the bugs and worms that liked to eat the same produce we do. The best way to spray was with airplanes. One had to admire the crop dusters of those days. Crop dusting was a dangerous business. All day long they flew only a few feet off the ground and often were obliged to fly under highline wires and skip over fence lines at the end of the fields. Some crop dusters were crippled or killed when they flew into those wires. Many got mortally sick from breathing the insecticide mist they sprayed on the farmer's plants. Little was known about the dangers of breathing that stuff, and most duster pilots despised wearing a mask. Some still sprayed with old Grumman Ag-Cats with the open cockpits. They flew airplanes with cool farmer-names like Air Tractor, Ag-Truck, and Ag-Cat.

When I had free time, I 'd fly along the Rio Grande looking for smugglers. All over among the fields of peppers, tomatoes, and onions were little airstrips, and parked next to many of them was a crop duster airplane. I'd land and talk to the pilots to find out what they knew about drug smugglers. Some of them were smugglers themselves. Some dusted crops by day and smuggled electronics into Mexico by night. Some smuggled drugs. They could fly low and pretend to be dusting, zip across the river, land at a strip, pickup the load, and be back across the border in minutes. No radar could spot them, and no one thought anything of seeing a crop duster flying along skimming the tops of the plants.

I flew with these pilots several times. They liked to show off their skills, and I learned from them. They showed me how to make those short, sharp turns at the end of a field. I called them "crop-duster turns." When a crop duster got to the end of a field, he'd pull the nose up sharply rapidly killing airspeed and roll into a ninety-degree bank turn with aileron and lots of rudder. The airplane was near stalling and the nose would fall into a steep dive, and in a second he was back on his airspeed skimming over the cabbages—a nice, easy, time-saving turn. I used that turning technique many a time in my work for DEA, especially hunting drug boats in the Carribean.

One of those pilots showed me how to "water skip." We'd fly over the Rio Grande or over a pond and let the tires skid on top of the water. If the pond was nice and smooth, it was fun, but if it was choppy, it'd rattle our teeth. This sounds dangerous but really isn't (at least not very) because the hydroplaning of the tires on the water made it difficult for the wheels to sink—but you better keep your speed up! That maneuver was of no use except to show off.

ONE LAST CHARACTER: BILL COLLAR. He wasn't from the Rio Grande Valley, but I include him because he was my supervisor while I was in south Texas. Also, because he was the most memorable of these—for me that is. Bill and I were good friends. At least I thought we were. I'm not sure he ever had any genuine "good friend." Bill was addicted to adrenaline. He loved to live on the edge of danger to stimulate the secretion of adrenaline into his bloodstream. He bought himself a Cessna 210, which he equipped with special long-range tanks so he could fly on vacations deep into Mexico and Central America. He liked to fly to remote places in the mountains and to back-country towns where no tourist ever went—so he could meet with "real people," he said.

One day he and I were headed for Corpus Christi in a Cessna 206. I was piloting the airplane and had filed for seven thousand feet where, according to the weatherman, we were supposed to be in the clear. When we got to seven thousand, we were not only in the clouds, but were rapidly taking on ice.

Collar said to me, "Don't you think we should ask for a different altitude?"

I jokingly said, "Well, I thought we'd experiment and see how much ice this airplane can take."

Any pilot in his right mind would have responded with a hell no, but Collar thought it was a good idea. He said with enthusiasm, "Yes, let's you and I play chicken with the ice!"

Collar won, I chickened out first. The ice slowly built up on the leading edges of the plane. I kept having to raise the nose to hold altitude. I opened the throttle. I kept bumping the controls to make sure the elevator, rudder, and ailerons were not locking up. The airspeed slowly bled down. Collar kept grinning at me excitedly. The ice was getting heavy. I could tell from the feel of the controls we were getting near stall speed. I knew I couldn't rely on the stall warning horn. It was frozen. Finally I began losing altitude even at full power, so I asked Houston Center for a lower altitude. We dived down, and immediately the ice began melting. Collar thought it was all great fun.

One time I was stationed with Collar on a TDY in Aruba. We stayed at a hotel in Oranjestad, a peaceful tourist town—too peaceful for Collar. We had been told to stay out of the town of Sint Nikolaas at the south end of the island, especially at night. That only made Collar want to go there—especially at night. When Collar went, he dragged me along, but I didn't enjoy it as much as he did.

One could get into trouble in Sint Nikolaas without effort. It was full of roughnecks from the oil fields of Venezuela. Full of sailors and grease monkeys and hard hookers. They looked upon stabbings and shootings as entertainment when they were drunk, and enlivened their sober moments with bloody bare-knuckle fist fights. When celebrating the holidays, they combined all these forms of recreation into a thundering shivaree. Collar seemed cut from a similar cloth. We walked around looking for Charlie's Bar, said to be a gathering place for the lowest of the above-mentioned riff raff. We wandered through the town. Whenever we heard gunfire, Collar headed in the direction of the sound. He simply had to find out who got hurt and how much and over what. We got thirsty and stopped in some bars looking for a place to have a few Amstels. Collar was not satisfied until we found a bar with blood on the floor. A knife fight had just sent two men to the hospital. Another man with a bloody rag wrapped around his fist was telling the crowd about the fight. That's where we sat down to drink. Collar drank in the stories as eagerly as the beer.

One day Collar came down to McAllen for a "supervisory visit." Drug traffickers were using airplanes to smuggle large loads of drugs all along the lower south Texas border. Collar was very interested in the kind of radar coverage we had. He said he was going to make a proposal to Washington to get more radar coverage "to plug the holes" so we could track any smugglers coming north. He asked me to write a detailed report about the radar coverage (or lack of it) from Brownsville to Rio Grande City. He'd attach that report to his proposal.

That night Collar went drinking with one of the secretaries from our office. Next morning she told me, "I really like your supervisor. He's a lot of fun. He's always smiling, and always has that bright look in his eye like a naughty little boy who is up to something."

He was up to something all right. It was more than a year before I found out what it was. By that time he had given up his supervisory job in Dallas and was the pilot in Charleston, South Carolina. I went there several times to fly DEA's DC-3 with him. We did several undercover deals and also several low-level sight-seeing runs over the ocean. Bill was a happy-go-lucky guy. As he held the yoke of the DC-3 he sang, "I don't go too fast, but I go pretty far," a line from a song about roller skates. He thought it fit the DC-3.

One day Collar called me in McAllen from Charleston and asked me to work an undercover deal with him. He'd been negotiating with some crooks in Brazil. We were going to fly a load of cocaine for them out of Manaus, a town on the banks of the Rio Negro near where it joins the Amazon. We would use DEA's Merlin IIIB as the undercover airplane. We'd make several trips to set up the deal, then a final trip to fly in the load. We'd arrest the receivers stateside, and the Brazilian authorities would arrest the traffickers in Manaus. Our undercover story would be we were pilots for a small airline out of Houston. We'd wear airline pilot uniforms. Collar took my body measurements on the phone. A week later I received in the mail several custom-made uniforms that fit me perfectly and also a nice set of gold airline pilot wings.

We were all set to go. Two weeks later I got a teletype from headquarters. We had clearance to do the trip. All was arranged with Brazil. I was packed and set to go. Then I got another teletype. It said there'd be a delay due to a lot of M-19 activity in that area. We were to wait until the Brazilians got better control. I had never heard of the M-19 in Brazil. They were a Colombian terrorist organization. It sounded funny to me, but I figured some bureaucrat at headquarters had screwed up and, as usual, was blaming it on something else. A little later, another teletype. The trip was back on. Then, on the morning when I was supposed to go meet Collar, I got a phone call from the head of the Air Wing: DEA Agent Bill Collar had just been arrested for smuggling cocaine from South America into the United States.

They apologized to me for jerking me around with all those teletypes. Here's what happened: An informant had surfaced who said Collar was smuggling cocaine into the country in his Cessna 210 (the one with the special long-range tanks). The informant said Collar had a partner, also a DEA pilot. The informant didn't know the partner's name, but the description he gave fit me exactly. The investigation seemed to indicate the informant was telling the truth. Other informants corroborated the information and added more. They said I helped Collar get past the radar in south Texas. The investigators had found my radar report in Collar's desk. It had never gone up to headquarters.

Finally they arrested Collar, and he cooperated immediately. He said he was expecting them. He told them about how he got me to write that radar report. He admitted the trips to Brazil were going to be smuggling trips, but that I knew nothing about his smuggling. He wanted me along because he thought I was their best Merlin pilot. He'd planned to bring back small loads he could hide in his luggage and in various compartments in the airplane.

The clever bastard! I still have that radar report. I had given him very exact information about the best places to cross the Rio Grande. I knew that south

Texas border better than anyone by then. I had taken the trouble to have Houston Center track me on radar as I flew along the river climbing and descending. They let me know at what altitudes I was visible on their radar. My report told about places a smuggler should cross, at what altitude he should fly, and what route he should take through the valley to avoid being tracked. I reported what could be seen on the weather radar at Brownsville. I reported on the radar coverage at Navy Kingsville and Navy Corpus. No smuggler ever had such reliable and detailed information for crossing a border as Bill Collar had when he flew his Cessna 210.

Collar carried the report with him on his smuggling trips. He told the investigators how he did it. He'd get a load in Central or South America and fly it over Mexico on a normal flight plan up to near the border. He'd land on an abandoned road, or an airstrip, or a clearing in the desert. He'd hide the stuff in the bushes. Then he'd complete his flight plan into McAllen or Brownsville and clear customs like normal. Then he would file a VFR flight plan to his destination in the states. He'd quickly fly back across the border, pick up his load, and activate his flight plan as he became visible on radar. Everything looked completely legal.

Collar went to jail. I hope he had an exciting time there and got his daily fixes of the adrenaline he so loved.

Chapter Twenty-Two

SHOW ME A BETTER JOB. I spent the rest of my DEA days flying surveillance and undercover missions for other agents. I was having the fun, but not the responsibilities of the case agent. I rarely went to court anymore. That was fine by me. After the Schaapveld case, I was fed up with lawyers, judges, and appeals courts. We got some real cream-puff assignments flying for DEA. They sent us out over the Caribbean Sea to look for drug boats. We patrolled the waters of the Spanish Main with our airplanes like pirates of old used to patrol those waters with their ships. Pirates looked for ships carrying gold and silver bullion from Zacatecas and Potosí to the Kings of Spain. We looked for boats carrying marijuana and cocaine from Colombia to the eastern shores of Florida. We flew out of places I could never have afforded on my own money. We basked in the sun on sugar-sand Bahamian beaches and drank Genlivet scotch in luxurious Virgin Island taverns without a care. Uncle Sam was paying. I'll always be grateful to the genius who thought of putting DEA agents to "work" looking for drug-smuggling boats in the Caribbean Sea and arranging it so Uncle Sam paid for it. Show me a better job.

The Spanish Main once referred to all the land that touched the waters of the Caribbean Sea and the Gulf of Mexico. The king of Spain claimed all the resources in that area—gold, silver, timber, even the people. This gave Spain the "right" to take the gold and silver of the Aztecs in Mexico and of the Incas in the Andes Mountains, the "right" to enslave the inhabitants of Colombia and force them to mine their mountains for emeralds, and the "right" to haul back to Spain any treasures they found. Not everyone recognized those rights. Some of Spain's European neighbors, like the Dutch and the English, got very jealous when they saw Spain hauling in the gold.

And Spain made bitter enemies among the indigenous people of the Spanish Main. Those abused people became rebels and revolutionaries. Often they had to flee to remote Caribbean islands to escape their Spanish masters. Mutineers from English and Dutch ships sometimes got themselves marooned on those same islands. And pirates who lost their ships to hurricanes and cannon fire found shelter on those islands. All these men ganged up and became the famous pirates of the Spanish Main. Generally they had a low regard for human life and a high regard for excitement. They developed a great contempt for kings, governments, and laws, and passed that contempt on to their descendants. Those descendants were now part of the drug trade of Colombia.

After Paraquat killed the marijuana business in Mexico, the Colombians filled the gap. Juan Valdez found growing marijuana easier than growing coffee for Folgers—and was about twenty times more profitable. The Colombians had already been practicing smuggling for years. They'd been smuggling drugs in small amounts mostly in passenger luggage on airplanes and boats. But now the demand was so great they piled multi-ton loads on big ocean-going barges and sent them north to the islands east of Florida. The Colombians found ready cooperation among the inhabitants of the islands, for the rebel blood of pirates still ran fast in their veins. They still despised authority, and they quickly saw the economic wisdom of defying American drug laws.

The big marijuana boats came off the Guajira Peninsula of Colombia. Some headed north toward the east end of Jamaica, then northeast through the Windward Passage between Cuba and Haiti. Others headed northeast toward Puerto Rico and went through the Mona Passage between Puerto Rico and the Dominican Republic. They anchored in international waters off the east coast of Florida or among the thousands of islands of the Bahamas. They unloaded their cargo in small portions onto innocent-looking leisure craft or shrimp boats and calmly sailed for the Florida coast. Or they loaded the cargo onto speedy little cigarette boats that could easily outrun the American Coast Guard. Those boats took their cargo into the hundreds of marinas, harbors, beaches, islands, and cays along the coast of Florida—impossible to police.

To catch drug boats coming off the north shore of the Guajira, DEA first stationed us at Aruba. I had several DEA vacations there, including that one with Bill Collar. We flew out of Princess Beatrix International. Every morning we'd fly along the coast of the Guajira and watch the activity in the bays. We'd try to identify and photograph boats that might be used for smuggling drugs. By the time I first got to Aruba, DEA was doing little good. Everyone knew who we were and what we were doing. I had been told (just like with Trizo) that we were to keep a low profile there. We were supposed to be tourists.

The second day I was there, the girl at the desk of our Oranjestad hotel says to me, "Oh, hi. You're one of the DEA agents."

"What makes you think that?"

"Oh, come now. You were drinking with the DEA agents last night. Everyone knows who you guys are."

"Is that right?"

"You're either a DEA agent, or a snitch, and if you're a snitch you'd better not hang out with those guys. You might not live long."

I thanked her for the advice.

Even the Colombians all along the Guajira knew who we were. We monitored their radio calls. Whenever we came buzzing along their shore, they'd radio to each other: "The mosquitoes are at it again this morning." They loaded their drug boats at night and left in the dark so by morning, when we came along, they were well on their way to the Windward or Mona Passes, while we took pictures of salt boats.

We spent our Aruba free time lying on the beaches, drinking beer, and watching New York ladies grill themselves in the sun. They'd arrive white as chalk, and leave a week later red as boiled lobster. The American tourists came expecting an idyllic, tropical island, lush with palm trees, coconuts, and bananas. But Aruba's a desert island. The tourists found low brush, cactus, and wild goats climbing among grassless rocks. And they got the forever-blowing trade winds that bend the divi-divi trees toward the west. The wind is so steady the divi-divi tree grows in that low-bent posture that makes it look like a large bonsai. The most interesting thing on the island (not for a tourist but for a geologist or paleontologist) was that among the enormous rocks were some caves with ancient petroglyphs on the walls, but no one ever figured out what they meant. And what tourist goes to look at petroglyphs?

We had a rental car we could use to drive to the airport and also see the sights on the island. The only sightseeing I did was to go to the lonely north shore of the Island and watch the Caribbean heave stupendous rollers against the jagged boulders. The waters foamed and thundered there day and night among massive volcanic rocks spraying roaring jets of water high into the air and making a constant movie of rugged snarling power that made me think the island should long ago have been swept away.

I liked the natives of that island. They were of African, Dutch, and Indian blood. From their Dutch ancestry they were assiduously clean. They kept neat little houses with white picket fences along the streets, and every morning the ladies swept and raked their sandy yards. They understood Aruba was a desert island and didn't foolishly force grass to grow where it did not belong, like Americans do. The ladies were wonderful cooks, but were hard to understand when they gave out their recipes. They spoke a weird language called "Papiamento," a confusing casserole of Spanish and Dutch lightly peppered with English and heavily salted with ancient Arawak words. I could usually communicate at least a little because many of my German words were close to their Dutch, and they understood some of my Spanish. I learned from them how to make *saté* (like a fried shish kabob) and the peanut sauce to dip it in. For desert: Windward Island pie crust with cashew filling.

About the time I learned all I wanted to know about Aruba, DEA sent us to other islands. They finally figured out we were wasting our time patrolling the northern coast of Colombia. We then moved into position to try to catch the drug boats as they went through the passes. To patrol the Windward and the Mona, we stationed out of Grand Turk of the Turks and Caicos Islands, and sometimes out of Puerto Rico and St. Croix. At Grand Turk, we flew out of the only airport on the island, an old airfield built by the U.S. Air Force during the Korean War. The airport was falling into disrepair. The only thing being kept up from the war days was a small weather station. There were a few British officials on Grand Turk, because the Turks and Caicos were still a British protectorate.

Some of our agents did not like staying on Grand Turk. The beaches there were not covered with bikini-girls like the beaches of all the other places where we stationed. On Grand Turk we were quartered in a military barracks instead of a fancy hotel. But I liked Grand Turk a lot. It was very quiet there, almost lonesome. It had the most wonderfully clear water and sugary beaches. Only a little way off shore were reefs loaded with shellfish, where in twenty minutes of snorkeling you could bring home a dinner of all the lobster you could eat. There was an old English tavern by the shore. The cook would prepare our lobster for us in grand style—though some of it was always missing. He took a commission. We played darts there in the tavern at night with the Brits. Hardly any American tourists were ever there. Accommodations weren't fancy enough, and there was a constant smell of stale saltwater from stagnant ponds all over the island. Also, they expected us to drive on the wrong side of the road (but there was only one road, and it had no traffic).

We gassed up our airplanes at South Caicos. During war time, our Coast Guard used to have a submarine tracking station on South Caicos, but that was closed now. When we parked on the ramp at South Caicos, we were parking right alongside drug smuggling airplanes, and when we went into the office to pay our bill, we waited in line with known drug smuggling pilots. Any smuggler could use the islands as a base if willing to pay the required bribe. They were all crooks around there. That included Norman

Saunders, who owned the fuel concession on South Caicos. He looked innocent enough. About my age, he wore glasses and a little mustache, and he was always friendly: shaking our hands, patting our backs, and smiling broadly. And well he could smile. He was rapidly getting rich. Norman Saunders was taking huge bribes from drug smugglers. You might ask: "Well, why didn't you call the chief administrator of the Turks and Caicos and have him arrested?" He *was* the chief administrator! He was the head of their government. When we talked to the Brits about Norman, they said they'd be happy to ask for his resignation if we could give them absolute proof.

Every morning we took off out of Grand Turk and looked for drug boats either anchored among the islands or sailing out in the ocean. We flew those missions under operation names like BAT, Trampa, and a half-dozen others. They were sold to congress as "drug interdiction" missions and were "enormously successful," because the operations claimed credit for any drugs seized or destroyed no matter under what circumstances. Any cases made by agents across the U.S. that involved the Caribbean Islands were claimed. If a drug airplane crashed on one of the islands because the pilot was drunk, DEA claimed credit. If a drug boat sank because an addled sailor pulled the drain plug, DEA took credit.

Identifying a drug boat from the air was a piece of cake. Drug lords like Pablo Escobar and Carlos Lehder were normally very smart, but in this matter they were entirely predictable. They knew some of their boats would get seized, so they didn't risk their luxury yachts. They bought cheap, old boats and hired crews of impoverished, uneducated Colombian sailors to sail them. Then they crossed their fingers.

When we patrolled for suspicious craft, we looked along the known routes. We looked for rough, weathered, dirty boats, flying under no flag and riding low in the water from heavy cargo. They usually had names that were faded, or painted-over, or had letters crudely changed. Some had no markings at all. We looked for boats with shy sailors. By "shy" I mean they did not appear on deck. If you buzzed a shrimp boat, a vacation yacht, or any honest sail, the people came out on deck and waved. They were out there by themselves on a vast, lonesome ocean and were happy to see a sign of human life. It wasn't unusual to see half a dozen people on deck waving and laughing and jumping up and down like children greeting Santa Claus. Ludlow Adams and I once made a series of passes on Royal Caribbean's Nordic Prince, and in a minute, the rails were lined with waving passengers. But when we buzzed a drug boat, it was different. The sneaky, reclusive crew didn't appear on deck. When caught by surprise, they slunk below and didn't show again.

When we found such a target, we swooped down, got her name (if she had one) and port of registration (if that was posted), her direction of travel, and her approximate speed. We relayed that information to the Coast Guard, who intercepted her and checked her cargo. Later we could find out through DEA's El Paso Intelligence Center (EPIC) what the results were. Boats carrying ten to twenty tons were not unusual, and the record was much higher than that. DEA celebrated each large seizure as though it was a great victory in "the war on drugs," but the Colombians barely noticed those losses. For every load we seized, dozens got through. Losing a few tons of grass here and there was nothing to them, and a ton of cocaine did not break the bank.

If the suspicious boat was anchored in a Bahamian harbor or if we found a suspicious airplane sitting on one of the island airstrips, we called out the helicopters of the BAT Strike Force. They had crews from the U.S. Air Force Special Operations Wing (later they had U.S. Army crews). Their helicopters had guns. The crew included pilot, co-pilot, flight engineer, and gunner. They usually had one DEA agent on board and four or five Royal Bahamian Strike Force soldiers. They had the dangerous part of our job. They made the arrests and seizures (when the authorities allowed it). These men often patrolled at night without lights, using night vision goggles, and followed airplanes into remote strips to see what they were up to. It was a nasty surprise for a drug-smuggling pilot to fly all the way from his Colombian jungle strip down by Rioacha and finally to make it to his secret strip on Ambergris Cay, only to find that a big Huey had landed right behind him with a bunch of cops on board, who informed him that his drug load now belonged to the government and, furthermore, he was under arrest.

Operation BAT (it stood for Bahamas and Turks and Caicos Islands) had DEA and Customs personnel stationed in several spots throughout the islands. They were supposed to get information from the locals about drug smuggling—not an easy job among these sons-of-pirates. They had radar sites to track smugglers and all kinds of other electronic equipment to spy on smugglers. They were always in need of parts and supplies for their electronic equipment. Since DEA could not use the commercial airlines to fly their secret stuff, I often got to play cargo pilot. The reason they didn't send the equipment by the airlines was because DEA always thought they were on a super-secret operation no one knew about, but was in fact no more secret than U.S. cops hanging out in donut shops. The local people always knew within a few days what was going on when DEA came to town. This was mostly because DEA agents couldn't keep their mouths shut. They bragged to the bar-ladies at night about what they were doing. Flying solo cargo missions was what I enjoyed most of all. I got to choose my routes, places to gas-up, and places to sleep. Headquarters never checked to see if I was flying the most efficient routes or staying at the most economical places. I could pretty much make the mission into a sight-seeing tour, as long as I delivered the goods.

I liked to fly solo. If I had passengers, I felt responsible, and if I had another pilot on board, he was often more hindrance than help. If he was a bungling incompetent (and DEA had plenty), I had to watch him like a hawk. And if he was an experienced pilot, we often had disagreements about flying techniques. I rarely got to fly with the really good military-trained pilots like Bishop, Vandiver, and McKelvey. I once flew with Agent Jarrell, who was Navy trained (or at least said he was), and when he made a pass on a boat and wished to turn around for another look, he'd roll into a steep bank turn without climbing and crank it around pulling hard G's and riding top rudder to help keep his altitude. I about puked to see a Navy man fly like this. When I got into the pilot's seat, I showed him how much easier, faster, and more efficient it was to make a crop-duster turn—and more coordinated. He wasn't impressed.

"What's the point of all that zooming and diving?" he asked.

"It saves time," I said. "The slower you go the faster she'll turn. And you don't have to pull all those G's."

"I guess you're not used to pulling G's," he said.

I let that pass, though I was pretty sure I had pulled more G's in one month of instructing aerobatics than Agent Jarrell had pulled in his life. Then he added for frosting, "And I guess you're not used to flying at low altitudes."

I let that go too. I said, "Suppose you lose your inside engine in that turn?"

"Well, then you just roll out."

"Yeah, if you don't get your lower wing into the water before you get a chance to react, and then you go cart-wheeling into hell."

"You have to be alert." He sniffed.

That's why I liked to fly solo.

WHEN WE WERE ON SEARCH MISSIONS we stopped at any island we wanted to visit. We did this under the guise of "doing reconnaissance and interviewing informants." Looking at the sights was "doing reconnaissance" and talking to anyone on the island was "interviewing informants." And so I got to visit most of the islands from Freeport on Grand Bahama down to St. George's on Granada. I resolved many a time that someday I'd go back to those places on a vacation. If a person had his own airplane or a sailboat, he couldn't do better than spend the rest of his life sailing among the islands of the Caribbean, learning the history, seeing the sights. There are hundreds and hundreds of islands, little gems all in a row from the east side of Florida down to Trinidad and Tobago, which lie off the northeast coast of Venezuela.

The people of San Salvador Island (it was listed as "Watlings Island" on an antique map I had) claimed Columbus first sighted land there in 1492. That claim was hotly disputed by the people of Grand Turk, who made the same claim for their island. However, the people of San Salvador had the upper hand. They'd taken the trouble of putting up a monument of solid rock with the engraving: "On this spot Christopher Columbus first set foot on the soil of the New World." That was enough for me. I don't argue with people who chisel their beliefs in stone.

At Rum Cay on a quiet day we could see a ship down in the water on the southeast side of the island. It was a huge thing, a British battle ship from back in Civil War times. Its hull had been torn out on the Rum-Cay reefs while underway from Jamaica to Bermuda. It looked like a wonderful place to dive, because she lay in shoal water, hardly more than ten feet beneath the surface.

For luxury the finest place we stationed out of was Nassau on New Providence Island. I don't remember ever doing any worthwhile flying out of there, but it was worthwhile living—the fanciest hotels, crowded with pretty New York girls who bragged about how many Bahama Mama Cocktails they could chug. Nassau chefs made the best conch fritters on the planet. St. Croix Island was okay too, but not nearly as fancy, and it was always overrun with empty-headed tourists off big cruise ships who took pictures of themselves to prove they'd been there.

For a DEA agent, the most interesting island was Norman's Cay. A DC-3 lay there in the water near the shore like a partially-submerged monument to air smugglers. It had crashed there one night when it tried landing on water instead of tarmac. That island was a perfect smugglers haven. It was near Florida and part of that confusing string of islands they called the Exuma Chain, reaching from Hog Cay, south of Great Exuma, almost up to Nassau. The island looked exactly like the dozens of other little islands in the Exuma chain, but this one was the hub of the drug traffic. It had a long, wide landing strip where they could land any airplane, even one overloaded with drugs. That fact was proven daily—well, nightly mostly. The island had a dozen handsome little coves and narrow harbors perfect for discreetly unloading boatloads of contraband.

The first time I went to Norman's Cay, Carlos Lehder, the Colombian drug lord, still owned the place—though I did not know it. I was still on the Schaapveld case and busy moving to McAllen and paid little attention to world-wide drug trafficking (I know—hard to believe for a DEA agent). I was aware one man owned a good deal of Norman's Cay, but I thought that man was golfer Greg Norman. I was with Agent Jerry Bishop, and he knew the real story. Carlos Lehder owned the whole island and directed an enormous drug-smuggling business out of there. He'd run every honest citizen off the island and had every one of the remarkably venal Bahama officials in his pocket. All Bahamian officials were merrily making tons of money aiding and abetting, and sharing in the profits of the Medellin Cartel.

That day I ran into Carlos Lehder on Norman's Cay, or I should say, he ran into me—literally. Bishop and I were going in to eat lunch at the hotel near the airport. As we entered, a group of men were leaving. At the head of the group was a laughing, pleasantly talking young man, clean shaven, starched white shirt, ironed blue jeans. I politely held open the door for him, but he bumped me aside as he swaggered by, and the men behind almost ran me down. He got into a new Corvette that was parked in front of the hotel with a very pretty, beautifully-tanned, lady driver. She wore big sunglasses and gave him a peeved look. Lehder had not yet closed the door when she stomped on it and spun the tires, spraying bits of coral all around as she fish-tailed down the street with her black hair fluttering in the wind.

Bishop said to me, "That's him."

"That's who?"

"Carlos Lehder! You should have punched him out for bumping you."

"Who's Carlos Lehder?"

Bishop gaped. "You call yourself a DEA agent and don't know who Lehder is?"

After Bishop finished telling me about Lehder's kidnappings and murders, his bloody body guards, and his intense recklessness, I was glad I was too much a chicken to take a swing at a man just for being rude, and I was just as glad he hadn't shot me for getting in his way. Next to Pablo Escobar, Carlos Lehder was probably the most famous Colombian drug trafficker ever, and at that time the most violent and most powerful. There was something likable about the guy, however. He was young and handsome and seemed to be having a tremendously good time. I wished I was in that Corvette with that gorgeous brunette driving.

As we flew over Norman's Cay from time to time, we saw airplanes being unloaded at the airport. The cargo often looked very much like bricks of cocaine. We saw boats being unloaded in the harbors, and the bundles looked suspiciously like bales of marijuana. But whenever we called out the Royal Bahamian Strike Force, they got there "just a little bit too late." They reported the plane had already left, or the boat was empty. They said they interviewed people and found out that the bricks were bags of sugar for the restaurants, and the bales were alfalfa for the cattle. They seemed entirely satisfied with their investigation into the matter, and Prime Minister Pindling—also a total crook—rubber stamped all the reports. Pindling allowed Lehder to operate as he did. Because of Pindling, Lehder could get by with murder on his little island. Lehder demonstrated that from time to time.

As far as I know, Mr. Carlos Lehder is serving 135 years in the federal pen at Marion. He'd probably still be on Norman's Cay if he had been smart. He began using so much of his own product he became paranoid, suspicious of even his best friends. Like so many traffickers, he became greedy and cut underlings out of the profits. He eventually got himself kicked out of the Bahamas, and went back to Colombia. He became so arrogant he made enemies of other drug dealers. Eventually even Pablo Escobar and the Ochoa brothers couldn't stand him. Pablo betrayed him. He told the Colombian authorities where Lehder was hiding in the jungle, and they extradited him to the United States. At Carlos Lehder's trial, George Jung, the man who had got him started in drug trafficking and who had been his friend all those years, testified against him. Carlos had cut George out of the business. George cut him back.

Chapter Twenty-Three

DURING THE NIGHT THE WIND came up aggressively. By dawn, under a ragged, gray sky, it was blowing a howling gale and driving little rain squalls over the water. It churned the sea into dark, angry rollers itching to swallow something. The boats anchored off the shore of the island were pitching and bucking in the heavy sea, pulling at their moorings like wild ponies. The surf was breaking high on the beach, in some places sloshing piles of foam among the palm trees. I thought at first we should cancel our search-flight for the day. Who would take a boat out in this weather? But we were patrolling the Yucatan Channel now, and any drug boat up here would have left Colombia days ago. And Ludlow said he had a feeling it would be a good day.

The Yucatan Channel is the opening between the Caribbean Sea and the Gulf of Mexico, the water between the eastern shores of Mexico's Yucatan Peninsula and the western tip of the Island of Cuba. We should have been flying out of Cancun, which is right by the channel, but after Trizo, we were no longer welcome in Mexico. We were forced to fly out of Grand Cayman—an unfortunate circumstance for us poor pilots. How we suffered there, lying on those sandy shores in patio lounge chairs by the Plantation Village Resort, watching the girls on the beach getting drunk on Cayman rum punches, which they drank through straws as they rotated their roasting red bottoms to expose them to the best angle of the sun. It was a grand place, Grand Cayman, a British protectorate, which meant a well-run, law-abiding place. In those days it was obvious as one traveled around the Caribbean islands that islands ruled by the Dutch or the British were mostly clean and orderly; those ruled by the French or the Spanish were not.

We had started to patrol the Yucatan because the Colombians, noticing we were patrolling the Windward and Mona passes, began to go through the Yucatan Channel instead. It was a longer trip for them because they had to go northwest from the Guajira until they got past Cuba, then turn almost straight east to get to the islands, but it avoided the Mona and the Windward.

Agent Ludlow Adams was with me on this tour. He was a jolly, plump DEA pilot, stationed in Atlanta. Other pilots called him Mudhole and warned me that he "talked too much." But I soon found Ludlow to be excellent company and a reliable pilot. Yes, he had some peculiarities. He hated to fly IFR, for instance. He said flying in the clouds was an "unnatural act," and anyone who enjoyed it (meaning me) must be some kind of pervert and should be examined closely by a psychiatrist for other dark flaws in his personality. He was indeed a chatterbox, but I found no harm in that.

One day he says to me, "I know I talk too much. I hope you don't mind."

I said, "I don't mind at all, as long as you don't mind if I sometimes don't listen."

He stared for a moment. Then a grin spread over his face. He held out his hand and said, "Deal!" We were friends from then on.

The nasty wind this particular morning was no real problem for flying. It blew straight down the runway. We took off with the rain rattling on the windscreen, and the Merlin jumping and yawing in the unstable air. The gusty wind tossed us around like a dry leaf. We headed straight south at first, then turned northwest to follow the likely path of a boat coming off the Guajira and headed for the middle of the Yucatan Pass. The Windward and the Mona are little more than fifty miles broad, but the Yucatan is double that, so we zigzagged back and forth for miles on either side of the path. Ludlow watched the radar, and I watched the ocean trying to spot any strange object.

The sea was boiling rough below, waves rolling high and the wind tearing sheets of foam from their tops and swirling them across the surface of the sea. Patches of low clouds fled before the wind, and we wound our way through them, depending more than usual on the weather radar. We ran into light rainsqualls, which did not improve our visibility. In a little while, Ludlow began to plan his lunch. He spent most of his waking hours thinking about food—another peculiarity of his. He'd eat any time of day. "Hunger is bad for you, weakens the immune system," he used to say. But he didn't take his eyes off the radar as he mentally built a sandwich of sliced beef, ham, Bermuda onion, swiss cheese and . . . "Wait a minute," he said. "Look at this." He pointed at a spot on the radar.

I rolled the Merlin into a steep bank and let her drop low over the water, and we headed in the direction of the target. Now we both looked outside. Ludlow wrote down her approximate coordinates adding and subtracting from our present position to pinpoint hers. With the low clouds, we could easily have missed her, but in a minute, there she was right in front of us barely visible among the foaming waves. No one was on deck, no surprise in this weather. Her prow soared and plunged as she bucked the mountains of water before her. She was smashing into waves that broke over the top of her bow, some washing clear across the deck. I felt queasy just looking. If I had been on that boat, I would have been sick as a poisoned dog. We made several passes on her but could not get a name. A sign on the stern had been painted over with tar. We saw some faded writing on her port side, but she was heeled over so far that, with the constant spray of the ocean and the waves curling over that side, it was unreadable. Ludlow called the Coast Guard, giving her position, heading, and speed. He must have done a good job because they intercepted her the next day—and she was loaded.

We found two more drug boats that morning. It was the best day we ever had. I had been on tours in the islands where we didn't find three boats in a month. That tour with Ludlow was the best. Having Ludlow on board was like having a chef and stewardess, and a good buddy and an excellent spotter. All pilots carried wide brief cases filled with maps, approach plates, and flight logs. Ludlow's was filled with sliced meats, cheeses, onions, pumpernickel bread, and gourmet mustard, which he slathered on his sandwiches in prodigious amounts. Ludlow was generous in sharing the bounty of his briefcase. My mouth still waters as I recall some of his creations in the cockpit. It was one of the few times I gained weight while on a TDY assignment.

That was a lazy, easy time on Cayman. We stayed in a luxurious apartment right by the beach. We worked mornings and lay around on the sand in the afternoon drinking beer with nary a care. We were finding plenty of boats, and the bosses were happy. Ludlow rubbed his Buddha belly with extravagant contentment. The days drifted by peacefully. Then about mid-month, the peace was broken by a phone call.

"Message for you at the office," Ludlow said as he was unfolding his lawn chair under a shady palm tree. "It says to call your stupid-visor."

I put off calling my supervisor until late in the day hoping that, whatever the crises, it'd go away. They were always in crises-mode at headquarters and often called half a dozen pilots and gave the job to whoever answered first. But this time the request was specifically for Ludlow and me. It was to do an undercover deal for Atlanta.

"We need you guys to go to Jamaica right away." As always the supervisor's voice was full of urgency on the phone.

Oh, no. Not Jamaica. We'd be going into Kingston and wading though a giant cesspool of bureaucrats to check into a country the size of a flea. Ludlow and I didn't hurry. It was always this way with supervisors—everything,

I mean everything, was a hurry-up emergency. Everything a crisis. They never planned ahead. Always putting out fires, never preventing them. Ludlow and I were having great success at Cayman. Plenty of pilots sat around in the States who could have done the Atlanta job. But the supervisor said the Atlanta office had specifically requested Ludlow for the deal.

Ludlow called the case agent in Atlanta, a friend of his, Agent Russ Jerkins. We made out arrangements with Jerkins. The supervisors always got things wrong. If we took their word for it, we might end up spending a week in Jamaica wondering why we were there. Agent Jerkins had been talking to a Colombian who said he could get us all the Colombian marijuana we wanted through his people in Jamaica. Jerkins wanted to get a load of 1,500 pounds and fly it to some dealers in Atlanta, then arrest the dealers when they came with their money. We'd get the Atlanta crooks, their money, and Jamaican authorities could arrest the source in Jamaica. That latter part of the plan was certainly up in the air. Jamaica had notoriously corrupt officials.

We had a one o'clock p.m. meeting at the embassy in Kingston next day. That meant we had to be airborne by mid morning. It was only a short flight to Jamaica, but it could take several hours to go through all the rigmarole of the Jamaican Airport Authority, with dozens of forms to fill out, and each one needing to be stamped by three or four pompous officials. I was in a bad mood that morning, dreading that nightmare-blizzard of meaningless paperwork. But after we got into the sky, and all was magnificent blue with only a few clouds on the eastern horizon, and the Merlin slipping smoothly along over an unruffled sea, I was put back in good kilter. In forty minutes we began descent over Montego Bay, landing at Norman Manley International in Kingston.

Security men swarmed over the Merlin like rats. We didn't flash credentials. We were undercover. We said we had come to take a load of Red Stripe Beer back to our boss in Houston. They grilled us about guns and *ganja* (their name for marijuana). They kept warning us smuggling *ganja* wasn't allowed on their island—such a preposterous lie Ludlow couldn't help smiling. This made their chief pull out a spiral notebook from which he read the law to us (it was written in pencil). The official tried to sound authoritarian. His sing-song delivery and heavy Jamaican accent made me smile, too.

Next came a team of officials from "the Department of Health of Jamaica." They wore faded, dirty uniforms, carried battered hand-pump pressure sprayers, and looked unhealthy. They sprayed us, fogged us, fumigated all around, in the most unlikely event we were carrying some bug they didn't already have in profusion on their island. Ludlow and I staggered outside coughing. They took great care to decontaminate our airplane, while the surrounding airport looked like a germ farm: flies buzzing around bits of rotting garbage, little piles of brown deposits left by dogs, cats—maybe humans?

Next a security officer led us around the airport where we had to visit everyone. Jamaican officials from Customs, Immigration, Health, Airport Authority, and other departments grudgingly shoved papers under our noses as if we had insulted them by showing up. They were surly and suspicious, asking again and again the purpose of our visit.

We survived all the stamping, folding, stapling, and questioning. We got to the American Embassy shortly after noon. There we met with officials from our State Department, from DEA, and from the Jamaican government. Agent Jerkins was a quiet unassuming agent, not at all the clamoring, anxious, aggressive type described by my supervisor. Jerkins wanted this deal to go with all his heart. But the whole thing didn't look good. The crooks were from the western part of the island. The Jamaican Army had complete control there, and the Jamaican police told us every army officer was corrupt. If we were to tell an army officer about the deal, it'd be called off, and the officer would be immediately richer. On the other hand, if we didn't tell the army and got caught, we'd end up in jail for months while the U.S. Embassy tried to bail us out. The Jamaican authorities didn't care whether we did the deal or not; they simply stressed they could give us no protection in that part of their country. The American authorities wanted to call it off.

Jerkins was beside himself. He'd worked hard to put this deal together, and now at the last minute it was evaporating into thin air. Ludlow did not want to do it. He was afraid he couldn't make sandwiches in a Jamaican-army jail. I wanted to meet the crooks, at least. I made this proposal: let's meet with the crooks and treat this just like a real deal. If the crooks can convince us we're safe from the army, we'll do it. If they can't show us the deal will be done in such a way the army won't interfere, we'll call it off. The U.S. Embassy officials said they'd have to talk to Washington first. Jerkins, Ludlow, and I checked into the Pegasus Hotel in Kingston to wait for a decision. I told Agent Jerkins I didn't think the deal was a go. Washington always took the easy way out on a decision like this. Calling off the deal was their easy way out.

To this day I don't know how the decision was made to go ahead with the deal. Somebody in Atlanta had great influence at headquarters. There was no way for surveillance to give us cover and, if the army got us, no way to get us out of jail without weeks of embarrassing international haggling. Either someone at headquarters didn't understand the deal (which is likely), or someone had some guts (which is unheard of). They said, "Go ahead, but you're on your own."

The next afternoon we met with two Jamaicans, Deebo and Nini, to negotiate the deal. Nini was a thin, slightly bent like an old man, but he was quite young and full of energy. He was black as tar and smoked cigarettes with a passion—as if each one would be his last. Deebo on the other hand was tall and straight, a brawny picture of health. He wore his shirt wide open in front showing a mat of hair like black steel wool.

Deebo I liked immediately. He was all business. Before he'd answer my questions, he wanted answers to his. He asked about how much flying experience I had, how old the Merlin was, and when it had its last annual and last one-hundred-hour inspection.

When he was satisfied, he said, "Now, what things do you need to know?"

"I need to see the field."

"Not to worry, mawn," he said. "Three thousand feet. Cool runnings, mawn." (Deebo always said, "Cool r-runnings, mahn," when he meant "everything's cool.")

"I need to see it."

"I show you on the map. You have no trouble finding the place. Big strip."

"I need to see it with my own eyes."

I had gone through this sort of thing before and wasn't about to take someone else's word on the suitability of the strip. Deebo looked a bit irritated. He hung his head awhile as if in deep thought. He tilted his head back and stared at me with his mouth pulled to one side. He took a deep breath and let it out.

"Okay," he said, "Let's go."

We walked to Deebo's car parked on a side street. Kingston was flooded with hazy, smoky sunshine, and with dark people dressed in brightly colored clothes. They walked with a lazy gait as though going nowhere in particular. All over were Red Stripe Beer signs, and Bob Marley pictures, Bob Marley music, Bob Marley books, and dreadlocks, pipes, and marijuana smoke.

Deebo drove. I mean he drove like a man possessed. His foot was jammed to the floor all the time—either full accelerator or full brake. Jerkins, Ludlow, and I were in the back. Our heads were either in the front seat from the braking or against the back window from the accelerating. If anyone was trying to follow, they were lost immediately, unless they were suicidal. The roads in Kingston were crowded with traffic: beat-up old cars, smoky snarly trucks, and people on foot with bundles on their heads, mules, donkeys, and ancient oxcarts with wavering wooden wheels. Blowing past everything on the road, we went west out of Kingston. We roared into Spanish Town and turned south. Suddenly there was no traffic—nothing.

Some large water tanks appeared on a hill to the left. Deebo pointed, "When you fly, look for the water tanks, turn straight south, one mile."

I was impressed. Exactly the type of landmark a pilot would look for. Deebo had done this before. Those tanks would be easy to spot from the air. We turned east into the trees and came to a fence with an iron gate. Deebo honked. Shortly a man stepped out of the trees and opened the gate. We drove onto a rutted gravel runway, sugar-cane fields on either side. Women and children were cutting cane. As we drove down the runway we passed women carrying enormous bundles of cane on their heads. I got out at the far end and kicked around in the gravel.

"Can't do it, Deebo," I said, "The Merlin will bounce on these ruts and the props will kick up the dirt. The engines will eat these little rocks and spit out parts we might need." I explained to Deebo that the Dash 10 engines on the Merlin are mounted upside down, putting the intakes on the bottom and with little clearance between the long propeller blades and the ground, the engines could easily ingest loose gravel on this kind of runway.

"Even grass would be better," I said.

"You like pavement?"

"Why, hell yes, I'd like pavement. But there are suitable runways that aren't pavement. This isn't one of them."

"You want pavement, I give you pavement."

The nightmare ride began again, only this time Deebo was in a real hurry. The roads were all dust and dirt but little traffic. In Spanish Town he turned west and streaked for May Pen. In May Pen he headed south again. I remain convinced Deebo took every corner on two wheels. We zoomed through shabby little towns of garbage and goats. People scattered like chickens in front of Deebo's flying missile. Women washing clothes in the creeks by the road looked up, then disappeared in clouds of dust. Soon the road was winding back and forth in brush country, veering crazily from side to side. Suddenly we burst out at the end of a vast, paved runway. I knew immediately where we were. I had studied the map—this was Vernam Field.

Vernam Field was an old World War II United States airbase. B-52s used to fly down here on training missions from Kansas. They used to hunt submarines out of here. But those days were long gone. The place was abandoned. All the buildings had been torn down. The seams between the cement slabs of the runway were sprouting tall weeds. Some of the slabs had heaved a little. I asked Deebo to drive down the runway to check for bumps. I had barely made the request, and we were flying down the field. There were a few thumps but nothing I thought would hurt the Merlin.

Vernam Field was good enough, but there were still a few details. I asked Deebo about the army. According to the information I had, an army base was not far away. I wanted to know if they had been paid off. Deebo admitted most traffickers on the west side of Jamaica used to pay off the army, but he said the officers were demanding way too much money now. He said the army was never a problem. They were too slow and too stupid to catch Deebo. He said we'd be loaded and gone long before an army unit could make it out of bed. "The army's stupid and slow, he said. It'll take them hours to get mobilized. It'll take them hours just to decide."

I was worried about the little village near the southern end of the field, but Deebo said the entire village was involved in drug trafficking and some of the villagers would be helping with the loading.

"This will do," I said, "We've found ourselves a runway."

Deebo grinned. "Okay, we load 1,500 pounds of *ganja* tomorrow at daybreak." He held out his hand to shake mine.

"We make a good team," he said. "I worry about my *ganja*, you worry about your airplane."

Nini was in charge of the loading. He said he'd have at least ten people to help. He showed us where he'd have the marijuana hidden in some thick bushes by the runway. He'd have a white sheet there on the side of the runway as a signal all was ready and safe to land. We were to park next to the bushes, leaving the engines running. Nini told me not to worry if I saw people running out on the runway from the village during the loading. They often came running, hoping to help load, so they could get paid.

Now my worry was that someone would run into a propeller blade. I said I'd shut down the left engine (the side where the door was), but both Deebo and Nini said no. Their men knew to stay away from the front of the engines. I could see they wanted us out of there as quickly as possible, which were my sentiments exactly. I was satisfied. Deebo had done a professional job of selling his operation. He was quick minded. I was confident.

We returned to Kingston the same way, with Deebo at the wheel, narrowly missing at least a dozen head-on collisions. I was the front-seat passenger this time—a big mistake. While passing other traffic Deebo played chicken with oncoming, monster trucks. The trucks usually lost the game and took to the shoulder at the last second, horns blaring angrily. On occasion, when he encountered a driver with some spine, Deebo would admit defeat and either pull back into his lane or would run the car he was passing off the road. Deebo relied on his horn far more than on his brakes. He simply honked his way through everything, leaving me clutching the dashboard, the seat, and my heart. And all the while he kept up a merry conversation about beer, *ganja,* and girls.

At five o'clock we got back to the Pegasus Hotel and we sat down for a beer. Trouble developed immediately. Nini wanted money up front for the loaders. We refused. Hell, we couldn't front money. Jerkin hadn't brought any, and besides who would front money to a Jamaican? Deebo was obstinate. He called off the deal and they left. They said they wouldn't be back unless we agreed to at least some front money. Jerkins was destroyed. He thought everything was lost. We cried in our beer for a while, and hoped they'd change their minds. Twenty minutes later they were back saying they were ready to do business. I grinned at Deebo, and he grinned back. He knew I was thinking he had blinked first.

We returned to Cayman, Jerkins along with us. We took some of the seats out of the Merlin and added thirteen hundred pounds of fuel. We checked all the fluid levels and were ready for an early morning go. The tower operator was Christopher, a squat, black man with a solemn, patient face. Christopher agreed to temporarily open the field at five o'clock in the morning. That'd give us enough time to be in Jamaica at daybreak.

Next morning at four, my alarm blasted me out of bed. Jerkins and Ludlow were already up. I called Christopher to make sure he hadn't forgotten. I took a quick shower. We'd eat breakfast on board—Ludlow sandwhiches. At 4:50 Ludlow and I were cranking the big Dash 10s. At 4:57 we were at the end of the runway ready for takeoff. It was still dark. My excitement was running high. At exactly at 5:00 a.m., Christopher brought up the airport lights. Without a word from me he said, "Merlin, you're cleared for take off."

We were rolling. We'd make it right at daybreak. Christoper announced he'd leave the lights on for fifteen minutes in case we had trouble. I liked that guy. The airport would open again shortly before seven, which was when we expected to be back. We'd top off our gas at Cayman for the trip to Atlanta. We began a climb toward the east. Right away things didn't look so good. A line of thunderstorms loomed in our path. That made the tension build. If we had to navigate around those storms, we might be late. Lightning was popping like flashbulbs all along the line. Every once in a while a dramatic flash would light up the entire eastern sky and hold it for a quivering second so we could see the mammoth cells scowling down on us. I looked at Ludlow. He was shaking his head. He dialed up the radar and a river of red showed the line was solid. I headed the Merlin for the thinnest point in the line and kept climbing. As we got above 20,000 feet, approaching the line we could see a little break. We made for the hole and kept in the clear as we entered the line. Turbulence tossed the plane violently for a few seconds, then suddenly we were through, sailing along in wonderfully smooth air.

The eastern sky was showing red as we picked up the lights of Jamaica. We dropped down to skim over the inky water. Ludlow set the radio at 123.4, the agreed frequency to contact Deebo. I tuned in the Ayr Hill Beacon and turned to intercept the 150-degree radial inbound. I didn't really need it. I knew where I was. Vernam Field was dead ahead twelve miles. Ludlow tried calling on the radio, but there was no answer. He called for Deebo. Silence. He called for Nini. Nothing.

Ludlow was upset. "Damn those idiots, they didn't bother to turn on their radios."

We were coming up on the runway. I could see the lights of the smokey little village winking through the trees. Still no answer. It was light enough now we could make out the runway, but there was no white sheet.

"Damn it, Russ," I said to Jerkins, "I can't land here without that white sheet, and at this altitude we're going to wake up the whole damned town and all the army units on this island."

"Oh, shit," he said mournfully, "Don't tell me." He was straining ahead looking up and down the runway for a sheet.

We were almost at the north end of the runway. We couldn't take the chance thundering over the trees like this and wake up the army. Then a man stepped from the bushes, frantically waving a white sheet.

"There's the sheet," Jerkins yelled, and I started a hard, right climbing turn. I brought back the power and continued in a 360-degree turn putting down the gear and flaps as the airspeed bled down rapidly. I dived for the runway. We rolled out on a very short final half way down the field and touched down almost immediately. I jumped on the brakes, and we came to a halt right where the man was standing with the sheet. Ludlow had left the cockpit and swung open the door as soon as the Merlin stopped.

A dozen men stepped out of the brush. Deebo and Nini were among them giving orders. The men marched to the plane in single file like a drill team. Bundles came flying into the back of the plane. As soon as a man had tossed his bundle, he about-faced and marched into the brush for another. The bundles came with the regularity of a conveyor belt. Ludlow and Jerkins had their hands full just throwing the stuff toward the front. I went through the before-takeoff checklist. I'd barely finished when I saw Deebo giving me the thumbs up. I began running in the power, holding the brakes. I heard the thump as Ludlow closed the door and, when I saw the door-ajar light go out on the warning panel, I released brakes. I swung the Merlin around reaching full power as we straightened with the runway.

We were on the roll—but what I saw ahead of the plane brought my heart into my throat. Men, women, children, dogs, chickens, and goats were charging down the runway toward us, streaming out of that little village by the runway. Ludlow said, "Oh, shit." Someone might run into a prop! But we couldn't stop now. There might be Jeeps full of Jamaican regulars tearing toward the airport. Ludlow was screaming, "Get outta the way." I was flashing the taxi light as the plane was gaining speed. As we approached the crowd, it parted like the Red Sea. We were clear except for one little goat caught running in front of the airplane. When he turned to the right he saw this big monster bearing down on him so he swung back to the left. When he did that, he could see the thing again, so he turned back right. He zigzagged like that in front of us and we rapidly overtook him. I didn't have liftoff speed yet, but I hauled back mightily on the yoke to bring up the nose and raise the propellers, hoping the goat would pass under. The nose came up just as the goat disappeared under the plane. He cleared the props but we felt a sickening thump as he hit the main gear.

"One dead goat," Ludlow counted.

The plane staggered into the air but settled back to the runway for more speed. I lowered the nose for a second and rotated again. This time she lifted off easily and sailed over the trees at the end of the runway. I put up the gear and flaps, and we were slipping swiftly through the sweet morning air. As soon as we were cleaned up, I banked to the west toward Grand Cayman. Below us ocean mists were falling away rapidly. Incredibly, we had spent less than five minutes on the ground. Jerkins and Ludlow were high-fiving it. We had the dope, the rest would be easy.

We delivered the marijuana to Atlanta later that day. That was the end of that trip for me. I went home. I heard from Ludlow later that the agents had arrested several people and taken their money when they came for the dope in Atlanta. Nini had come to Atlanta and was among those arrested. The Jamaican Police had tried to set up a meeting with Deebo in Jamaica but he never showed up. Deebo was too smart. He could smell a rat like a terrier.

Cool r-runnings, mawn.

Chapter Twenty-Four

Early one morning while makin' the rounds
I took a shot of cocaine and I shot my woman down
Went right home and I went to bed
I stuck that lovin' forty-four beneath my head.

Got up next morning and I grabbed that gun
I took a shot of cocaine and away I run
Made a good run but I run too slow
They overtook me down in Juarez Mexico
~Johnny Cash song, by T.J. Arnall,

To make cocaine you need the coca bush. More specifically, you need the leaves of the coca bush. There are several varieties, but the best ones grow in South America on the eastern slopes of the Andes Mountains. Cool temperature and the rainfall are just right there to make the plant happy. It's an innocent little plant, no more harmful than a coffee bush, and less poisonous than the tomato plant in your garden. The ancient tribes of the Andes, like the Incas of the altiplano, chewed the leaf long before the white man ever began chewing tobacco—and with less harm. They steeped the leaves in hot water and drank the brew for as long as Chinamen have had their tea. Using coca without abusing it means using it like a native of the Andes. To abuse the plant, you have to get out a chemistry set and make it into something else—something it wasn't meant to be. You can process it into coca base and into cocaine. Then you can use it like Len Bias and Whitney Houston. And you'll surely become addicted. And you, too, could die.

Americans had a flowery romance with cocaine. Here's part of that sweet story, how the romance fell apart, and how we made fools of ourselves (again): As the sun rose on the decade of the 1980s, it was setting on the Age of Aquarius. The flower children who had tried living off the land in communes found it was not as easy as they had thought. They learned that "Mother Earth" was not at all like their real mother. She did not give them free stuff. Mother Earth was rather a tight-fisted miser who demanded payment in the form of manual labor. These children, the baby boomers, didn't like that kind of labor. They turned to (horrors!) capitalism. They were now competing in the marketplace and were doing well. They wore starched white shirts instead of tie-died kimonos, oxfords instead of sandals. They wore the suits and ties they had so much despised and drove to work in expensive new cars. They sat behind mahogany desks in elegant offices overlooking downtown. But they remembered the good old days, and they still held the belief the really good times came through the use of drugs.

Now they had money and could afford the best. They wanted something a bit zippier than pot and not as zany as LSD. They didn't like heroin much—that was for back-alley street bums to stick in their arms with dirty needles. They discovered cocaine. It was nice and white and clean, and they could suck it up their noses through a rolled-up twenty dollar bill and look ever-so-smart at an office party. The baby boomers sent a river of American greenbacks, wide as the Amazon, flowing to South America. They made Pablo Escobar ever so happy. The Colombians had for a long time been smuggling small quantities of cocaine in false-bottom suit cases, in statues of the Blessed Virgin, in hollowed-out wooden legs, and in the coat pockets of dead bodies in coffins. They had sneaked in small loads in balloons swallowed by mules, who came into Miami starving themselves so the balloons would not pass into their diapers before they had a chance to get by US Customs and get to a hotel room where they could encourage the happy event with doses of castor oil. But these methods were insufficient to meet the great baby-boomer demand. Now tons and tons were required.

At the beginning of the decade of the 1980s, all over the Southern U.S, informants were telling DEA and Customs that multi-ton loads of cocaine were coming in by air, but we didn't believe them. The best we ever got were one-hundred-kilo loads. How far ahead of us the Colombians were became obvious in the spring of 1982 when U.S. Customs officers at Miami International Airport tripped over some boxes being unloaded from a TAMPA Boeing 707 just in from Colombia. The cargo was "wearing apparel." The officers poking around the boxes noticed some white powder running out of a punctured box labeled "JEANS." These ingenious, ever-curious officers thought maybe this deserved further inspection. It occurred to them that jeans didn't normally leak white powder. They found two tons of cocaine—really good cocaine. The innocent acronym, TAMPA, had probably fooled many into thinking it was an American airline out of Tampa, Florida, but it belonged to a Colombian cargo company that had been flying their "cargo" into Miami for three years. The acronym stood for Transportes Aéreos Mercantiles Panamericanos. They hauled cargo for a company in Medellin that belonged to Pablo Escobar and the Ochoa clan.

The snitches were right. Cocaine was coming in by the ton. We were getting a very small part of it, like getting a few drops of river water while trying to stop the Amazon.

Miami was the U.S. city nearest to all those Caribbean islands populated with sailor bandits, who could sail a sloop in a storm and find a certain hidden cove on a dark night among hundreds of coves along eight thousand miles of Florida shoreline. Miami was also the first stop of all the "legal" commercial airliners coming from Colombia. The Medellín and Cali Cartels were taking advantage of this, and had no trouble keeping ahead of DEA and Customs. All our patrolling, intercepting and interdicting did nothing. The seizures we made under operations like BAT, Grouper, Tiburon were considered by Pablo Escobar and the boys as simply cost of doing business. Brutal competition among the cocaine traffickers blossomed in Miami. The result was dead bodies on street corners of the city every morning or floating in the green waters of the Everglades—collateral damage of doing business.

Miami boiled with Colombian traffickers. Miami was wild-west Dodge City, Al-Capone Chicago, and Cuerno-de-Chivo Culiacan multiplied by a factor of ten: the Mac-10. In Miami they used the Mac-10 in place of the Kalashnikov to do business. A Mac-10 is a cute little machine pistol just made for hoodlums. They could hide it under their coats, easily unload a thirty-two-round clip of monster .45 caliber slugs in two seconds, and punch every one of them through a car door as easily as if it were the front page of the *Miami Herald*. With a suppressor mounted on the barrel, it made no more noise than a printing press. But the Colombians much preferred it without the suppressor. That way it made enough noise to wake the dead. The Colombians wanted that noise to wake up Miami to the fact that a new order of criminal was taking over the trade. Bodies were left lying in pools of blood in plain sight to make the front page of the *Miami Harold*.

Usually the popularity of a drug doesn't last long. Drugs cycle through fads like ladies' apparel. The big-three in the cycle are heroin, cocaine, and amphetamine. In between are minor fads like methoqualone, PCP, ecstasy—anything that comes handy. But the baby boomers stuck to their coke a long time. They went through different styles of using it: trying it in their noses and eyes, freebasing, and smoking it in the form of crack. It was the in-thing. They openly wore solid gold coke spoons and gold razor blades on neck chains. The bolder ones had little vials with a white powder inside (it may have been baking soda, but it looked so-oo brave and trendy). Baby boomers thought themselves forever young and indestructible. They held a general belief cocaine was harmless and "only mentally addictive"—if at all.

Cocaine was lifted out of the gutter and into the penthouse. Before, it had been a pimp's drug—used to keep whores in line. Now it was associated with glamour, wealth, and power. By the time I got settled into my station at McAllen, cocaine was "the champagne of drugs." It was preferred by aristocrats, stars, and artists. A 1981 issue of *Time* magazine had a cover story about cocaine. On the front cover was a beautiful martini glass full of gorgeous white powder. The message was: "it's just like a martini, only you snort instead of swallow." *Time* said cocaine was the drug of choice for solid, conventional citizens. They clearly linked coke to smart, classy people who knew how to make money, and how to party. So many rumors circulated of cocaine use by the Dallas Cowboys (who called themselves "America's Team") people began calling them "South America's team."

The magazines *High Times* and *Rolling Stone* rolled with the times. *High Times* had centerfolds featuring cocaine. It was all such fun! *Rolling Stone* could not extol the virtues of cocaine and crack enough, and only rarely conceded there might be a little down side. The cool people, they said, used cocaine, and didn't have any trouble with it. "Intelligent people do drugs intelligently." At one point the magazines were promoting crack-smoking over snorting the powder, "because it was a more natural form of cocaine" (and we all know that anything "natural" is harmless).

But then, good Lord!—some very inconvenient warnings began to surface. In big cities we began to hear of crack houses, and they sounded suspiciously like the old opium dens of Chinatown. One crack smoker explained the problem this way: "It's much more addictive than the old snort. The stuff gets to your brain instantly, and you get a blast way more intense. You become an addict right then and there. Your will-power doesn't mean shit, maturity doesn't mean shit, backbone doesn't mean shit. You sucked up and now you're fucked up. All you want is more!"

Probably the first time normal people heard about freebasing cocaine (by normal here I mean the ones who didn't have a lifetime subscription to *High Times* or *Rolling Stone*) was when comedian Richard Pryor set himself on fire while freebasing at his California home and, being completely screwed up from the drug, fanned his fire by running down the streets of LA yelling for help instead of trying to snuff it out. People stared, and wondered if he was practicing his comedy act. The cops jumped him and put out the fire, but not before burns covered half his body. He spent six weeks in recovery at the burn center in the Sherman Oaks Hospital.

But even this incident was treated lightly. When he got back on stage Pryor said, "Funny thing, when you're on fire and running down the street, people will get out of your way." And fellow comedian George Carlin mentioned the incident later at a Carnegie Hall performance. He said, "An update on the comedian health sweepstakes. I currently lead Richard Pryor in heart attacks two-to-one. But Richard leads me one-to-nothing in burning yourself up." Considering Pryor's burn damage, Carlin added: "Fuck that. I'm having another heart attack."

As the decade progressed, things weren't so funny anymore. Cocaine began losing its glitter. In big cities gangs were formed that sold crack, and there was violence over turf wars, and lots of guns and blood and bodies in the streets. TV documentaries about the down side of cocaine appeared. The beautiful people were coming out of the cocaine closet and confessing. Hollywood celebrities admitted they were actually cocaine addicts and needed help. Hollywood doctors were finding "coke noses" on their patients—yes, on those beautiful, sophisticated, and smart noses. Chronic cocaine sniffers developed holes in their nasal septums, and doctors were scratching their heads about how to patch them up. A voluptuous blonde was less alluring with a hole in her nose. (That was in the old days; nowadays she bores the hole herself and sets a platinum nose screw in it with a 14K diamond to make sure everyone notices.)

And then some sports heroes began actually to die. There had already been cocaine corpses found in crack houses and getting in the way at hospital emergency entrances, but those were just stupid junkie kids and poor blacks. Now real people were dying! Len Bias, University of Maryland basketball superstar, died. Just like that. One day he's playing great basketball, next day he's dead. He would have made millions in his life. Len Bias, a healthy giant, six-foot-eight, over 200 pounds, down as if struck by lightening. Only a week later, lightning struck again. Down went Don Rogers, Cleveland Brown defensive linebacker, another healthy giant.

The worst thing about the cocaine epidemic for cops was that the coke heads of the street turned into real assholes. They weren't laid back like the heroin addict and pot smoker. When they were on a high, they thought they could fight the cops, fight the army, fight the world. They became paranoid and saw cops everywhere so they were always ready. Many were reduced to sitting on the couch watching TV while clutching a loaded shotgun—safety off. I was used to the passive junky who sat around all day in his bathrobe and dozed in a heroin stupor or a marijuana haze, but these cocaine abusers were fiercely aggressive, like mainline speeders, and thought nothing of challenging with their bare fists police officers holding drawn pistols. I was glad to be in the Air Wing because I was seldom required to go along and kick in the door on one of those crazy maniacs.

The public began to yell at their congressmen to do something. Congress went into the usual frenzy. In a short time they passed the mandatory minimum laws in dispute to this day. In the antidrug hysteria of 1986, Congress declared crack cocaine one hundred times worse then the powder variety. Offenders got five years in jail for selling five hundred grams of the powder cocaine, but it took only five grams of crack to get the same sentence! Public pressure makes politicians do crazy things. They pass crazy laws and demand crazy action.

That's how DEA got themselves into operations like Snowcap and Blast Furnace in South America. During the rest of my career with DEA, I spent most of my foreign flying time in support of those programs. Like Trizo these were operations only city slickers could dream up. They blamed the problem on the farmers. United States bureaucrats decided to "attack the problem at its source." They sent us to South America to help local officials destroy coca bushes and arrest farmers all along the eastern slopes of the Andes. We searched the lowland jungles for cocaine labs and destroyed what we found.

To understand how complicated these operations can get in a foreign country, one has to know something of the people and the history: The farmer of Bolivia was no different from the farmer of Stearns County. He earned his bread by the sweat of his brow. He ploughed his fields and tended his orchards to make money to feed his family. He didn't care about world politics, didn't care about (was almost surely not even aware of) the cocaine problem in the United States. When buyers came to his farm and offered to pay him ten times as much for a coca crop as for a corn crop, he planted coca.

And why not? It is impossible to convince an Andean native there was harm in the coca bush. It grew wild in the Andes. The natives of Peru and Bolivia, especially the royalty, had chewed its leaves since the time of the Inca and the Aymara. They'd domesticated the plant thousands of years ago.

The Spanish, when they conquered this area, found their Indian slaves in the silver mines of the altiplano could suffer the cold, hunger, and brutal labor better when they chewed coca. They promoted the cultivation of the bush, and its use spread among the common people. The farmers of the Andes regularly chewed wads of coca leaves as they worked their fields. Their wives used it for headaches, stomachaches, muscle aches, and various other ailments. They administered it to their children.

And just as with the poppy in Mexico, for years the United States had been encouraging the growing of coca and had been buying tons of the leaves from Bolivia to make pharmaceutical and other coca products in the United States. Many common U. S. medicines were made from coca and so were many popular "soft drinks." In the early 1900s our Coca Cola Company was using cocaine in their super secret drink. People often called it "Dopa Cola." A drink called "Wiseola" made you smart. "Koca Nola" made you forget all your troubles. Many believed (and that included doctors) cocaine was good for your health and it could safely free you from the addictions of opium and whiskey. In the early 1900s we were merrily downing over ten tons of coca a year in the U.S.—and that was when the population was only ninety million. In those days as much legal coca leaf shipped to the States as illegal leaf shipped when I began working for DEA. And now suddenly, along comes the United States government and tells the Bolivian farmer he can't grow the stuff anymore. It was like telling a Stearns County farmer he can't grow corn.

The Bolivian farmer wasn't the one making the cocaine powder; he was growing rows of pretty coca bushes in beautifully terraced, peaceful fields on the mountainside. He wasn't getting rich. He grew the stuff because it paid better than other crops. He sold the coca leaves to cocaine traffickers, and they made the real money. Sometimes the farmer made the leaves into coca paste, but only because it made shipping easier. The paste took up far less room, and unprocessed leaves tended to get moldy. The paste was cheap to make, requiring only kerosene and soda ash. The farmers mixed it in "maceration pits" and drained off the liquid leaving a greenish, pukey paste, which was shipped to the labs.

The money makers in this business were the ones doing the shipping, the processing, and the smuggling. In Bolivia the chief of these was Roberto Suarez. When I was down in Bolivia looking for cocaine labs, Roberto was the undisputed Cocaine King. Roberto was different from the drug kings in other countries. He didn't start out poor. Roberto was from a family that was rich and influential. The family had gained most of their wealth in the rubber business in the early 1900s. And Roberto never gained the bloody notoriety of men like Rafael Caro Quintero who killed DEA Agent Camarena in Mexico or of Pablo Escobar who bombed judges and blew up airline passengers in Colombia. When we were in Bolivia, we saw Roberto sometimes at night in the bars and nightclubs of Trinidad and Santa Cruz, but we didn't arrest him. We were told not to bother him, nor his platoon of body guards, nor his bevy of girlfriends. We bothered the farmers, and when we got lucky we bothered an occasional cocaine lab in the jungle, and those were almost always abandoned.

The Suarez family had at first been living in Santa Cruz and had social and political prestige there. Old grandpa Suarez wanted to be a cowboy. He moved the family to the northern part of Bolivia and claimed large tracts of land there. The claims weren't disputed. Much of the land was Amazon flood land—a tangle of vines and trees. The place was crawling with caimans, anacondas, jaguars, and (as described by the Bolivian Army captain telling me this) "a few worthless Indians." With the help of his brothers, grandpa either killed the natives or scared them off their lands. The Suarez boys settled down to raising cattle on the vast stretches of belly-high grass that extended between the patches of jungle. Son, Nicolas, the father of Roberto, did not care so much for cows. He took up selling quinine, widely used to treat malaria in those days, and not widely available except out of the heart of the Amazon jungle. When rubber became popular, Nicolas went into that business. He discovered the Suarez land had thousands of rubber trees growing in the wild. Cattle, quinine, and rubber were shipped in Suarez steamboats down the Beni, the Mamore, and the Madeira rivers to the Amazon, where the cargo went east to the shipping ports of Brazil.

Attempts to raise rubber on plantations failed. Henry Ford came down to Brazil and tried to grow rubber for his car factories. He started a huge plantation called Fordlandia, but his rubber trees, grown close together on plantations, died. The trees growing wild, and separated by other jungle plants, prospered. The Suarez rubber business boomed. With the profits they bought more land. I read a Bolivian government report that said the Suarez family once owned six million hectares of northern Bolivian lowland. That's about fifteen million acres (one hectare is almost 2½ acres).

Eventually the British figured out how to raise rubber in Malaysia and other countries. When Roberto Suarez came of age, the rubber business had collapsed, so he went back to the old cattle business. By the time he got married, he owned vast herds of cattle and commanded hundreds of cowboys. The Bolivian Army captain who told me this stuff said Roberto was "highly respected in Bolivia." The captain admired Roberto Suarez for his honesty and said sometime in the seventies, Pablo Escobar came down from Colombia and talked Roberto into entering the cocaine business. Pablo corrupted Roberto.

It may be hard to believe a good, rich, honest man could be corrupted merely by a visit from Pablo Escobar. Keep in mind that growing coca in Bolivia didn't have any stigma attached, and at first Roberto only grew the plants. He shipped the paste to Pablo's cocaine labs in Colombia. Roberto's business grew by leaps and bounds like the appetite of North Americans grew. In a short time Roberto had a squadron of airplanes and full-time pilots to fly them. He built airstrips in the remotest parts of Northern Bolivia. He built sophisticated cocaine labs and brought chemists down from Colombia to run them. He no longer needed Pablo Escobar.

How rich Roberto became is anyone's guess. Upon leaving on one trip to Bolivia, I was told by headquarters Roberto Suarez was making 400 million dollars a year—but DEA officials tended to exaggerate. I do know he became rich enough to spread money among the poor, and came to be called "the Robin Hood of Bolivia." He helped to build hospitals and schools. He became rich enough to buy the politicians of his country. It was said he once offered to pay Bolivia's entire national debt (in the billions of dollars). It was widely known he was the money behind the 1980 military coup (called the "Cocaine Coup") that made the bloody General Luis García Meza president, and made Roberto's cousin, Colonel Luis Arce Gómez, minister of the Interior. Those two politicians were roundly hated all over Bolivia. They brooked no opposition, banned political parties, exiled or jailed their opponents, and booted reporters out of the country. They acted just like South American dictators. They weren't in office long, but during that time Roberto's cocaine shipments had government protection and any Bolivian coca trafficker who didn't pay bribes to the government had his product confiscated and handed over to those who did.

For Washington bureaucrats to deal with Bolivian presidents was not easy. The presidents changed so fast. A new one came in every few months—that is if you counted all the acting presidents, chairmen of Juntas, interim presidents, and provisional presidents that popped up as a result of revolutions, coups, mutinies, and revolts. Bolivia was only a little over 150 years old, but it had already had nearly 200 military coups. When Bolivians do elect a president, they usually repent in a month or two and send him fleeing to Argentina or Uruguay, and then they spend ten years trying to get him extradited back to Bolivia to stand trial for human rights violations. A petition to a Bolivian president has to get sent down there quickly or it'll be addressed to a man who has gone out of style and out of the country.

The U.S. kept requesting—kept demanding—that Bolivia stop the illegal coca business. The Bolivians either ignored the requests or made false promises to appease the U.S. politicians. U.S. demands were always made under threat of cutting off foreign aid. But that foreign-aid threat doesn't work as long as trafficker bribe-money exceeds foreign-aid money. And it also doesn't work because everyone knows we never cut off foreign aid.

But by the mid 1980s the drug traffickers in Bolivia were so powerful the government began to fear a takeover. Roberto Suarez already owned land the size of New Jersey and could buy more whenever he felt like it. His private bank account was more than Bolivia's reserves in the Central Bank of Bolivia in La Paz. His private army was better equipped than the Bolivian army (which isn't saying much), his fleet of aircraft was more modern than the Bolivian Air Force (which is saying even less), and his navy was bigger (which is saying he had several boats that didn't leak).

Victor Paz Estenssoro became president. He won by legal election! Our government celebrated that unique event. We were still cautious however—no election in Bolivia is final. The man with the most votes, if he doesn't have at least fifty percent, can still lose, because the National Congress can step in and pick someone else, and the military can step in at any time and override the National Congress. But Señor Estenssoro had been around the block. He'd been in politics for more than fifty years. He'd been president several times before. The last time he was president, Estenssoro had to make a run for the border because army generals were determined to shoot their president (they did this whenever they got upset). This time he had the army and the Congress behind him. In the past he had a love-hate relationship with the United States. This time it was love.

Reagan was president of the U.S at the time, and Estenssoro liked him. Both were in their declining years, though Reagan was a child compared to Estenssoro then in his doddering eighties. Estenssoro was well aware of the power of coca traffickers like Roberto Suarez and of military generals like Luis Garcia Meza. So he invited us to come down to help fight the coca traffickers.

He did this, of course, not for his love of Reagan, but for his love of the money and equipment that would pour into Bolivia to help fight the traffickers.

And that is the story of how we got the Bolivian version of "Operation Snowcap," which was a DEA counter narcotics program that lasted an eternity and accomplished nothing. And we got "Operation Blast Furnace," which temporarily brought the U.S. Army to Bolivia to help in this accomplishment.

Snowcap in Bolivia was organized into two main strike forces: a Coca Strike Force and a Lab Strike Force. The Coca Strike Force was made up of DEA agents, Bolivian OMOPAR troops, and Bolivian Army soldiers. A few U.S. Army Special Forces personnel also helped, but no one was supposed to know that; they were "not officially there." The Coca Strike Force was destroying coca bushes in the Yungas and Chapare regions. The Lab Strike Force was made up of men from the same units and joined for a while (during Blast Furnace) by troops of the U.S. Army. They had the job of hitting cocaine labs mostly in the Beni and Santa Cruz departments.

Almost all the missions I flew in Bolivia were to support the Lab Strike Force. I called those "potato runs," because so often we were hauling a planeload of potatoes, onions, and carrots to the Strike Force's forward base. They were simply transport missions, a job that didn't require a trained DEA Agent with fifteen years of experience. But my, what a wonderful way to dissipate taxpayer money! I got to visit places I would never have seen in my life were it not for the generosity of United States taxpayers and the splendid stupidity of Washington bureaucrats. I'm forever grateful.

DEA Headquarters loved Operation Snowcap. In the annals of DEA it will always be trumpeted as a great success. But among the working agents in Bolivia, it was known as "Operation Snowjob" (whenever DEA Headquarters was briefing Congress) or as "Operation Snowcrap" (whenever the agents were thinking of how much they were accomplishing); and later when the operational head of it took to lying up all day in his hotel room in Trinidad with the barmaid of the Ganadero—it was "Operation Blowjob."

Chapter Twenty-Five

AT FIRST WHEN THEY SENT ME to Bolivia it was to fly the Merlin, which is a twin turboprop made by Swearingen in San Antonio. It could easily be flown by one pilot, but the Air Wing supervisors usually insisted on using two—a more profligate spending of taxpayer money. This was done because they themselves didn't feel comfortable flying the thing alone, and they sent pilots down there who couldn't fly a Piper Cub alone. Later in Bolivia, we flew the CASA, a neat little cargo plane like a miniature C-130, made in Spain by the company Construcciones Aeronáuticas SA, which is where the name CASA comes from. That airplane did require two pilots, because one could not reach all the switches from the left seat. The CASA had a big, rear cargo door through which we could load and unload in seconds, and was a great improvement over the Merlin for transport, but it was horribly slow, and kept reminding me of the jokes told by Air Force pilots about the T-41.

For me, a trip to Bolivia usually went like this. I flew out of McAllen in the Cessna 206 up to Air Wing Headquarters at Addison to pick up the airplane for the trip, and then headed south usually with another pilot. We normally gassed up at Cozumel or, if I was alone, I gassed up at Grand Cayman and delivered twenty cases of Coors Beer to the Royal Cayman Police. They were happy to pay for the beer because it wasn't available down there, and they had it cemented in their heads it was the best beer in the world. Next we'd fly into Panama or into Bogotá to deliver supplies to the DEA offices there and to get gas. Then we flew down the line of the Andes Mountains into Lima where we got more gas and sometimes delivered supplies to the embassy. Next into La Paz to clear Bolivian customs, and finally on to Santa Cruz or Trinidad depending on which was our base at the time. In both of those towns I was greeted by signs painted on walls that said *Yanquis Afuera* (Yankees get out!).

La Paz is more than twice as high as our "mile high city," Denver. The airport is at an elevation of well over 13,000 feet. The first time I flew in there I had Agent McCravy with me, and he had a friend meet him at the airplane with an oxygen bottle. The air up there on the altiplano is very thin. It's also dry as a desert, but very cold. Down in the lowlands only a few miles to the east it's hot, and they get plenty of rain. It is hard to believe anyone would choose to live up there on that sun-blasted mountain where nothing grows, when he could live in the lowlands and eat coconuts, oranges, and bananas out of his back yard. But the Incas, who founded that city, worshipped the sun. There are few places on earth where the sun shows itself with more grandeur and glory than the high Andes. The morning light shows up in La Paz long before the sun. The eastern cordillera of the Andes hides the sun until mid morning. One waits and waits in the shadows, shivering in the dawn. Then suddenly the sun bursts over a mountain and sprays its glory and benediction on the city, and one instantly feels warm—and grateful to the sun god.

The air is so dry the body accumulates great charges of static. In the La Plaza Hotel I could walk around in the dark and light up my room with blue sparks by touching metal. I used to run my shower on hot for half an hour to get some moisture into the room. I often had an altitude-headache in La Paz. I'd go down to the restaurant and drink *mate de coca*, a tea made from the coca leaf. It felt good in my stomach and cleared my head. It was strange and creepy to think that in the United States—land of the free—I could be arrested for having that tea.

The first time I filed out of La Paz for Santa Cruz, the man who signed my flight plan said, "Watch out for Ilimani. She is hiding again this morning." He was talking about the great mountain to the east, which rockets above the other peaks to a height of over twenty-one thousand feet. The great mountain with its three snowy peaks stands along the route between La Paz and Santa Cruz. It's more than a mile higher than anything we have in the Rocky Mountains, and, Lord, it's a sight to see when the sun's setting over the western cordillera and has thrown everything else into shadow except those three snowy peaks, which then appear in blazing white, with the margins lined with gold of the evening sun—looking like an apparition of the Holy Trinity.

Ilimani was on everyone's mind at that time because on New Year's Day, just a few months earlier, Eastern Airlines Flight 980, a Boeing 727, hit that mountain as it was coming in from Asuncion. All aboard were killed. I clearly remember reading a newspaper account about the crash, because the reporter made the most superfluous statement in the history of the printed word: "The pilot did not follow the prescribed airway."

The flight data recorder and cockpit voice recorder from that crash were never recovered. The plane had hit the mountain way up in the eternal ice and snow, where the winds blow forever at a hundred miles an hour and makes searching impossible. On clear days, when Ilimani wasn't shrouded in mist, from some parts of La Paz (if you had binoculars) you could still see parts of the wreckage, dark against the snow. The bodies are up there to this day.

We often stationed at Trinidad. We could take off from La Paz, and as soon as we cleared the eastern mountains we could begin our descent because we had two miles of altitude to lose to reach Trinidad down on the floor of the grasslands of the Beni region. In Trinidad we stayed at the Ganadero (Rancher) Hotel, the best place in town. It was so named because it was in the heart of the cattle country, and any cowman with money stayed at the Ganadero. My first time there, I got a room on the third floor. The front-desk clerk assured me it was the best room in the hotel. They had built the Ganadero to specifications the Bolivians thought was sumptuous luxury. They had put thick carpet on the floor and halfway up the walls. That included in the bathroom! They shouldn't have done that. Cattlemen didn't aim well when drunk, and the carpets smelled of old, dry urine. Don't put carpet in a cowboy's bathroom unless you want to change it every Monday.

It was an oppressively hot day the first time I came to Trinidad. I was thirsty when I got to the Gandero. Across the street was a man selling Coca Cola. I had no Bolivian money, so I asked the girl at the desk to change a twenty.

She said, "Oh, I'd have to give you the official government exchange rate. You can do much better on the black market."

"Where is the black market?" I asked.

She pointed through the glass doors at a ragged man strolling along the street with a dirty knapsack on his back.

"There," she said, "he'll give you a good rate. But don't change a whole twenty. It gets too bulky. Don't you have a five?"

For five dollars, the black market money exchanger gave me five rolls of money as big around as tennis balls. The rolls were tied with rubber bands and were in denominations of 100,000 pesos bolivianos. I started to count one of the rolls, though I had no idea what I was counting. The exchanger waved me aside.

"No, no count. Is all correct," he said. "All the same."

He started to move on, but I pulled at his knapsack. I said, "Wait, wait. How do I know the count's right?" I was sure I was being cheated somehow, though he had given me more money than I ever dreamed of.

He began to scold me in Spanish. I did not understand what he was saying, for he talked like a machine gun. I tried to argue, but he kept shaking his head and turning his back to move on. People were stopping to watch the show.

One man stepped up and asked me how much I was exchanging. I said five dollars. One glance at my money and he said, "He's not cheating you."

I said, "Well, all I want is to buy a coke."

He said, "See that man over there? Give him one roll, and he'll give you a bottle of Coke and some change." He patted me on the shoulder and gave me a wry smile, "And you better hurry. The longer you delay, the less change you'll get."

The inflation rate of Bolivian money at the time was so crazy no one could keep track. In the U.S. we thought anything above nine percent was a national crisis, and Jimmy Carter's double digit inflation was Armageddon. In Bolivia the rate was over 20,000 percent. I know you think I'm crazy, but it was so. The government set the rate higher twice a week, but that didn't nearly keep up with the real inflation. The *peso boliviano* had been the currency of Bolivia for a long time. The government had once tried to stabilize it at something like twelve thousand *pesos bolivianos* to the US dollar, but that didn't work. It kept climbing and climbing until it was a joke.

For one dollar I had bought over a million *pesos bolivianos.* The bottle of Coke cost me three quarters of a million. The street vender handed me the Coke. He didn't count the money in the roll. He simply riffled the corners, gave me a handful of loose 100,000 *peso boliviano* bills. There was no trying to cheat. It wasn't worth the trouble. In Trinidad a thief might steal your watch, or sneak a candy bar out of your pocket, or take the buttons off your shirt, but he'd likely leave you with your *pesos bolivianos.* It would take a truckload to make the stealing worthwhile. On a later trip I once got two million *pesos bolivianos* for one US dollar. Then on another trip shortly after that, everything had been simplified (relatively speaking). President Estenssoro's government had created a new monetary unit, the *boliviano.* They made one *boliviano* worth one million of the old *pesos bolivianos,* so that now for one US dollar you got just two *bolivianos.* You could carry your money in your wallet again, instead of a wheelbarrow.

I worked mostly with the Lab Strike Force. The labs we hunted were in the Beni and Santa Cruz departments, which cover the eastern portion of the country where the lack of population and the thousands of acres of extremely thick jungle made an ideal hiding place for cocaine labs. Trinidad was the capitol of the Beni Department. Santa Cruz was the capitol of the Santa Cruz Department. There were hardly any roads in eastern Bolivia, and the trails they called roads weren't worthy of the name. The Beni did not need roads in the old days. It was so spider-webbed with rivers they could get almost anywhere with a boat.

Trinidad was a cow town. There were a few signs of money in that town and lots of signs of grim poverty. The town was like something out of a Clint Eastwood spaghetti western: most of the buildings a very faded shade of pink, blue, or green, the rest beige or dirty white; cement walls all cracked with large missing patches; brick walls pitted and crumbling at the corners. Open sewer ditches ran in the main section of the town with planks laid across in front of the houses so the women carrying loads of firewood did not have to jump across. Dogs and hogs searched the ditches for tidbits, and sometimes we would see a naked child sitting in a ditch laughing happily as he splashed in the stinking water. The streets in the center of town were of cobblestone, but there was so much mud dropped from the wheels of vehicles coming in from the country that the streets were thick with mud when it rained, and thick with dust when it was sunny. Only the big ranchers had pickup trucks. Poor farmers still used carts drawn by ox or horse, but they had modernized the carts by nailing old tires to the wooden wheels. We often saw a farmer coming into town on market day walking next to a sleepy ox using a stick to keep him awake and moving along.

The favored way of moving about the streets of Trinidad was on a *moto* (a small motorbike). The bikes were built to accommodate one skinny man, but they were often seen carrying as many as four, always with one precariously balanced on the handlebars. The *moto* had a very narrow seat, and if a fat man was riding on one with his jiggling buttocks drooping over the sides, the seat was hardly visible, and then we held our breath anxiously as he passed, thinking if he hit a large bump that seat would disappear completely and might require surgery for its removal.

The poorest sections of the town lay on the outskirts. Those had streets of dirt and no sewer at all. The people dumped in their back yards or hauled buckets into town and dumped into the open sewers. In those decrepit sections, men moved around with a slow sadness, a surrendered look about them, and about their houses. The houses were cobbled together from wood, cardboard, and tin, and had a blanket or piece of canvass for a front door. Many of those people were from Indian families that had lived forever in the surrounding jungles but had been driven off their lands by European and *mestizo* landlords who now owned practically all the country. The poorest ones had no indoor heat, and when a cold *surazo* blew, they warmed themselves by their backyard cooking fires or huddled together in blankets, and prayed for the return of the warm north wind (we are south of the equator here, and the temperature of the winds is reversed). The lucky ones were able to get work and save enough money to buy a house in the main part of town, where they could live by a sewer ditch and a dusty cobblestone street.

Armando, the fuel man at the airport, was one of those lucky ones. He and two of his buddies had the job of putting gas into the airplanes. They made a good living because only the rich had airplanes and the rich (that includes DEA agents) were generous in tipping. The bar maid at the Ganadero had also found work. She lived on the generosity of the drinkers that came to the cave-like bar in the basement. It was a narrow, windowless place, and the maid, a stunning beauty, moved like a dark leopard in the gloom behind her counter. She called you "*carino*," and "*mi amor*" and smiled and looked at you from the corners of her eyes. She knew how to flirt better than any bar maid in America. She was young and had saved no money. She lived with her parents, and all her money went to feed the family. She felt her poverty keenly, bitterly. She apologized for wearing the same monotonous clothes. She had only two dresses good enough to wear to work. She said she was communist, but when I asked her questions about Marx or Lenin, she'd never heard of them. She wanted socialism, communism, fascism, or any ism that would change the country. If one lived in hopeless squalor and grinding need, any change was a life line to a drowning man. She had beautiful white teeth, but her attempts to smile always had a kind of sadness like smiles at wakes and funerals.

One day she asked, "How do you like Bolivia?"

I said, "I like it fine, except I don't like all those signs painted on the walls that say 'Yankee go home.'"

She gave me that joyless smile and said, "The young girls here say it too. But they say, "Yankee go home, and take me with you."

The Ganadero was next to the Cathedral, which had a big clock on its tower. The clock was perpetually stuck at a quarter after twelve. The Cathedral had a bell to call people to morning Mass. The bell had a harsh clanging sound, not at all the sanctified tone of a mellow cathedral bell, but more like the profane banging of a famer on a plowshare. In front of the Cathedral was the main plaza of the town. There, every few days a smelly old sloth let himself reluctantly down from his high perch in a palm tree, relieved himself with great patience on the grass and, in laborious slow motion, made his tedious way back up to his humble home in the branches to search for food—a living allegory of the torpor, poverty, and smell of the poorest section of Trinidad.

But poverty never kept a New-World, Spanish-speaking human from keeping a dog and a rooster. Rich or poor, anywhere from Paraguay to the Rio Grande, people had to have these two decorations if they wished to call their hovel a home. Rich dogs slept in the sun by the master's house in fat contentment; poor ones, always hungry and skinny and mangy, haunted the garbage dumps. On a quiet morning, if we took our breakfast on the flat roof of the Ganadero, we could hear roosters crowing from all directions and dogs barking at them to shut up. Only the clanging of the cathedral bell before Mass drowned them out.

Even though almost everyone in Trinidad, indeed in the Beni, was Catholic, only a few old ladies responded to the morning bell of the cathedral. Jesuit and Franciscan missionaries had gone through this region in the fifteen and sixteen hundreds like a prairie fire, and made Catholics out of everybody. Not real Catholics, you understand, that believed whatever Rome said, but Catholic enough to give money to the missionaries to help build big beautiful stone cathedrals of old Spanish architecture in even the poorest towns. A map of Bolivia shows the missionary influence: San Lorenzo, San Miguel, San Rafael, San Pedro, San Javier—to name just of few of the blessed towns. There are rivers like the San Ramon, the Madre de Dios, the Santa Elena, the San Simon. It was almost a relief to see a river with a venerable old native Indian name like Tipuani or Tahuamanu. The name Trinidad too is of Jesuit origin. It was originally La Santissima Trinidad (the Most Holy Trinity), but that was shortened after the Jesuits were expelled from the country. The capitol of Bolivia, La Paz, was originally Nuestra Señora de La Paz (Our Lady of Peace).

Those holy missionaries "converted" Indians all over the New World from Argentina to Canada, often with less-than-holy methods. One can always tell conversions done at gunpoint—the change is no deeper than changing your shirt. The Jesuits left a trail of the most colorful and entertaining variations of Catholicism. The Indian made a show of praying with the priests. He let them pour water over his head. But in his home and in his heart he leaned toward the old beliefs of his forefathers. In Bolivia, when the Amazon River backed up into all its tributaries, and the flood threatened his house, the Indian prayed with the missionary at church, but he took out insurance by praying to his old, tried-and-true gods at home. The missionary god was fine for normal problems, but emergencies required stronger medicine.

One afternoon the fuel man, Armando, invited me to eat at his house, for he had caught a huge Surubí fish in the Mamoré. His wife proudly showed me holy pictures she had pinned on the walls—Catholic pictures, she said, but they were nothing like our holy pictures at home. God the Father had a surprised, bug-eyed look and had rays of sunshine shooting out of his ears, making him look very much like the Inca sun god in La Paz. A picture of the Virgin Mary had her dressed exactly like the virgin of the Inca religion who was supposed to be the daughter of the sun god. Armando had painted a kindergarten-crude picture of a snake on the side of his house.

I asked, "Who did this?" thinking it was a prank.

He said he himself had done it, and proudly pointed to other artistic achievements of snakes he had wrought on neighbor's houses.

"It's for protection against lightning and thunder," he said.

Evidently the gods of lightning and of thunder were afraid of the snake god, and so the house was secure. Armando was of Quechua ancestry and visited the "house of God" at fiesta time to see his friends, but he did his praying at home. Armando did believe in the power of the Blessed Virgin. He and a neighbor had once made the long pilgrimage to the town of Loreto about thirty miles south to ask the weeping Virgin Mary there to work one of her many miracles and cure the lame foot of the neighbor's baby boy. Armando's type of Catholicism was common in Bolivia. To see this colorful mix, go to Trinidad at the time of the Fiesta de la Santissima Trinidad, and watch their parade. The fiesta comes right after Pentecost Sunday. A Catholic from Stearns County would be surprised at what appeared in that religious parade (and think it pagan) and would hardly recognize anything except possibly the devil, and even he is weirder, fiercer, and scarier. He makes our devil look pretty tame.

One night I woke up startled. I bolted from my bed. The Ganadero was on fire! The smoke in my room was heavy enough to sting my eyes. I jumped into my jeans, ran barefoot down the hall, and down the stairs to the lobby. Smoke all over the place! There sat the night clerk calmly reading the paper and chewing her bubble gum like a contented cow. She looked up and raised her eyebrows and pulled her head back when she saw me standing there bare-chested.

"Where is the fire?" I asked.

"Oh, eet eez out on the llanos," she sang with bored indifference, "far awa-ay."

She was referring to the great savannah land of the Beni they called the Llanos de Los Moxos. We flew over those grasslands all the time to the north and west of Trinidad. We saw vast herds of cattle up to their horns in the tall grass. Every once in a while the cowboys cleared off the cattle and set the grass on fire. This cleared out the sprouting brush, and the grass came back thick and green and rich in the nutrients that made the Beni beef the best on earth. You can prove this to yourself by eating the two-inch slabs they serve all day at the Churrasco Restaurant. The prairie fire burns the grass fast and clean, but the stumps, the peat, and the rotting logs smoke for weeks like hell's kitchen. When the wind comes from the direction of the smoking llanos, Trinidad disappears in a bank of smoke. Then for a few days you can enjoy breathing smoke instead of the fragrance of horse manure and sewer. The smoke combined with morning fog, and then you couldn't turn a wheel at the airport. You could barely see enough to drive on the street.

Early one morning at the Ganadero, as I was gathering my stuff to go fly, I smelled something exceptionally revolting in the air—something *new* exceptionally revolting. I stuck my head out in the hall—no, it was only in my room. I sniffed around the bathroom. It was not from there. It seemed to just hang in the air all over the room, like something had died. When I got back in the evening, it was still there, but worse. During the night it seemed to weaken and strengthen in cycles. I couldn't make it out. In the morning I complained to the front desk. They sent a boy up, evidently the hotel blood hound. He sniffed around the whole room but never picked up the scent. He speculated I had a nose overly sensitive to street smells. I complained to the manager and said I wanted another room. He said the hotel was full. When I got back from flying that night, they said they had solved the problem.

They were partially right. The maid had doused the room with cleaning fluid so it almost covered the smell. But by the next morning it was insufferable. I told the manager if he did not give me another room, I wished I might join whatever had died in there. He promised to have the room searched from top to bottom and also the surrounding rooms. That night the smell was gone. They had found a dead rat in my air conditioner—a very dead rat.

Chapter Twenty-Six

THE LAB STRIKE FORCE WORKED with the UMOPAR. That unit was part of the Bolivian National Police. It was only a few years old. It too had been funded by U.S. taxpayers, when Congress woke up and smelled the cocaine problem at home. The acronym stood for *Unidad Móvil Policial para Áreas Rurales*, which means Mobile Police Unit for Rural Areas. They were sometimes referred to in nickname as "Los Leopardos," which means "The Leopards." It was a name the U.S. news media just loved and could not repeat often enough in their coverage of Blast Furnace. DEA agents always referred to them as the UMOPAR because that's how they were known in Bolivia, and because the DEA guys had made up different meanings for the acronym—some not complimentary, and need not be repeated here. Few of the UMOPAR troops could speak good Spanish. Almost none spoke any English, causing some of our agents to conclude they were stupid, illiterate dolts. It's true some were illiterate, but the fact was that Colonel Linares, the Comandante, had put them on the force because they spoke Quechuan and Aymaran and were often needed as interpreters when working in the hinterland. They were by no means stupid.

The Lab Strike Force kept moving its forward base to locations around the Beni where the troops were within helicopter range of suspected cocaine labs. They called the forward base the "FOB" (Forward Operating Base). For a while Josuani Ranch, 140 miles northwest of Trinidad and roughly ten miles west of Laguna Rojo Aguardo, was the FOB.It was easy to find because of the conspicuous cluster of lakes around the Laguna and because it was the only place far and wide that could possibly be called a ranch. But finding its airport was another matter. Did I say airport? No, airstrip—no, not even that—the Josuani Ranch landing place was a cow pasture, and a rough one—even for a cow. It was a grassy, lumpy, guttered bit of pasture guarded on both sides by termite mounds as solid as fire hydrants. Hitting one of those mounds would likely put an end to a flying career and roast the load of potatoes and carrots. It was best to recall sins and make an act of contrition while descending into Josuani. The first part of the landing roll was a jarring, tire-testing experience that set eyeballs to chattering in their sockets, and loosened fillings in teeth.

The Merlin wasn't designed to land at a place like this. I didn't have to be an engineer to figure that out. The long blades of the propellers just barely cleared the ground. Every time that front strut bottomed out, a propeller might hit a rock and fling it up where the engine intakes could suck it up and wipe out the turbine fins—an unhappy event on takeoff when beyond critical engine failure speed with a load of colonels and government ministers in the back. Why the engineers put the intakes at the bottom of the engine instead of at the top, I could never figure out. The Merlin was designed to land at LaGuardia, not in a cow pasture. The airplane sat high up on spindly legs that looked as if they'd snap off like toothpicks. After my first landing at Josuani, I called Washington and said the gear on the Merlin wouldn't withstand a month of landings out there. Their answer: "If the gear gives out, it will have to be replaced."

Josuani was still a working ranch. It had belonged to a cocaine trafficker a few days ago, but was now property of the Republic of Bolivia, which probably meant it now belonged to President Estenssoro or to his minister of the Interior, Fernando Barthelemy Martínez. The cowhands had been kept on, and all the animals were still there: cows, chickens, pigs, goats, and a pair of unhappy llamas. The Strike Force tents were scattered among the trees in the dusty barnyard. When I taxied up the first time, I wasn't aware of the dust. When I swung the plane around to face the wind for shutdown, the propellers raised a brown cloud of dust and dried animal manure, which drifted nicely across the yard and sifted down on the tents and the cooking fires.

"Thanks for the seasoning," said a familiar voice as I got out. "We were wondering what we could use for pepper."

It was good ol' Billy Martin from our McAllen office back home. Was I glad to see him! I'd worked with him undercover on a case in Weslaco and had grown to like him. There's something magical about seeing a buddy's face four thousand miles from home. He introduced me to some of his friends, and they sarcastically added comments like: "I'm sure you brought cold beer to wash down that dust," and "Be sure to do your engine runup here too."

But they weren't upset. We were bringing them supplies. We had guns and ammunition and sacks of carrots, potatoes, and onions. Meat they had—good, fresh, Beni beef, and it was free—well, maybe not. Somehow the U.S. taxpayer was always paying. I looked at the corral. Milling around in there were cows and pigs. One large sow had a pink bandana tied around her neck.

"Who puts a bandana on a pig?" I asked.

There was a roar of laughter from behind me.

"God damn, look at him," said Billy. "He's here five minutes and already he's got his eye on the colonel's sow." He put a hand on my shoulder. "Now look here, that sow's marked because she belongs to the colonel. Nobody is to touch her."

More laughter. Morale was high in spite of the conditions. The ranch was a hellhole of heat, red dirt, and mosquitoes; pig manure and cow pies all over the yard; spiders and ants crawling on bits of gut, horn, and hide; flies, bees, and wasps circling in the dusty sunshine. The only grass grew in little depressions in the red dirt. Next to the ranch house a fire smoldered under a barrel. The cowboys were making soap. The odor and the smoke drifted slowly among the trees. It smelled like they were cooking garbage. The ranch house had two noisy guard dogs chained to the porch.

The Josuani Ranch might have been plucked out of California in 1880. The ranch house walls were of thick adobe and the roof of red tile. It was now a wonderful scene of contrasts. A dusty cowboy, slapping his chaps with a lasso, drove a steer to the corral; hard by among the trees was parked a modern helicopter and a twin turbo-prop Merlin IIIB; on the porch of the ranch house a grizzled, stubble-faced man sat braiding horsehair into a rope; a few yards away on a stump a shiny-jawed army private sat cleaning an M-16. The ranch still had no washer, dryer, toaster, but camped here were members of the world's most powerful military with all the latest in weapons and machinery.

The Josuani "airport" had originally been "built" for the *carniceros*, Bolivian beef haulers. They came into Josuani on occasion with a DC-3 to haul beef carcasses up to La Paz. At the approach end of the runway, not far from where the Merlin was parked, stood a structure of tall posts with a thatched roof. The crossbeams of the rafters were hung with meat hooks and ropes. That was their slaughter shed. A holding pen was attached to it. The animals were killed right there, loaded up immediately and flown up to La Paz. The area had the stench of putrid blood and manure. In the days to come, while preflighting the Merlin next to that slaughter barn, we sometimes had to kick dried cow guts out of the way for fear of getting it caught in the propellers.

Throughout the Beni were many airstrips like the one at Josuani. All of them had little holding pens next to the runway. No roads or railroads connected that area to civilization. There was no electricity out in the hinterland—no refrigerator, no freezer, no ice. A cow slaughtered out there, where they had vast herds of them, was worth little. But that same cow was gold up in La Paz. The *carniceros* made their living flying beef carcasses out of the Beni in old World War II cargo planes. They were like the electronic smugglers of the Texas/Mexican border except they were legal. They hauled out of Trinidad too, but there the carcasses were delivered in trucks to a paved runway. On a hot day you could smell their planes from the other side of the airport. The ceilings of the planes had rails with sliding meat hooks and the floors were dark with blood from dripping beef.

I stayed overnight at Josuani just one time—and that was enough. Everything there was calculated to disturb sleep. I slept on the floor of the Merlin that night, at first with the door closed against the mosquitoes, later with it open to get some air. I was roasting in there and would have been beyond well-done by morning had not a breeze come up during the night and cooled the plane a little. When it was completely dark, a semi silence finally reigned over the army camp. Suddenly shouting came from the four directions of the compass: "*Uno, dos, tres, quatro!*" From up at the ranch house, the dogs went into a barking frenzy that lasted some five minutes. Then everything was quiet again. I could hear occasional low murmurs from the tents, sometimes the breeze rustled the leaves a little, and sometimes I heard the soft hoot of a night bird. I began to doze. "*Uno, dos, tres, quarto!*" Damn, there it was again! And again it set off the dogs.

The sentinel-guards of the camp called out every half hour! Twice an hour into the peaceful darkness: "*Uno, dos, tres, quarto*" (if all four were awake); sometimes one of them didn't answer, and they would start over shouting louder: "*Uno, dos . . . quarto,*" and repeating until a sleepy voice finally filled in the *tres*. Always the dogs added to the din, and the tents swore at the noise. By about three in the morning I'd gotten so used to this routine I actually fell asleep in spite of it. Then I came awake to grunting, bawling, and the clashing of horns as cattle in the corral got into a scuffle. Pigs squealed as they got kicked out of the way. Of course dogs set up a shivaree that made the former barkings seem like lullabies. The scuffle in the corral was soon over, but the dogs kept up full-throated approval for another ten minutes drowning out even the sentinels. Eventually quiet again. I settled in.

I got no sleep. In a short time a rooster crowed. I thought, surely this is too early to be heralding the dawn. It was still long before first light. He crowed again. Surely he'd realize his mistake and retire in embarrassment. But he persisted, and soon he convinced others, and they started a competition. I was raised on a farm, but I had never heard such a cacophony of constant crowing. They filled the air with lusty calls from high in the trees, from the top of the ranch house, and from every fence post along the corral. Some were just young up-starts, the kind that begin their calls with a big macho boast and then taper off to a pathetic, abortive shriek. This did not shame them in the least. Crowing standards were not high at Josuani Ranch.

After a while the low murmur of swearing came from the tents as the men decided to give up on sleep and begin the day. The men got busy stoking fires, setting up coffeepots, and cursing the roosters, the dogs, the cattle, and the sentinels. I got up too and did a preflight. We were supposed to fly Interior Minister Fernando Barthelemy up to La Paz. He was there to look over the camp and wanted to return to his headquarters as soon as we had light enough for take off. The sun was already lighting the tops of the trees. I squatted by a campfire across from Billy Martin to drink coffee. Billy was sitting barefooted. His boots lay on the ground next to him.

He said, "Ah, well, the noise is the same every night. I'm used to it."

Another agent, I think he was from New Jersey, said, "This whole show is another DEA snafu. We're not getting tons of cocaine like Bradley's telling everybody. And I don't trust any of these foreign bastards." He was looking toward the corral where Interior Minister Barthelemy stood inspecting the cattle. "That includes Fernando," he added.

Billy knocked the heel of his boot on a tent peg, checking for scorpions. "You're absolutely right," he said. He looked at me, squinting one eye against the rising sun. "But we don't complain. Who else pays you for going camping?"

After breakfast a couple of cowboys on horseback came to the corral to cut out a steer to slaughter for the Interior Minister to take back home. Their ponies were used to the cattle and quickly isolated a fat steer and drove him out the gate. As soon as the animal realized he was free, he broke into a run, but the one cowboy's horse started right with him. The cowboy had his lasso ready in his hand. As his pony drew alongside the steer, he deftly dropped the rope over the horns, and as they approached the next tree the pony went on one side as the steer passed on the other. The pony cut sharply back, leaped over the rope and in a blink the cowboy had the steer tied to the tree. The men around the campfires roared approval and applauded. It was done neat as a circus act, but was routine for the cowboys. They paid no attention. In a few minutes they had butchered the steer and had fifty pounds of the choicest parts in a bloody gunny sack which they handed to Barthelemy. One of the soldiers carried it to the plane for him. The soldier left a drop of blood on the ground every few feet. I put a piece of plastic on the carpet in the Merlin, and the soldier threw the bloody sack on top. By the time Barthelemy and his aides got loaded up, a little puddle of blood had formed next to the sack on the plastic. I realized some of the blood might leak onto the carpet, but I figured if Washington didn't care about the Merlin's gear, why the hell should I care about the carpet?

At La Paz, when Fernando took up his bloody sack, he saw that there was a large blood stain left on the carpet. He ventured the opinion the carpet might smell if it wasn't cleaned soon. I had to agree with him, but I wished he might at least have apologized. Evidently he was generally lacking in manners. Only a few months later he was in trouble for raiding a garden belonging to the Augustinian Recollect Nuns at Sucre. The mendicant nuns were raising herbs for their dinner table, and someone thought the herbs might be marijuana. A few months after that Estenssoro fired him, though that was more about corruption then about pestering nuns. Fernando had been extorting bribes from the Bolivian cocaine traffickers in exchange for his official protection.

The suspicions of that New Jersey agent were well-founded.

Chapter Twenty-Seven

THE GREATEST SHOW I EVER SAW was when the United States Army helicopters came into Santa Cruz for Operation Blast Furnace. We were loading up groceries at the Viru Viru Airport that afternoon. The tower had told us we had to park at the extreme south end of the parking ramp because a "very big plane is coming in, and he will need much room to turn around." That was no exaggeration. Big indeed. There was thunder overhead, and in came an airplane as long as a dairy barn and as wide as a cow pasture. Everything at Viru Viru came to a standstill. Groups of people gathered to point and wonder. Cars stopped on the airport road with their doors open while their occupants stood on the road with their mouths open.

The plane was a U.S. Air Force C-5A Galaxy, and I couldn't help feeling that, considering its size, they must have been inspired when they named it. The enormous craft had four huge engines with intakes big enough for a grown man to stand in, and the noise they made shook the earth as the plane swung into its parking spot on the ramp. It parked right in front of us and a little to one side as if to give us a front-row seat for the show. The only obstruction to our view was a group of U.S. and Bolivian officials and members of the press who came to meet the airplane. The big rear cargo door came down. Immediately a storm of activity looked like a stirred anthill. The whole front end of the plane opened up like a clamshell so I could see daylight through the fuselage like one massive culvert. Soldiers were unloading front and back. Not one stood around and looked at the scenery. In thirty minutes those men unloaded and set up six Black Hawk helicopters—yes, I said six! Not only that, in another fifteen minutes three of those choppers were airborne and on their way to Trinidad with a load of soldiers and equipment. The other three followed a few minutes later. Anyone watching that show must have said to himself, "If it ever comes to war with that bunch, I believe I'll pass, and if I'm forced into it, I'll make my will."

Had the spectators known the origin of the personnel in this performance, they might have been impressed even more. The C-5A Galaxy came all the way from Dover, Delaware. It belonged to the Eagle Wing (the 436th Military Airlift Wing) of Dover Air Force Base. The choppers were from the

U.S. Army's 210th Combat Aviation Battalion, and the soldiers were from the U.S. Army's 193rd Infantry Brigade out of Panama. God bless America.

When we got back to Trinidad that night, the U.S Army had changed the airport from a sleepy hamlet to a swarming city. A long row of tents had popped up along the east side of the taxiway. The airport had a pleasant smell of canvass and rope. Some men were driving the last anchor pegs. One of the tents was a huge cook tent (the mess tent) with a long serving counter along its front and a water buffalo parked nearby. A U.S. Army water buffalo was a big drinking-water tank on wheels, with a faucet for filling cooking pots, wash buckets, and canteens. A truck was unloading groceries purchased at the Trinidad market. A little farther down, the soldiers had excavated a long ditch, and a dozen men were building a row of toilets with lumber from the town.

Trinidad was a boom town while the US Army was there. As the days went by, it was overrun by a stampede of reporters from every major newspaper and magazine in the States: *Time*, *Newsweek*, *Boston Globe*, *New York Times*. They all stayed at the Ganadero. For a month or more the hotel was filled with the biggest congregation of lazy, incompetent, bungling reporters—writers of half truths, amplifications, and ignorance—ever convened in one place. (I mean up until that time. Since then, conventions of that kind have become routine, and the reporters have the same virtues.)

The best thing the army brought was the field hospital, a horse-shoe tent with inflatable walls kept filled with insulating air from a pump. Even on the hottest days when the airport was sweltering at 100 degrees, that tent was cool as a basement. I stopped in there, whenever I could, on a hot afternoon, but I had to sometimes bribe the doctor with a bottle of beer smuggled from the Ganadero for the privilege. General Taylor didn't allow his men to go into town except for specific supplies, and beer was not on the list.

But Taylor ran a great chow tent. The baker made fresh buns for nearly every meal. The aroma from his ovens drifted down the line promising excellence—and delivering every time. The army could buy all the beef they wanted from the town, but they couldn't get enough eggs, so breakfast often consisted of terrific fried strips of beef with not so terrific U.S. Army powdered eggs.

The Army also brought MREs. A civilian never heard "MRE," but soldiers heard it every day. It meant "Meals Ready to Eat." The MRE was the army field rations that recently replaced the Army's canned meals, "C-rations" or "Charlie Rats." The Army called them"Meals, Combat, Individual Rations." C-rations came in a can. MREs came in plastic pouches. When the FOB was close enough to Trinidad, the soldiers ate hot food sent in by chopper, but when they were farther away, they ate MREs. I know this reflects negatively on my image as a bon vivant, but I have to admit I not only ate with the soldiers, but I liked their hot food and even their MREs. The army was very generous with food. General Taylor said we could eat at the chow tent any time, and the sergeants passed out MREs by the armload. When I flew the CASA with Agent Terry Sawyer, he discovered if we threw the meat pack from the MRE on top of the black instrument panel of the CASA when we started up in the morning, the heat of the sun would have it nice and hot by noon.

What happened when other pilots were there, I don't know. Things may have been different then. I can only say what happened while I was working for Blast Furnace in Bolivia. I've read DEA accounts that imply the labs we hit were mostly discovered by DEA. That wasn't true while I was there. Most of the labs we hit, especially the hot ones (those currently in operation) were found when Major Howard and I did our afternoon recon flights. The DEA-informant sites we hit were often not only cold (not operating), but had sometimes been hit before. This didn't matter to Agent Bradley and the Snowcap bosses. They sent in reports to Washington that said we had hit a lab capable of processing so much coca paste per month, and could turn out so much cocaine blah, blah, and that by this fortunate strike we had reduced by such-and-such many tons the amount of cocaine that would reach the shores of our great country and the noses of our precious young citizens. They didn't mention the lab wasn't operating or that it had been hit before. They sent in these reports, confident the DEA bureaucrats in Washington would be too lazy to scrutinize them, and too eager to show Congress how effective their money-sucking program was.

From Agent Jesus "Jesse" Gutiérrez I learned how to spot a cocaine lab from the air. Jesse was the head of the DEA office in Santa Cruz at the time. He had an informant who said there was a big lab in the Huachuca area near the Brazilian border. Jesse had confirmed this by finding the lab's airstrip from the air. He flew with me and showed me the place. We circled high above and I studied it. I could see nothing but a little airstrip and a side trail that disappeared into the jungle. As we headed back to Santa Cruz, I said, "Jesse, I think your information might be off. There was only that airstrip. No lab building, no barrels of chemicals, no generator that I could see. There are little ranch strips like that one all over this country. If there is a lab there, it must be a very small one."

But Jesse said, "It's there, and it's not small. You saw how freshly used that strip was, and you noticed that well-used path going into the jungle. The fact there were no buildings: no ranch house, no corral, and no cattle is the very indication of a lab. That trail leading into nowhere but thick canopied jungle is the best indication of all. They have a lab hiding there under the canopy."

The light came on in my head. It was so simple I was astounded I had not thought of it myself. There were indeed little air strips like that all over the wild parts of Bolivia. Every little cow ranch, fishing camp, and lumbermill had one. But they all had a house, a barn, or at least a corral near by. This strip at Huanchaca was a pattern for a cocaine lab: remote location, no buildings, no cattle, and a trail leading to nowhere. To disguise their labs the traffickers should have put up a ranch building and a corral by the strip, and should have hired a farmer to walk around with a shovel and a hoe.

Major Howard and I used this model to find labs. Howard saw the wisdom of it immediately. As Major Howard and I searched for cocaine labs, he liked to recall his days as a chopper pilot in Vietnam. He talked about places like Phu Kat, Pleiku, and Tan San Nut, all names with which I was familiar from my stint in the Air Force. He had signed up for several Vietnam tours. He said, "I kept flying around there hoping for the proverbial million dollar wound, but those fucking people couldn't hit a bull in the ass with a scoop shovel. After a while I gave up and went home."

He said, "I recommended to the Army we bring the new Apache can opener down here and surprise these labs with the hellfire, but the brass didn't like the idea of a crazy man with a real weapon. (By Apache he meant the Army's new twenty-million-dollar anti-tank chopper with the hellfire missiles.) "But we're only here in Bolivia for show anyway. This is not war."

I said, "I guess that's why they sent a laid-back general like Taylor."

"Yeah, he knows we're only here to put on a play for the politicians. But don't let Taylor fool you. He can be a real warrior when the guns begin to shoot."

Howard kept ribbing me about the pansy Air Force pilots who never saw a real battle in Vietnam, and I ribbed him about how the Army soldiers lay around the rice paddies smoking pot and opium. To that he responded, "Yeah, well, when you're over there and hear about all those ass holes demonstrating against the war at home, and you wonder if anyone cares you're over there fighting for your country, and then, to add to your joy, your girl writes you a Dear John letter, you can't blame the guys for turning to drugs. Morale was low, and opium and grass was so damned cheap and easy to get. But we're on vacation here in Bolivia. Moral's high. The soldiers know this is a show. One of the principles of low-intensity battles is that whoever has the will of the people wins. This so-called war was lost before we came here. Bu-ut, well, we can still make it look good."

Later we sat at Doc's inflatable hospital and drank Paceña beer Howard's men had smuggled down from La Paz. The doctor said, "We're missing another principle of war here. You must always have a final objective so you can make a clear-cut definition of victory. We don't have that definition here, and the brass can't come up with one that'd sound reasonable to the boys."

I loved those days working with the Army, but sitting in the cramped cockpit all day was hard on a man's body. My bones often ached when I crashed at the Ganadero at night. Many DEA agents (mostly ones who had not been in the military) didn't like working with the Army. They considered them a bunch of kids who didn't know anything. Most of the resentment was that, while the Army was in Bolivia, we had to keep our nose to the grindstone and weren't able to take a day off whenever we felt like it. We hit a lab every day, sometimes two. After the Army left, we hit that many in a month.

The Strike Force kept moving the FOB. The best FOB they ever had was the Roca Ranch. This too had allegedly belonged to a cocaine trafficker, but was now the property of the president. It was far out on the Llanos de los Moxos, the great savannah. It didn't have all the mosquitoes of Josuani, and had only three roosters. Living was easy there. Most of the officers and the agents slept in the big ranch house, and many of the soldiers found shelter in the out buildings. The land around was endless flat grassland, so a sentry could see for miles. And Roca Ranch had an honest to goodness airfield. It was a wide, smooth, long strip. Not paved, mind you, but a vast improvement over Josuani. It was another place easy to find. It had a big lake right at the head of the runway. I made many a trip into there flying army chow from Trinidad to the ranch and picking up the major to look for cocaine labs.

One day at the Roca Ranch, I was resting with some of our soldiers in the shade of a couchillo tree near the runway. It was blistering hot with the sun scorching the land. I was surprised to see a man out in that heat on the shimmering runway. I said, "That guy looks like an Air Force sergeant. What's he doing out here in God-knows-where, Bolivia?"

The sergeant had a mysterious instrument and a bag with him, and he seemed to be collecting something. The soldiers shrugged. "He says he's testing the runway."

I thought they must be kidding. The runway was hard as pavement, dry as a bone. My curiosity got me out of the shade and onto the furnace runway with the sergeant.

"Testing for what?" I asked. "I've been flying a Merlin in and out of here for a week, and now you're coming along to test the runway?"

The sergeant gave me a look of benevolence and sympathy, as one might look at a dim-witted child. "A Merlin? Your Merlin is a flea compared to the elephant we're thinking of bringing in here. We're talking about a real airplane, a C-130."

I stomped on the brick-hard surface. I said, "Well, I've brought my flea in here fully loaded and it hasn't even left tire tracks."

The sergeant continued to regard me with deep compassion. He looked down, shook his head and scratched it as if to say, "This kind of stupidity I have never met before." With a sigh and a voice dripping with patience he said, "Your airplane weighs about six tons. A Herk (a C-130 Hercules) weighs about seventy tons. Your airplane costs less than a half million. A Herk costs more than a hundred and twenty-five million. This surface has to be better than the ICAO load classification number 25 or the Air Force won't allow its baby in here, and then those choppers'll be spending all their time hauling blivets."

A blivet is a collapsible rubberized bladder as big as a car. The army choppers were slinging them under their bellies to haul fuel to the FOB. A blivet held five-hundred gallons of gas, which sounds like a lot if you're operating a John Deere farm tractor, but that wasn't enough to gas up two Black Hawks. The only fuel at the FOB was what they hauled there in blivets. And if a target was beyond their operating range, they had to refuel from a blivet they had dropped along the route to the target. That made a strike more difficult, made it take far more time, and made it much more likely the crooks would be alerted. First a chopper took off with a full load of fuel and a blivet. They'd drop the blivet at a landing site along the route to the target, then return and load up with fuel and personnel. They'd fly out to the blivet, top off their tanks, and finally hit the target. On the way back to the FOB they'd top off at the blivet, pick it up, and finally head for home. The C-130 in one trip could provide as much gas as six blivets, not counting what might be siphoned from the main tanks.

I said to the sergeant, "I'd venture to guess you could bring one of your Galaxys in here even after a rain."

The long-suffering sergeant said, "The Air Force is unlikely to make their decision based on your guess."

A few days later as I was leaving Roca Ranch for Santa Cruz on a potato run, they asked if I didn't want to wait to watch the C-130 come in. I said, "Naw, I've seen C-130s land before," like I was above that kind of child's play.

What an idiot! I should have stayed. I missed a show. When I got back from Santa Cruz, I first made a low pass over the runway to have a close look. Something wasn't right. A C-130 was parked very near the approach end of the strip. It was cock-eyed, one wingtip sticking up in the air the other resting on the ground! I landed a little long to clear the C-130, and as I taxied back I saw the problem. The right main landing gear was completely buried in mud, the plane resting on its belly and on its right wing tip. It had broken through the hard top layer of ground, and was moored in the soft mud below. All four propeller blades on the right outboard engine were severely bent.

It was a bad blow to operation Blast Furnace, but a delight to the U.S. Army privates. They had a great time making fun of the Air Force. This type of bantering between military units was constant, but here was gravy. They had the Air Force dangling like a piñata and happily pounded it like Mexican children. However, the Air Force captain who'd piloted the C-130 wasn't crushed. He posed for pictures leaning on his airplane and smiling like Christmas morning.

I said, "I don't think this is good for your career."

The captain laughed, "I don't give a shit. I'm not a career man, and I was following orders. It might not be good for the guy who certified the runway though."

I said, "I don't think he was testing down here by the lake."

"Then my instructions should have warned me not to taxi down here."

When I was getting ready to leave, the captain said, "Hey, Bloch, look at this picture I'm sending to my dad."

He had a picture of himself standing by his crippled airplane, arms folded, chin high, proud as an Indian chief. Under the picture he had written: "Yes dad, I did this all by myself!"

SOMETIMES THE STRIKE FORCE stayed only a day at an FOB, then moved on. I don't remember them all, but I remember San Javier because we supplied the whole town with gasoline one day. The Strike Force was moving and had an extra blivet half full of gas. Agent Sawyer and I were flying the CASA. Sawyer says, "Well, let's top off the CASA," which we did, but we had taken on fuel at Trinidad, so there was still over a hundred gallons of gas left in the blivet. They were thinking about where to dump it, but one of the UMOPAR guys went into town and rang the bells at the old Jesuit Mission. when people came running to see what was going on, he told them they could get free gas out in the pasture where the Strike Force troops were unpegging their tents. What a stampede there was! The whole village turned out from grandmas to toddlers. Gas cans, oil cans, sprinkling cans, coffee pots, soup pots, rusty pork-and-bean cans came out. One little boy came along with a large water dipper, though I doubt he got much of his load back to the house. The people drew themselves into a nice, orderly line and the chopper pilots pumped gas.

Since I spent only a month at a time in Bolivia, I never saw many of the forward bases and wasn't part of many of the raids. Other pilots flew the same missions when I was home in Texas, so I missed some of the most exciting raids. I'd been hoping to see the raid on Huanchaca. I wanted to see if Jesse's informant was right about how big the lab was there. General Taylor had stuck a special pin in his map at the Huanchaca site, because Jesse had convinced him it was a hot lab, and a big one. But that pin was way out there in east Bolivia all by itself near the Brazilian border, whereas the Beni had clusters of pins. It'd take a week to hit Huanchaca, because they'd have to set up a trail of refueling blivets across the country to get there, then set up an FOB in the area before they could hit the site. During that week they could hit a dozen labs in the Beni. And so the Strike Force didn't hit Huanchaca until it was forced by public pressure to do so. That's a whole other story.

I was home during October of that year. I didn't see the famous raid on the little town of Santa Ana, but I saw reports in the paper and on TV. The *Los Angeles Times* had this:

> Bolivian and U.S. drug agents raided this town Friday in search of cocaine traffickers, then fled during a protest by hundreds of angry residents, some shouting, "Kill the Yankees!" No arrests were made and no cocaine was seized. Authorities said there were no reports of injuries. Bolivian officials, assisted by U.S. troops, have been raiding cocaine laboratories at jungle ranches in Bolivia for the last three months. Friday's raid marked the first time a town was the target of the joint crackdown on drugs. The raid was prompted by reports that several major cocaine traffickers were hiding in Santa Ana, a town of about 5,000 people in the Beni tropical flatlands where most of the country's cocaine laboratories are based.

I had flown over Santa Ana many times. It was halfway between Trinidad and the Josuani ranch on the west side of the Mamoré where the Yacuma River meets the Rápulo. It was another one of those Jesuit Mission towns, but its church was smaller than most, even though the town was quite large by Beni standards. It had a little airstrip on the southwest side where our Strike Force landed for the raid that morning. When I got back to Bolivia the next month they were still talking about it. Believe me, this raid was a huge embarrassment for the Bolivian authorities and for DEA, though it wasn't painted that way in DEA reports. Agent Trouville, the boss of our DEA office in Cochabamba, was in charge of the DEA agents on that raid. He said, "What a fiasco this was. It was a bomb ready to blow. We were lucky to get out of there alive." Colonel Linarez, the UMOPAR comendante, said it was the most humiliating experience of his life. That was saying a lot. Colonel Linarez had once been involved in a failed coup attempt against the government in La Paz, and on that occasion he had to get out of Bolivia until the heat cooled down.

The brilliant idea of the Santa Ana raid came from DEA Snowcap bureaucrats. Our boys went into Santa Ana that morning with a handful of search and arrest warrants. The town was basically another Beni cattle town, but several of its most popular citizens were now in the cocaine business. Word was the houses of some of the good Jesuit Christians in the town were being used as warehouses for coca products. The Strike Force moved in at dawn with airplanes and helicopters. They began to question residents and to search homes and cars. In a short time the Mission bells of the little church began a fervent pealing that rolled across the sleepy village and brought the citizens pouring into the street. Word of the raid spread like fire on the llanos. Under the continual pealing of the bells, came shouts in Spanish: "Yankees get out. Kill the Yankees. Yankees go home. Kill them all! Don't let them leave!" A large crowd, numbered anywhere from three-hundred to three-thousand (depending on who's telling the story) armed with axes, shovels, and hoes advanced on the troops. The DEA guys knew enough to throw in the towel and make for the helicopters. The Bolivian officers tried to disperse the crowd by firing tear gas and bullets into the air, but that was gas on the flames. The angry mob chased the Bolivian troops to the airfield. They blocked the runway and crowded around the choppers until the mayor of Santa Ana was allowed to board the aircraft and verify that no residents were being flown out as prisoners.

DEA was always ready to say "Mission Accomplished," but this beat all. Here was a desperate effort to put lipstick on a pig: The *Los Angeles Times* under a sarcastic title of "MISSION ACCOMPLISHED" reported that a DEA agent, speaking on condition of anonymity, proclaimed the raid a success. They quoted him: "Part of the mission was accomplished in that the

Bolivians have shown their resolve they won't allow this kind of thing to go on in their backyard. It was a success in the fact that the mission was accomplished at all."

I said, "I wonder who that jackass was."

Sawyer was with me. He said, "Sounds like Bradley."

I said, "No, Bradley wouldn't have asked for anonymity."

Sawyer said, "Yeah, you got a point there. He'd've been proud of it. Well, whoever it was, he'll be promoted for this bit of brilliance and sent to Washington." He paused, then added, "Where he belongs."

Chapter Twenty-Eight

I flew into Chimoré in support of the Coca Strike Force. Coming in to Chimoré for landing or climbing out on takeoff, you had a view that stayed with you always—a gorgeous area as thick with lush green jungle as the Beni was with grass. To the west rose the misty Andes, snow capped, and wreathed with drifting clouds that draw moving shadows slowly across the dark green valleys of the mountainsides, while high above their snowy tops shone a brilliant white in the sun. The runway was cut into the jungle. In the landing flare, we'd flush flocks of parakeets that swirled and disappeared into the trees. When parked, we were entirely surrounded by a wall of trees. Along the runway we would sometimes see a tree covered with big macaws flashing their foot-long tails and stunning colors as they squawked and preened.

I loved flying into Chimoré because of the scenery, but I didn't like the mission being executed there. Destroying laboratories of rich cocaine kings was one thing, but tearing up the coca plants and jailing farmers trying to make a living from their crops was another. These weren't rich people. Some were miners recently forced down from Potosí on the altiplano. The government was closing the mines. There was no other work on the altiplano. Years ago the Spanish had taken their forefathers up there in chains and forced them to work the mines as slaves. The miners were no longer slaves (strictly speaking), but they were making a bare living on a salary of thirty dollars a month. Estensorro's government said it could no longer pay such extravagance. The miners were fired—about twenty-seven thousand at one time.

You can't live on the altiplano unless you have money. It's cold as the moon up there, and as fertile. You need heat to stay alive. Nothing grows but little patches of sparse grass that only an alpaca could love. There's no wood to make a fire, no garden to raise vegetables. There is only the clear, blinding, unchanging, cold-hearted sun. President Estenssoro didn't pass out food stamps or workman's compensation. Suddenly thousands of miners and their families were beggars. Many of them moved to the coca growing regions to get jobs in the coca fields. Others moved to cities like Santa Cruz to beg and to look for work. There was little work, but at least in that warmer climate one could exist without heat.

Barely exist. Some resorted to stealing. We flew out of Santa Cruz a lot. Our hotel was just across the street from the prison. At the big gate of iron bars along the front of the prison the prisoners begged for food and money from the people passing in the street. They stuck their hands and arms through the bars and called out in the name of God. Almost every day a dutiful little Indian wife came plodding along with a pot of soup for her husband. He ate it through the bars, while other prisoners begged for some.

The girl at the front desk of the hotel told me, "Don't give them any money, that fat guard will take it away."

I saw a lot of beggars from Potosí on the streets of Santa Cruz. The editors of the Santa Cruz paper, *El Mundo*, scolded Estenssoro for dumping the poor on their city. They said Santa Cruz had enough poor people as it was, without adding homeless miners and their children. I met one of the children in the street. It was a chilly day, the streets shiny wet from drizzle and gloomy with fog. She was about fourteen (I really couldn't tell), hollow-cheeked, skinny, dark eyes set deep into the skull as if retreating from the world. She wore an unwashed, ragged skirt that dragged on the wet cobblestones. Her shoes were made of paper with a piece of cardboard for a sole, all wrapped up with twine. Her poncho was a piece of plastic with a hole in the middle. She had a look of deep anguish as she held out her hand to beg—it was heartbreaking. She was hungry, she said. I had a chocolate bar in my pocket, but it was all smashed and gooey. I offered it. She tore into it so quickly I was startled. She took a bite like a hungry wolf, stripped off the wrapper, and gave the rest to an old man sitting against the wall behind her. She licked the wrapper clean like a dog finishing his bowl. The old man, who had been hunched and staring down at his feet, suddenly came to life. In a few seconds he gulped down the chocolate. The man was obviously not well. Skeletal and trembling, cadaverously pale and spiritless, he looked like someone from a Nazi death camp. The girl gushed with gratitude. She spoke rapidly. I had a hard time following. She said her name was Marisol, and I think she said the old man was her grandfather and needed medicine. What he needed was a hospital.

I had only a few *bolivianos* left, but I had just bought a wood carving of the Madre India from a shop across the street. I told the girl to wait. She kept saying "Si, si," to everything I said, but I wasn't at all confident she understood my Spanish, because when she spoke to the old man, she talked in some other language. I returned the carving to the store and the lady gave me my money back. When I told the lady I was giving the money to the beggar girl, she gave me some sausages she was frying up for lunch. It was *chorizo Beniano* (Beni sausage), a feast for a king. I gave the beggar girl the money and the food.

That night I was drinking Ducal beer with some of the other pilots at the hotel. I told about the girl, and that I gave her about twenty dollars. One of the pilots was good old Jimmy-jet, his own cynical self—and very much like himself, he said, "Fish!" to indicate I was a sucker. I couldn't blame him much, though. At that time a gang of thieves operated in Santa Cruz who posed as beggars, but those guys were easy to spot. Their clothes were all patched and dirty, for show, but the clothes were of warm wool. And no one could fake that starving look and keen glitter of pathetic-want in the eye that comes from hopeless hunger. The deep despair one can feel in the genuine article is absent in the fake.

A week later I was in the same area. The girl wasn't there. I asked another beggar about Marisol. He said he knew her well and her family. He had come down from the mountain with them. The grandfather had died a few days ago and he said the girl had gone back up the mountain to find her uncle.

I got home from that trip just before Christmas. Bea had all the Christmas trimmings up, trees and wreaths, lights and candles, fire in the fireplace, and our house looked warm and bright. The TV was on. Dan Rather was giving the evening news, and he practically wept as he reported about poverty in our country. He showed a "homeless family" in California living in a garage. A plump wife was cooking supper in several steaming pots on an electric stove. A refrigerator stood next to the stove. The two children were bouncing on a bed in the back of the garage while watching cartoons on a color TV. They all looked well-dressed, no patched clothes, the beds big and comfortable, the garage obviously heated. The woman was saying how hard it was with her husband out of work. They couldn't afford their old apartment so they moved into a friend's garage. That was Dan's report on the homelessness in the United States of America.

Oftentimes at night, when the winter wind is rushing cold in the trees by my window, I'm all snuggled down in the quilts, the furnace is softly purring downstairs, and Bea has her electric blanket on, I remember that beggar girl in Santa Cruz. The girl with the paper shoes.

Chapter Twenty-Nine

YOU NEVER HEARD ABOUT THE MURDER of Noel Mercado. Bolivian officials didn't like to talk about it. They thought it might discourage tourists from visiting their Huanchaca National Park (now Noel Kempff Mercado National Park). DEA didn't like to talk about it. It was another embarrassment out of Operation Snowcap. (All DEA operations are a booming success, you know.) This much is certain: the murder of Mercado was not the fault of DEA, but the newspapers in Bolivia, many owned by cocaine lords, were able to make it look that way. The murder might have gone unnoticed by the press, but Mercado was a well-known, distinguished biologist in Santa Cruz. The writings and yellings of "*Yanquis afuera*" increased a hundred-fold as bits and pieces of wild speculation, unfounded rumor, and outright lies leaked out.

I've already mentioned the beginning of this story: Agent Jesse Gutiérrez and the suspected lab at Huanchaca. We were getting around to hitting that lab when the following episode put the spurs to the operation. What I relate here is the true story—maybe the only true one existing. It comes from newspaper accounts, from Vicente Castelló (the only survivor of the massacre at Huanchaca), from police reports, and from memories of my trip with Jesse.

It was springtime, early September, and the sun as usual rose hot over the eastern jungle. Noel Mercado must have thought this might finally be his lucky day as he scanned the northern horizon from his home in Santa Cruz. Not a cloud in that part of the sky. He needed that clear sky because he wanted to fly to the north on a hunt. He had been planning his trip for a month. He was on his way to study the flora and fauna of the region of Bolivia called Huanchaca. A fellow scientist, Vicente Castelló from Spain, was going with him. They hoped to catch a glimpse of the "White Stag" that had been seen by natives of Huanchaca. They'd hired Captain Juan Carlos Cochamanidis to fly them to that area.

They loaded their notebooks into a Cessna 206 and took off with their pilot and a guide. The plane roared into the sky and turned to put the sun on the right wing. Huanchaca was little more than two hundred miles ahead. They flew over heavy jungle. An occasional clearing with a thatched hut and maybe a pig or a cow tied close appeared, but it was a rarity. Only the largest rivers gleamed between the trees, everything else was completely roofed over by the unending, triple-canopy green.

The jungle thinned out a little as they approached the cliffs of Huanchaca. On the eastern side of the Paucerna River the pilot found an airstrip. He was delighted to see the strip so well-groomed. Noel was delighted as well. He saw a nice little trail leading into the heaviest part of the jungle. There was water there too; they could see it flashing through the leaves here and there as the plane circled. The pilot landed and parked the plane. Everyone got out and stretched. Mercado, eager to get started, took the guide (his name was Franklin Parada) with him and followed the path away from the runway into the jungle. Vicente Castelló lit a cigarette and listened to the peaceful droning of jungle insects. He moved to the shade of the airplane wing and leaned against the spar. The pilot broke out his thermos and poured himself a cup of coffee. Vicente smoked, Juan sipped coffee as they chatted.

Suddenly, Juan stopped in mid-swallow. He frooze, mouth open, staring at the path taken by Mercado and Parada. Vicente, puzzled, spun around. What he saw struck terror through him down to his boots. Mercado and Parada were marching toward the airplane, holding their hands high in the air. They were covered by several men with submachine guns. The pilot threw his cup of coffee and bolted for the jungle. Vicente followed suit. Immediately all hell broke loose. The quiet air was riven with the thunder of gunfire. Bullets flew in all directions. Vicente ran, trying to keep the plane between himself and the guns. At one backward glance he saw Mercado, who had also begun to run, go down. To his right he heard the pilot grunt and stagger as he got hit. Bullets whined and snapped all around, smashing leaves and bits of vine. He ran and ran, zigzagging, lungs burning, gasping, falling, stumbling on. Finally he felt his heart would take no more. He dived into some bushes. He lay still, trying to quiet his breathing and his pounding heart. He heard the bandits searching. Sometimes they came so close he could hear them talking. They had killed the other three, and had similar plans for him.

The search went on through the heat of the afternoon. Toward evening, the bandits dragged the three bodies under the airplane wings. They opened up the fuel drains, and let the gas run over the bodies. They set the whole thing on fire, then disappeared up the path into the jungle. Vicente wanted to run as far as he could in the opposite direction. But the opposite direction was the border of the Brazilian State of Mato Grosso, and that was even more remote and wild and lawless than Huanchaca. He'd never find his way back. No map, no compass, no food, no safe water.

The flames of the fire shot high into the air, burned the rest of the evening and died down as night came on. Soon all was darkness. Vicente didn't move. His only chance was a rescue plane. He was confident a plane would be sent out as soon as they were discovered missing, and he was pretty sure they could find the airstrip. Their pilot had found it easily enough, and the bodies, he thought, would smoke for days and act as a marker for a rescue operation.

That was on a Friday. In Santa Cruz on Saturday morning, the women came down to the police station. Something was wrong. The four missing men would not have remained out in the jungle overnight. After a morning of confused planning, another Cessna was launched to search. The pilot knew where to look. As he approached the Brazilian border he saw smoke, found the airstrip and recognized the burnt out wreckage of the airplane. As he passed overhead to turn downwind, he saw a man run out of the brush waving frantically—survivors!—at least one. The pilot landed. During the landing roll Vicente Castelló ran up like a crazy man, waving and raving. He ripped open the door while the plane was still rolling, and dived in shouting, "Take off! Get out of here! Murder! Murder! They'll kill us all!" The pilot saw bandits come running. He took off on the remaining runway with bullets striking his plane as it got airborne. They returned safely to Santa Cruz.

The next day Santa Cruz newspapers, the *El Mundo* and the *El Deber*, carried reports of the murders under headlines like: "MASSACRE AT HUANCHACA" and "WHAT MADNESS!" They speculated the dead men were victims of cocaine traffickers who had a lab at the landing strip in the jungle. The public was furious, but the fury had just begun. The real storm came when it was discovered that DEA knew all the time a cocaine lab was at Huanchaca.

In the days following that September morning, the U.S. Drug Enforcement Administration in Bolivia was accused of helping the drug traffickers murder one of the beloved citizens of Santa Cruz. After all, if they knew there was a lab at Huanchaca, why had they left it alone? DEA's collusion in the murder was obvious. In a country where bribery was a way of life, the only answer could be that DEA had taken bribes from the lab operators. It was another of the lovely ironies of life that many of the accusers were doing exactly what they were accusing DEA of doing.

The Strike Force immediately turned their attention to Huanchaca. They hit the place a few days later, but by then the crooks had taken away their cocaine and had wisely moved on to who-knows-where. They'd most likely skipped across the border into the Mato Grosso of Brazil. The huge lab buildings and the hundreds of barrels of chemicals showed what an enormous cooking operation the crooks had going at Huanchca. It was nothing like the colossus of Tranquilandia in Colombia, but was the biggest lab ever hit in Bolivia. The Bolivian senate, to please the voters, launched an "investigation." They eventually put out an arrest warrant for Agent Jesse Gutiérrez who's only crime was that he had developed the informant who had pointed out the lab at Huanchaca. We flew Jesse out of Bolivia.

That's the true story of Huanchaca. Ignore all those stories about conspiracy, bribery, and collusion. If you ever visit the Parque Nacional Noel Kempf Mercado on the Brazilian border in eastern Bolivia, you can recall the story of the great cocaine lab and the massacre. They won't talk about it out there.

ALL THIS HAPPENED WHILE I was at home in McAllen. I didn't know about it until I got a call from Air Wing Headquarters. They said I was to go down to Bolivia and check the runway at Huanchaca to see if it was safe to fly the Merlin out of that airstrip. When the Strike Force hit the lab, they had left a contingent of UMOPAR troops to guard the place. The traffickers, in their hurry to disappear, had left behind hundreds of barrels of valuable chemicals. And DEA had left behind a Merlin IIIB damaged in a landing. Air Wing Supervisor Charlie Martinez, in charge of the Merlin rescue, said, "It was a mistake to fly in there with the Merlin. I think the runway's too short, too narrow, and too soft. But go look at it. If you think it's okay, we'll send down the mechanics with engines and propellers to fix it up. But if you think it's too dangerous, we'll just blow up the airplane along with the lab to keep the crooks from getting hold of it."

I wasn't worried. I'd seen that strip from the air with Jesse. Granted, we had been five thousand feet above it. From that altitude we couldn't see rocks, ruts, or mud ponds, but I thought it couldn't possibly be as bad as the strip at Josuani. When I got to Trinidad, the U.S. Army was still camped there. Agent Kelly McCullough, the San Antonio pilot, was with me. An Army Blackhawk flew us to Huanchaca. Even before the chopper settled on its wheels, I knew there was no problem. The runway had a longer usable surface than Josuani. The surface was harder, wider, with fewer obstacles by its sides. There were a few trees at the far end of the runway, but they were not tall enough to be a problem, and about a half mile beyond the trees was a nice clear spot where a person could make a forced landing if he blew both engines on takeoff.

I thought the supervisors were idiots to even think of blowing up this airplane. I did not tell Kelly. Kelly and Charlie were good friends. And well they might be. Four years earlier they'd gone through hell together. They had been kidnapped by some Colombian crooks from their room at the Don Blas Hotel in Cartagena and been driven out into the country to be murdered. Luckily the crooks didn't have their guns in working order, nor their brains. Both agents were wounded, but while the crooks were trying to figure out how one goes about an execution, both agents escaped. From that time on Charlie and Kelly were close. So I went through a show of stomping on the runway, stepping off the width and length (it was over three thousand feet long) and pretending to be pondering the decision. Finally I said I thought it was safe. Kelly passed it on to Charlie. When the engines and propellers got to Trinidad, we were all set to go.

The morning we were to launch out of Trinidad for Huanchaca came on in gloomy drizzle. We were up well before dawn. I went down to Agent Bradley's room at the Ganadero and got a .38 revolver and a pocket full of shells from him. There were rumors the crooks were planning their own raid on Huanchaca to retrieve some of the expensive equipment they had left behind. The UMOPAR guards at Huanchaca reported they could hear the constant drone of generators to the east.

At the Trinidad airport that morning everything was wet. Between the mess-tent clatter of dishes I could hear a constant drip, drip, as moisture fell from the palm leaves. The soldiers' slickers in the chow line glinted shiny-wet in the lamplights. The chopper pilots were preflighting their machines.

I ate my breakfast standing up and talking to the chief master sergeant who was also eating his, his slicker thrown back over one shoulder where his M-16 hung by the strap. He saw the .38 sticking out of my belt and mockingly said, "I see you're going fully armed." (He was always making fun of us for carrying "peashooters.") I said, "Well, this time I have to admit I'd rather be carrying one of those." I pointed at his rifle. Without the slightest hesitation he unslung the gun and hung it on my shoulder. I thought he was joking, but he wasn't. He would not take the gun back.

I said, "Don't I at least have to sign for it?"

He said, "Just give it back to me when you're done fooling with it."

So then I said, "Well, since you're so generous, I've always wanted one of those caps with the chief master sergeant chevron on it." I was referring to the cap he was wearing, and I was being funny. But he immediately took it off his head and placed it on mine. And again he refused to take it back, saying he could get plenty more any time he felt like it. I still have that cap and enjoy the thought of that sergeant's generosity every time I wear it.

Kelly and I and the three Air Wing mechanics loaded our junk onto the helicopters. We took off as daylight came. Our chopper rose, hovered a moment, tilted forward and began to move quickly. As it gained speed, it gained lift from the airflow over the fuselage. It climbed into the clouds. In a short time we cruised at four thousand feet and 150 knots. The clouds thinned and brightened. Soon we burst into bright, glorious sunshine. Right away I could feel the heat. The pilot said over his shoulder, "It's gonna be a hot son-of-a bitch out there." He was a prophet. By the time we got to Huanchaca the place was sweltering. The UMOPAR guards kept mostly to the shade.

The first thing that struck me when the engines shut down and we got out stretching was that the air by the runway reeked fiercely of rot. A gravesite bordered the runway marked with a crude wooden cross made of two broken sticks tied at the middle with rope. It must have been a shallow grave for it leaked badly. The whole place had an eerie feeling, with that gravesite there and with the charred remains of that Cessna, burned pieces of which lay by the side of the runway, and with that sad Merlin on the far end of the runway with the bent props. We unloaded, and the choppers left. We were cut off and about as far from civilization as one could get on planet earth.

Before you take a vacation to Huanchaca there's one thing you should know: insects. Maybe it was just that time of year, maybe it was a once-in-a-century irruption, but the air was thick with them—flies, mosquitoes, beetles, and bees. The bees looked a lot like our honey bee at home, but these bees buzzed around our heads aggressively as if we were the last source of nectar on earth. They landed on us, in our hair, on our faces, and on our lips. Like honey bees, they didn't sting unless we tried to brush them off or smash them. They took that personally and speared us to repay the insult. I raised honey bees back in McAllen and understood the temperamental little bastards, but the mechanics kept getting into trouble with them because mechanics don't like to have bees crawling around their eyes while trying to read the line on a torque wrench. After the first day, each mechanic had several lumps to show for his day of working in the bee swarm. We cut up our mosquito netting and made veils for them to hang over their faces while they worked. This obstructed their view a little, but at least they could turn a wrench without constantly swatting the air around them.

If those bees made honey, I resolved not to eat any. They were the most careless feeders. Carrion or caviar was all the same to them. When we took a leak, the bees started buzzing around our urine stream, and by the time we turned, they were gratefully feeding on the wet spot on the ground. They did the same when we took a dump. They came swarming around as if we had rung the dinner bell. We had to be careful when we wiped so we didn't trap a bee in the paper, or we'd get its barb in a very tender place.

The sun at Huanchaca was a blast furnace. Unless you were a camel, it was impossible to survive without shade. The mechanics rigged up a large tarp over the wings of the Merlin so they could work in at least part-shade, but it was still so hot they spent half their time drinking water. The rest of us went swimming morning and afternoon in the cool river that ran by the cocaine lab. The lab was less than a quarter mile from the runway in a beautiful shady spot. Only an occasional pinpoint of sun winked through the canopy of trees. The lab was just as the workers had left it. Bolivian politicians were still trying to decide whether to blow it up to please the U.S. politicians, or leave it to please the cocaine lords (bribe-bids from both sides were still being considered).

One had to admire the ingenuity and hard work of the cocaine lords to get all this equipment out into the remotest boondocks. They had brought in huge generators to power the drying lights, and hundreds of fifty-gallon drums of ether, kerosene, and sulphuric acid, all neatly stored under the jungle canopy. They had built a house for twenty to thirty people including a large dormitory with bunk beds and a kitchen with gas stoves and a long table. They had the most clever, refreshing toilet. It had been built so it projected way over the river. You could sit there, doing your morning chores, and watch golden-collared macaws preening only a few yards away and listen to strange bird whistles in the trees all around and hear far away the call of howler monkeys. Below was the soft gurgling and swirling of the river as it carried off the waste. By the time you zipped up, you saw nothing but clear, cool, sparkling water. They should have kept that place intact and sold it as a resting haven for New York tourists, but the military blew the whole thing up shortly after we left. What a sight it must have been to see 12,000 gallons of ether lift the jungle canopy into the air.

In the evening the UMOPAR liked to boil dried peaches in a big, black pot for a day-ending dessert. The pot had to simmer a long time before the peaches were ready. They stirred with a long wooden paddle a mess that looked like dirty laundry and smelled a little like it too, but it was delightful to eat, especially with the crackers from the MREs. The UMOPAR chief asked me one night, "How do you like Huanchaca." I told him it was okay, but I didn't cherish all the mosquito bites I got on my butt from defecating in the jungle.

At this, the chief launched into a seminar on how to take a dump in the woods. All the UMOPAR troops immediately gathered round and began to laugh, though the chief delivered his lesson with all the gravity of a priest preaching salvation. It was a little skit he put on for new recruits, and it was so hilarious we all laughed until we hurt. I didn't understand all his Spanish, but I think that made it funnier. He went into the minutest detail, demonstrating every move. He showed how to squat so as to hold your pants in the right position to uncover only as much of your bottom as absolutely necessary with no danger of falling backward. Your left knee had to be up, your right knee down, your right buttock resting on the heel of your right boot. He showed with his finger how your product would then pass safely just past the heel of the right boot. Next he showed how to protect your boot with a banana leaf when you had diarrhea and how to rock back and forth and side to side to stimulate the process when you were constipated. Last, he had one of his men bring some leaves. He told us which were safe to use for toilet paper. He bent over and demonstrated how to wipe properly.

It was wonderfully peaceful at Huanchaca in the night as soon as the air cooled. The bees were gone to rest. The mosquitoes called a truce. The sound of that far-away generator wasn't intrusive. The smoke from the UMOPAR campfire drifted lazily around our tents, the smell of the cooking, the occasional low rumble of men in conversation, and the far-off, lonely sounds of the jungle sent me to sleep in seconds.

We did engine run-ups during the day to test the hydraulic and gas lines, and to make sure the RPM, EGT, and torque gauges were within limits. The mechanics fixed anything not right. Some of the run-ups lasted several minutes at full power. After one run up, as I was getting out of the airplane, I noticed one of the mechanics was behind the plane and just in the act of pulling up his pants and buckling. When I asked what in the world he was doing back there, they said he was constipated and was tired of allowing the mosquitoes to feast on his buttocks while he made attempts to work things out, so he had taken to sitting behind the airplane during run-ups where the prop wash kept the mosquitoes off. He preferred having his bottom peppered with the flying sand rather than mosquito bites.

We finally got everything working. We took one of the damaged propellers and planted it as a permanent marker at the grave by the runway, replacing the stick cross. The four long blades resembled a cross. It was late in the day, so we decided to wait until morning before heading to Santa Cruz. I didn't sleep much that night. I wasn't worried about the runway at all. This was the dry season, and it was in perfect condition. I had only one concern and that was I might make some mistake and let down those three mechanics. I was confident the mechanics had done their best and I wanted to do mine. Kelly and I were going to leave the gear extended—there was no way to test that out there in the jungle as we had no airplane jacks. If we lost an engine on takeoff, it was going to be a bit tricky. I'd never flown the Merlin on one engine with the gear down. I got up for a while and sat with the UMOPAR guards eating peach sauce. It was after midnight before I went to sleep.

I woke with a start. Had I heard thunder? I stepped outside. Sure enough: a low rumbling and lightning glimmering in the west. Damn—the last thing we needed was rain to turn the runway into mud. Pretty soon we could see the tops of thunderclouds in the moonlight. It was only a small storm and was moving toward the north. We weren't in the path. I went back to bed.

Dawn came as beautiful as ever. We loaded. Kelly ran through the checklist, and we cranked. At full power all the gauges looked good. A mechanic on each side of the runway looked under the airplane for leaks. Both gave a thumbs up. I said, "Let's go," and we jumped off the brakes. I let the plane accelerate way beyond take-off speed before lifting off. I thought if we lost an engine I'd do one of those hammerhead crop-duster turns and let the good engine bring us sharply around and back onto the runway. One of the mechanics had stationed himself near the far end of the runway. He was thumbs up all the way. As we passed, he jumped up and down doing a celebrity dance.

For making that flight out of Huanchaca they gave Kelly and me the DEA Administrator's Award. I've already mentioned what I thought of that award. I think we got the award for three reasons: one, the supervisors, as usual, were not fully aware of what was going on in the field; two, the supervisor who put us in for the award was a good friend of Kelly's; three, Administrator Jack Lawn was looking for any excuse to give the award to an Air Wing pilot because that had not been done before. If I deserved an Administrator's Award for flying the Merlin out of Huanchaca, I should have received the Legion of Merit for working undercover with Jimmy-jet in Colombia, and I should have received no less than the Medal of Honor for letting Air Wing Pilot McCravy do a take off in the Merlin from the pasture at Josuani. And really, it was the mechanics who deserved the award. They hooked up all those hoses and lines and torqued all the nuts and secured them with safety wire and had to do all this under the constant attack of an army of ornery Bolivian insects dead set against this entire project.

Chapter Thirty

Air Wing pilots also flew in support of Snowcap in Peru. Like its neighbors, Peru had kicked out the Spanish in the early 1800s, but that made no change for the natives. The *criollo* elite, who had resented the Spanish control, stepped in and took over the reins, leaving the Indians in the same place they were before. Simón Bolívar worked on changing things for a while, then he gave up and went to retire in Colombia. Unrest and instability ruled in Peru as in Bolivia. During the first forty years after Bolívar left, Peru had thirty-four presidents, twenty-seven of them military officers. The economy was completely tanked. What saved their economy? Bird shit. No kidding. There was a bird-shit boom. Well, they don't call it bird shit. The stuff was known as guano, and it was shipped all over the world. The excrement of the billions of seabirds that visit the islands off the coast of Peru was the best fertilizer. Spain fought a war over guano, the Chincha Islands War. In Peru people still talked about the good old times, "the Guano Age," of their grandfathers. It's true birds have been pooping all over the world since forever, but a little rain leaches out many of the ingredients that make it good to sell as fertilizer. Along the coast of Peru, it doesn't rain. Mountains of well-preserved guano have been growing there for a million years.

But I didn't mean to write about bird shit here. My point was that Peru never had a decent economy except during those guano boom years. When I got to Peru, the economy was as bad as ever. Commercial fertilizers had nearly killed the guano business. It was still going, but wasn't as profitable. You could smell the guano at Lima International Airport. The airport was in the suburb of Callao, right by the Pacific Ocean. As we approached minimums on the ILS to the southeast runway (and we always flew the ILS because a cloud of brown pollution obscured the runway and most of the town), we began to smell something like a very old chicken barn. The smell got stronger and stronger. By the time we landed, we wondered if this stuff could kill us—the smell from the guano factories and shipping warehouses of the harbor. It was the smell of money—money that never got far from Lima. The farmers in the mountains to the east were dirt poor. In the valley called the Huallaga, where coffee, tea, and sugarcane could effortlessly be grown, the farmers were easily persuaded to plant coca because getting their other products to market was too expensive. They had no decent roads or railroads. And the Huallaga River ran the wrong way—away from Lima and away from the coast where ships could have hauled their produce to markets.

The inflation in Peru was so frantic that, if a farmer took his product over the mountain to Lima, even if he got a good price, the money was worthless by the time he made the trip back to his valley. To give an idea of the inflation: The first time I went to Peru, the monetary unit was the *sol*, and we bought our goods at the market with *soles*. The next time I went, I still had about seven hundred *soles* from the first trip. They had switched their currency to the *inti*. My seven hundred *soles* did not buy even one *inti*. And then the *inti* inflation also went up like a rocket. In a short time it was worth three cents. The last time I went to Peru they had switched again. Now it was the *nuevo sol*, and you had to have one million *intis* to buy one single *nuevo sol*. That meant that one *nuevo sol* was worth one billion of those original *soles* I still had at home. Since I had only seven hundred—well, you do the math. It's too much for me.

The travel books said Peru was the poorest country in South America. As far as I could see, Bolivia was worse. But those Peruvians in the mountains were definitely poor and definitely unhappy about it. As we flew down the Huallaga Valley, in every tiny village (there was no other kind) we'd see a beautiful red flag with the bright yellow hammer-and-sickle of communism fluttering over the mayor's office—if they had one. Sometimes it was nailed to the side of a building, or it hung from the steeple of the church. Like the bar maid at the Ganadero, they probably didn't know what communism was, but they longed for change of any kind. That's why they supported the coca traffickers and the Sendero Luminoso (Shining Path) Maoist guerillas. And that's why they didn't support the Peruvian Army and the Snowcap Strike Force. Those two represented the government, which represented oppression, which represented no change for them.

The Huallaga River runs out of the Andes on the east side and empties into the Amazon basin. For a while the upper part of the Huallaga Valley produced nearly half of the world's coca crop. The leaves were turned into paste and flown to Pablo Escobar's labs in Colombia. We flew missions into the Huallaga in support of the Strike Force. Stationed out of Lima, we got confusing orders from the DEA office in the American Embassy, not from the Strike Force.

That Huallaga Valley—what a mess! DEA and the police were "fighting" the coca traffickers. The Peruvian military, mostly a gang of torturing thugs, was fighting the Sendero Luminoso. The coca traffickers sometimes fought, sometimes helped the Sendero Luminoso. They fought or sometimes bribed the Army commanders. When the Army commanders weren't busy fighting, they were busy bothering the coca traffickers for bribe money. In the upper part of the valley, where the best coca grew, the traffickers showered the Sendero Luminoso with money so they would keep the military busy. The Peruvian Army didn't view the traffickers as a problem. They were the problem of the stupid gringos. The DEA gringos wanted the army to fight the traffickers; the army wanted to fight the Sendero Luminoso. Those *malditos* didn't pay bribes. Any young man from Lima who wanted a job could go up to Tingo Maria and hire on with any of a dozen different groups. But it was risky work. The Shining Path guerillas left a shining path all right—shining with blood. It was wise to take out life insurance before going into the Huallaga Valley.

We flew into the little valley town of Tingo Maria until the U.S. government wasted a ton of money and constructed a base at Santa Lucia. The base was abandoned a few years later (it only cost fifty million U.S. dollars). Into Tingo Maria we had no instrument approach. Still, one would think it an easy place to find, anchored on the east bank of the Huallaga River right where the Monzón comes in. But it was hidden in a very narrow part of the valley, the Andes on one side and the Blue Mountains on the other. There were some jolly times trying to find that little airport in the rainy, foggy, cloudy climate. I made several approaches into Tingo by simply descending blind through a cloud deck—and smiling when it was still there.

The agents called it "Chingo Maria." I don't have to translate *chingo*. If you speak Spanish, you know what it means; if you don't, you can substitute any adjective as long as it is not complimentary. And if you look in a dictionary, you'll easily find a translation for *chingo*, but good luck finding one for Tingo. I asked a hundred people. No one knows what it means. No one knows how it got applied to that little valley town.

One thing I remember about Tingo Maria. They didn't have good plumbers. To be fair, that was true of most any town in Spanish-speaking America. Toilets were always clogged. Faucets always leaked. They dribbled the same amount of water open or closed, and there was no such thing as hot water. Often there was no such thing as toilet paper, which left it up to one's imagination how others got by. Bathrooms were slovenly, dirty, stinking holes. Usually we could tiptoe through the mess holding our noses, do our business, and make a fast exit. That wasn't possible at the Tingo Airport.

Sawyer and I were there one morning with the Merlin. When he saw me coming out of the jungle at the side of the runway carrying a roll of toilet paper, he said, pointing at the terminal and laughing, "Don, there's a toilet right in there."

I said, "If you'll carry me in there, and wade through that cesspool of urine and paper, and hold me over the bowl, and have an oxygen tank on standby, I'll go." He declined.

Duty in Peru was a nice living for Air Wing pilots. We got to see the tourist sites and got to fly into remote places. If anyone from the embassy wanted to look for coca fields, we were there for them. If anyone from the embassy wanted to go sightseeing, we took him, and the ticket was free. I got to fly to places like Tarapoto an hour north of Lima, which sits on a high jungle plateau on the east side of the Andes and has the best scenery for sharp cliffs and high waterfalls anywhere. One day we searched the area around Mazamari and Huancayo. We found nothing of coca fields but were satisfied we had found some of the best mountain scenery in Peru. Another day we flew some Peruvian Army brass down to Arequipa. We fooled away most of the day sightseeing. On the way down, a colonel came up to the cockpit and asked if we had seen the Nazca Lines. When I said, "No," he said, "Fly over this way and descend." We flew over an area that must be the most barren desert in the world, but it had those mysterious "Nazca Lines," which are some very ancient and very large and very bad pictures of a monkey, a spider, and some birds. No one has ever been able to explain how they got there. On the return trip the colonel directed us to fly over the ancient ruins at Machu Picchu. We had a directive from the Air Wing to "fly embassy personnel wherever they want to go." I've always been grateful to that colonel and that directive.

The most fun I had on any of these trips was when I was with Sawyer flying out of Lima. DEA Agent Terry Sawyer was a great companion both in the cockpit and in the tavern—skillful on the throttle and the bottle as Major Mac used to say. Sawyer was intelligent, had a good sense of humor, and he was generous. He wasn't at all like Jimmy-jet; he didn't examine a beggar's teeth or require a resume to give alms. He handed out fistfuls of money and was happy as Santa Claus. We always had our pockets stuffed with money when in Lima. We were getting lots of per diem and Haz Pay, and with the inflation in Peru, we never knew what our money was worth anyway. We gave up counting money. Any time we got change, we stuffed it in the glove compartment of our rental car. The glove compartment was always so packed that, when we opened the door, handfuls of bills fell on the floor. Whenever we stopped for a light at a street corner, Sawyer rolled down the window and handed out money to beggars and to venders selling cigarettes and bananas. When we drove off, the venders would shout that we had forgotten to take our purchase. Sawyer was a smoker, but he did not like Peruvian cigarettes, and he didn't eat bananas.

As always, the poor suffered the most from the inflation. Lima had more than its share of them. The road we took to go to the airport had a bridge on it. A sign by the bridge read: *Tirar basura estrictamente prohibido* (Littering is strictly forbidden). It might as well have read "city dump" because everyone threw their garbage off the bridge maybe hoping the next rain would wash it away. Since it never rained and the creek bed was always bone dry, the garbage piled up. Our nose told us when we were approaching the bridge. Skinny children played and hunted among the rusty tin cans and dirty plastic bags from early morning to late night. Some poverty is so desolate, so desperate, you wanted to throw up, and I don't mean from the smell of the garbage, but rather from the sight of the bitter, squalid, everlasting damned wretchedness of the people. Sawyer regularly cleaned out the glove compartment as we passed over the bridge and let the money snow down on the children.

One morning when we crossed the bridge we saw a dead donkey lying on the sand below. Some little boys were standing around the donkey poking at it with sticks. The next day one of the hind quarters was missing and a cloud of flies swarmed around it. The children played close by, unbothered by the flies. Vultures circled over the children. Sawyer closed his window against the smell. The following day the smell was worse. The children still played nearby. Vultures still circled. On the way back that day a cloud of black smoke boiled around the bridge. They had set the carcass on fire. The thick smoke smelled worse than the dead donkey, and I wretched out the window. Some boys were up on the bridge throwing cans and rocks into the smoke. They grinned broadly as we passed showing twisted rows of brown and black teeth.

The heart of Lima was an awful place. Dirt, smoke, poverty, and the smell of urine on every block. For some reason the men in Lima thought it okay to urinate on the streets. I'm not so naïve to think this never happens in our own cities, but in Lima it doesn't rain. The smell is as permanent as the cobblestones. And in Lima the men do it in public, in broad daylight and with ladies passing by, never bothering to look for an alley or even a tree. However, the man always holds his penis with his left hand curled over the top to hide it from passersby, as if this bit of modesty somehow redeemed the act of sending a stream of urine splashing on the sidewalk or spraying against a wall.

Except on Sundays, downtown Lima was a roaring pandemonium of buses and people. The buses were always overloaded, always decrepit old tin cans, clumsy, rumbling things with people hanging on the sides and riding the bumpers. They leaked a brownish diesel smoke from their undersides. On occasion some of the smoke actually made it through the exhaust pipes. If you attempted to elbow a way through the downtown maze of Lima, you might see a person attacked on every corner by aggressive fake beggars and predatory street venders, who followed a person for half a block, then cursed him for not shelling out money.

But Sawyer and I lived far away from all that. We had apartments in one of the suburbs. It was a nice, clean area not anything like downtown. They were bright, comfortable apartments with full cooking facilities. Every day the landlord's pretty young daughter came around to ask us if we needed anything. We spent the lazy days lying in the sunny, sheltered courtyard, drinking Cristal beer, eating rotisserie chicken from a nearby restaurant, and wondering when the embassy might call again. (Lima, by the way, has the best rotisserie chicken in the world. They call it *pollo a la braza.*) We went to horse races and the city fair and drove out in the country to see the sights.

Those were the good old days of Snowcap in South America.

Chapter Thirty-One

I HAVE SKIPPED OVER THINGS going on back home, and one of those was by far the most significant event of my twenty years as a federal agent: the murder of DEA Agent Henrique Camarena Salazar down in Mexico. I barely knew Agent Camarena. He was one of the agents stationed at the U.S. Consulate in Guadalajara. I was the closest Air Wing pilot to Guadalajara, and when that office needed a pilot, they often sent me down. I had met Agent Camarena a couple of times at the Consulate, but only in passing. He had that usual Latin-male swagger about him, and some of the people at the Consulate called him "the Black Rooster."

I got to know him a little better when I flew co-pilot on a tech-run with Agent Dave Kunz in the DC-3. Kiki (that was his nickname, or Kikque in Spanish) hitched a ride with us from Guadalajara to McAllen. He came up to the cockpit, rode the jump seat and told us about working in Mexico. Kiki had reasons to be a proud "rooster." He had spent several years working at one of DEA's most difficult and dangerous posts and had made a lot of big cases. He had a pilot friend, Captain Alfredo Zavala, who sometimes flew search missions for him out of the Guadalajara airport. They were finding marijuana fields bigger than anything seen before. No longer the tiny patches hidden in secluded canyons like we used to find in the Trizo days in Sinaloa, these were huge hundred-acre plots out in the desert, where they had to be watered by very deep and very expensive wells.

Kiki said that some of the biggest drug lords in Guadalajara were the ones we had chased out of Sinaloa ten years ago during Operation Trizo. He called them the Guadalajara Cartel. He rattled off some names. I recognized one: Rafael Caro Quintero, the one the Professor called *ese pendejo* (an unflattering appellation) when we were in Culiacán. He was part of a gang of young, loud, arrogant Culiacán cowboy drug traffickers. In Guadalajara the Sinaloa boys operated their drug business as openly as they'd done in Culiacan.

The hardest part about working in Guadalajara, according to Kiki, was trying to tell the police from the traffickers. The police officials sold their badges, credentials, and uniforms to the traffickers. If a man had police credentials, it meant he was either a real policeman or a trafficker with good police connections. It was not uncommon for a trafficker's body guard to have authentic police credentials, or for an authentic policeman to serve as body guard for a trafficker.

Dave Kuntz asked, "Then how can you tell a crook from a cop?"

Kiki said, "You really can't, unless you've known the guy for years. Even then you never know when he'll turn and take the money."

Dave said, "I don't see how the hell you can work that way."

Kiki shrugged, "You just have to take a chance. Otherwise you sit in the Consulate all day *rascando la panza* (scratching your belly)."

But Kiki was tired of dealing with corrupt police officials in Mexico. He was getting out. He had his orders to go to San Diego, his post of choice. He said he was happy to get his wife and kids out of the Mexican hellhole.

Jaime Kuykendall was the resident agent in charge of the Guadalajara office. Most of what I write here about Kiki's murder and about Guadalajara came from Jaime. When we picked up Kiki in Guadalajara, Jaime told me it was getting hard to get DEA agents to volunteer to come to Guadalajara. A year before there had been a long list of candidates, but the list dwindled fast as the candidates heard about the danger. A few months earlier, the Guadalajara traffickers had machine-gunned Agent Roger Knapp's car as it sat in front of his house while Roger and the family were inside eating breakfast.

Jaime said Kiki was the best street agent in Mexico and knew more about drug trafficking in that country than anyone, including Ed Heath, DEA's country attaché in Mexico City. "On second thought," said Jaime, "that isn't much of a compliment. Most of the agents think Ed doesn't know much about what's happening in Mexico."

The Guadalajara Cartel had all the authorities in their pockets. They paid off every Mexican official who got in their way: the Mex Feds, the PRI ruling-part politicians, the Guadalajara police, and the DFS (Dirección Federal de Seguridad), who were a gang of thugs like the KGB of the Soviet Union. The Mexican officials were so well paid off by the traffickers they not only ignored the trafficking, but helped move the drugs. The Cartel had especially good connections with the heads of the DFS, whose written job description was "to preserve the internal stability of Mexico against all forms of subversion and terrorism" (they had their own peculiar way of doing that). The Cartel ruled Guadalajara with their money and with sadistic gunslingers like Manuel Salcido Uzeta, called "El Cochiloco" (the Crazy Pig).

Rafael Caro Quintero, not the smartest, but certainly the flashiest of the Cartel leaders, drove around Guadalajara in the latest, most expensive automobiles dressed in the finest cowboy gear, glittering with heavy gold jewelry, and always with his teenage girlfriends by his side. He bought mansions all over town. He bought ranches around Jalisco and gave Arabian horses as gifts. He bought car dealerships, and often passed out brand new Gran Marquis to his crooked cop friends. The Cartel also owned bars and restaurants including the notorious La Langosta and El Yaqui, both hangouts for narcotraffickers and crooked cops.

The Guadalajara Cartel also had excellent connections with the Medellín Cartel in Colombia. That got started with Trizo. When our beloved U.S. pot smokers found out there might be Paraquat in their Mexican smokes, for a few years they refused to buy Mexican pot unless they were really hard up. Colombians filled the gap by raising more of the product in Colombia and, because of the heat of our Caribbean operations, they shipped via Mexico. When the Colombians saw how efficient it was to move their product through Mexico, they began to pay the Mexicans to transport cocaine for them. Falcon jets loaded with cocaine came into Guadalajara International on a regular basis and were unloaded right under the noses of the police, often with the help of Mexican Customs and Immigration workers.

The Mexicans also imported Pablo Escobar's mantra *"o plata o plomo?"* meaning "do you want the bribes or the bullets?" and they added Mexican fervor to that refrain. When they dispensed *plata* (silver), they shoveled it out by the suitcase full, and when they dispensed *plomo* (lead), they thundered out clip after clip, and tossed a few hand grenades after for good measure. In very little time all the Guadalajara police understood the advantages of choosing silver over lead.

DEA considered Agent Camarena one of their best. Unfortunately for him, so did the Guadalajara Cartel and the corrupt Mexican police. Whenever one of their loads got busted, they laid the blame on that accursed Agent Camarena. They blamed him for the raid on the notorious Buffalo marijuana ranch up in Chihuahua near the town of Búfalo—though Kiki had little to do with that. DEA agents had known about the ranch for a long time and about the police protection it received, but they had never been able to convince the brass in Mexico City and Washington there was a big marijuana plantation out in the middle of a dry desert. Finally, under great pressure from DEA, the Mex Feds and the Mexican Army reluctantly hit the place.

I read reports written by the Mexican Army and by DEA about the raid on the Buffalo Ranch. They estimated the value of the annual production there at eight billion dollars (that's dollars, not pesos). They seized ten thousand tons of plants and of processed marijuana. Twelve thousand people from all over Mexico and Guatemala worked there. Experienced marijuana farmers had been shipped in from Sinaloa and Oaxaca to work the fields. All the equipment for planting, irrigating, harvesting, drying, packing, and trucking was seized. (At least temporarily seized—you never know in Mexico). That raid cost the traffickers a lot of money. It also embarrassed all those Mexican police officers in Jalisco, Zacatecas, and Chihuahua who had been taking bribes and guaranteeing the safety of those drug operations.

Kiki's reputation as a star agent, along with his habit of pointing out the corruption of Mexican officials, including members of the PRI, Mexico's ruling party, was a crime that couldn't be ignored. The Buffalo ranch was raided around Thanksgiving. It was still a sore point two months later when the raid was discussed at a Guadalajara drug-dealer bash. The Guadalajara Cartel held grand parties. They brought their favorite *corrido* music bands from Culiacán and flew in their friends from the Sierra Madre. They made a point to invite the corrupt officials around Guadalajara and feasted with them like old buddies. They had one of those parties on the fifth of February, a little over two months after the Buffalo raid. All the main cartel crooks were there that night, including Rafael Caro Quintero and the Crazy Pig, and also some Mex Feds, some Guadalajara policemen, and members of the beloved DFS. During the course of the evening, they talked about what ought to be done about Agent Camarena. That was on a Tuesday night.

On Thursday morning, as Kiki Camarena left his office to go to lunch, he was stopped on the street near the U.S. Consulate by five men, some of whom had DFS badges. They shoved Kiki into their automobile and disappeared. It was the last time any of his friends at the Consulate saw Kiki alive. The same day Kiki's informant, Captain Zavala, was abducted near the Airport. His friends never saw him again either.

It didn't take long for word to get around that Kiki was missing. The Guadalajara agents kept close track of each other, and usually went out in pairs. But the hunt for Kiki proceeded at a nerve-wracking snail's pace. Our Guadalajara agents immediately suspected the Cartel was responsible for the abduction, but they couldn't get any cooperation from the local police. Pressure had to come down from the caverns of Washington to the catacombs of Mexico City, and finally into the labyrinth of the Guadalajara police.

If you read the story about the Mexican investigation of the Camarena case, you'll find it so shot through with lies, fraud, and deceit you'll think the whole thing must be a lie. DEA sent dozens of agents to Guadalajara to do nothing but investigate the case. Those agents were stymied at every turn by Mexican officials. If our agents wanted to talk to one of the crooks, he was always out of town. Witnesses disappeared or refused to cooperate. The crooks were better informed about what was going on then our agents were. The Mexican cops spent more time spying on the DEA agents than on the crooks. All the cooperation offered by the police was fake. They produced tutored witnesses. They offered fraudulent informants. They gave false leads just to keep the DEA busy and off the backs of the crooks.

In my flight logbook are several entries that say, "Looking for Kiki Camarena." Those flights were a waste of gas. The informants involved were police frauds. The flying time on one of those missions was 7.5 hours in the Cessna 206; the date February 14, 1985, flying out of Laredo, Texas. With me that day was Agent Jaime Kuykendal, and a Mex Fed informant. The informant had told Jaime he could point out the ranch where they were keeping Agent Camarena and Captain Zevala. By that time I knew how to smoke out a fake informant: nail down the details before take off. I spent half an hour with him drawing up a detailed map of the ranch, the house, barn, corral, stock tank, surrounding area. He tried to be as vague as possible—a sure sign. I told Jaime the guy was a fake.

"I know that's likely," Jaime said, shaking his head. "But he's the only lead we have right now, and I owe it to Kiki and his family to follow up on every clue no matter how hopeless it looks." Jaime looked very sad.

So we went up. South of Laredo we circled and circled. Jaime directed the ground surveillance to several ranches. No luck. We went back to Laredo and got more gas. The informant kept insisting the ranches looked so similar from the air he had made some mistaken identities, but he was sure we were in the right area. We looked some more. When the informant pointed out a ranch, Jaime would say something like, "You said the ranch had a big stock tank—where is that?" Then informant would stutter around and say, "No, no, that's not the one. It's more over this way." And then we would go "this way," and the fraud would point out another ranch but with no barn. And so on. That fraud was able to tie up a dozen DEA agents for an entire day.

I felt bad for Jaime. He took this thing personally and was overworking himself. He couldn't help feeling some responsibility for the loss of one of his agents, and the frustration of this kind of futile searching was driving him crazy. After a while the Guadalajara agents knew they were no longer looking for Kiki, but for a corpse. That didn't lessen their zeal in the hunt.

They kept up the pressure. They bothered all the authorities, Mexican and American. They called them at their offices, at their houses, and paged them in restaurants. They bothered the Jalisco governor, the U.S. Ambassador who bothered Mexican President de la Madrid. The Mexicans could never figure out why we'd make such a big fuss over losing one lousy DEA agent. "We lose a hundred drug-fighting agents every year," they said.

The American press was all over Guadalajara by then, and the stories they were printing about corruption were a huge embarrassment to the Mexican president and a hindrance to Mexican tourism. That put more pressure on the Mexicans than our politicians in Washington ever did.

Weeks went by. Our agents thought if they could just find the body, they might determine through forensics what had happened, and maybe how, and maybe who. They demanded Mexico either produce Agent Henrique Camarena or at least his body. For a carrot to the donkey, they hinted that they'd drop the investigation and go home if they could just find the body. That was a brilliant carrot. The cops and the crooks got together to devise a way to deliver the body without implicating themselves.

On the last day of February, Comendante Pavon of the Guadalajara police, suddenly produced a mysterious (and anonymous) letter postmarked out of Los Angeles, California. The letter said that Camarena and Zavala were being kept in a lemon orchard on El Mareno Ranch near the town of La Angustura in Michoacan. Pavon had been receiving hundreds of phony notes and letters, but he seemed to put remarkable credence in this particular one. Pavon said his men would do some surveillance on the ranch and would raid it in a couple of days. He invited DEA to go along on the raid.

La Angustura was a small country town about a dozen miles east of Lake Chapala, not far off the road that runs from La Barca to Zamora. That meant at least a two-hour drive from the U.S. Consulate in Guadalajara. The next Saturday morning (two days after the letter arrived), agents got the word the raid was on. They were surprised to find Pavon and his men had started out hours ago. When the DEA agents got to the ranch, they found a slaughter. Six people were dead, including one federale. Comendante Pavon said when his men arrived at the ranch, they were met with a hail of gunfire. When one of his men was killed he had to give the order to return fire.

But the whole scene looked phony. The Bravo-Segura family living in the house looked like they were shot execution-style rather than in a gun battle. Some were shot in the back, some in the head at point blank range. And the dead federale, Manuel Esquivel, had thirteen bullet holes from an AR-15—mighty good shooting for a family roused out of bed on a Saturday morning. Comendante Pavon produced ammunition, shotguns, and assault rifles that were used at the ranch, and also a goodly supply of cocaine they found hidden in the house. The agents searched the lemon orchard and found nothing.

The Guadalajara press flashed headlines about the raid, taking their news directly from Pavon. They painted the Bravo-Segura family as a gang of mean, drug-dealing, cop-killing kidnappers. Comendante Pavon gave the DEA agents the serial numbers off the guns found at the ranch. The numbers were all incomplete and unusable. On Wednesday, a few days after the raid, a man walking along a path near the El Mareno Ranch, found two bodies partially wrapped in plastic bags. He ran to La Angostura and told the constable. The bodies were transported to the coroner's office in Zamora for identification. That was a mere formality. The police and the press immediately announced the bodies were those of Camarena and Zavala.

And they were right—of course. When our FBI forensic experts finally got permission to examine the bodies, they confirmed the identification. They also found Camarena had undergone the most barbaric and brutal torture that could be devised by sadistic savages. I don't have the stomach to cover it here. I'll only say, for agony, it must rank with a crucifixion. If you are inclined to read about that sort of thing, you can easily find an account in the official records and news reports. Every story about Camarena's death had the lurid details. Later, sworn testimony in U.S. courts revealed that corrupt cops including a member of the DFS sat at the door to listen to the torture. Among those listening was the governor of Jalisco and the Mexican secretary of the Interior, both PRI politicians. They wanted to know what Camarena would say about their own collusion with the drug-traffickers.

I got called to Guadalajara to transport cadaver dogs from Tuscaloosa, Alabama. An FBI soil expert figured out from the soil samples taken off the bodies they must first have been buried in the Bosque La Primavera forest, which was west of downtown Guadalajara, and later were dug up and moved to near the El Mareno ranch. The Bosque was a rugged forest with brushy thickets and deep hidden canyons—an ideal place to hide a body. The bodies would never have been found had they been left there. The dogs were brought down to pinpoint the original grave site and possibly find other bits of evidence in the area. A good cadaver dog would alert on any bit of decaying human flesh and on soil or clothing that had been in contact with the flesh. The dogs found the gravesite and also several other gravesites. Evidently the Bosque was a popular cemetery, although bodies buried there were not in caskets, and mourners didn't follow the usual Mexican custom of putting headstones and plastic flowers on the graves.

I wanted to go watch the dogs search, but they were in a big hurry, and I had to check in with officials at the airport. The search went on without me. Since I had plenty of time, I determined to check into Mexico without handing out a half dozen twenty-dollar bribes like I usually did when I came into Guadalajara. The required ceremonies for entry into Mexico were a marvel of inefficiency. First I had to go to the Flight Plan Office to close my flight plan. I filled out a form in triplicate giving the aircraft name, model, tail number home station, owner's name, pilot's name, and pilot's license number. After I made the first few entries, I signed and pushed the forms across the desk. The official pushed it back and pointed out some more "required" entries. This back-and-forth went on for fifteen minutes. (None of this was required if you passed a twenty on the first push).

Next I had to go to the Migra (Immigration). That official wanted my passport. (I knew he also wanted a twenty, but I was stubborn). He sat down at a typewriter and slowly pecked out a visa with his right forefinger, nodding his head each time he punched a key. Sometimes he stopped and looked at me with his head cocked to one side. He wanted a twenty. I looked back. He went on. After a while he was done pecking. He had me sign. Then he signed. Another official came from a desk in the back. He brought out a badly worn stamper and stamped the visa. Then he stamped each copy of the flight plan. He applied each stamp so-oo very carefully, rocking the stamper back and forth on each application so that his chair groaned as he shifted his weight.

They directed me to the Airport Authority Office, which I had never visited before. If you passed out twenties, you never got that far. There, sitting at another ancient typewriter was an officer with a form I had never seen before. The form was put out by the Secretary of Communications and Transportation of the United States of Mexico. It was an "Aircraft Entrance Form." The officer began filling it out with a most vigorous pounding at the keys. There were so many carbon copies he had to pound out the letters with great determination to make sure they got through the carbons. The letters appeared on the form one by one with long pauses between as the officer searched the keyboard for the next letter. Sometimes he stopped and looked at the ceiling as if trying to remember where the next letter was stationed on that keyboard or if it was one of those that always seemed to move to a new place. Then he'd lunge at the typewriter and peck out two or sometimes even three letters right in a row without stopping. Every few poundings he would stop to look at his bottom copy to make sure the typing was getting through. Finally he pulled out the copies and laboriously stamped each one. There were five copies of this most important form.

After some thought, this official directed me to sign the front and the back of each copy—ten signatures! I thought now we must be finished, but I had to go to another room where two more officials were holding forth. One was from the great Office of Inspections of Airplanes. He placed his official seal on each copy and, as a special favor just for me, he signed over each seal with impressive flourishes. Then it was the turn of the Customs Inspector. He kept his seal in a leather pouch strapped to his belt. Out of his briefcase he took a dented inkpad. He opened it on the desk. He unsnapped his leather pouch and extracted the great seal. He stamped each copy.

Now back to that deeply thoughtful Airport Authority officer. He inspected each copy. The forms were now all blotched up with purple ink and scribbled up with signatures. The stamps were smudged and unreadable in spite of the exaggerated attention used in their application. The official seemed happy with the forms, but he was still thinking, his head down, staring at the floor to one side of his chair. His head came up, his face bright with a question: did I have my Airworthiness Certificate?

I was already reaching for my wallet to get out a twenty (which would have been close enough to an Airworthiness Certificate), when I remembered my determination to forgo the bribing. I told the man I didn't think a United States Airworthiness Certificate was required in Mexico. I felt I was on good ground, since I'd never before been asked for one. Everything stopped! All the officials gathered round to assure me an American pilot must have a United States Airworthiness Certificate to fly in Mexico. I went out to the Merlin and dug out the Airworthiness Certificate. The official seemed disappointed when I handed it to him. He scrutinized it very carefully, even turning the paper over and inspecting the reverse side which was blank. He thought some more. The other officials were watching him closely.

A light came on. "Do you have insurance?"

I told him the airplane was insured by the Government of the Untied States of America.

"Yes, I understand. But do you have Mexican insurance."

I told him that the U.S. Government insured that airplane anywhere in the world.

He looked very sad. "But, Señor, you must have Mexican insurance." He hung his head in sorrow. "It is the law, Señor."

His regret was immeasurable. The others nodded. His grief was so genuine I almost put my hand on his shoulder to comfort him with the promise of getting Mexican insurance straight away. Instead I slowly reached into my pocket and extracting a twenty and two tens. I slipped them between the copies in front of him. I was a defeated man, broken in body and in spirit. Take me to the hospital on a gurney and let me die.

The Airport Authority official completely ignored the money. It accidently slipped from between the papers and fell into his open desk drawer as he stood up. He tore off the green copy and handed it to me, saying we would overlook the lack of insurance. He handed the yellow, the blue, and the white copies to the other officials. The buff copy was for himself. That went into his desk neatly covering the money. He smiled and said, "That is all, Señor," He seemed entirely pleased with the expeditious way my entry into Mexico had been accomplished.

The dog handlers, Tuscaloosa Police Officers Ted Sexton and Mike Everett, had expected to stay in Guadalajara for only a day, but they were there for several. On the trip home, Ted sat with me in the cockpit. Mike slumbered in a back seat. Their three dogs slept in the aisle. Ted said they were out of dog food. I said, no problem. I had to land at McAllen anyway to clear U.S. Customs. We could get a bag of dog food there. Ted said that wouldn't work. The dogs were on a strict diet. They had to eat the special food stored at the kennels in Tuscaloosa. The only exception was that they could, in a pinch, eat a few hamburgers from Burger King—not Wendy's not McDonald's—only Burger King. Anything else could make them sick as a dog. I said my wife could meet us at the airport with the hamburgers.

Ted looked puzzled. We had no cell phones in those days, and I had to explain to him I could call this place in Cedar Rapids, Iowa, on the high freq radio, and Cedar Rapids would give me a phone-patch to my house. He was relieved. But he cautioned the hamburgers must be plain—no dressings, no onions, no pickles. Ted said, "If there's even a little mayonnaise on a hamburger, the dogs can't have it. Tell her a dozen plain hamburgers." That's only four for each dog, but it will do until we get them home.

After I leveled off at cruising altitude, I called Atlas Radio in Cedar Rapids and got a connection with Bea. I told her what I wanted. When talking on the high freq, you always kept everything as short as possible because the whole world could listen in. So I just ordered a dozen hamburgers from Burger King with nothing on them. Now Bea had been around long enough to figure out I was probably returning from Mexico, was probably clearing customs at McAllen, and was in a hurry to get somewhere else yet that night. She assumed I had passengers on board. She also knew I always ate cheeseburgers and insisted on extra onions.

So she says, "Cheeseburgers, right?"

"No, hamburgers, just plain."

"With onions."

"No, no onions, no pickles, no mayo, no nothing."

Bea, thinking I was ordering for several people and that I was just trying to keep the order simple for her, said, "Why don't I bring three cheeseburgers with onions, and the rest plain. It's no bother."

By now the man running Atlas must have thought she was a bird brain. I'm sure he had the order straight from the start—twelve hamburgers with nothing on them.

I repeated, "One dozen hamburgers, just plain."

She said reluctantly, "Oka-ay. Just trying to help."

I parked by the terminal at McAllen's Miller International and went in to clear customs. Bea was there with the hamburgers. I brought her out to the plane so she could meet the Tuscaloosa officers and could watch them feed the cadaver dogs. The officers had the dogs out and were allowing them to run around on the grass by the tarmac. The dogs were not allowed to eat the buns. The officers took the patty out of each bun and flipped it into the air over the dogs. The dogs were big German shepherds, and they leaped up and swallowed the meat with one gulp before their front feet were back on the ground. Bea said, "Why didn't you tell me the hamburgers were going to the dogs? I thought it was for you and your buddies."

We had to wait for the gas truck. The officers put on a little show for Bea. Ted Saxton held the dogs by the plane. Mike Everett had a little block of wood in which there was imbedded some flesh cut from a human cadaver. He walked off a ways and hid the piece of wood in some tall grass by the airport fence. He came back and we talked a while. Then Ted loosed one of the dogs and told him to go search. The dog sniffed back and forth on the ground. In about thirty seconds he alerted on the piece of wood. Mike threw the wood off into the grass and the dogs always fetched it back. I smelled the wood. I couldn't smell anything. The officers said that, from our position at the terminal, the dogs could have smelled out a cadaver even at the far end of the airport.

It was already dark when we took off out of McAllen. Officer Ted Saxton warned me the dogs would be passing gas from the hamburgers. He said for some reason hamburgers caused a horrible smelling gas and that, with three big dogs breaking wind in harmony, it could get kind of thick inside the cabin. I laughed it off as a joke. But it wasn't a joke! As we climbed, the drop in cabin pressure caused the gasses in the dogs to expand. The cabin and the cockpit began to fill with a horrendous stench. The smell was so bad I had to stick my nose into my armpit to get at some breathable air. Ted kept saying, "I told you!" The dogs lay in the aisle, resting their noses on their front paws, cheerfully releasing gas. Occasionally they shifted a little and grunted contently as they gratefully expelled an exceptionally large fart. And then they smiled, too, I thought. I tried releasing some of the cabin pressure to vent the smell out the back, but that raised the cabin altitude and made the dogs fart more. I kept looking back at Officer Everett to see if he was still alive. He was breathing into the crook of his elbow and laughing.

When we got to Tuscaloosa, it was near midnight, and then I had a scare. There was no airport! There was a town, and I knew where the airport should be, but it was missing. I rechecked my calculations. Did I have the wrong town? I rechecked the navigation instruments. This had to be Tuscaloosa. I circled and got out my flashlight to look at the airport data sheet. I had not bothered to read all the details. It said you had to click your mike button to turn on the runway lights. I clicked three times and, hallelujah, just below me I saw an explosions of lights like the Fourth of July and as beautiful as a Christmas tree. I put down the gear and landed between two bright rows of lights. The cadaver dogs were home.

Chapter Thirty-Two

DURING THE REST OF MY CAREER with DEA there were numerous trials connected with the Camarena case both here and in Mexico. Most of the villains that took part in the crime were sent to jail. And many of those who didn't go to jail were sooner or later found dead somewhere in Mexico—a precaution on the part of the Guadalajara Cartel. Seeing the murderers go to jail was little consolation for DEA agents. Mexican jail punishment was inversely proportional to the amount of money one had, and the Cartel had plenty. While in jail, they lived the life of Riley. They had all the whiskey and women they wanted. They had their friends in for big parties, and informants said they sometimes appeared at parties back home in Culiacán.

Whenever a DEA agent got killed, agents across the country discussed the death in bars at night with much speculation and rumor. This was especially true in the Camarena case. Some agents told the story as if they were there and saw how it all went down. After midnight and a few beers, speculation and rumor was sworn to as fact. That got passed on, and soon the whole story was a myth. The kidnapping and murder of Kiki Camarena has become such a myth. The nearest anyone will come to the truth about the Camarena case, is to ask Jaime Kuykendall. Even DEA's own historical website about the murder has misleads and inaccuracies. The most egregious of these is this whopper: "The 1985 torture and murder of Agent Camarena marked a turning point in the war on drugs." If that statement meant "Kiki did not die in vain," and was written solely as consolation for Kiki's family, it deserves applause. But if it was the usual bureaucratic attempt to portray utter failure as blessed success, it deserves contempt. You have only to consider what happened in Mexico after the murder and what is still happening to this day to realize the magnitude of that lie. The power of the drug lords, the number of drug killings, the corruption among politicians make the days of Kiki Camarena look like Utopia. Ironically that statement contains a grain of truth if by "a turning point" is meant a turn for the worse. They should have recalled Voltaire: To the living we owe respect, to the dead we owe the truth.

One day I got a call to go to Guadalajara. This was long after Kiki was dead and gone. The other agents were also gone—mostly transferred back to the States. New agents had taken their place. The new guys had an undercover deal going. Some Guadalajara crooks were to deliver 600 kilos (1,320 pounds) of cocaine to the airport at Tamuin in the state of San Luis Potosí. We were to fly the cocaine out of Tamuin and deliver it to buyers in San Diego. When the San Diego crooks showed up to buy the load of cocaine, San Diego DEA agents would arrest them and seize their money. The Mex Feds and the Guadalajara DEA boys would arrest the crooks that set up the delivery to Tamuin. This was the same plan for cases I'd so often been part of before. But this time I was a bit more nervous than usual about the deal. It was the first time I was doing anything undercover for Guadalajara since Kiki got killed. Also the undercover agent told me the Mex Feds helping on the deal were new, and he wasn't positive about how much help they'd be. He said, "Now, you don't have to do this, if you think it's too dangerous."

I said, "I have one question. Are you going along?"

He said he and the informant would both go with me in the airplane. That was good enough for me. I hated deals where the case agent said, "Go to Belize and meet with the crooks, and they'll bring you a ton of cocaine." Unless the case agent was a trusty old friend, I didn't go. I had a rule: if the case agent went along, I did the deal. I figured the case agent didn't wish to get shot any more than I did. That's why I was content to do Agent Jerkin's deal in Jamaica, and why I was willing to do this one.

I said I was a bit nervous about the deal. As it progressed, I got a lot nervous. The agents were all new to Guadalajara and weren't as wary of the Mex Feds as the older agents like Roger Knapp had been. I met with the undercover agent at a drinking hole near the Guadalajara Consulate. He laid out the plan. We'd fly into Tamuin in the early morning. The crooks would be at the airport with the dope. We'd leave engines running, quickly throw in the bundles and take off. As we rolled down the runway, the Mex Feds and the DEA agents would come sweeping in and arrest everybody and pretend to try to stop the plane as we took off. They'd drive alongside the runway firing shots over the airplane to make it look good. That way if there was any communication between the Mexican crooks and the San Diego buyers, it'd look like the airplane had escaped with the dope and was on its way.

What also worried me was the informant. The agent said the informant, whom they called Ciego, would shortly be joining us in the bar to meet me.

I asked, "Why do you call him Ciego?" (Ciego means blind.)

"Everyone calls him Ciego. He can't see worth a damn."

By way of illustration he told me one night they were sitting at a table in a dimly lit bar drinking with Ciego. A red-and-white coke machine stood against the wall behind Ciego. It happened that the waiters in that bar wore red-and-white uniforms. At one point when Ciego's beer mug was low, he looked around for a waiter. Seeing the coke machine, he ordered a round of drinks and told the machine to be quick about it, and then admonished it when it did not move immediately.

In a little while Ciego showed up. He was large for a Mexican, jolly and plump. He walked along very cautiously and constantly squinted around as he moved, trying to make sense of what his eyes were telling him. He had a stick, but didn't tap around like a blind man. He used it mostly to scare people out of his way. He was brim-full of confidence about the cocaine deal. It was all set, he said, everything according to plan. I noticed as he sat down in his chair that he was packing. Later I asked the undercover agent about this.

"Why are you letting an informant carry a pistol, and a blind informant?"

"Aw, Ciego insists on carrying a gun. But don't worry. There's not going to be any trouble, and if there is, Ciego can't see enough to hit anything."

I said, "Yes, that's just it. I don't want to be in the same county when Ciego starts to shoot."

"The gun's just for ornament. Makes him feel like a big man."

I got up at three o'clock next morning. We wanted to be in Tamuin at sunup, and the town was more than an hour's flight in the Merlin. It was nearly four by the time we got Ciego rousted out of bed and were ready to go. The airport was supposed to be open twenty-four hours—it was all locked up. For half an hour we walked around knocking on windows and doors. Finally a sleepy Mexican came to a door and let us in. I went directly to the flight planning office. In Mexico you had to file IFR if you wanted to fly in the dark. There was no one there. I went back and asked the sleepy Mexican how I could file. He came back to the flight planning office with me and shouted "Jose!" several times. A back door opened. Jose came out, walking wide legged, zipping up his pants. He scratched himself and combed his hair with his fingers. I filed IFR for Tampico (the airport authorities did not need to know where we were going).

It was still dark as we headed east out of Guadalajara International and climbed to altitude. It was a beautiful morning with dazzling starlight so we could see the outline of the mountains. In a short time a rosy glow appeared behind the Sierra Madre Oriental. Then dawn came on fast for we were flying to meet it. The undercover agent got on his radio and began communications with the ground. I circled to the west of Tamuin until the undercover agent said everything was ready. The crooks were at the airport, the surveillance ready for the bust. As we descended into Tamuin we could see the crooks' pickup truck at the far end of the runway. The airport was not officially open and there was only a light breeze that morning, so I landed downwind, rolled out, and swung the plane around by the crooks' pickup.

The undercover agent immediately opened the door and jumped out. I did the after-landing check and the before-take-off check. I could hear the thumping back there as the cocaine bundles were being loaded into the plane. I could see the back of the truck and as the last bundles were thrown in, I began to run up the power. I heard the loud clunk as the undercover man slammed the door. I watched the cockpit door light go out indicating the door locking lever was in the locked position, and I released brakes. We began rolling down the runway. Immediately I could see vehicles storming in from all sides to make the arrests. A pickup truck came racing alongside the runway. The officer riding shotgun was firing his pistol out the window and two men standing in the bed of the truck also fired in our direction. The field beside the runway was uneven. The truck was bouncing crazily, and it wasn't hard to imagine the bullets meant to miss the airplane might puncture a fuel tank and make the whole show all too real. But that drama took only a few seconds, and we left the truck behind and lifted off.

Immediately I knew I was in trouble! Something was dreadfully wrong! The nose of the airplane over-rotated on lift-off, and even with the stick full forward it was coming up still further with the airspeed bleeding down. The pressure was enormous! With full-forward trim and all my might, I was still having trouble holding it. I snapped on the autopilot, but it wanted no part of this. I turned it on, it kicked itself off. I turned it on again, it kicked itself off again. It seemed to say, "You got yourself into this, you figure your own way out." I could not leave the cockpit. Had I been alone in that airplane I would have been a dead man for sure.

"Throw that cocaine up here or we're going to crash!" I yelled at the top of my lungs. It had been Ciego's job during loading to pitch the cocaine bundles toward the front of the cabin to distribute the weight, but he had forgotten that part, and I had been too stupid to check before we got going. We were badly out of balance. Fortunately, when I yelled, Ciego came to the front to find out what I wanted. He was fat, and his weight greatly relieved the pressure on the stick. I made him sit in the co-pilot's seat while the undercover man straightened out the load. He was pitching with one hand and talking on the radio with the other. After we were back in trim, he came up to the cockpit and informed me the Mex Feds wanted us to go to Tampico, and his boss, the resident agent in charge at Guadalajara, had ordered a change of plans.

I said, "What the hell for?"

"They want to weigh, photograph, and mark the dope."

I said we could do that when we gassed-up at Mazatlán. The undercover man shrugged and threw up his palms. "I already tried that. We have to go to Tampico."

I said, "I'm not landing this load at Tampico until our agents are at that airport."

He was agreed, and he got on the radio to tell them.

When we landed at Tampico we witnessed a long argument between DEA and the Mex Feds. I stayed out of it. The Mex Feds had changed their minds. We were now flying the dope to Mexico City where they said they would incinerate the stuff. They had some phony excuse about the San Diego part of the deal being blown. I did not give a damn. I was so tired of this Mexico BS. We loaded up and flew to Mexico City where Mexican authorities took custody of the cocaine. The Mex Feds had played us for fools. Of course, DEA would never call this operation anything but a great success—after all, we "seized" 1,320 pounds of cocaine!

The Mex Feds had played DEA like a Stradivarius. Here's what I think happened: The Mex Feds set up the deal with the crooks, telling them they had a pilot who would fly the dope to San Diego for them. Then they told DEA they had a big cocaine deal, but needed an undercover pilot (which they knew DEA would provide). Once the DEA pilot got safely out of Tamuin with the cocaine, they called it back with their phony excuses. We brought it to Mexico City for them where they repackaged it and sold it back to the crooks from whom they had stolen it in the first place. It was brilliant. They got rich on this deal. They got front money for protecting the cocaine. They got a fee for providing a pilot—a lot of money. Drug pilots did not come cheap. A thousand dollars a pound was not unheard of. Then they got the money selling the cocaine back to the crooks which was easily two thousand dollars a pound. Or if they could arrange to smuggle that cocaine into the States, they could get more than triple that. I think the Mex Feds to this day must still chuckle when they remember that good old Tamuin cocaine deal.

I have always wondered if Ciego was in with the Mex Feds on this deal or if he was a dupe like I was. I never saw Ciego again, but DEA was still using him after the Tamuin deal. I heard about him four months later in mid August, four months since the Tamuin fiasco. I got a call from Agent Tony Ayala, the agent in charge at Guadalajara. He asked me to go immediately to Tucson to pick up Agent Victor Cortez and his family and take them wherever they wanted to go. Victor had been sent to Guadalajara after Kiki was killed. Victor had been working undercover with Ciego. They had a meeting set up with the crooks at the Bolerama Bowling Alley in Guadalajara. DEA Agents Benny Maestas and Alan Bachelier were inside the Bolerama covering the meeting. They waited and waited—way past the appointed time. Victor and Ciego didn't show. They went back to the Consulate. Victor was not there. The office hadn't heard from him.

Immediately the two agents went back to the bowling alley to interview people. They found a man who said he had seen the police take the two men away. The man had a partial license number. This started to sound just like the abduction of Kiki Camarena. Tony Ayala immediately informed the Attorney General of Mexico. The whole DEA office began calling around to police stations. All the police denied having Agent Cortez. Tony went to the station indicated by the partial license number. They were just releasing Victor because they had been called by the Attorney General of Mexico.

Agent Victor Cortez, just like agent Kiki Camarena, had been abducted in broad daylight along with his informant—abducted by the police. Victor and Ciego were both taken to the police station and tortured. They blindfolded Victor, stripped him naked, tied his hands behind his back, doused him with water, and began the standard Mexican police "interview," which even in its mildest form included the use of cattle prods and seltzer up the nose. And again the police "knew nothing" when they were first called. It was highly likely that, had Ayala not called the Attorney General promptly, Victor and Ciego would have ended up in the Bosque de la Primavera cemetery. Ironically, on that same day, while the Jalisco State Police were torturing a United States federal agent, President Ronald Regan and President Miguel de la Madrid were meeting to negotiate more foreign aid for Mexico.

DEA immediately transferred Victor and his family, and Ciego across the border to Tucson. Jack Lawn, the head of DEA, told the press Agent Cortez would be taken to "an undisclosed location" for a rest. I flew Victor and his family to that undisclosed location. I saw no scars on Victor's face or hands when I met with him in Tucson. He was a weight lifter, and looked a young man in prime physical condition. I saw no physical scars, but one can't see the scars on the mind—psychological scars inflicted by human torture. Those scars are deeper than the physical ones. Those scars do not heal.

Chapter Thirty-Three

THERE WAS MORE VIOLENCE, and it spread across the Rio Grande into Hidalgo County. Colombians were now shipping most of their cocaine and marijuana through Mexico. The porous South Texas border was getting more popular and more murderous. Everybody had a gun. No self-respecting crook would venture forth without that insurance. At McAllen the number of arrests and of drug seizures were up. Gun seizures were way up. On Halloween of the year following the murder of Agent Camarena, Manny Segovia of the Hidalgo County sheriff's office was shot to death by a drug dealer. Our DEA agents had often worked with Manny. He had been with the McAllen Police department's Narcotics Unit before he went to the Hidalgo County Sheriff's Office. He and some of his fellow officers were executing a search warrant at a house in Mercedes. When they entered, one suspect ran to the back of the house, grabbed a gun and shot through the wall killing Segovia.

On the last day of that same year, New Year's Eve, a drug dealer shot Willie Ramos. Willie was one of our McAllen DEA agents in Group One, and I knew him well. We called him "Bro," because of his habit of addressing other agents by that name. He flew with me a couple of times. Once he and I went up in the 206 and spent an hour clicking photos of several ranches belonging to drug traffickers in Starr County. When we got back to the office we discovered we had been snapping an empty camera—no film. We had to go back up and do it again. I liked Willie. He was sort of humble and shy in spite of all his accomplishments. Only thirty, he had already received a law degree from the University of Arizona, had been a prosecuting attorney in Mojave, Arizona, been a U.S. Border Patrol agent, and was now a DEA agent. He had been assigned to our office only the year before.

I had just returned from Dallas that New Year's evening. Bea and I were sitting at home by the fire trying to find something decent on TV. It was New Year's Eve and all the networks had those stupid programs showing people drinking and going nuts. The telephone rang. It was Benny Pierce, the Group One supervisor in a panic and grasping at straws. He said Willie Ramos had been shot and one of the men involved had fled the scene in his car. Benny wanted me to take the plane up and look for that car. I had to explain to him it was completely dark out. From an airplane I could see nothing but lights, and unless someone on the ground found the vehicle, I couldn't follow it, and if someone found it, I'd be useless for an arrest. He said okay and would call me back. I didn't expect him to call back, and he never did.

Next day, Wednesday, we had off for New Year's Day. People kept calling to see if I was home and if I had heard that Willie had died in the hospital. By Thursday morning when we got to the office everyone including the secretaries knew about the killing. A funereal gloom hung over the place. All talk was in low voice with the usual comments: "and so young . . . his poor wife . . . such a nice guy . . . and she with those two little girls . . . how in the world could this happen." The agents said the shooting took place in Las Milpas, a dinky little dirt-street hamlet south of Pharr, only a few miles north of the river. There was an easy crossing there when the river was low. The crooks liked to do deals in Las Milpas because it was a quick escape back into Mexico should the cops get on their tail. I heard conflicting versions of how Willie got shot. I went to Agent Joe Watkins to get the straight story. He'd been there and was a level-headed agent. He wasn't likely to panic and not likely to embellish his role in a case. I base my story on what Joe told me.

It was already dark when they got to Las Milpas. The town was quiet except for an occasional "pop, pop" of firecrackers from New Year's Eve celebrations. Only a few street lights were on in the town. The parking lot at the grocery store where Agent Willie Ramos was meeting with the crook, was poorly lit—mostly with Christmas lights on the front of the store. Joe was in a car with Agent Angel Perez. They had the eye on the undercover car. They could see little else except dark silhouettes moving around between the cars in the parking lot. The bust signal was the trunk lid opening, and they could see that plainly. Other surveillance agents were stationed across the street. Those included Agent Mario Alvarez, Supervisor Benny Peirce and the new guy, Agent Walter Morrison.

Willie Ramos was in the undercover car with two informants, one of whom Joe knew as "Roberto." The deal was for 250 kilos of grass. The crook had showed up driving a van with the grass in it. The crook was now in the undercover car sitting in the back seat on the right. Willie was in the driver's seat. They talked a while, then both the informants got out of the car. They went to the rear and opened the trunk.

Joe radioed, "The trunk's up! Let's hit it."

Joe and Angel got out and walked casually toward the undercover car to give the other agents time to move in. Suddenly Joe noticed both informants running back to the undercover car, and Joe could see a struggle going on inside.

Joe began to run. He could see shadows bobbing up and down in the car. Several shots rang out. One informant staggered back (hit in the hand). The popping sound of the shots was not conspicuous because it sounded just like the firecrackers going off around the town. Joe thought only three shots were fired, however, after the struggle, when they opened the revolver, they found four expended shells in the cylinder. Joe knew immediately when he shined Willie with the flashlight that he was badly wounded. His chest was running red, though he still clutched at the crook's wrist. Joe's anger flared. He would have shot the crook but was afraid of hitting Roberto, who was still in the fray. Joe pressed his gun right in the crook's eye and forced him down on the back seat. By this time Mario had opened the other back door, and he stepped on the crook's arm and took the pistol away. It was Willie's .38 service revolver.

Joe yelled to Benny, "Call an ambulance." Benny got on the radio. But Joe had just recently waited a long time when his father-in-law needed an ambulance, so they decided to take Willie to the hospital themselves. Angel got in with Joe, and they drove hell-for-leather to the Valley Memorial Hospital in McAllen. Willie was unconscious. The new McAllen Hospital was a few blocks closer, but Joe wasn't acquainted with the entrances. Besides he had read that Valley Memorial had by far the best trauma unit in the valley. Nurses came out immediately. Joe wanted to make sure they didn't think this was just some bar bum they brought in from a New Year's Eve fight, so he told them the man was a federal narcotics officer shot in the line of duty. The petite nurses were struggling to get Willie out of the car. Joe pushed them aside and picked up Willie bodily and placed him on the gurney (Joe was a weight lifter. He could bench press four hundred pounds.)

As they wheeled Willie into emergency, Joe heard one nurse say, "Oh, God no! It's a chest wound."

Angel called his wife and told her to go to the Ramos house and sit with Willie's wife, and they'd call as soon as they had word on Willie's condition. In a short time the hospital security guard came out to the waiting room and said, "They have little hope." A few minutes later he came back. He said, "He passed away."

Then the doctor came out. He beckoned to Joe to come with him into the operating room. He said, "Come, I want to show you what happened here."

There lay Willie. They had cut open his chest side to side just below the heart. The cavity was propped open. The doc showed Joe where one of the subclavian veins had been completely shattered by the bullet. He said, "There was nothing you could have done for him after that shot was fired."

No vital organs had been scathed. The doc said. "Look, his heart is perfectly good," and he cradled Willie's heart in his hand to show Joe.

Benny and Angel went to the Ramos house with the bad news. Benny had also called his wife and told her to go. It happened that Willie's mom, who lived in Puerto Rico, was there on a visit. She went into such hysterics, they called a doctor, who came out and gave her a sedative.

That killing happened on New Year's Eve, a Tuesday night. The funeral Mass was held on the following Friday evening. Bea and I got caught in "snowbird" traffic and would have been late for the Mass, but the body was even later. Two police guards stood at the doors of the little Catholic Church waiting for the coffin. Thanks to Ceballos Funeral Home, we waited an hour before the hearse came along with the coffin. The pall bearers were uniformed local officers from the police departments of McAllen, Pharr, Mission, and from the Hidalgo County Sheriff's office. They wore their uniforms with badges and decorations, all pressed and polished, and looked wonderful as they slow-marched into the church with the flag-draped coffin. The church was full of policemen from all over the valley, and there were DEA agents from Houston, Brownsville, Monterrey, Laredo, and San Antonio. The bosses were there from Dallas and Washington, D.C. They made speeches about what a great guy Agent Ramos was, though I don't think they knew Willie from Adam.

A FEW DAYS LATER I WAS in Benny's office. He was looking glum. It wasn't good to have an agent in your group get killed. I thought I would give him some comfort.

I said, "Too bad how Willie screwed up that night."

Benny said, "Huh? What d'ya mean, he screwed up."

I said, "Well, trying to make that arrest by himself and not waiting for surveillance."

Then Benny said one of the dumbest things I ever heard from a DEA supervisor: "Oh, I don't call that a screw up. When I'm undercover, I don't like to have the surveillance agents do my dirty work for me either."

Here's why that's stupid: Surveillance agents love to make that arrest. They sit boring hour after boring hour waiting for that trunk lid to come up so they can swoop in and stick a gun in the crook's ear and slap the cuffs on him and break the news he's headed for jail. Seldom will human beings act with the eagerness and enthusiasm equal to that of a band of DEA agents storming in for the arrest. Nothing is more satisfying to the undercover agent than to see his buddies come streaking in from all directions and taking over the situation. To say the arrest is dirty work for surveillance is like saying that opening Christmas presents is dirty work for children.

But to finish the story of Willie (and to add another twist). DEA Special Agent William Ramos of the McAllen District Office, was shot and killed on the last day of December. The trial opened four months later. The man who shot Willie was Felipe Molina-Uribe. Molina's defense attorney came up with one of the most bazaar defenses I ever heard, a half-baked conspiracy theory that left me scratching my head. According to the defense, the agents of the McAllen District Office hated Agent Ramos and set up the New Year's Eve deal to assassinate him. They planted the gun in the undercover car hoping that, when Agent Ramos tried to make the arrest, Molina would find the gun and shoot him. Failing that, they intended to kill Ramos as they came in for the arrest. Willie Ramos was a victim of the hatred of his fellow agents.

The defense attorney offered no evidence to support his theory. In fact, he painted Ramos as a shining gem of a DEA agent and offered nothing to show that anyone disliked him, or even could dislike him. The jury did not buy the story. Molina was convicted of first-degree murder.

Later I was drinking beer with some of the agents from Group One. Joe Watkins was there and so was Mario Alvarez. When I declared the defense attorney was nuts when he said the agents didn't like Ramos, they said that if I had been in Group One that defense might not seem quite so crazy. Willie was in fact not well-liked. If the defense had done some investigating, they might have found an informant or two to testify he was not popular in Group One. With some more investigating, they could have found Willie was always filing EEO complaints. He had just filed one only a month before he was killed. Investigating further, they would have found Willie had been kicked out of the Border Patrol for stealing. In order to show the jury a pattern in DEA, the defense might have been able to slip in the fact that, only a few years ago, DEA Agent Sante Bario "choked" on a peanut butter sandwich while in jail after DEA arrested him, and many thought Sante Bario had been poisoned to shut him up. The defense might have found an agent like Mike Levine to testify he thought Sante Bario was assassinated by government agents.

Joe said, "If consul had brought all that into court along with his 'crazy' defense, he might have introduced reasonable doubt in the jury's mind."

Mario agreed. "It only takes one to get a hung jury. We might be sitting here right now wondering when the next trial will be or even how Willie's killer got off scot-free."

THE VALLEY WAS GETTING more dangerous all the time, but I still felt basically safe at our house on Houston Avenue. We did have a few scary incidents. We had a cathedral window on the west side of the house. One night someone hurled a rock through it, exploding the big window pane to smithereens. Another time someone pitched a brick through the window in the hall. The pitcher must have been standing right by the window, or he had one hell of an arm, because the brick went through the window with such speed that it bent the steel frame and knocked a hole in the wall on the other side of the hallway. Then one night in bed Bea woke me. She thought she heard an unusual sound outside. I took my pistol and walked to the big sliding door that led outside from our bedroom. It was dark out, but a quarter moon shed enough light so I could see two dark silhouettes moving toward the house. Two men, crouching low, waddled right toward me, evidently unaware someone was standing by the door. Our house was wired with a burglar alarm. As soon as I turned the lock on the door, the alarm sounded. The two men spun around and ran like rabbits out to the street.

I told Bea to call the police and grabbed my clothes and ran out the door, skipping as I hopped into my pants. I jumped into the car and drove down the street in the direction the two had taken. When I got to the first alley I turned in. I could hear dogs barking. I figured those men must be in the alley or had run through there. I had a spotlight in the car that threw a beam as bright as the sun. I scanned the alley. Nothing moved. A McAllen P.D. cruiser pulled in behind me, and two cops got out with their guns drawn. I threw my pistol on the seat and held both hands out the window to show I was unarmed. I had no credentials, but it was easy for them to believe who I was, because they had the call from Bea, and I was driving a car with hidden lights and siren. They told me to go home. They would handle it from here.

The next morning at breakfast a cop stopped by the house. He said they had found the two hiding in the tall grass by some trash cans in the alley. They had a cache of stolen items hidden there and were evidently waiting for a truck to come pick them up and take them into Mexico. (This was a common burglar method in McAllen.) The two had already stolen some lawn ornaments, two bicycles, and some tools. The police distributed the entire load among the neighbors who identified the stolen items as theirs.

Still I felt pretty safe. I did not think these incidents were necessarily connected to my work. The broken windows could have been pranks by kids. The burglars weren't armed. However, I wanted to take Bea to the firing range and have her practice with my guns. She refused. She didn't want to kill anyone. I asked what she was going to do if someone tried to break in when I was gone. I was surprised to find she'd given this a lot of thought. She showed me how she'd run down the hall to the bathroom in the back corner of the house. She'd open the casement window, squeeze through, and crouch down among the bushes. It was a good hiding place. If no one was on the street, she'd easily slip across the alley to Lalo Ramirez's house. Lalo was a good friend of ours and a wise old Mexican. He could handle any situation as well as I could.

I liked Bea's plan. She was smart. No sense confronting a crook if you didn't have to. I did insist she learn to work my Remington 870 pump shotgun enough to jack a shell into the chamber, even if she did not plan to pull the trigger. It was my opinion that, if any burglar was feeling his nervous way around our house in the dark and he suddenly heard the "clack-clack" of Bea wracking the shotgun, he'd make an immediate exit and go home to change his underwear—and would resolve to go for easier pickin's next time.

Through all this I was always aware that working as a pilot for DEA was safer than working as a street agent. I felt far less exposed sitting in a cockpit than sitting in a bar with a crook, or sitting on the witness chair in court with the crook and all his friends looking on. Not to say there was no risk in flying. I had some scary moments in the cockpit too, though I have to admit some of those were my own fault.

I was on my way to Dallas one day to pick up an airplane to fly to Bolivia. It was summer in the valley, hot and humid. As I climbed out of McAllen International, I could see no cloud in the sky except the usual cumulus building over the Gulf of Mexico. To the north, where I was going—severe clear. The early-morning air was still smooth, not a ripple of turbulence. I had the Cessna 206, the same one I'd used for hundreds of hours and was as comfortable as a pig in mud. I paid no attention to the gauges on the instrument panel—which was always a mistake. I got up toward Three Rivers and was contemplating the Choke Canyon Reservoir wondering how the fishing was down there. The air seemed to be getting hazy or maybe the windscreen was getting foggy. As I tried to wipe it, I became aware of the smell of burning oil. This was smoke!

I looked at the oil gauge. Shit. It was bottomed out. The smoke was coming from under the instrument panel and coming out now in waves. The damned airplane was on fire! I pulled the throttle to idle and rolled up on one wing to look for a landing area. This was flat country and I could land just about anywhere. Right away I saw a little clearing next to a field that was perfect. I had plenty of altitude. I opened my window to clear the smoke. I lowered half flaps, shut off the engine, and turned off the master switch.

As I circled to lose altitude, I could see no smoke trailing the plane, so I thought the fire must have gone out. The plane touched down, rattled a bit on the rough field and came to a stop. I got out. Only a little smoke came from the engine compartment. My scare was over. I didn't run for cover as pilots did in the movies, and then the burning plane blows up just as they dive into some bushes. I looked underneath. The whole bottom of the airplane from stem to stern was dripping oil.

I saw a farm road at the edge of the field where I was parked. A little to the north, a ranch house. I headed there to find a phone to call the Air Wing and tell them to come get their airplane. An old pickup sat in front of the house. I felt the hood as I walked by. Cold. Not driven that morning. All was quiet.

As I approached the front porch, I got a bit uneasy. Two dogs slept near the door. Guarding the master, I thought. I planted my boot firmly on the first step and expected the hounds to explode into action. But no. One raised his head and looked at me, the other opened his eyes but didn't move. I took another step. The livelier one (if one can use that description for a lazy hound) got up and gave his tail an unenthusiastic wave. When I got to the door, the other dog sat up and waited to see my next move. I knocked. No answer. I knocked again rather loudly. At that knock, the lively one raised his nose to the sky and gave a sound like a bark that trailed into a loud, long wailing howl. Then, evidently deciding he had done his duty, he lay down to rest himself.

I was about to leave the porch to look around the ranch when I heard a thump inside. Shortly I heard the creaking of the wooden floor. The door opened to reveal a young lad hopping around on one leg while he was trying to pull on a boot.

"Just a minute," he said, "While I get these damned boots on."

I had obviously roused him out of bed: hair uncombed, shirt half buttoned, fly open. When he got his boots on, he looked up, but he didn't look at me. He was looking around in the yard behind me.

"Where the hail did you come from?" he asked in astonishment.

Then I realized he was looking for a car, truck, bus, bicycle or something that would explain my presence out here in the country.

I pointed down the road to the field where the airplane sat.

He stuck his head further out the door and seemed even more astonished.

"I had trouble with my airplane," I said, "and had to set her down. I hope you don't mind. I need to call my office to let them know where the plane is."

I got no response from the lad. He stood on the porch staring at the plane with his mouth open.

I tried again. "I was wondering if you have a telephone."

He turned and seemed to get a focus on me for the first time. "Telephone?" he shouted as though I must be crazy. I had a sinking feeling there was no phone at the ranch. But then, as though he had a sudden revelation, "Why sure you can use the phone. C'mon in."

He showed me where the phone hung on the wall. I spun the dial and asked the Addison secretary to give me maintenance. As she was switching me over, I covered the mouthpiece and I looked at him.

"Where are we?" I asked. I knew that was the first thing maintenance would ask, and I didn't want to admit I was lost.

"Huh?" he said, leaning toward me, frowning and cocking his head as though he didn't think he could have heard me correctly.

"Where are we?" I asked again.

"Why," he answered pointing at the floor, "We're right here."

I couldn't help laughing, and just then the head of the maintenance department came on the phone. I explained the problem with the airplane.

He swore. "You don't have to be so god damn cheerful about it."

I said, "I wasn't laughing about the airplane. It was something else."

I was able to pinpoint the location of the airplane by asking the young man what was the nearest town, how long did it take to drive there, and which road he normally used when he went. By the time I got off the phone, I decided he was mentally challenged. I asked him if he could take me to the nearest airport. This, too, took a while to filter into his brain, but we finally got under way.

That day I learned that a person might seem stupid simply because you haven't asked him anything that peaks his interest. As we got into his truck he yelled, "C'mon, Blue," and one of the hounds loped over and jumped onto the seat. We got in and the hound put his head on his master's lap. The lad stroked the head lovingly as we bounced along.

"What kind of dog is that?" I asked.

A miracle took place. Before my eyes, this bumbling dim wit, who barely knew the name of the high school he attended, was transformed into a genius. The dog was a rare cross between an Australian Blue Healer and a Red Tick English Coonhound. I was given a lecture on the virtues of each blood line and how they manifested themselves in this present hound. This boy knew all about the dog's daddy and granddaddy, and about the mother's side of the family. He told of famous incidents in the lives of the ancestors. Then he stopped. The well was dry. We rode in silence.

I primed the pump, "What's your favorite hunting dog?"

Another light went on. This boy continued with a knowledge of dogs that could only be equaled at the Westminster Dog Show. When he dropped me off at the Live Oak County Airport by George West, I handed him a twenty-dollar bill. He wouldn't take it.

"I just want to pay you for your gas and your time," I told him.

He said, "Mister, around here we don't take money for helping a man who's in trouble."

I stuffed it in his shirt pocket saying it wasn't really my money, that it was the government paying him. It was their airplane.

Still he reached to give the bill back. I said, "Buy something for old Blue there."

Then he smiled and patted his shirt pocket. "By God, I'll do it." He waved and walked to his truck.

ANOTHER SCARE I HAD was most certainly of my own making. I was coming back from Bolivia. I had a long, hard month and wanted to get home. I delivered the Merlin to the Air Wing hangar at Addison. They were just finishing installing a new ILS in the Aerostar and wanted me to take it to McAllen to do an undercover deal for Corpus Christi next day. The plane had not been test-flown, but I was eager to get home. It was past sunset, almost dark. The weather in Dallas was shitty: rainy, foggy, drizzly. Toward McAllen to the south, it was even worse. Most of the valley had ceilings and visibility near minimums. I had a hard time finding an alternate. I put down Corpus Christi. I needed 600 feet for an alternate, and they were calling for 700 until ten o'clock, then lowering ceilings till morning. I put down Corpus as an alternate, though I knew I'd be arriving there after ten and would also be low on fuel if I had first shot a missed approach at McAllen.

Like an idiot, I pressed on.

I kept checking the weather after I got airborne. I checked everything from Del Rio to Corpus. I didn't like Corpus for an alternate because I was stretching the fuel. By the time I got to San Antonio, Brownsville was saying, "Sky obscured, indefinite ceiling at 100 feet and half mile in drizzle and fog." That was scary. I thought I better land at San Anton, which was now at 300 feet and one mile. But just then Harlingen suddenly opened up to 700 feet and a mile! I pressed on and switched my alternate to Harlingen.

I was less than a half-hour out of McAllen, when I heard a Continental Airlines pilot go missed approach at Harlingen. Damn! I checked Laredo.

It was below minimums. McAllen was now the only place in the valley not below minimums. That was scary too. I knew at McAllen they often carried a ceiling of at least 200 feet and a mile until all the DC-3s had returned from Mexico from their smuggling trips. That way the DC-3s could land at McAllen legally. I looked at the gas gauges. I had barely enough fuel to make one approach and then go to Corpus Christi.

A DC-3 landed at McAllen and reported the ceiling and visibility were right at minimums. Small comfort. I knew that pilot. I figured he had just busted minimums and didn't want to say so. My stomach got tight. Every time I calculated my fuel, it seemed less likely I could make it to Corpus without getting into emergency fuel. What a fool. I was in an unfamiliar airplane with new electronics, not tested in flight, flying in bad weather, and low on fuel.

I was nervous and overshot the McAllen ILS as I came in. I was used to a south wind at McAllen, but tonight it was from the north. At the outer marker I had the HSI centered, but got no signal. Either McAllen's outer marker transmitter was out or my receiver was. But I was on the glide path and on course. I looked at the fuel. Suddenly a very calm feeling came over me. There was no more decision to make. I wouldn't go to Corpus. I could be in the same boat there, plus be low on fuel. I felt a great peace. I was going in here even if it was in a ball of fire. At 300 feet I thought I saw a light and my heart leaped. But the light disappeared instantly into thick fog. The tower still said the field was at minimums. As I passed 200 feet my fingers were nervous on the throttles, and I was swallowing hard. I passed 100 feet and was no longer breathing. Suddenly the fog all around me glowed brightly as it did over lights. A second later, bam! I was over the approach lights. I pulled the throttle to idle and the wheels squeaked on the runway. The airport was clobbered with fog. I had to search to find my own hangar. I don't know what I would have said if the tower had asked me about the weather. But the moment I touched down, the tower announced they were closed.

That scare was over. I resolved if I did anything this foolish again, I'd go to confession first, and take Communion too, and any other sacrament available. Last rites didn't seem unreasonable, and I would carry a large St. Christopher medal—one with oak leaf clusters.

Anyway, I was back home in the Golden Valley of the Rio Grande where the weather was always beautiful, and nothing ever happens.

Chapter Thirty-Four

DAD USED TO SAY, "*Was dich nicht umbringt macht dich stärker*" (What doesn't kill you makes you stronger). When I was a teenager I considered that absolute foolishness. I would say, "Okay, then I should take a dose of strychnine every so often to get stronger?" I didn't say that out loud though, or Dad would have given me a dose of something to make me stronger on the spot. At Crosier seminary, Father Bosch used to try to tell me the same thing with the adage: "Tragedy often turns into treasure." Now, years later, I look at those adages as wisdom that should be carved in granite. They have been tried and proven in the crucible of my life. Three major events occurred, which at the time seemed the worst and most painful things in the world, but which turned out to be the best things that ever happened to me.

First I developed back problems. Bad back problems, to the point where I had to crawl out of bed in the morning, make my way to the dresser on all fours and pull out the drawers one by one so I could claw my way up to a standing position. Once on my feet I could function, although with pain. The doctor took X-rays and told me I had a herniated disk and had to have surgery. I was afraid of the knife so I declined. I said I'd see if it would get better.

The doctor said, "Oh, yes, go right ahead. It'll only get worse. You'll be back in a month begging me to do it." I didn't like that doctor.

I knew a physical therapist who practiced in northern Texas. I called her.

She said, "Don't listen to the doctor. You don't even know if you actually have a herniated disk."

I said, "He saw it on the X-ray."

She said, "X-rays can be misinterpreted. And even if you do have a bulging disk, it's highly likely you can get things straightened out by doing stretches."

She sent me a booklet with stretches to do for the spine. My progress was very slow, but in three months I was back to normal. I kept up those back stretches. Thirty years later, though many of my old comrades are plagued by back problems, I rarely have any. Only through the motivation acquired from that spinal episode have I been able to stay with the stretching all these years.

Also, that episode made a big decision for me. The therapist had told me part of that spinal problem came from my sitting so many hours strapped in the pilot's seat of an airplane. I decided not to buy an airplane when I retired as I had been planning. I was getting near retirement and had been giving the matter a lot of thought. I didn't want to quit flying, but neither did I want to fly for someone else. I'd seen those corporate pilots at airports doing crossword puzzles as they waited for the boss to show up. I'd seen them flattering the boss's wife and carrying her luggage around. They might be in their glory when in the air, but on the ground they took a position lower than a cab driver. Either I had to buy my own plane or quit flying. That decision was made for me when I had that back problem.

Next tragic event: I became a lunatic. (Bea doesn't like for me to say it that way). I developed mental problems. Something went awry in my brain. I'll tell this story with a bit of detail so that, if it ever happens to you, you'll recognize it for what it is, and not for the end of the world—though it will seem like it. I was at the time of my life when I should have been the most content. I had only a few years left until retirement and was respected in my job. My stress level was low. I had almost ten thousand hours of flying time, and little about an airplane could scare me. I still worked undercover, but the most stressful parts of that (dealing with the informant, writing the reports, and preparing for trial) were usually not my responsibility. The Air Wing had just decided to make me an aircraft-accident investigator, which was great. I always liked playing detective. I often thought I should have been a homicide investigator. Finding the clues that cause an accident was similar.

On a clear, sunny day over the Rocky Mountains, I was on a commercial airliner out of Denver headed for Los Angeles to go to a class as part of the training for aircraft accident investigator. The air was smooth; we were high above the mountain-turbulence. People were watching movies, sipping drinks, eating snacks. I was reading *Huckleberry Finn*, and all was well. Of a sudden, a little wave of anxiety washed over me. I was puzzled. I looked around. Had I heard a warning sound in one of the engines? Everything seemed normal. I dismissed it and went back to reading. In a little while it happened again. A stab of fear—but nothing caused it. Was it an omen? Was I clairvoyant? Were we about to crash? I made a trip up and down the aisle. I could see nothing, hear nothing, smell nothing that could cause alarm. I dismissed it again.

That night in my hotel room it happened again. Just a few seconds of alarm, then gone. I never had anything like it before. In the following days as I sat in the classroom it happened again and again. Each time the dread became a bit stronger. After I got back home it continued. I began to worry. I became anxious. I was afraid I was going crazy. The more I worried, the more anxious I became. The more anxious I became, the more I worried. It was snowballing out of control until I was anxious all the time. The only relief I got was when I was totally immersed in my work, but even then I worried my flying skills might be affected by the confusion in my brain. The next time my supervisor called to send me on to Bolivia, I felt I had to tell him. I did not want to be in a situation where a bad decision of mine could get someone else hurt.

DEA already had an "answer" for this. They had a special psychologist on staff in Washington, D.C. She called me. Her voice was oh-so-soothing, her manner so very assuring. I was not alone in this. It happened to a lot of DEA agents. "We savage ourselves in our work," she said. She gave me the number of a psychologist in McAllen.

I saw that man several times, but he was no help. He had never had anything like this himself and did not seem to understand how it felt. He had all kinds of fancy names for it: battle fatigue, shell shock, post traumatic stress syndrome, and soldier's disease. After I told him I didn't think my job was that stressful, he kept trying to get me to admit I had been sexually abused as a child, as though that was the only other possible cause for such a thing. I finally told him to go to hell.

Then they gave me the name of an "eminent" psychiatrist who had a small office in northern McAllen. It was a dingy, dark, depressing office. As I sat in front of the man's desk, I expected cave bats to come fluttering by. This man had a degree from somewhere in Mexico, and his English was challenging. He put me on a drug called Nardil. I soon wished he had put me on cyanide. All my anxieties got worse. I was having panic attacks. I couldn't sleep. Now I *was* crazy!

The shrink in Washington had told me much of my problem came from being away from home so much and not having a normal, settled life. Since this was a possibility and since I was planning to quit flying anyway in a couple of years, I resigned from the Air Wing. They offered me a position at Air Wing Headquarters where I wouldn't travel much, but I didn't want to move from McAllen just then. I went back on the street. My mental problems continued. Whenever I told the psychiatrist about any side effects I was having from the Nardil, he said it wasn't from the Nardil but from the anxiety. And when I said the Nardil wasn't working he upped the dose. When I called the DEA shrink in Washington, she was no help. She told me to stick with it. She just kept repeating her favorite mantra: "We savage ourselves in our work." Then she went back to filing her nails.

I suffered in this hell for eight months—and it was *hell*. I remember praying, "God, take an arm, take a leg, but don't make me suffer like this. Give me leprosy if I must have something." After seven months I had to admit my Mexican psychiatrist was a total quack and was poisoning me. I quit going. I quit the Nardil. I began reading up on health and nutrition. I began eating regular meals, not stuffing myself every night after starving all day. I took vitamins. I ate only one bowl of ice cream instead of three. I drank only one beer a day. In a month I was back to normal.

That mental tragedy resulted in several advantages. I credit those mental problems with my present good health, both physical and mental. So far I don't have the blocked arteries, diabetes, and the aches and pains of arthritis and rheumatism many people my age have. I don't suffer the anxiety, fear, and depression that often comes with old age. That bout with lunacy also got me to thinking about suffering and why God allows man to suffer. This led to my third great tragedy, which in turn resulted in the greatest treasure of all.

I began to question my religion. Believe me, this was a painful process. To call into question the deep beliefs that had been the comfort and safety of my youth, and the bastion of my parents, grandparents, and God knows how many generations before them, seemed like I was taking that strychnine dose—with only a vague hope it might make me stronger. I learned about spirituality, especially from the writings of the great Trappist monk, Thomas Merton. It was a first step. I came to realize spirituality and religion weren't the same. One can have a religion without being spiritual and be spiritual without a religion. I began to suspect some of my beliefs were actually a hindrance to the spirit. This slowly brought change into my life the depth of which I can't describe in words. It brought me the peace and freedom I've always sought.

If you never suffer, you'll always be a shallow human being. You have to experience back pain yourself, or you will always think people who complain of back pain are shirkers. You have to have mental problems yourself before you quit thinking people with mental problems should go to the nut house, and if you're steeped in the safe cell of an established religion which you never question, you may never realize true spirituality and may always think people who question the religion are traitors.

I DIDN'T MEAN TO DRIFT into a sermon. I'm way off my narrative. I meant this to lead into what it was like to be back on the street again and now in the Golden Valley of the Rio Grande. It was quite different from the streets of Minneapolis. To get a feel of what it was like, you must know about some of the people: the cops and the crooks. The violence from Mexico had crept into Hidalgo County, and so had the corruption. There was just too much money in the drug trade.

At work older agents were retiring, younger ones coming in. One of those younger agents was Ralph Palacios. I liked him. He was fun to work with, was tireless, and had especially good connections with the local police departments. He had been a McAllen patrol officer before he came to DEA. Ralph and I, Officer Roy Padilla of the Pharr City Police, and IRS Agent Max Galvan formed a little informal task force. We used to meet in the early mornings at the Tejas Restuarant near the corner of I Road and 495 in Pharr to plan our day while we pigged out on *huevos rancheros* and *migas*. Roy loved to eat. This was his favorite eating place, and you couldn't start a day better than by sitting down with a smiling Roy Padilla to eat Mexican food at the Tejas. Roy was a total professional at anything he did: backing you on the street, keeping you company over a beer, or eating stacks of hot tortillas at the Tejas.

Roy Padilla had initiated the Pharr P.D. Crime Stopper's Program. He carried the Crime Stopper telephone with him day and night. We had good times investigating the tips Padilla got on his phone. Roy freely shared his information with Ralph and me. Some DEA agents didn't trust local officers and certainly the FBI didn't. It's probably true there is more corruption among the locals (though not by much), but there is also more information. They have more informants. They know the people.

Ralph and Roy didn't display the petty jealousy so often present between two law enforcement agencies—jealousy that always impedes investigations. Ralph, Roy, Max, and I worked on a lot of cases together with no disputes over who got the credit. I was better at writing and so wrote up a lot of the reports. I was glad to have Ralph as the case agent, for I was trying to avoid being called back to court after I retired.

It was easy to make cases in those times on the border. The valley was flush with drug money. I don't think another stretch of river anywhere in the world had as many crimes being committed as on the one hundred and fifty miles of Rio Grande border between the Falcon Reservoir and Port Isabel. A hundred easy crossing places existed, especially during the dry season. When it rained, the river was high and a good place to dump a corpse. The corpse would find its way to the Gulf of Mexico in a short time—where the fish erased the evidence.

One smart crook who knew how to make use of that river was Rafael "Rafa" Longoria. People who had a disagreement with him often had the misfortune of drowning in the muddy river water. He lived south of Weslaco near South Texas Boulevard. Roy was getting information about him regularly on his magic telephone. Rafa was very fat. We could not find a strong enough adjective to do justice to his corpulence so we simply called him "The Fat Man." He was beyond fat. He was unsightly obese and did not carry the lard well; it hung on him loosely like oversized clothing and shuddered and wobbled in blubbery rolls as he moved about like a walrus. Every day we heard more stories about him—not about being fat—but about drugs and murder. I had the pleasure of seeing him arrested just as I retired, but I wasn't there to see Assistant U.S. Attorney Pat Profit bring him to court.

A few of those Golden Valley crimes were being committed by the sheriff himself. Sheriff Brig Marmolejo was the Hidalgo County sheriff the entire time I was in McAllen. He came into office just as I came to McAllen and went out of office and into jail just as I left ten years later. When I first came to the valley, he was considered one of the finest law enforcement officers in Texas, known to be dedicated, hard working, and incorruptible. He was also known to hate the feds, especially the FBI.

Brig established his reputation during his first term in office. He had Hidalgo County District Attorney Oscar McInnis arrested. Brig had the evidence on tape. The attorney was indicted for solicitation of murder and was disbarred. That made Brig forever "incorruptible" in the valley press. However, through this case Brig made the FBI mad. They thought they should have been invited along on the case. And he made the Texas Rangers mad. They supported the district attorney and said Brig framed him. (The attorney, by the way, pled guilty to a lesser charge and later his law license was reinstated.) Brig also made DEA mad when he dropped the remark publicly that DEA hired nothing but thieves and drunkards. Brig didn't lose popularity with local law enforcement officers over that. They didn't like the feds either.

But there were always whispers about Brig's shadiness swirling around the valley like wisps of fog that floated up from the river at night. Even before he was sheriff, it was said he had helped the big marijuana dealer from Edinburg, Juan Frank Garcia, in his business. It was also whispered that, as sheriff, he helped Ramon Martinez, the famous Donna, Texas doper, get started. Brig lost no votes over this. Men like Garcia and Martinez were popular in the valley. Like the dopers in Sinaloa, they used their money to good advantage among the local citizens. They weren't considered a danger to the community (though there might have been second thoughts when Garcia's body was found shot full of holes by Colombian marijuana dealers who were eliminating their competition). There were whispers Brig and some of his deputies were taking bribes from dopers to let loads pass through the valley. But no story about corruption at Brig's office could get traction in Hidalgo County. Brig-supporters said the feds were ginning up rumors. Brig won the 1980 election by an avalanche.

We kept our prisoners in Brig's jail. The prisoners were coddled there. Brig let them run their drug business from his jail. He let them have Texas-style *pachangas,* and visits from girlfriends. Brig had better access to our prisoners than we did. He made friends among them. He had better information about their activities then we did.

Because of his spending habits, McAllen DEA agents were certain Brig was skimming money from drug deals. DEA was trying to make a case against Brig, but it was tough. Brig knew exactly what was going on in our office. We still had agents (one or two Texas good ol' boys and some naïve new-comers) who shared information with Brig's deputies. Edinburg was the county seat. That's where Brig had his office and his jail. Edinburg was where the Echo Hotel was. The hotel's Echo Bar was a popular meeting place. On a Friday night, drug traffickers, defense attorneys, and Hidalgo County deputies drank together. Sometimes a DEA agent joined them.

I was getting information from two different sources about the corruption of Brig's chief deputy, Bob Davis. The sources said Davis was selling information to drug traffickers. I wrote up a DEA 6 about it. A few days later I got a telephone call from Deputy Davis demanding the names of my informants. Someone from DEA was leaking him information. Davis thought I was obligated to tell him who my informants were, because he was a "fellow law enforcement officer." I wrote another DEA 6 adding to that information. This time an angry Davis called on me the very next day, called on me in person. He was waiting for me on the street by our office. He sat in his car with the window open and yelled at me as I came to the front door. He said he was going to sue me for defamation of character. He said he had already talked to an attorney and was about to get me for libel and slander. Then he stomped on the accelerator and squealed off in his car. I waved him goodbye. He waved back. I used five fingers to wave, he used one.

When I accidentally met Deputy Davis in the hall at the Hidalgo County Jail next day, he informed me he knew where I lived. I thanked him for that information, but said I wasn't inviting him over for a beer. I told him however, I would gladly be pallbearer at his funeral if he wished for me to have that honor. I added my hope the happy event would come off in the near future.

Brig kept winning elections no matter what he did. DEA finally made a little headway against him. Our agents identified properties Brig was buying. He was spending money no one on his sheriff's salary could possibly afford. We sicced the IRS boys with the green eyeshades on him. This made Brig still more popular. Valley citizens didn't like the IRS either. Brig kept on winning.

McAllen DEA agents didn't like that we had to house our prisoners in Brig's jail, but, ironically, that was the very thing that finally brought Brig down. It all started in the little town of Donna, Texas. That town was famous for one thing: their Redskins football team was once the All-time Texas State Champion of the AA Conference. They were the only team from the Rio Grande Valley ever to accomplish such a feat, and what made them proudest was that their team had been made up mostly of scrappy little Mexican-Americans considered too small to play football with the big boys. A battered old sign by the railroad tracks said, "Home of the Texas State Football Champions - Conference 16 AA." Many in Donna fondly remembered those good old days when their boys "kicked gringo ass" and "bloodied gringo noses" on the gridiron.

Maybe it was in the Donna milk. On the corner of Business 83 and Victoria Road in Donna was Thompson's Dairy Farm. You could buy butter there and get milk in old milk bottles made of thick glass—milk in quart bottles, cream in pints. Milkmen still drove Thompson's Dairy Farm trucks and delivered to the front porches of Donna houses. One of those milkmen was Ramon Martinez. But Ramon had a peculiar style of delivery. He also delivered marijuana to some front porches (by previous arrangement in the bar at night). Ramon became famous as El Lechero (The Milkman). To this day old timers talk about El Lechero and how good things were back then.

El Lechero became rich. He quit driving the milk truck. The ton quantities of marijuana he was moving didn't fit in a milk truck. He got a fleet of trucks and delivered to warehouses in Oklahoma City. And El Lechero no longer needed the milk truck for cover either. He had Brig, and he had the people of Donna. El Lechero was selectively generous. He knew where to donate money to gain popularity. He was lavish in his donations to the church and the school and the football team. He created a real estate boom by buying up dozens of properties around Donna at premium prices. He gave scores of Donna citizens employment and paid thousands in hush money. The happy citizens of Donna often referred to him as "El Patron." The city itself got a reputation as a drug-smuggling center. The Donna city motto was, "The City with a Heart in the Heart of the Rio Grande Valley." The cops said it was "The City with the Dope in the Heart of the Rio Grande Valley."

Roy Padilla's telephone had been gleaning a lot of information about El Lechero. El Lechero had branched out into cocaine and heroin, and he could now deliver enormous amounts of any drug to any place in the United States. He laundered his money through the Casas de Cambio in Mexico and brought it back to banks in the U.S., especially the Citizens State Bank of Donna. He bought race horses, and fighting roosters—and politicians.

A boy in a poor Mexican family in Donna, Texas, couldn't help admire the evolution of El Lechero from milkman to millionaire. One of those poor admirers was Gilberto Salinas. Gilberto was raised in poverty. He was a smart boy and well-behaved. They made him an officer in the Donna police force as soon as he became of age. But Gilberto wasn't happy with the money he made. He saw that drug dealers like El Lechero did much better. He watched El Lechero with hungry eyes. He often met him around Donna, and they became friends. Gilberto moved to the Weslaco Police Department where the pay was better, but it was still not enough. He began supplementing his income the way El Lechero did when he worked for Thompson's Dairy. In a few years he was fired from the Weslaco police force for, among other things, "selling drugs out of his patrol car." He was known as "The Little Milkman."

He was not "little" for long. The Little Milkman's career progressed even faster than that of the Big Milkman. By the time we arrested El Lechero, Gilberto Salinas was big enough to fill in the void. But he did make a mistake one day. He showed up in a truck at the Whataburger in Brownsville with $405,000 hidden in a spare tire. The money was a down payment for 3,000 pounds of marijuana that Gilberto was buying. But the seller was our informant. DEA was in on the deal.

Gilberto jumped bail on that charge (it was only $100,000), fled to Mexico, and kept on expanding his business. In a short time he was set up on the Yucatan Peninsula of Mexico in the beautiful state of Quintana Roo. He was smuggling tons of Pablo-Escobar cocaine into the United States and was working as part of the Juárez Cartel of Amado Carrillo Fuentes. Our El Paso Intelligence Center considered the Juárez Cartel the biggest and richest drug organization in the world by then. When Gilberto finally was stopped two decades later, he was wanted all over the United States for drug violations and was making twenty-two million dollars a year as a lieutenant for Amado Carrillo Fuentes. He was sentenced finally in U.S. District Court in New York City to a term of twenty-seven years.

Before ending my story about Gilberto Salinas and the Juárez Cartel, I want to pass on a warning to doctors: don't volunteer your services to anyone in the Juárez Cartel. Doctor Francisco Jusino, a McAllen obstetrician of sterling reputation, delivered a healthy baby boy one day. The mother died of complications in the delivery. She was a wife of Gilberto Salinas. A little more than a month later, the doctor was assassinated in a hail of bullets. Though it happened in broad daylight at a busy intersection near some large apartments in McAllen, no witness ever came forward. About a year later Mexico City doctors were doing liposuction and plastic surgery on Amado Carrillo Fuentes, boss of the Juárez Cartel. Amado died on the operating table. A few months later two barrels were found on the highway between Mexico City and Acapulco. The bodies of the doctors who assisted in that operation were in the barrels, encased in cement, hands and feet tied, gagged, strangled, and shot. There were other signs of torture: the bodies covered with burn marks, nails ripped out. Don't do business with the Juárez Cartel.

Okay, forget the Little Milkman. Back to the big one: El Lechero. And back to the shenanigans of Sheriff Brig Marmolejo and to what brought him down. DEA was finally able to arrest the famous El Lechero of Donna. When he came to court for his bond hearing, Donna citizens, including the mayor, lined up to testify what a sterling citizen he was. They all declared El Lechero too honest to jump bond, but the judge kept him in jail anyway. El Lechero sat in his cell and thought over his prospects. He faced a ninety-two count federal indictment and was likely to get an eon of jail time. He decided, "I better sing."

He did, and it was a beautiful song. It was about Homero Beltran Aquirre. DEA had known almost nothing about Homer Beltran. El Lechero was a gold mine of information. Homer Beltran was El Lechero's chief supplier and the supplier of other big drug dealers along the border. Homer was smart. He kept a low profile. He lived in Monterrey and kept his assets in Mexico. He seldom crossed the Rio Grande, and when he did, he took care of business quickly and went home. He didn't hang out with dopers at the Echo Bar or any other public places. He didn't buy show-off mansions in the States. He didn't buy race horses, roosters, and U.S. politicians.

El Lechero dropped this bomb: Homer's source was the cartel in Guadalajara, part of the gang who engineered the murder of Agent Kiki Camarena.

That set every agent on the border looking to get Homer. It didn't take long. Homer Beltran Aguirre was arrested in San Diego, California, and shipped to the Hidalgo County jail where McAllen DEA agents could have a chat with him. Homer knew what was happening in the drug world along the lower Rio Grande. But Homer was not ready to talk to DEA. Life was too easy in Brig's country-club jail. So DEA shipped him to a federal pen in Alabama where he could contemplate his sins in a more austere environment.

Another reason we shipped him out was because he was too important a prisoner to trust to the Hidalgo County jail. The U.S. marshals had paid for improving the security of Brig's jail, but none of that money went to improving the moral character of the jailers. One Saturday morning two of our federal prisoners were allowed to walk out of jail and escape into Mexico. Brig wasn't there that particular morning and, of course, knew nothing about it. He said he "would get to the bottom of this thing, right away!" He never did. It was Brig's Chief Jailer Mario Salinas and Brig's boot-licking Deputy Bob Davis (my buddy) who allowed the escape. Brig did not fire either of them.

When Homer found that staying in Uncle Sam's jail wasn't as amusing as staying in Brig's jail, he started to think about his future and about how he might like to see his grandchildren grow up. Homer decided to talk. We told Homer to make a drug case on Brig, but Homer said that was impossible. Brig never touched the dope or the money in a drug deal. Homer did think we could get Brig for taking a bribe. We brought Homer back to Brig's Hidalgo County Country Club where he could enjoy the sheriff's hospitality again. Homer paid Brig $6,000 a month for special treatment, and another $1,000 every time he wanted to enjoy connubial bliss with his wife or adulterous ecstasy with his girlfriend. The payments were made by Homer's brother-in-law, Juan Antonio Guardado, a Mexican police officer. After a pattern was established, we wired up Juan Antonio and put a video camera in his truck. The next time he paid Brig, we got pictures and audio. Brig was sunk. Finally, by combining this with all the other evidence, DEA had a case against the sheriff. It was July 15, 1993, only a few months before my retirement.

Sheriff Marmolejo and four of his deputies were arrested. What a pleasure for me: my buddy, Deputy Bob Davis, was among them. The prosecutor, Assistant U.S. Attorney Greg Surovic, knew he could not find in Hidalgo County twelve good men, honest and true, willing to send their incorruptible sheriff to jail, so he had the trial's venue moved to Laredo. I retired from DEA just as the trials were about to begin. Ralph Palacios and Roy Padilla kept me posted.

The trial judge cut two of the deputies loose; he did not think their crimes fell under the federal law, but he hinted the state ought to charge them. My buddy, Deputy Davis, pled guilty to selling confidential police information (just as I had reported earlier in a DEA 6). Only Brig and one deputy (his trusty chief jailer, Mario Salinas) went to Laredo for trial. Prosecutor Surovic charged the two officers under the deadly RICO Act (Racketeer Influenced and Corrupt Organizations Act). It was a great move. RICO gave the prosecution a lot of leeway, and it scared the hell out of defense attorneys. RICO was still young, and the courts were still testing it.

Prosecutor Surovic had Homer Beltran for a star witness. Homer was excellent on the stand. And Surovic had a pretty little ace in the hole: Homer's girlfriend. Surovic put her on the witness stand, and the fascinated jury leaned forward in their chairs as she told how she had sex with Homer in Sheriff Marmolejo's office while the good sheriff stood guard at the door.

The Laredo jury found Sheriff Brig Marmolejo guilty of two counts of violating RICO, two of accepting bribes, three of money laundering, and one of interstate travel in aid of racketeering. They found Deputy Mario Salinas guilty of one count of conspiracy to violate RICO, and two counts of accepting bribes. Both men appealed to the Fifth Circuit, but that court affirmed the convictions. Deputy Salinas was somehow able to bring his case all the way to the Supreme Court of the United States. That shows how much money he had. However, it did him no good. The Supreme Court ruled against him, and affirmed the judgment of the Fifth Circuit.

All this court stuff took place while I was already retired. I no longer worried about such things—and was glad.

Chapter Thirty-Five
A DEA Christmas

JUST BEFORE THANKSGIVING, the electricity of the holidays was running free through the office. The agents were going through their yearly ritual of slowing down the work. When informants called, they were told to wait till after Christmas. Agents avoided cases like the plaque. Those with far-off families were planning to go home, some for Thanksgiving, some for Christmas, some for both. It was a time of cheer and good will. And Ralph got carried away.

"I sure would like to find a way to let the Romos get to see their kids during Christmas time," he was mumbling. "The trouble is the U.S. marshals don't want to cooperate, and I really can't figure how we can do it without getting into trouble."

Mr. and Mrs. Romo were both in jail. They had been involved in the drug organization of Rafa Longoria, the Fat Man. We had tried to get their cooperation in testifying against the Fat Man, but they were afraid of him. It was said he had already murdered several potential witnesses. They would have walked scot-free if they had testified, but they chose jail.

"Better a live jailbird then a dead snitch," was Ruben Romo's answer.

Ralph's idea grabbed me immediately. We could do a good deed for Christmas, and at the same time could show the Romos we were good guys and cared for them personally. It might be the very thing to flip them.

"Ralph, that's a great idea," I said. I walked over to his desk scratching my head. "Why couldn't we have the U.S. attorney bring them down here for an interview on the Fat Man's case? During one of the interviews you can have grandma bring in the children. We can say we didn't know she'd show up."

Ralph perked up momentarily. "We could bring them over here to the office." But then he slouched back into his chair. "Naw, that'd make it obvious. The marshals have already warned me. If I get caught arranging a meeting between prisoners and family, I'll be in big trouble."

"No," I said, "blame me. If anything gets screwed up, it was my idea. I'll be retiring soon. There's nothing they can do to me. Let's at least get them down here. We'll say we thought they had changed their minds about cooperating."

I had long-ago learned that in a bureaucracy it was easier to apologize than to get permission. Ralph got on the phone immediately and during the next few days made arrangements to have Ruben and Jackie Romo brought to McAllen "for debriefings in regard to the *United States v. Longoria.*"

The trouble with Ralph was he was a young agent, and he was so full of enthusiasm he was unable to contain himself. Often he told too many people about what he was doing. And so, Assistant U.S. Attorney Pat Profit got wind of the plan long before she was supposed to. She called us in and went through the same warnings Ralph had gotten from the marshals. We didn't think it would do any good to try to fool her. She was sharp. Sharper than the marshals. So we admitted the whole scheme and tried to get her in on it. We reminded her of how valuable the Romos could be to her case against the Fat Man and also that it was the season of love and good will and cheer, and all that stuff.

"C'mon, Pat, it's Christmas time," Ralph kept saying. "There are two little kids out there who want more than any other Christmas present the chance to see mommy and daddy."

I kept calling her a scrooge.

I knew it wasn't easy for Pat to say yes. I told her I'd take the blame, but that was small comfort. It was risky for her. Prosecutors weren't allowed to arrange special treatment for prisoners. She didn't like it, but she decided to go along with the plan. She even let us set the meeting in the conference room at the U.S. Attorney's office.

On the tenth of December, Ralph informed me the Romos were on their way, and he had set the meeting for Monday the 20th. But Ralph had court that Monday so he asked me to help Max Galvan in conducting the meetings. Max had been helping us with the case. Max knew the Romo family from way back. He made all the arrangements with grandma. Grandma was to bring the children to the federal building in McAllen. She was to stay in the restaurant downstairs until we had dad in the conference room. We couldn't leave grandma and the kids in the conference room because we didn't want the kids to see us bring dad into the room in handcuffs. The plan was to give dad thirty minutes with the kids and then give mom the same.

The U.S. marshals wouldn't allow us to take both prisoners at one time. We had to take one, do our interview, return that one, and only then could we get the other. There were very strict rules about having two prisoners together, about having two agents per prisoner, and so on. Max and I were trying to break as few rules as possible while breaking the big rule of conducting prisoner visits. We had no business doing this because, in the strangling world of federal bureaucrats, this was the job of courts and prison officials, and there was no chance of getting approval any other way. But it was Christmas, and (we told each other) we wanted to get the Fat Man.

I met Max at the Federal Building on the morning of the twentieth. A huge Christmas tree glowed brightly in the lobby. As we passed the restaurant, we saw Grandma Romo in there with the two kids. We got on the elevator where the people were cheerier than normal. They greeted each other and chatted together instead of staring straight ahead as they did the rest of the year. We could hear "Silent Night" coming up from the bank offices on the first floor. Max and I went up to the U.S. Marshals Office and got Ruben Romo out of jail. He had ankle chains on and was handcuffed behind his back. We asked the marshals to take off the ankle chains because we had to go down a flight of stairs to the U.S. Attorney's office (we did not want to use the elevator—low profile, you know). They removed the chains and warned us to be careful. The prisoner was now entirely our responsibility. We brought him down and led him through the U.S. Attorney's office, where all the secretaries sat at their typewriters. Pat was not in her office. She was up in court. The secretaries had put up Christmas lights, ornaments, and tinsel all around. The entire office sparkled with Christmas delight.

We brought Romo to the conference room at the far end of the office. The secretaries took little notice; it wasn't unusual to see a handcuffed prisoner in the U.S. Attorney's office. We closed the door of the room and took off the cuffs. Max hid them under the cushions in the couch. I put dad in a chair facing the door and I stood to one side talking with him while Max went to get grandma and the kids.

A moment later Max walked through the door followed by a pleasant-looking, gray haired lady who led by the hand a little boy of about three years and a little girl of about five. As soon as the door opened the little girl screamed, "Daddy!" and charged her father with both arms stretched out. He scooped her up in his arms, and she clung to his neck almost choking him with her enthusiasm. He was laughing and trying to kiss her face but she clung so tightly to his neck he couldn't turn his head. Meanwhile the little boy climbed onto dad's lap, turned around, and sat there totally content as if he had been there all morning. The children's faces were bright with joy, and the little girl kept saying "Daddy," over and over.

Max and I stood off to the side. The hugging and kissing and squealing went on for several minutes, then the girl began to calm down. Max asked about the children's names and when they might be starting school, but mostly we kept out of the conversation of the family.

Grandma stood and watched calmly. "Don't forget, you have a present for daddy," she said after a while.

The girl leaped from her father's arms and ran to grandma. She stuck her hand into grandma's purse and pulled out a little package wrapped in Christmas paper.

"Nope," she said, "That one's for mama." She reached in again and came out with an even smaller package. She turned and ran to her dad.

"Open it, Daddy, it's for you."

Ruben Romo looked reverently at the package. He slowly opened the gift while the little girl stood in front of him clapping her hands. It was a new pencil and a scarred, old pen. The girl was dancing with joy and Ruben acted as though it was the most wonderful pencil and pen he had seen in his life. The little boy sat on his father's lap playing with the buttons on Ruben's shirt.

Grandma had agreed to help us limit the visit to thirty minutes. Max and I thought this was important or we might end up with long sessions, and make it easier to get caught. I saw the old lady looking at her watch. When thirty minutes were up, she announced that it was time to go.

"Daddy has to go now," she told the children. "He has to go with these men."

"But I don't want daddy to go," wailed the little girl, tears welling up.

Mr. Romo had gotten to his feet. He was trying to hand the girl to grandma, but she clung to his neck so tightly he couldn't pull her off. The little boy stood on the floor with both arms wrapped around his father's right leg. He was crying and pleading with dad not to go. Finally Grandma was able to wrestle them away from their father with promises that they would get to see mommy, if they came with her.

Grandma smiled kindly at us, but we felt like heels. She led the two children out of the office holding their hands tightly. Both children were weeping and walking sideways as they waved a continuous goodbye all the way through the office. Grandma calmly dragged them by the hand, smiling and nodding at the secretaries as she went.

When they had disappeared, Max took out the cuffs. We gave Ruben a little time to dry his eyes before we cuffed him behind his back. He had shown no sign of crying while the children were in sight. When Max had snugged the second cuff into place he looked up at me. He had tears in his eyes too.

"Damn, Don, I don't mind telling you this is tearing me up," he said. "I have kids about the same age."

"Yeah, I know, Max," I said, "I didn't think it was gonna be this rough."

"Mr. Romo," I said to Ruben, "You have two of the nicest kids I've ever seen."

Romo looked proud. "I can't thank you two enough for this chance," he said.

"Ah, hell," Max blubbered. "We know how it is, being it's Christmas and all. I'm just sorry it couldn't be longer, but we have to get your wife in here too."

As we marched Ruben Romo through the U.S. Attorney's office I became aware everyone was looking at us, and several of the secretaries had tears in their eyes. They had heard all the wailing and had found out what was going on. This was turning into a real sideshow, and it was supposed to be a secret.

We brought Ruben up to the jail and turned him in. We checked out Mrs. Romo and the whole pageant began again. This time everyone was watching as we led Jackie Romo through the office to the conference room. Mrs. Romo was a petite little thing, but she had a proud way about her. Some people have a knack for looking dignified, even in handcuffs. I took the cuffs off, and Max got grandma and the kids. This time it was the little boy who made the biggest fuss. He led the way in greeting mama.

Jackie Romo's tears flowed freely, and the situation was not as comfortable as when Ruben was with the children. The little boy kept asking mama why she was crying, and she only cried more. Shortly, she got better control. But she had barely stopped crying when the little girl got her present from Grandma's purse and, as she handed it to her mother, the crying started again. The package contained a blue neckerchief. Jackie thanked the children again and again.

"Now I won't be so cold at night." she told them.

The whole thing was so heart wrenching I am sure Max and I wouldn't have been able to separate mother and children. Thank God for Grandma. She was strictly business. When the thirty minutes were up she made the announcement and dragged the children away. Grandma was a rock. This whole thing would have been a mess without her.

We had to wait quite a while for Jackie Romo to compose herself. During that time one of the marshals burst into the room. He was flushed and obviously excited. He pulled us aside and yelled that he had heard what was going on, and we had better get the prisoner back right now.

"I could lose my job over this kind of chicken shit," he blurted. "I thought I could trust you people, but evidently that's not the case." Max and I assured him we would bring her up to jail immediately.

We apologized many times, but we were never sorry for what we had done.

Jackie heard most of what was said, and now she was aware we had stuck our necks out to get this meeting to take place. She kept telling us how grateful she was, and we kept trying to shut her up. Too many people already knew what we had done.

After we got Jackie back in jail we went down to the U.S. Attorney's office to talk to Pat. She was back from court. We got the warmest reception you could imagine. Now everyone knew the story. They had heard the marshal making a fuss. The marshals had yelled at Pat too, but she was still happy we had done it. Max and I stood there in the middle of the glowing Christmas lights and the warmth of smiling secretaries. I don't think I ever got slapped on the back so often. It was really like Christmas.

Ralph would tell me several months later that the judge had found out from the marshals what had happened, and he chewed Pat out in court right in front of the defense attorneys. It was long after the holidays, but I think Pat still remembered that Christmas feeling, and I don't think she minded the judge.

Epilogue

Forgive, O Lord, my little jokes on Thee
And I'll forgive Thy great big one on me.
~Robert Frost

I HAVE TRIED NOT TO PREACH (and failed at times), but I can't leave off without indulging. I'll have to answer some questions that arise from this book anyway. So here is a short treatise on religion, on drugs, and on retirement:

On Religion
(I refer mostly of the Catholic religion of the U.S.)

MANY CHANGES OCCUR in a man's lifetime. When I came back to Stearns County in my retirement, I rejoiced to see some things were still the same, but I lamented that much had changed. The county is rapidly changing from a farming to an urban society. The small dairy farms like my father's are almost gone now. The German language is no longer heard and, if you try it on a young person, the effect is the same as Chinese. But the most remarkable change of all is people's attitude toward the priest. When I was little, the priest was the most respected citizen in the community. The priest wore the Roman collar all the time. Out on the street he had it on; when he answered the door of the parish house, he had it on. The Roman collar was revered above any symbol—even the stars and stripes. The priest was the representative of Jesus Christ here on earth. While I was gone from Stearns County (and it wasn't that long) the clergy somehow squandered that reputation. The Roman collar now receives no more appreciation than a farmer's red bandana.

Even the priests themselves no longer respect their profession. Benedictine monks of St. Johns Abbey no longer wear the robe as they walk around the university campus. You can't tell a monk from a student. The parish priest no longer wears the collar. The pastor answers the door in his bathrobe. The assistant walks down the street in flip-flops, torn T-shirt, and shorts. They don't want to be called "Father" anymore. It reminds them of their priestly duties, which they find tedious. They want to be called "Joey" or "Jimmy," and want to be one of the boys. They perform the Mass with robotic apathy, drone out plagiarized sermons in dreary boredom, and pass out Communion as casually as dealers flip blackjack cards in casinos. They tell jokes in church. They try to emulate Johnny Carson, not St. Francis.

The venerable old pipe organ that used to play the sacred hymns of Mozart and Bach stands silent up in the choir loft in the back of the church. They bring guitars in for Mass, and drums, and play up front so everyone can see them performing. They bring in that big burping tuba and the wheezy old concertina and have a "polka mass." The tunes and rhythms that used to be background for getting drunk at the New Munich Ballroom on Friday night are now background for honoring God in the church on Sunday morning. They've drained the reverence and the awe. Mass is now a grand social event.

The priest is no longer the community's spiritual director, no longer the moral compass. He's been relegated (or more honestly, has relegated himself) to the rank of mere functionary who performs baptism, marriage, and funeral. The Church hierarchy laments this loss of esteem, but they have greatly contributed to it. They've protected priests who sexually abuse young people and have sworn priests to silence on the matter. In my lifetime, they have made changes in doctrine that are so confusing and contradictory that they have overloaded the circuits of any reasonable man's belief system.

First of all, they decommissioned some of the sins. When I was little, I could commit more sins on a weekend than a person can now commit in a month. And I was not even skillful in the field. The city kids were far more proficient (but they had the advantage of having nuns for teachers and knew more sins than I did). The docket of sins we could choose from in the old days surpasses today's by far. There were two distinct kinds of sin back then: mortal and venial. A mortal sin was like a major felony; a venial sin was like a misdemeanor. The angels in heaven kept a rap sheet on us. If we died with a mortal sin on our rap sheet, we went straight to Satan's fiery jail, and the sentence was—not ninety-nine years, not life—but *eternity,* with no possibility of parole! It was a mortal sin in the old days to eat meat on a Friday. Today you can fry up a big steak and a pound of bacon on a Friday morning, and eat breakfast in happy contentment—and smile thinking about how things used to be (and also wonder where some of your forefathers are spending eternity).

It used to be a mortal sin to miss Mass on a Sunday morning. Now you can go on Saturday if you want, and if you miss, well, try again next week.

And back then, you had to go to the Latin Mass. Now you go to the English Mass and frown on those ignorant followers of Pius X who still go to that old Latin Mass. In the old days we had to fast from midnight on to receive Communion on Sunday morning. That could be as late as noon. That included no water! It was a mortal sin to receive Communion without that fasting. Now you can eat a bag of potato chips as you stand in line for Communion, and your belly can be full of beer when you receive the Host. And you can chuckle to yourself to think how granddad used to starve himself out of reverence for the Blessed Sacrament.

I've been told I'm a traitor for some of the things I say about the Church, and at times I feel that way myself, especially when I consider that almost all my high school and college education came from monks and priests. But mostly I feel it's the Church that's betrayed me in what they told me back then and what they tell me now. Maybe the Church hierarchy was in a humorous mood when they made those original rules, or maybe when they made the changes. I feel they should restrain themselves: humor is out of place when dealing with a billion souls and with eternal life.

When I was young, swearing was not a mortal sin unless you were really good at it, but masturbation was always a mortal sin even if you weren't. Masturbation was worse than lying or stealing. It was the most grievous and unhumorous sin a kid could commit—a number-one major felony that made the angels in heaven weep (though they still remembered to put it down on your rap sheet). But today masturbation isn't so bad. I recently talked to a priest about it. He said, "Well-ll, you kno-ow, the Church has loosened up a bit on that one. If the drive is so strong in you that you can't resist, then it's only a venial sin, if that."

Now that's unfair! If I'd been born a decade ago instead of seven decades, I could have done all that experimenting with only misdemeanors on my record instead of felonies. I want my rap sheet expunged! I'll pay for the erasers, if I have to mortgage the house.

Yes, things have changed. The Catholic Church of my youth is no more. The question "Is the Pope Catholic?"—once humorous and strictly rhetorical—is now given serious consideration.

On Drugs
(Not a pun.)

THIS IS NOT A PLEA for the legalization of drugs. It's merely a request that some of the following facts be taken into account when the subject is debated. Our adult culture is obsessed with drugs. Consider what happens on TV: one drug commercial after another hawking over-the-counter and prescription drugs—and all so romantic. The people laugh and sing and dance and walk on the beach, are so much in love, and are ever so handsome and happy. You, too, can be like this, if you take our drugs! The government makes the drug companies tell about the possible side effects of taking their drugs, but those warnings are mentioned while showing people smiling and healthy and happy. Don't worry about these little side effects!

Those commercials are pushing legal drugs, but all the young people know that illegal drugs can be even more fun.

If you allow your children to watch movies that glorify drug use, and you send them to schools where professors think it's cool to use drugs, they'll use drugs. They won't care what the law says. If dad idolizes football stars that snort cocaine, and mom adores movie stars that smoke crack, the children will use drugs. Drug use is a cultural problem, and relying on law enforcement to solve it is futile. Only in a police state where authorities have absolute power is it possible to keep drugs out of the hands of citizens. The United States already incarcerates more people than any other nation. A free people will always have drug users among them. The police can't change that. Unfortunately, part of freedom means freedom to be stupid, freedom to be self-indulgent, and freedom to do harm to oneself.

Law enforcement makes the problem worse. It raises the prices of the drugs and makes dealing far more profitable. If a young man wants an exciting challenge and likes money and has a yen for expensive cars and fast women (and what young man doesn't), smuggling drugs is a grand career. Enforcing drug laws is a challenging career also, but it doesn't have the other benefits. The police will continue to put your children in jail if you insist. It's a wonderful game—an adult form of cowboys and Indians. If the purpose of drug laws is to provide entertainment for the police, it is a good system.

Making drugs illegal turns into a violent trade what could be a peaceful one. If drugs were legal, an addict wouldn't feel the need to pack a pistol when making a buy. He'd be getting his drugs from the doctor or the pharmacist instead of from the Bloods or the Crips. Instead of going on the assurance that "this is really good shit, man!" he could judge the quality of his drugs from the label on the bottle.

Taking our law enforcement to foreign countries is even worse. Again it's a matter of the culture. The farmer in Colombia, Bolivia, Mexico, and Peru does not give a damn about the welfare of "spoiled brat children" in the U.S. He views his own government as crooked and oppressive and, when our officials come to his country to "cut off drugs at the source," he considers those officials an invading force that has joined with his corrupt government. Drug dealers, who are viewed in the States as depraved villains, are idolized there as brave heroes for defying the oppressive power of their government and of the United States of America. Pablo Escobar of Colombia, Roberto Suarez of Bolivia, Caro Quintero of Mexico, and dozens of other drug lords have songs written about them that are sung in their countries like national anthems. Their pictures hang on walls in little villages all over their homelands. In our attempts to enforce drug laws, we make the drug lords rich and famous, and powerful. We also help to corrupt their governments. The drug lords become so rich they can buy the politicians. They become so popular they can win elective office.

While the American government is providing millions to the governments of source countries to stop the illegal drug trade, American citizens are providing *billions* to the drug lords to keep the trade going. Who do you think is going to win?

The reason you think law enforcement is effective is because our government tells you so. They show you statistics, not results. So many tons of marijuana seized! So many kilos of heroin and cocaine confiscated. Oh, my, how effective! But the only true measure of success must be the decrease in the use of the drug, not the increase in the number of seizures, the number of prisoners, or the number of tax dollars spent. Politicians don't tell you how many more young people are now taking drugs and how many more have gone into the drug business since their "successful" operations have been going on. Politicians crow about success when a drug lord is jailed or killed. They don't tell you another has just taken his place. When Pablo Escobar was shot down like a dog in the streets of Medellín, the price of cocaine was affected not a penny. Colombia's Cali Cartel simply took up the slack.

On operations like Snowcap, I met some of DEA's finest agents. There were of course, as always, the slackers who were there just to collect the per diem and hazard pay. But the good ones were exceptionally brave men devoted to the idea of "attacking the problem at its base." (The real base of the problem, of course, is the drug user.) Those brave DEA agents will point to the seized drugs, trucks, airplanes, and ranches as proof of our great success. Those men will tell how we forged close ties with our law-enforcement counterparts in the host countries. All this is true, but while we made friends with a few dozen officials of the government, we made enemies of huge masses of the common people.

The men who grow the poppy, who cultivate the coca, who work the maceration pits, and who sail the dilapidated drug boats are not the true narcotraffickers. They're laborers trying to make enough money to rise out of their squalor. But those laborers are the men who get arrested on our foreign drug operations. The big drug lords aren't bothered by those arrests. There is so much poverty in their nations that new peasants are always ready to fill the jobs. The people see the drug lords as benefactors, providing jobs and money to the local communities. When a drug lord dies (especially if he is killed by law enforcement), shrines are erected to his memory. Go to Sinaloa and look at the cemeteries. The drug lords are commemorated with huge mausoleums made of Italian marble. The buildings are air conditioned for the comfort of the crowds of mourners. They resemble basilicas more than sepulchers.

If DEA's 1980s darling operations in foreign countries had been effective, there would have been less cocaine for sale on the streets of our big cities. When there is less cocaine, the price goes up. When there is less cocaine, the purity goes down (the dealers mix in more cut). During the 1980s the opposite happened. Prices went down, purity went up. At the beginning of the decade the national wholesale price for a kilogram of cocaine was somewhere between $45,000 and $70,000 depending on the city. By the end of the decade the price was between $10,000 and $40,000.

And have we convinced our neighbors to the south? Let's see. In Bolivia they have elected Evo Morales as their president. Evo is a staunch supporter of the coca industry and a consistent critic of the United States. He likes to adorn his hat with coca leaves, and he wears necklaces made from the plant. He was a coca farmer in his younger years. He became popular campaigning against U.S. and Bolivian attempts to destroy the coca industry. He was arrested many times for leading protests against our eradication efforts in Bolivia, which he denounced as an imperialist violation of indigenous Andean culture—a very valid point. Our Operation Snowcap made him president.

With great pleasure he kicked DEA out of his country. Coca rules in Bolivia more than before.

And what is happening in Mexico? As I was still writing this manuscript, Fox News was reporting that Rafael Caro-Quintero had been released from prison in Mexico—an obvious stick in the eye of the North American beast. Our government immediately put out a five million dollar reward for information that would put Caro-Quintero back in jail—no takers. And Jesus Malverde, the Mexican narco-saint of Culiacán, is more popular than ever. Now there are shrines to him in many other places in Mexico including the nation's capitol. In Sinaloa drug trafficking is more lucrative than ever. Only a few years ago Joaquin Guzman Loera (known as "El Chapo") the head of the Sinaloa Cartel, was listed in *Forbes* as one of the richest men in the world and by DEA as the biggest drug dealer on this earth. El Chapo has been arrested several times, but he always manages to escape from jail (from Mexican "maximum security jail"). He was arrested again in Mazatlán in early 2014. Not a shot was fired. U.S. politicians were ever so glad to get this dangerous man off the street. El Chapo "escaped" again little more than a year later. He's still dealing. He's still admired. He will be arrested again when he fails to meet his bribe obligations.

In Peru the Shining Path rebels, who tried to convert Peru into a Maoist state, have instead been converted by Peru into cocaine traffickers. They no longer want to follow Mao, they want to follow Pablo Escobar.

During my years with DEA our country gave the source countries billions and billions of dollars to "fight the drug war." That money does not fight drugs, it corrupts political leaders in those countries. Most of that money went into the pockets of the politicans in the receiving countries. Perhaps our bureaucrats in Washington will start up another Operation Snowcap. This time it will require much more money. They'll say the reason we have failed so far (if they ever admit failure) is because of underfunding. And they will paint you a wonderful picture of how many tons of drugs are seized and people arrested and properties confiscated, and you'll be happy to hear it.

Even the moral argument against legalization (which I have often used) is completely fogged up. In Colombia and in most of Mexico the Catholic Church had tremendous moral authority, but it did not seem to be able to make up its mind about which side it was on. The newspaper in Medellín often showed priests arm in arm with Pablo Escobar. Medellín priests like Father Lopera and Father Cuartas walked around with Pablo bestowing beneficence and benedictions on the people. Bishop Cardinal Lopez Trujillo didn't have a problem with this obvious endorsement of Pablo and the Medellín Cartel. The cardinal attacked anyone who questioned how he ran his diocese and seemed to put himself on the side of the traffickers. In Mexico, Father Jose Raul Soto Vazquez became famous when he gave a sermon in the Basilica of Guadalupe in Mexico City in which he remarked that Catholics should be as generous as drug traffickers like Rafael Caro Quintero and Amado Carrillo.

The argument that legalization is morally wrong because it will cause suffering, is valid only if you ignore the suffering that is caused by our efforts to enforce our present drugs laws. Never let anyone tell you we need more drug laws. The United States has by far the best laws for fighting crime anywhere in the world. Our conspiracy statutes are superior to any other country's, and the criminal penalties more severe. This is the question you must consider: is the child better off with daddy at home smoking pot and selling drugs or with daddy in jail for twenty years?

The argument that millions more will use drugs if they are legal is a weak one. In this country anyone who wants a fix can get one with little effort. Ask any rock star or Hollywood actor. Am I saying we should legalize drugs? I don't care. At my age I no longer have a dog in this fight. I'm just saying that in a free society drug enforcement doesn't work. It's not effective—unless you measure *effective* strictly by how many people are put in jail. When I began working for DEA, we had less than a quarter million people in jail for drug violations. By the time I left, there were well over two million.

The only thing that'll work is a change in the culture. And don't tell me that can't be done. It was done with tobacco, it was done with alcohol. When I was young smoking was cool, romantic, even healthy! Some doctors recommended it for asthma. Not so long ago getting drunk in public and driving under the influence wasn't only tolerated but considered to be very funny and good entertainment. All that has changed.

It's contradictory and hypocritical to call ourselves free in this country, when we have made it a crime to possess a harmless coca leaf, or to grow the beautiful opium poppy in our gardens. A farmer in Stearns County is a criminal if he grows hemp, which is one of the oldest and most useful commercial plants on earth, and also one of the most profitable. We import about a half billion dollars worth of hemp products every year, but can't raise it ourselves simply because our elected bureaucrats don't know the difference between hemp and marijuana.

Among DEA agents there probably aren't any who are for legalization. The zealots among them see themselves as protagonists on a great drug-fighting crusade that'll bring at last an end to society's greatest problems; they would not give up that role for anything. And the slackers among them oppose legalization because they're afraid they'll lose their place at the government trough. After having a lazy snout deep in that rich government slop, it's hard to imagine life on normal feed again.

On Retirement

WHEN MY NIECE ASKED, "What do you feel is your greatest accomplishment in life?" I answered, "I was able to successfully retire." She thought it was a joke. It wasn't. All the other retired DEA agents I've kept track of went back to work. Almost all the retired old men I know around our neighborhood are restless in their retirement, are going back to work, or wish they could go back.

I was lucky. I foresaw that retirement would be such a great change that I had to prepare for it ahead of time. I'd have to adjust to it as one does to a new job. I slowed down on my job with DEA, and I quit flying ahead of time. So retirement was not such a shock. And I was lucky I had a friend who recommended a book that set me on the right path. That book showed me that true retirement isn't just retiring from the job, but more important: retiring from the ego. The book tells how to shed that ego. There are hundreds of books about retirement. They're about managing money, about how old people can have fun, about proper exercising for old goats. If you haven't learned those things after living for sixty years, a book won't teach you. Give it up and try again in the next incarnation—if there is one. If you want a book about real retirement, get *The Power of Now*, by Eckhart Tolle. You can find that great peace that St. Paul says "surpasses all understanding." You can find that narrow gate mentioned by St. Matthew that leads to life, to peace, and to freedom.

When I was little, playing in the ground, catching frogs by the pond, watching the clouds by day or the stars by night, I felt a deep sense of peace and freedom. A child doesn't suspect this feeling can be altered, for it seems to be part of life itself. But as we grow into adults, we allow our minds to dwell so constantly on the pressures of adulthood we lose that joyful sense of self. Consistent dwelling on regrets about the past, anxieties about the present, and worries about the future cover up that joy of life. I never suspected I could think myself into a completely different state from the one I felt in childhood. Someone should have told me that—someone at school, at church, or at home. I had to find out the hard way. I had to suffer a long time. Finally in my declining years, I've found again that old freedom and contentment. Only now it's better. Now I know what it is like to lose it. I know the suffering that comes from losing one's self in the world. I know the freedom that comes from returning home.

present, and worries about the future cover up that joy of life. I never suspected I could think myself into a completely different [illegible] the one I felt in childhood. Someone should [illegible] told me that—someone at school, at church, or at home. I had to find [illegible] the hard way. I had to suffer a long time. Finally in my declining [illegible] found again that old freedom and contentment. [illegible] its better. Now I know what [illegible] I know the suffering that comes from losing one's self in the world. I know the freedom that comes from returning home.